# THE PUBLIC IN LAW

**The Edinburgh/Glasgow Law and Society Series**
*Series Editors*: Professor Emilios A. Christodoulidis and Dr Sharon Cowan

**Titles in the Series**

**The Many Constitutions of Europe**
*Edited by Kaarlo Tuori and Suvi Sankari*

**Law as Institutional Normative Order**
*Edited by Maksymilian Del Mar and Zenon Bankowski*

**Law and Agonistic Politics**
*Edited by Andrew Schaap*

**Public Law and Politics**
**The Scope and Limits of Constitutionalism**
*Edited by Emilios Christodoulidis and Stephen Tierney*

**Transformations of Policing**
*Edited by Alistair Henry and David J. Smith*

**The Universal and the Particular in Legal Reasoning**
*Edited by Zenon Bankowski and James MacLean*

**Law and the Politics of Reconciliation**
*Edited by Scott Veitch*

# The Public in Law

## Representations of the Political in Legal Discourse

*Edited by*

CLAUDIO MICHELON
*University of Edinburgh, Scotland*

GREGOR CLUNIE
*University of Glasgow, Scotland*

CHRISTOPHER MCCORKINDALE
*Glasgow Caledonian University, Scotland*

HARIS PSARRAS
*University of Edinburgh, Scotland*

Routledge
Taylor & Francis Group
LONDON AND NEW YORK

First published 2012 by Ashgate Publishing

2 Park Square, Milton Park, Abingdon, Oxon OX14 4RN
711 Third Avenue, New York, NY 10017, USA

*Routledge is an imprint of the Taylor & Francis Group, an informa business*

First issued in paperback 2016



**British Library Cataloguing in Publication Data**
The public in law. – (Edinburgh/Glasgow law and society series)
1. Sociological jurisprudence.
I. Series II. Clunie, Gregor.
340.1'15–dc22

**Library of Congress Cataloging-in-Publication Data**
The public in law / by Claudio Michelon ... [et al.].
p. cm. – (Edinburgh/glasgow law and society series)
Includes bibliographical references and index.
1. Law—Philosophy. I. Michelon, Claudio.

K235.P83 2011
340'.1—dc23

2011039327

ISBN 9781409419099 (hbk)

ISBN 978-1-4094-1909-9 (hbk)
ISBN 978-1-138-27396-2 (pbk)

*For Lilian Moncrieff – for her inspiration*
*and with best wishes for her young son, Herman Earnest*

# Contents

*List of Contributors* *ix*

Editors' Introduction 1

1 On the Necessarily Public Character of Law 9
*Neil Walker*

**PART I CONSTITUTED PUBLICS**

2 Rediscovering 'The Public': The Curious Case of Benjamin Constant 35
*Christopher McCorkindale*

3 Democracy, Political Parties and the Will of the People 53
*Andrew Maloney*

4 Between Contract and Constitution: International Organizations and the Protection of Global Public Interests 69
*Richard Collins*

**PART II UNCONSTITUTED PUBLICS**

5 'Unconstituted Publics'? 89
*Scott Veitch*

6 A Dilemma for the Civil Disobedient: Pleading 'Guilty' or 'Not Guilty' in the Court Room? 99
*Piero Moraro*

7 Justifying Civil Disobedience With Reference to EU Public Consensus 115
*Haris Psarras*

**PART III EXCLUDED PUBLICS**

8 Excluded Publics – Included Privates: The Janus Headed Nature of the Liberal Public-Private Divide 133
*Daniel Augenstein*

9 The Prisoner's Right to Vote: The Creation of an Abnormal and Excluded Public 147
*Vanessa De Greef*

10 Subjects to Citizens: 'Native' Enfranchisement in Reconstituting the Imperial Public of the British Empire, c. 1887–1914 161
*Coel Kirkby*

**PART IV PUBLIC/PRIVATE**

11 The Public/Private Dichotomy and the Unity of Capitalist (Re-)production 177
*Gregor Clunie*

12 The Public Nature of Private Law? 195
*Claudio Michelon*

13 Between the Public and the Private: Banking Law in 1830s England 205
*Iain Frame*

14 The Public-ness of Development in the World Trade Organization 219
*Stephanie Switzer*

**PART V EMERGING PUBLICS: THE ROLE OF THE VICTIM IN INTERNATIONAL CRIMINAL JUSTICE**

15 The Impact of the Distinction Between Situations and Cases on the Participation of Victims in the International Criminal Court 235
*Ania Salinas and James Sloan*

16 Addressing the Interests of Victims: Perspectives from the Office of the Prosecutor 263
*Olivia Swaak-Goldman*

17 Victim's Access to the International Criminal Court: Much Remains to be Done 287
*Gilbert Bitti and Leïla Bourguiba*

*Index* *303*

# List of Contributors

*Daniel Augenstein* is Assistant Professor in Legal Philosophy at the University of Tilburg.

*Gilbert Bitti* is Senior Legal Adviser to the Pre-Trial Division of the International Criminal Court.

*Leïla Bourguiba* is Associate Legal Officer to the Pre-Trial Division of the International Criminal Court.

*Richard Collins* is a Lecturer in Law at the University of Sheffield.

*Gregor Clunie* is a PhD candidate and Tutor in Jurisprudence in the School of Law at the University of Glasgow.

*Vanessa De Greef* is a PhD candidate in the Centre for Public Law at the Université Libre de Bruxelles.

*Iain Frame* is a SJD candidate at Harvard Law School.

*Coel Kirkby* is a PhD candidate in the Faculty of Law at the University of Cambridge.

*Andrew Maloney* is a PhD candidate in the law school at the University of Dundee.

*Christopher McCorkindale* is a Lecturer in Law at Glasgow Caledonian University.

*Claudio Michelon* is a Senior Lecturer in Law at the University of Edinburgh.

*Piero Moraro* is a PhD candidate in the department of Philosophy at the University of Stirling.

*Haris Psarras* is a PhD candidate and Tutor in Jurisprudence in the School of Law at the University of Edinburgh.

*Ania Salinas* is a PhD candidate in the School of Law at the University of Glasgow.

*James Sloan* is a Lecturer in Law at the University of Glasgow.

*Olivia Swaak-Goldman* is International Cooperation Adviser in the Office of the Prosecutor of the International Criminal Court.

*Stephanie Switzer* is a Lecturer in Law at the University of Dundee.

*Scott Veitch* is Professor of Jurisprudence at the University of Glasgow.

*Neil Walker* is Regius Professor of Public Law and the Law of Nature and Nations at the University of Edinburgh.

# Editors' Introduction

'The public' is a crucial concept in the disciplinary division and doctrinal understanding of the legal realm, whilst also animating much scholarly exposition of the relationship between law and society. This work provides a synoptic overview of the instantiations of 'the public' which appear in a number of legal spheres, and attempts to ascertain whether the notion can maintain a coherent essence in spite of the heterogeneity of its application. A key question framing the contributions relates to the work which is done by 'the public' in structuring the relationship between law and society – the extent to and manner in which it allows the interests and opinions of social groups to be represented and reflected in legal discourse. A related, and subsequent question, concerns the ability of the legal system to effectively impose such collectively-generated imperatives upon political and economic actors.

It is clear that the notion of 'the public' plays a 'gathering' role in relation to law and legal research that pertains to issues such as: the production and management of public goods; the mediation of the relationship between citizens and state agencies, and the rights and responsibilities entailed therein, and the process of constitutional democracy that produces consensus from the interplay of a plurality of opposed political interests. What is less certain, however, is whether 'the public' functions in reality as an interface between law and the political community, or rather inaugurates a process of self reference whereby the legal system reproduces its own guiding logics. To the extent that 'the public' does genuinely operate as a hinge between the legal system and the collective demands of an extra-legal political community, it should further be considered whether the interests and identity of the latter are distorted in their transversal of this boundary; is 'the public' deformed by its refraction into the legal? If the movement from the ground zero of the population at large to the rising edifice of 'the public' is one of selective filtration, what can be said to have been *lost* in this process of reduction? Further and related issues arise as to whether law's function can best be understood as *representative* or *constitutive* – questions which bear on the fundamental relation between law and politics and the ontological (and thus analytical) priority accorded each. In addition to these questions, the volume will explore more broadly whether the notion of 'the public' is immanent to the form and function of law as an institution, a discourse or a sub-set of social relations – whether law has a *necessarily* public quality.

The papers brought together in this collection interrogate the operation of 'the public' in a range of different legal (as well as illegal and arguably a-legal) spaces and are written by scholars from diverse disciplinary backgrounds. Such a composition is reflective of an understanding that the role of 'the public' in relation to law is not exhausted by the conventionally demarcated field of 'public law', nor are public lawyers the only commentators with an interest in this relationship. The volume also productively brings together scholars at different stages in their academic careers, from exciting young researchers to well-established academics.

The volume is introduced and broadly framed by Neil Walker's chapter 'On the Necessarily Public Character of Law'. Walker asks whether, beyond the selective doctrinal and disciplinary senses in which law is designated as 'public', we can understand law more generally to be of a public character. His study blends historical and normative approaches, whilst deploying as an analytical device a distinction between first (positive) and second (pre-positive, constitutional) orders of law. Under this framework, the liberal legalist public/private dichotomy operates as a first order distinction, behind which Walker attempts to establish law's second-order *publicness*, using as a pivot the constitutive relationship between law and public authority. Further, he engages with contemporary narratives which emphasize the decentring of the state as the primary locus of political power, assessing whether second-order publicness may be de-moored from the state as a mobile virtue in the age of globalization.

The remainder of the book is structured into five parts: Constituted Publics; Unconstituted Publics; Excluded Publics; Public/Private, and; Emerging Publics: the Role of the Victim in International Criminal Justice. The first section (Constituted Publics) considers constitutionally-bounded spaces and institutional formations for the articulation of the voices and interests of political communities. Christopher McCorkindale's chapter opens the discussion by revisiting the political philosophy of Benjamin Constant in an attempt to excavate a republican moment. For McCorkindale, Constant's thought cannot be reduced to an anatomy of liberties ancient and modern and the accordance of priority to the latter, such as the readings of Isaiah Berlin and Philip Pettit would suggest. Rather, precisely at the moment when Constant asserts the primacy of modern liberty, he returns to the liberty of the ancients and the (re-)constitution of the public realm as the remedy for the ills of modernity. McCorkindale further engages with the republicanism developed by Pettit and Quentin Skinner, arguing that the latter, in tailoring their vision of liberty as non-domination to the ideological hegemony of liberal modernity, jettison too much of the republican tradition. For McCorkindale, freedom cannot be negatively framed, requiring instead the positive exercise of political liberty, courage and the public-minded virtue of *zoon politikon* being necessary conditions of non-domination.

Andrew Maloney investigates the role of the political party as a form of constituted public representing the aggregation of interests in the context of the tense complementarity of electoral and liberal conceptions of democracy. The chapter centres on a critique of the decision of the European Court of Human Rights in *Refah Partisi*, which concerned the dissolution of the party of that name on grounds of lack of respect for secularism in terms of the Turkish constitution. Maloney argues that the decision in *Refah* constituted a subversion of core principles of liberal and electoral democracy, especially the principles of equal respect and equality of influence as the basis for majority rule.

In the final contribution to the *Constituted Publics* section, Richard Collins considers the role of international institutions as a site for the formation and articulation of an *international* public interest. Collins identifies within the institutional structures of Inter-Governmental Organizations (IGOs) the reproduction of a tension between the increasingly 'public' content of international law and its underlying contractual form. These structural tensions are explicable in view of the application of Weiler's notion of geological layering, such that we may recognize in international law a Westphalian base, a 'communitarian' infrastructure and a regulatory/governance superstructure. Collins evaluates the potential for productively harnessing the tension between organizations as actors and as agoras (forums and enterprizes), arguing that the constituted politics of the IGO as multilateral arena should be regarded as provisional or relatively autonomous spaces understandable by reference to Arendt's concept of the political.

The second section, *Unconstituted Publics*, addresses the potentialities of the formation and activity of political subjectivities outside of (and in opposition to) institutionally-framed economies of representation. A key issue in this regard is whether there are instances or moments in which constituent power can, through an organic process of self-organization, gain purchase on the legal and political landscape in such a manner as to reveal foundational contradictions in the dominant legality and undermine existing lines of inclusion/exclusion. Scott Veitch, in the opening paper of the section, problematizes the very notion of the 'unconstituted public', arguing that different senses of 'the public' are always already constituted by the operation of institutional logics. Indeed, the primary relevance of 'the public' may be regarded as its role as a normative horizon and regulative signifier. However, Veitch argues that there remains space for contestation in the dialectical relation between the demarcated spaces of the 'constituted' public and the residual energy of that which is left behind.

Piero Moraro's paper considers the position of the civil disobedient – she who acts illegally or against command, yet (purportedly) in the interests of the (a) public – with specific regard to the question of whether she should plead 'guilty' or 'not guilty' at trial. Contrary to traditional accounts, in which first, the civil disobedient signifies her 'fidelity to the law' with a guilty plea, and second, the court affirms her status *qua* civil disobedient with a reduced sentence, Moraro persuasively argues for an alternative. For him, a 'not guilty' plea may be preferable insofar as it provides an opportunity for the civil disobedient to prove the prosecutor's charges to be inappropriate and persuade the jury and political community of the compatibility of her actions with the public interest. The paper confronts the assumption that the interests and identity of a political community can be distilled into a *legal* public and that the civic virtue of political action may be determined solely by the operation of law's cartographic lines of (il-)legality. Indeed, the development of the identity of the community and the pursuance of their interests may necessitate action outside of the law, as in the case of civil disobedience. In this context, the question of how the disobedient should plead goes to the heart of our understanding of the capabilities and orientation of the legal form.

A 'guilty' plea could demonstrate the inability of the law to accommodate the diverse expressions and interests of a political community, thus symbolically undermining the very notion of legal justice. In contrast, a 'not guilty' plea would suggest an appeal to the reflexive qualities of law, a belief that dissent or protest can be (and *should* be) accommodated by (and contained within) the legal system.

Haris Psarras, in the final contribution to the *Unconstituted Publics* section, considers a different question of civil disobedience, this time in the context of the European Union. Psarras asks whether the EU's polycentric governance model creates the conditions whereby an official may disobey the orders of a hierarchically superior officer in the name of values promoted by the law. In essence, the paper assesses the opposition between political and legal prescriptions – both of which purport to represent the public interest – in a decentralized command system, the investigation proceeding against the background of the case of *Bernard Connolly v Commission.*

The third section of the book, *Excluded Publics*, considers the role of law in creating the public sphere, investigating the process by which the public space of politics (the *polis*) is defined and policed through a series of inclusions and exclusions. The chapters consider in different contexts how legal lines dissect the political environment, framing identities and both enabling and restricting communicative possibilities. These cartographical lines attribute legal personality, determining who may suffer harm (or put otherwise, whose suffering may register legally) and who may have recourse to legal mechanisms to assert their rights and offset the wrongs they have suffered. Key issues include the relationship between patterns of legal inclusion/exclusion and processes of economic distribution and cultural (mis-)recognition, while the debate is crucially informed by the tension between circumscribed spaces of constitutional discourse and the imperatives and articulations of constituent power.

In the first contribution to the section, Daniel Augenstein investigates the dynamics of exclusion accompanying the operation of the liberal public-private dichotomy in the context of religious practice/observance. Augenstein questions the existence of a neutral secular public space, noting that the operative notion of 'publicness' is often impregnated with Christian and national values. Such an arrangement facilitates the practice of assimilation and intolerance in the guise of secularism and the promotion of social cohesion. However, Augenstein contends that rather than abandoning the public/private divide as a foundational ontology of liberal democracy in view of its failure to accord 'equal' public recognition to 'private' differences, what is required is rather its re-conceptualization as an open, reflexive space for negotiating diversity. He argues that the dichotomy provides paradoxically the very basis for the *inclusion* of the religious other in a pluralistic political community, whilst further operating as a lever upon which such minorities can challenge majoritarian accounts of the public.

The chapters contributed by Vanessa De Greef and Coel Kirkby both consider instances of exclusion from 'the public', or else the construction of alternate, subordinate 'publics' through processes of disenfranchisement legitimized by criminalization (in the case of prisoner's voting rights) and racialization (in the context of the formation of the Imperial Public of the British Empire). In both cases, law is instrumental in the construction of a self-other dichotomy, the delineation between 'inside' and 'out', included and excluded. The insight that neither the 'ins' nor the 'outs' constitute an identifiable group when decoupled from their opposite highlights the central role that processes of boundary construction and maintenance play in the formation of collective identity. De Greef, in her paper, contests both the possibility of and the logic underlying the identification of prisoners as a homogenous, subordinate public whose active citizenship may be legitimately suspended. For her, the taxonomy dividing voters into 'law-abiding' and 'law-breaking' publics is simplistic, the one distinguishing between 'normal' and 'anormal' voters is senseless since the 'normal' voter, supported by law, does not exist. Coel Kirkby's historical analysis of the institutionalization of 'an imagined public sustained by law' at the beginning of the twentieth century suggests that the distance between the promotion of a cultural identity and the legitimization of cultural racism is not large; particularly, when the formation of a consensus-based public domain entails the political and spatial segregation of people who would otherwise be treated as equal subjects under a unifying authority. Kirkby identifies the practice of exclusion as a constitutive element in the formation of the cultural borders through which the fictitiously homogeneous public space of the British Empire attempted to define itself.

*Public/Private* is the title of the fourth section of the volume, which brings into sharper focus the foundational ontology which crucially prefigures the work as a whole. In the opening chapter, Gregor Clunie challenges the conventional understanding of the public sphere as a space or moment which exists independently of and prior to the private. This conception, which animates much political and legal theory, identifies the 'private' as a secondary, derivative realm which is framed and constituted by the public. Adopting a different approach, Clunie appeals to the analytical tools of Marxist political economy in order to investigate the operative relevance of the public/private dichotomy from the perspective of capital accumulation. Demonstrating the organic interpenetration of relations of production and social reproduction in capitalist society, he argues that the commodity form comes progressively to structure the emergent totality. Building on the dialectical jurisprudence of Evgeny Pashukanis, Clunie further contends that this unity is mirrored by the formal coherence of public and private law, such that all law may be regarded as being of a fundamentally bourgeois character, its deep structure and logic being that of the commodity form. From this perspective, the dichotomy between public and private appears as a first order distinction operating to facilitate and rationalize the reproduction of the social conditions which ground capital accumulation. Demonstrating the limitations of the legal form in rectifying the social contradictions which emerge out of the system of generalized commodity production, Clunie argues for a revolutionary transformation of the mode by which society organizes production and reproduction.

Claudio Michelon, in his paper on the public nature of private law, challenges the liberal vision of the private sphere as a realm in which agents are justified in acting without taking into consideration anyone else's interests. Michelon argues that the private realm cannot be thought in isolation of private law, which should in turn be conceived as an embodiment of the mutual interest of the members of that group in the flourishing of one another. The paper criticizes the liberal conceptualization of the private sphere for treating it as unavoidably impenetrable by the deontic considerations that prevail in the public domain. With that in mind, Michelon invites us to consider private law as an enterprise that further enhances the political interaction between free and equal actors.

Iain Frame's chapter uses an illuminating example from English economic history – the banking law reform that followed the 1825 banking crisis – to illustrate the extent to which financial innovations are reliant upon a certain market and property environment facilitated by the implementation of legal rules and the encouragement of particular legal practices. Frame's argument is supported by carefully scrutinized historical data and a subtle analysis of certain aspects of the interpenetrative relation of law and economics. Crucially, the paper attempts to recover an understanding of the market as an instituted process, arguing for the centrality of law to financial transactions in all contexts, rather than solely at those moments of crisis which necessitate bold legislative interventions. Frame thus demonstrates the inherently public character of areas of economic activity which are often regarded as the exclusive domain of autonomous private actors.

Stephanie Switzer, in the final chapter of the section, considers the public-private divide as it is reflected in the tension between multilateral and unilateral approaches to the meaning of 'development' as a process and a commitment within the World Trade Organization. Switzer argues in favour of a multilateral conception of development, emphasizing the potential of such a model to grasp development not only as a process driven by efficiency considerations, but also as a commitment to the community of all WTO Member States. Through her defence of the multilateral approach, Switzer captures the concept of development in the WTO context in terms of a public discourse that can still accommodate elements of private decision-making.

The final section is entitled *Emerging Publics: the Role of the Victim in International Criminal Justice*. The three papers in this section approach from different perspectives the role of victims in proceedings before the International Criminal Court (ICC). The question of the appropriate role of the victim in criminal proceedings finds divergent answers in different domestic contexts and is centrally engaged in such pivotal issues as: whom does the law address, and; how and under what conditions does 'the public' appear in the court room? May the interests of the victim be said to coincide with and be adequately represented by the prosecution, or are there circumstances which necessitate the more direct participation of victims, free from institutional mediation? The founding of the ICC has re-posed these difficult questions in an international context as the court attempts to marry the interests of an emerging public with the idiomatic peculiarities of the criminal trial. While considering at a procedural level and in valuable detail the integration of the victim into ICC proceedings, the papers in this section cast new light on themes which frame the work as a whole, revealing in a complex, developing context tensions which are fundamental to the concept of 'the public'. Specifically, the reader is invited to revisit the question of the efficacy and appropriateness of law as a mechanism for the mediation and reconciliation of often divergent interests – here, for instance, the interests of the victims of a particular crime as against the more general interest of the public in the efficient operation of the criminal justice system. Further, one is obliged to consider whether the legal system, with its limitations of form and procedure, is capable of operationalizing in a coherent and integrated manner the outcomes of political contestation. If this question receives a negative response, then the operation of law – revealed in the courtroom in its most fundamental, adversarial form – must necessarily appear as arbitrary: a coercive force grafted problematically onto a contradictory terrain of political discourse. 'The public' is then revealed as at best an uneasy and fragile compromise and at worst a vacuous signifier which functions only to legitimate the rule of political and economic elites.

In the opening chapter, Ania Salinas and James Sloan consider the Rome Statute's recognition of the role of victims in ICC proceedings as a significant step forward, yet highlight the pragmatic problem of the conflict between the victims' right to access to justice and the necessity for the Court to function efficiently, without unreasonable administrative burden. Moreover, they identify the substantive tension between the victim's rights to participate and the accused's right to a fair trial. In view of the fact that the Rome Statute does not provide specific guidance on some key aspects of victim participation, in particular on the problem of the stages at which the victim's right to participate can be exercized and on the modalities of such participation, the ICC has called upon itself to provide such guidance. Salinas and Sloan map the landscape drawn by ICC jurisprudence on victim participation, identifying questions left unanswered.

In the second chapter of the section, Olivia Swaak-Goldman provides an analysis of victims' participation from the perspective of the Office of the Prosecutor (OTP). Her paper focuses upon the OTP's policy, with specific emphasis on prosecutorial strategy and how the OTP has influenced jurisprudence and court-wide policy making on victims' participation. The paper details how the OTP has attempted to navigate a path between the imperative to allow victims to take part in ICC proceedings and the necessity to ensure the latter's safety from the harm that might ensue from this process of participation.

The volume's concluding chapter, written by Gilbert Bitti and Leïla Bourguiba, closes section five by assessing the difficulties experienced in practice by victims attempting to access the ICC. The chapter focuses on (a) the obstacles to victims' effective access to the Court and (b) the challenges to their protection and the impact of those challenges on participation. The authors survey a variety of different sources, ranging from court decisions to NGO reports, in identifying particular obstacles to and structural limitations impacting upon effective victim participation. Bitti and Bourguiba demonstrate how these emerging publics articulate themselves beyond strictly legal contexts and, in so doing, provide an account of the shortcomings of the current victim participation procedure.

# Chapter 1
# On the Necessarily Public Character of Law

Neil Walker

## Introduction

Noone would deny that the adjective 'public' has much to contribute to our understanding of the nature of modern law. Just how much is less clear. There are certainly various senses in which we can consider *some* law, or some laws, as possessing a public character, but is there any significant sense in which we can consider *all* modern law as having a public character? And what connection, if any, is there between these two measures of law's public character? Does the difficult case for the public character of all law – in other words, for law's *necessarily* public character – gain support from any of the indisputable ways in which some law displays a public character – in other words, from law's *selectively* and contingently public character?

My answer to both questions is a qualified yes. In the first place, there is a significant sense in which we may consider all law as having a public character. It is a fragile and disputed sense, and one that is under more threat than ever in today's world. Yet, however elusive the idea of the necessarily public quality of law, it remains a central theme of our attempts to make sense of law today as well as an important point of departure in our efforts to imagine the legal future. In the second place, that necessarily public character of all law is related to at least some of the ways in which law can be understood to be selectively and partially public, although the connections are indirect and have to be carefully traced.

In unpacking this argument below, we proceed from the more modest to the more ambitious claims. We begin by looking at the different ways in which the public label can be applied selectively to law. Then, in the light of what that tells about the relationship between law and 'publicness', we move to examine the proposition that law in some significant sense has a necessarily public character.

## False Beginnings

Before embarking on this line of inquiry, however, we should pause to note, and to set to one side, one relatively *insignificant* sense in which law can be said to possess a necessarily public character. If, as Wittgenstein famously argued, we cannot imagine such a thing as a private language (Wittgenstein 1953: para 256 et seq), then, by close analogy, we might also hold such a thing as a 'private law' to be unimaginable, and by this route assert law's 'public' quality to be necessary and inevitable. What Wittgenstein was alluding to was the idea that language is an undeniably social accomplishment, and that it is so in a double sense. It is both the case that language's basic purpose is the social one of communication and that the achievement of that basic purpose depends upon the successful social activity of arriving at a common or at least overlapping sense of what is meant, or signified, by the symbols making up a language. So, too, law may be conceived of as a social accomplishment in a double sense – both in its aim and in its method. Its basic purpose is the effective articulation and communication of a common normative framework (van Hoecke 2002), and the achievement of that purpose depends upon the development of some shared or overlapping sense of the meaning of norms, or at least some shared or overlapping sense as to how we should arrive at an authoritative version of the meaning of these norms.

Such a quick conclusion, however, begs more questions than it answers for anyone investigating whether law necessarily possesses a 'public' character. In the first place, it assumes that the opposite of 'private' is always 'public', or, more strictly, that the non-private is by definition public, thereby exhausting all categorical possibilities. But that assumption risks stretching the meaning of 'public' further than we want, and in so doing rendering the claim that law is necessarily 'public' over-inclusive and even trivial. After all, we have argued nothing more here than that law is intrinsically social; and if anything that is 'social' is by definition 'public', then the claim that law has a necessarily public character adds nothing to our understanding of law.

In the second place, if the issue is approached from the opposite direction, then the claim that law can never be 'private' goes against deep conventional usage. There may be much theoretical controversy about the proper *conception* of private law, but there is very little dispute about the significance of the core *concept* or idea of private law (Cane 2005). The term 'private law', as generally understood, specifies a disciplinary field of law that deals with those relationships between individuals with which the state or a similar 'public body' has no direct concern. Simply to ignore *this* 'private' aspect to law, which would be the consequence of reducing and restricting the private to the realm of the mentally interior and non-social in the Wittgensteinian sense, would be to deny much about how we understand the disciplinary division of the legal world. What is more, that same disciplinary division yields, on the other side, the domain of 'public law', which suggests a very different, and as we shall see, much more significant conception of legal 'publicness' than one that rests merely on law's social quality.

## The Selective 'Publicness' of Law

There are two key ways in which we conceive of the 'public' character of law in a selective fashion. First, we consider law to be selectively 'public' with reference to various aspects of legal *doctrine*. This involves the characterization of some legally relevant feature of the world – a form of property, an office, an action, a service, a policy, a location, a relationship, an interest, a benefit, a duty – as somehow 'public' The point of the attribution of 'publicness' here is particularizing and practical. It is particularizing in that its focus is on a specific norm or complex of norms. It is practical – that is, it involves the application of practical reason[1] – inasmuch as it is concerned with working out what that norm means and how one should act on the basis of that norm.

Secondly, as already noted in the Introduction, we think of law as being selectively 'public' with regard to the *disciplinary* division between private law and public law. What we are concerned with in this case is a distinction that can be made within any and all legal systems between two basic branches or fields of law – a distinction that turns upon whether the state or similar 'public body' is or is not directly involved in the matters regulated. The point of the 'public' attribution here, therefore, is not particularizing and practical, but generalizing and theoretical. It is generalizing in that its aim is to allocate a legal norm or set of legal norms to one rather than another broad disciplinary category – public rather than private. It involves the application of theoretical reason inasmuch as it is concerned with the regulation of *belief* about the law rather than of *action* within the law; in particular, with developing a better understanding of the nature of the legal universe, its internal structure, and how it fits with the social and political world in which it figures.

Of course, these two senses of publicness – doctrinal and disciplinary – are closely interconnected, but they remain distinctive in ways that tend to be underappreciated. First, while much of the discipline of 'public law' covers how we invoke notions of the 'public' in legal doctrine, the fit is far from perfect. For it is also the case that, as we illustrate below, many doctrinal invocations of 'publicness' take place within the disciplinary field of private law (contract, tort, trusts, etc.); likewise, many state or other public bodies that we locate within the disciplinary field of public law engage in particular legal activities and relations that we primarily associate with private parties (procurement, employment, etc.). Secondly, and more importantly for present purposes, as is suggested by the distinction between practical and theoretical reason, while the use of the 'public' in a doctrinal sense is *internal* to the domain of positive law, the deployment of public law in a disciplinary sense is *external* to the domain of positive law. It is concerned with how, as students, practitioners, authors or subjects of the law, we grasp and make sense of the legal world – with how we comprehend the anatomy of the legal order, and in particular, with the contribution of that part of the legal anatomy known as 'public law'. In a nutshell, where publicness as doctrine is concerned with authority *within* the many particulars of the law, publicness in the disciplinary sense is concerned with the surface forms and, at root, the deep structure of authority *of* the law in general. And, as we shall see in due course,

1 The distinction between theoretical and practical reason has its origins in classical Greek philosophy, most prominently in the writings of Plato and Aristotle. For an overview, see Wallace 2008.

this distinction between the internal and the external, as well as that between the particular and the general, leads us to draw different conclusions about the contribution of the two selective perspectives on law's publicness – the doctrinal and the disciplinary – to the argument about law's necessarily public quality.

*'Publicness' in legal doctrine*

If we now turn to consider in rather more detail, first, the doctrinal dimension of publicness, what is immediately striking is the sheer variety of ways in which ideas of publicness impinge upon the law. This is not simply a function of the vast range and diversity of situations in which the characterization of some legally relevant feature of the world as public makes a difference to how implicated agents may or should act. Rather, it reflects a more fundamental truth. As Raymond Geuss has powerfully argued, 'there is no such thing as *the* public/private distinction, or, at any rate, it is a deep mistake to think that there is a single substantive distinction here that can be made to do any real philosophical or political work' (Geuss 2003: 106). Instead, it is a division that has grown over pre-modern and modern times, bringing together '[d]isparate components – conceptual fragments, theories, folk reactions, crude distinctions that are useful in highly specific practical contexts, tacit value assumptions – from different sources and belonging to different spheres' (Geuss 2003: 10).

So various yet historically interwoven are the strands from which our modern contemporary distinction between the public and private is constructed, indeed, that they defy easy classification, as do the ways in which these strands map on to legal doctrine. Nevertheless, we can distinguish a number of different if overlapping broad frontiers of meaning. The most venerable basis for the distinction, originating in classical times, concerns modes of access to or control over property or (of increasing relevance in the modern state) information (Geuss 2003: 7). Property or information which falls on the public side of the divide – across a boundary that itself can be blurred and uncertain – carries with it both legal privileges and legal restrictions. On the one hand, the publicness of property or information implies common access and availability. On the other hand, there are constraints of decency, of orderly behaviour, of modes of assembly, of non-discriminatory exclusion and inclusion, of state security, etc., as regards the enjoyment of public property and public access to information which do not apply to property or information in private ownership or possession.

Secondly, there is a more capacious idea of publicness which specifies the realm of matters and affairs that concern everyone as opposed to purely personal or group concerns and interests (Geuss 2003: chapter 3). Again, this is of classical vintage, and again it is greatly expanded in the modern age. The legal doctrinal manifestations of the recognition of this special public sphere – of *res publica* in its expansive meaning[2] – are many and varied. Again, the implications of the attribution of publicness may be either burdensome or advantageous. It may impose higher standards, deeper obligations and wider responsibilities. Alternatively, it may involve the granting of immunities or the bestowal of other benefits. What is covered here includes the expansive public-regarding duties of care of public authorities in tort and their distinctive susceptibility to judicial review on grounds of procedural fairness and substantive rationality, as well as the latitude granted to public authorities just because of the range and diversity of their obligations and their scarcity of resources (Oliver 1999); or the special legislative (and sometimes common law) powers attaching to certain officials as opposed to private citizens to carry out key tasks of state – for example the police and security services – as well as special offences, supervisory regimes and sanctions associated with the abuse of these special powers;[3] or the greater immediacy of legal responsibility associated with the perpetration of certain acts by public rather than private bodies, including the 'horizontal direct effect' of EU legislative directives on public bodies, and the imposition of a direct obligation on public bodies to act consistently with human rights under current British legislation.[4] In all of these cases, moreover, again the definitional question of the boundaries of publicness, and so whether a particular entity or act belongs to the public sphere, can prove controversial. Different, inconsistent and sometimes mutually contested lines of doctrine exist. They variously emphasize one or more of legal source and pedigree, institutional form and location, autonomous or unilateral authority, functional or purposive remit, range of interests served, or target constituencies, as more or less influential upon or decisive of the question of publicness of the entity or act in question.[5]

Thirdly, there is a sense of publicness in legal doctrine the function of which, in the tradition of modern liberalism, is to define the limits of the private domain conceived of as a protected area of activity and choice (Geuss 2003: chapter 5). This might appear simply to be the flipside of the previous distinction, but the underlying rationale and point of departure – the negative aim of establishing the

2 The fact that *res publica* as originally and narrowly conceived referred only to public 'property', as in our first formulation of the public/private divide, is, of course, itself a good illustration of the historical fluidity and interconnectedness of ideas of 'publicness'. See Geuss 2003: chapter 3.

3 For a recent discussion of the police case, see the exchange between Malcolm Thorburn and John Gardner in Thorburn 2008, 2010, Gardner 2010.

4 Human Rights Act 1998: s6.

5 These debates are probably most fully developed and engaged over the question of the scope of judicial review. Here, as elsewhere, the doctrinal position is often complicated by the fact that judges seek a balance between universalism and particularism – between a sense that the general rationale of the public-private divide should be similar across jurisdictions, and so foreign precedents should be considered as persuasive authority, and a sensitivity to distinctively locally rooted conditions and considerations. See, for example, in the context of the treatment of the supervisory jurisdiction under Scots and English law, McHarg 2006.

outer boundaries of a universal private domain rather than the positive aim of establishing the contours of the public domain – is somewhat different (Geuss 2003: 76–80). Here, to take but a few examples, we may be talking about the *contra bonos mores* qualification of the right to enforce private contractual terms or conditions of a will, or the public interest defence to defamation, or restrictions on the right to privacy on grounds of public safety, or restrictions on the freedom of conscience or religion in order to protect public order, health or morals.[6]

Within legal doctrine, then, we see many different, if complexly overlapping rationales for classifying certain things as public, which rationales inform an immense range of different legal propositions. What is more, legal doctrine is no mere passive receptor of these rationales. Rather, it exhibits a degree of reflexivity in debating and developing the meaning and location of the various threshold distinctions – public property, public space, public order, public safety, public interest, etc. – upon which the applicability of the relevant legal propositions depend. That reflexivity only serves to reinforce the sense that, from a doctrinal perspective, the boundaries of the public and the location(s) of the public/private distinctions are drawn *within* the law – supplying a range of internal cuts and divisions – rather than being coterminous with the boundaries of the law itself. There is no question, then, that when we consider publicness as a doctrinal category, it invariably involves a partial and selective claim about the public nature of law rather than a comprehensive and necessary one.

### *'Public law' as a disciplinary field*

When we come to consider 'public law' in the disciplinary sense, these qualities of partiality and selectivity are even more palpable, and so may seem on first view yet more remote from any claim that publicness is definitive of law in general. Whereas private law, as we have already noted, designates the field of law that deals with those relationships between individuals with which the state or similar 'public bodies' have no direct concern, public law designates that field of law in which the state or similar 'public bodies' are in direct relationship with individuals and other legal persons, or in which different organs or agencies of the state or similar 'public bodies' are in relationship with one another. In other words, the very disciplinary definition of public law implies its merely partial coverage of the legal field.

What is more, given that public law, when used in this disciplinary sense, essentially serves as an organizing category offered as part of an external perspective upon the legal field in general, its basic analytical mode is a broadly descriptive one, and one that tends to take for granted the validity of the underlying framework within which that description takes place. The depiction of the public domain, in other words, is preoccupied with the surface 'what'

6 The last two examples are drawn from Articles 8 and 9 respectively of the European Convention on Human Rights.

rather than the deep 'why' of law's anatomy. As that depiction is not concerned with particular doctrine or its legal consequences, it need not closely attend to the various specific and in some measure inconsistent distinguishing criteria of publicness – pedigree, authority, function, interests, etc. – to be found in legal doctrine, and with the harder questions these more precise tests raise about the rationale for the public/private divide. Rather, the focus of the disciplinary view is on the core rather the periphery, on the undisputed heartlands rather than the disputed boundaries of publicness. For these purposes, the deep-rooted institutional connection between publicness and the apparatus of the modern state provides a definitional short cut that reinforces the tendency to curtail the more difficult questions, and the more revealing answers. The regular addition of 'similar public bodies' to the definition, therefore, is not typically intended to highlight complexity and inviting examination of difficult margins. Instead, it is often no more than a casually tautologous addendum to an unquestioned basic definition.

## The Necessary 'Publicness' of Law

### *'Public law' as law's constitutive discipline*

Yet this is not the whole story. There is also a body of work that *is* more concerned with and detained by the deep 'why' rather than merely the surface 'what' of the disciplinary quality and integrity of public law. Much of this literature, and much of the thinking that animates this literature, is not in the English language or tradition, but in that of other European continental countries. This is due in no small part to the different developmental trajectories of different national legal systems. Aspects of the evolution of national law have had the effect of making the public quality of law, considered as a distinct field, a more salient consideration in continental Europe. These include the modern tradition of foundational constitutionalism and the institutionalization within civilian legal systems of separate sub-systems of administrative law and administrative courts – 'administrative' referring to the administration of governmental power and so being a category itself conventionally dependent upon a distinction between the exercise of public and private power (Oliver 1999: 16–19). However, more recently – notwithstanding the absence of these features from our domestic legal traditions – there have been notable attempts to deepen our understanding of the disciplinary idea of public law in the British context which draw upon this wider European stream of thinking.

The contribution of Martin Loughlin is of pivotal significance here.[7] In a nutshell, the manner in which his work, and the European tradition he draws upon,

7 See, in particular, his two key monographs *The Idea of Public Law* (Loughlin 2003) and *Foundations of Public Law* (Loughlin 2010a). In what follows, I will instead concentrate on a few articles that offer cogent and concise statements of his ideas.

seeks to make deeper sense of the discipline of public law is by showing how it can be understood as underpinning the legal system as a whole. Drawing upon older notions such as *ius politicum*, *droit politique* and *Staatsrecht*, Loughlin argues that beneath the topsoil of the field of public law considered as *constituted*, and so as positive law, there is a deeper layer of public law considered as *constitutive*, and so pre-positive and even pre-Constitutional. Public law, in this prior, deeper sense, is precisely "that which confers the right to govern by way of positive law" (Loughlin 2009: 5). Of crucial importance, then, in terms of forging the link between a selective and a necessary understanding of law's public quality, Loughlin's field of public law, while it is still only one part of the legal universe, now becomes its framing and therefore indispensable part.

But what does this deeper and constitutive layer consist of, and in what sense is it 'public' and in what sense 'law'? The deeper layer consists, most basically, of the set of regulative understandings that establish the sovereign character of the modern state. That is to say, it embraces the claim of the state, composed of the familiar troika of demarcated territory, ruling authority and people (Loughlin 2009: 5–6), to institute the autonomy and absolute authority of the political sphere – which sphere we also call 'public' as it is synonymous with that of *public* affairs rather than *private* force or property. And even though they are pre-positive, these concepts of state and sovereignty, must, for Loughlin, remain juristic concepts – concepts of public *law*. This is so, first, because sovereign political or public authority cannot be understood as an abstraction but must be secured and expressed in institutional form, and this is achieved by vesting or presupposing an original "rightful power" (Loughlin 2009: 5) in the state and its office of government. Secondly, not only the form but also the medium of sovereign state authority is legal, since the power that is conferred or presupposed is of an order that 'equips government with an unlimited competence to govern through the instrumentality of [positive] law' (Loughlin 2009: 5).

Loughlin's aim in seeking to retrieve this pre-positive notion of the field and discipline of public law – a subject that he claims 'seems to have fallen off contemporary maps of knowledge' (Loughlin 2008: 47) – is to trace the deep structure of legal and political authority to the idea of the state itself and no further. By so doing, he wants to challenge various misconceptions of the place of law and politics in the modern order of things that have filled the gaps left by the evacuation of the field by his preferred *Staatslehre*. In particular, he wants to reject, on the one hand, the idea of the state as the 'agent' (Loughlin 2009: 5) of some other and higher authority, whether metaphysical or constitutional, and on the other hand, an 'essentialism' (Loughlin 2009: 10) that treats the state as the embodiment of some prior existential unity of the people. Instead, he seeks to show that the state, considered as a juristic idea in its own right rather than as something either merely post-Constitutional and so positive law or as mysteriously pre-legal, is the framing 'scheme of intelligibility' (Loughlin 2009: 8) through which peoplehood and positive law are mutually and reflexively constructed and reconstructed over time. There is, in other words, no law that stands above the state and the political realm, but equally and reciprocally, there can be no articulation and operationalization of the state and of the political *qua* political other than through and in the form of law. Public law, then, in this deeper form, is neither the servant nor the master of politics. Rather, it *is* politics, conceived of in its generative rather than its programmatic mode.

In looking to the juristic idea of the state and no further, Loughlin seeks to account both for what is distinctive about the modern political and public realm as compared to pre-modern systems of authority and for what the modern retains from the pre-modern. On the one hand, the very defining modern character of the political as political, and so of the public sphere as a public sphere, depends precisely upon its autonomy from other world-views. It supplies a new 'representation – from a distinctive perspective – of the entire society' (Loughlin 2008: 57), in so doing claiming to possess a self-constituting and so only *self*-limiting character that stands independent of any prior metaphysical or traditional forms of authority. Of course, *res publica*, as we have seen, has a pre-modern etymology, and at the doctrinal level this continues today in a whole range of operational indicators of what belongs to the domain of public affairs and what does not. However, only in the modern age does the idea of public authority also become the master or 'second order' category for deciding the nature of the 'first order' split between public and private affairs. That is to say, the very decision as to what are public affairs and what are private affairs does itself become for the first time in the modern age a 'public affair', so to speak. On the other hand however, the framing of the autonomy of the political through the mechanism of a pre-positive public law inherits and adapts through a process of 'secularization, historicization and positivization' (Loughlin 2009: 5) some of the core assumptions of earlier conceptions of natural law; in particular, it retains and sustains the idea of a level of law that is framing rather than framed – positing rather than posited – supplying an irreducible and indefeasible basis for life in society.

There are many aspects of Loughlin's thesis that enrich our understanding of the public quality of modern law. Certainly, his central argument that there is a deep public law basis for the whole of positive law, including that part of the whole of positive law which also attracts the label 'public' in both the doctrinal sense and in the shallow disciplinary sense, contains a key insight. It suggests that we can and should understand law's publicness at two levels, at both a deep and necessary 'meta' level and also as a selective 'object' of positive law. Yet while this captures something important about the public nature of law, certainly as historically understood, we have to push still further, both challenging and building on Loughlin's views, in order to gain the fullest sense of what this has amounted to and what it might amount to in the future.

This impulse to question and to push matters further is provoked by the methodological premises underpinning Loughlin's work, and so by the strengths but also the limits of the kind of exercise he believes himself to be engaged in. His exploration and explication of the foundations of public law, for all that this is a significant and increasingly densely documented and intricately woven body of historical scholarship,[8] is not intended as a closely observed comparative empirical exercise – one looking at 'the detailed arrangements of particular regimes' (Loughlin 2008: 50). Nor, however, is it offered as a study in purely ideal theory – intended to elaborate "the structure of some ideal constitution" and so instruct us as to how the modern relationship between politics and law *should* be conceived. Rather, it is a kind of stylized reconstruction, a simultaneously deep and encompassing account of a dominant conception of state-building that allows us better 'to understand the ways in which existing constitutional arrangements can be said to work' (Loughlin 2008: 49). Yet, for all the attractions of such an approach as a way of conveying a broad explanatory message, and for all Loughlin's success in exploiting his methodology to provide an insightful account that retrieves a deeper sense of public law, the fact that the emphasis is neither on detailed empirical patterns nor on matters of ideal theory does leave certain questions hanging. And it is these questions, as we shall see, that prompt us to look beyond his own methodological prism to reframe and augment the question of the necessarily public quality of law.

Let us begin, then, with the question of the empirical range and credentials of the kind of reconstructive thesis that Loughlin proposes. Historically, just how broadly encompassing has the tradition of pre-positive public law been? If it is supposed to be a defining feature of modernity and modern law *tout court*, how, for example, do we account for the British case, where the constitutive idea of public law seems most emphatically to "have fallen off the contemporary map of knowledge" and where, indeed, it is harder to discern its consistent outline even in historical maps? For Loughlin, the most notorious indicator of British singularity, namely the fact that the United Kingdom lacks a written constitutional pedigree, need be no impediment to its inclusion within the wider tradition of *ius publicum*, since such written constitutional law is itself merely the highest form of positive public law. As he acknowledges (Loughlin 2009: 14), a documentary Constitution might, nonetheless, be viewed as a key product, and so as an important marker of the "scheme of intelligibility" and regulatory world-view that the deeper, pre-positive sense of public law encapsulates. Yet if we recall Loughlin's understanding of the relationship between the constitutive law of 'state formation' and the constituted law of the 'formed state' as being reflexive and iterative, the 'big bang' documentary constitutional moment is neither the unique such marker nor even an indispensable component of the positive manifestation of an underlying constitutive public law. Rather, Loughlin stresses how the unwritten British constitution, centred on the idea of parliamentary sovereignty, can, like that of Britain's continental neighbours, be understood to have gradually evolved out of a new state-centred way of thinking about public authority that is the functional equivalent of *ius politicum* (Loughlin 2010a: chapter 9).

---

8 Especially with the recent publication of the 500 page *Foundations of Public Law* (Loughlin 2010a).

Two difficulties, however, remain not only for the British case but for the historical record more generally. In the first place, however plausible the idea of a constitutive public law as the *leitmotif* of a comprehensive narrative about the generation and validation of positive law in the new age of the modern state, it is by no means the only narrative available. Typically, the positive law recognized by the modern state according to the deeper public authority of the *ius publicum* includes elements other than those documentary constitutional norms and legislative instruments that can be regarded as directly 'constituted' through the state. Other norms, including the common law and public international law, are instead recognized by the state system of positive law through homologation, incorporation or delegation. But there surely are other candidate narratives of generation for these extraneous elements. As Patrick Glenn persuasively argues, the common law itself is central to one such alternative narrative (Glenn 2005). Here understood broadly to refer to a diverse stream of law, including elements of *ius gentium* and customary law as well as the various nominal forms of 'common law' that have developed alongside or across different state laws, the common law's key and defining feature in this generic mode is a claim to be common 'in relation to' (Glenn 2005: chapter 1) law that is particular to a specific and bounded domain – primarily, the particular constitutional law and statute law of the state. The idea of 'in relation to' covers many possibilities. These range from the nurturing or supplementation of the particular law by the common law within the domain of the particular law, to efforts through the common law to qualify or challenge the domain or content of the particular law, and also to attempts through common law to generalize and extend beyond the domain of the particular law. In all cases, the common law *sensu largo* is the repository and the expression of a set of claims to constitutive legal authority, typically grounded in conceptions of morality, in ethical constituencies, or in communities of practice which transcend the state, that, while not (necessarily) denying a parallel claim to constitutive legal authority on the part of the state, challenge the claim of the *ius publicum* to provide through the pre-positive legal form of the state the *exclusive* source of positive legal authority within its jurisdiction.

Of course, there is no compelling reason why the common law narrative of authority – of legal world-making – should be preferred over that of the *ius publicum*. But that is beside the point. Rather, the very fact that an alternative juristic narrative of authority exists to that of a state-based public authority has to be taken seriously. Because it is an account that is nurtured and sustained within some relevant epistemic communities (e.g. amongst judges, other constitutional officials and jurists), because it tells a plausible story about the sources of authority of at least some of those laws that are generally recognized as positive law within the community, and because its narrative may be more prominent in jurisdictions such as those of the United Kingdom where the 'common law' carries a longstanding nominal significance as an additional category of positive law and where some of the more obvious juristic props of state-centred public authority are absent, (such as a written constitutional tradition and a special terminology to distinguish pre-positive 'Law' [*ius*, *le droit*, *das recht*] from positive 'law' [*lex*, *le loi*, *das gesetz*]), the claims that Loughlin makes on behalf of *ius publicum* have to be reassessed. The public authority-centred pre-positive account and authorization of the world of positive law that he reports remains a persuasive one, but it is not the only such claim 'out there', and it has to be recognized that other deep accounts and authorizations of the world of positive law exist, and as a matter of historical fact provide alternative and in some respects rival schemes of intelligibility through which to construe that legal world.

A second, and more urgent empirical difficulty surrounding the narrative of *ius publicum* concerns the contemporary effects of globalization. There is no doubt today that the global pattern of positive legal authority is an increasingly interconnected one. The growth of transnational collective action problems and state 'externalities' in a word in which persons, goods, capital, services, communications, cultural forms and political regimes increasingly circulate across state borders has meant that more and more legal initiatives involve parties other than single states and affect populations other than those of single states. This is evident in the rise of supranational law in Europe and other regions, in the development of global jurisgenerative institutions such as the UN and the WTO, in more citizen-centred rather than state-centred forms of international law in human rights and criminal law, in the development of new forms of transnational 'administrative law' (or 'Global Administrative Law') where forms of governance absent or attenuated from a formal Treaty base abound, and in the growth of forms of functionally specific self-regulation lacking the pedigree of any state or state-like 'public' authority in areas such as sport and the internet (Walker 2008).

As Loughlin points out, none of this necessarily means, as many scholars of globalization too quickly assume, that, by world-historical standards, however measured, the nation state is in decline, or even that it exerts less overall influence than once it did (Loughlin 2009: 17). What it does mean, however, is that the manner in which states individually and collectively exert legal authority, and the kind of legal relations and 'irrelations' they inhabit with regard to other non-state polities and agencies, are altered. It follows that the deep juridical map of the post-Westphalian age in which, with *ius publicum* as its key, states provided the relatively self-contained and mutually exclusive sovereign centres of authority, is less appropriate than once it was. It is no longer just a question, therefore, as in the historical example of the claims of the common law family of concepts, of there being a supplementary account of legal world-making that might challenge the *ius publicum* model at the margins. Rather, the basic model is itself under threat. The very way that we think of constitutive legal authority – how far state-centred, how far pooled across states, how far based in non-state settings, how far still a property of the state parts rather than the global whole – is now under challenge.

Loughlin is by no means unaware of this challenge. He is also correct to point out that the series of answers to that challenge provided by many of those who perceive or advocate the progressive shift of *constitutional* authority to non-state sites is often inadequate. For Loughlin, these increasingly numerous and influential postnational constitutionalists often tend to mistake symptoms for causes, superstructure for base. They are apt to treat constitutions as purely normative entities and constitutionalization as a purely normative process; that is, as consisting only in the development of forms of non-state positive law that are in different ways – form, structure, content – analogous to the positive constitutional law of states. As Loughlin says, unless the connection is retained or remade between the positive constitution and the underlying material constitution of public authority, this kind of approach cannot get beneath the surface of the problem it purports to address. Rather than answering the question of constitutive public authority reframed in the context of the new globalization, the emergent postnational constitutionalism often merely begs it (Loughlin 2009: 17–28, 2010b).

Yet the lack of a satisfactory alternative to Loughlin's preferred *staatslehre* does not rehabilitate the latter by default. It remains the case that present forms of legal and political globalization sharply question the sufficiency of a state-centred conception of public law as the constitutive basis of contemporary positive law. Here again, we come up against the limits of Loughlin's approach. Just as the evidence finally runs out in any attempt to make the historical case for the dominant constituent role of *ius publicum* against all-comers, so too, and more obviously and urgently, the adequacy of the state-based public law account as a way of understanding the contemporary world of positive law is profoundly challenged under conditions of increased transnationalization of legal authority. In the end, with his emphasis on the deep and general explanatory character of his thesis, Loughlin bequeaths to us a persuasive, but by no means irrefutable, account of the indispensably public historical basis of modern law, together with a version of the public foundations of law in today's world that increasingly threatens to be undercut by the forces of globalization.

If we want to continue and build upon the argument for the necessarily public quality of law as part of a two-level conception of publicness, we must recognize the restrictions imposed by a purely explanatory paradigm. As noted, Loughlin sets his stall out against ideal theory. He does so on the basis that its aspirational and ideological lens distorts understanding of how the world is (Loughlin 2008: 50–54), and also because, in concentrating on the 'ought', ideal theory can be inattentive to the gap between 'is' and 'ought' and so to the issue of whether and how that gap may be bridged.[9] Yet, is there not a middle way? Can we not have an approach that that blends explanation, evaluation and ideal projection – that comprehends the real in light of the ideal and the ideal in light of the real? Can we not acknowledge the grounding of the idea of 'publicness' in certain historical and contemporary conditions of authority yet still try to find an ideal vantage point

9 For example, in his critique of the excessive normativism and attendant neglect of the underlying material constitution in much postnational constitutional writing, he stresses how little attention is paid by the exponents of this approach to the necessary preconditions of the realization of their ideal conception of constitutionalism. See e.g., Loughlin 2009: 17–28.

appropriate to these conditions for evaluating and criticizing or justifying these extant notions of publicness? Can we not in this way provide a more compelling account of why publicness has been important to law and why and how it might continue to be? And if we follow this approach, cannot the evaluative dimension be added to the balance sheet in assessing the merits of rival historical understandings of the law, as well as supplying guidance in our working out whether and how we might retain or restore the public foundations of contemporary law under conditions of globalization?

The following subsection will set about trying to answer these questions in the affirmative. It is only possible to explore the deepest resonance and full potential of law's publicness, this paper will argue, if that evaluative dimension is introduced. However, the consequence of so doing is not to resolve the question of law's character under globalization but merely to open that question up to a wider range of possible answers.

### 'Publicness' of Law as Democratic Ideal and Aspiration

In recent work Jeremy Waldron has begun to address the challenge of considering law's publicness from a morally committed standpoint. He has sought to identify the necessarily public quality of modern law understood not only as a living practice, or as a legacy of past practice, but as a quality *ideally* suited to modern law (Waldron 2008). Where and how does he locate this ideal dimension?

For Waldron, the key benchmark of appropriateness – of ethical adequacy – of contemporary law, is supplied by the idea of democracy. We now live in an age in which, as Amartya Sen points out, the democratic ideal of collective self-rule has ceased to be understood in its various localities as a purely local need and has come instead to be endorsed as a 'universal commitment', and so as a 'normal' template of government (Sen 1999). Democracy sets the basic standard of our political times, and our legal system, just like all our other modalities and institutions of government, should respect and reflect that basic standard. And if, according to Waldron, we duly pursue the imperatives of a 'democratic jurisprudence' (Waldron 2008) then we will conclude that modern law should indeed exhibit, amongst other things, a necessarily and irreducibly public quality, but one that is best expressed through the presence of key input and output dimensions of the democratic ethic of collective self-rule; that is to say, modern law should function through '(i) ... norms that purport to stand in the name of the whole society, and (ii) ... that address matters of concern to the society as such, not just matters of personal or sectional concern to the individuals who happened to be involved in formulating them' (Waldron 2008: 39).

We should note that, for Waldron, these standards mean both less and more than that each and every particular legal norm should emanate from a democratic source. While this may be an important way, indeed often the best way of fulfilling his first, input-based criterion, it is neither a strictly necessary nor a sufficient condition of the publicness of individual legal norms. It is not necessary because norms that are claimed to be made in the name of the whole society might be issued in good faith by those who have no formal democratic mandate but who can nevertheless plausibly claim to be 'guardians of the public good' in particular contexts of action. It is insufficient because a democratic source is not enough for the law to be properly 'public' unless it also meets the output-based criterion and effectively presents itself as oriented to the needs of society as whole; that is to say, unless it '*purports* to promote the public good' (Waldron 2008: 39–41).

Waldron's approach is only sketchily developed. It is not explicitly concerned to pursue Loughlin's central insight and distinguish between different tiers – constitutive and constituted – of public, democratic authority. Moreover, it does not directly engage with the question of non-state forms of public authority. Nevertheless, it supplies a highly suggestive platform for building a more normative element into the Loughlin conception of publicness.

In the first place, the choice of democracy as a key background evaluative standard for publicness avoids the charge of remote or contentious idealism. More so than any other candidate ideal, the democratic standard is one that is both immanent within modern society and the modern state system, and, in principle, if not in practical detail, is relatively uncontroversial.

In the second place, the particular link forged between the ideal background standard of democracy and the modern historical development of law's constitutive public authority is a plausibly intimate one in which the real and the ideal are mutually informative. On the one hand, the real nurtured the ideal. Historically, the innovative modern idea of law as a constitutive public authority – so central to Loughlin's analysis – was at least proto-democratic in quality. It was based on a notion that certain matters should be treated as of general 'public' concern just in view of the fact that the interests of all members of society were affected. This, in turn, presupposed that the interests of all mattered and were to be taken into account, and the cultivation of such sentiments would lead eventually and after much social struggle to the development of modern institutional forms of representative democracy. Indeed, to recall the question of the historical credentials of law's necessary publicness, that proto-democratic quality – the germ and prospect of the ideal in the real – is one of the reasons why, in accounting for what is distinctive about modern law, we might favour a narrative that locates the constitutive basis and self-authorizing narrative of modern law exclusively in the principles of *ius publicum* over a narrative that embraces wider 'common law' sources as constitutive. On the other hand, and completing the circle of mutual influence, the ideal may be deployed to reshape the real. The modern democratic imagination that emerged out of the social reality of the development of a constitutive conception of public authority, and which, however tentatively and unevenly, has become consolidated within the mature forms of that constitutive framework, may be and has been reciprocally deployed as an ongoing critical standard against which to test and guide that sense of publicness in state-centred and state-decentred frameworks of contemporary law alike.

In the third place, just as we understood the public character of law within a two-tier model as both the generative framework of all positive law and the selective object of that generative framework, so we may adapt and apply Waldron's insights in order to comprehend the standard of democracy associated with publicness in similarly two-tier terms. Most basically, the background standard of democracy, itself rooted in the constitutive sense of public autonomy, speaks to the importance of collective self-rule as a meta-principle of political organization. That is to say, the very framework conditions of the 'political pact' (Loughlin 2009: 20) – the constitutive sense of the proper subjects, territorial and functional jurisdiction, and key offices of the political which, in Loughlin's terms, make up the pre-positive juridical structure of the state – should so far as is possible, and even though they are by definition prior to the constituted forms of democratic rule, themselves be democratically mandated or homologated and be thus responsive to democracy's input standard.[10] Yet it does not follow from that constitutive democratic standard that every positive law duly constituted and every wide-ranging, public-affecting legal capacity duly created under positive law must or can itself meet the input standard of democracy. Sometimes there are reasons of principle why this is the case. Requirements of expertise, of impartial decision-making, of disinterested administration, of immunity from short-term electoral pressure, as well, of course, as the need – recognized in the very double articulation of modernity's publicness at the comprehensive 'meta' level and selective 'object' level – to preserve significant spheres of private and associational autonomy within society, may militate against democratic forms of representation and accountability in and under the law. In these cases Waldron's second, output-based criterion of publicness – that the norms generously and inclusively reflect and respond to concerns of society as a whole and not just particular sectional interests – may be in tension with and may override the case for democratic input standards. Furthermore, as we shall see, even where there is no such clash of principle, even when democratically inclusive 'output' is not jeopardized by democratically narrow, short-term or divisive 'input', there may nevertheless be practical impediments to the development of forms of democratic input, in which case attention to democratic output standards can still be of significant compensatory value.

Fourthly and finally, these considerations generate a decidedly mixed message for the prospects of a democratically informed standard of publicness under conditions of globalization. On the one hand, the Waldron approach is flexible in

10 Loughlin himself fully appreciates the incipiently democratic quality of the second-order 'political pact'. Indeed, he explicitly states that this pact rests on the principle of consent and, as such, also implies 'some notion of representative, responsible, and accountable government' (Loughlin 2009: 13). For him, however, this remains part and parcel of the 'real', and so a proper object of his explanatory thesis, rather than some ideal extrapolation from the real and benchmark for reinterpretation and refashioning of the real. On the difficulties associated with the idea of a democratic theory prior to and about the terms of establishment of the *demos*, see Walker 2010.

terms of what democratic jurisprudence demands of the public quality of law at the derivate, first-order level of individual legal norms. The fact that the democratic indices of publicness are about output standards as much as input standards allows considerable scope for forms of institutional design of positive law in which the link to a particular state-centred constituent people may be somewhat attenuated. On the other hand, if democratic pedigree is to count as the highest input standard, then it must be considered as especially important, perhaps even indispensable, at the basic, second-order level of the very constitution of publicness. That is to say, unless first-order legal norms and capacities of positive public law, whose own democratic credentials may only be output-based, can be ultimately traced back to an original second-order source of authority that exhibits incipiently democratic characteristics, then the link upon which law's constitutive sense of publicness depends is broken, and with that severance the very idea of law's necessary publicness is jeopardized.

It is this mixed message that underwrites the open-ended, contested character of the question of law's necessary publicness under contemporary conditions. The prospects of a normatively informed idea of the necessary publicness of law in a globalizing age depend on just how these various first- and second-order issues of the relationship between democracy and public authority are approached and addressed. Crudely, we can distinguish three broad positions. First, there is a state-centred position in which the second-order publicness and the qualities of constitutive democracy associated with the second-order publicness of a state-based *ius publicum* remains the exclusive key to law's necessarily public character. This is a position we can associate with Loughlin's elaborately developed theoretical model, but also with a whole generation of state-centred thinkers within constitutional and international law.[11] It holds that we can continue to conceive of the legal world in necessarily public terms only to the extent that non-state based positive law, whatever balance of input and output democratic qualities it might possess, can in the final analysis be understood as a delegation of authority from the original authority of the states.

A second position is one that, by contrast, pays no or less attention to questions of second order publicness and instead concentrates on the public qualities of first-order legal norms across the dispersed network of global governance. The advocates of this position, of whom we find prominent examples under such

11 Loughlin nevertheless emphasizes the difference between his own more fundamental critique of post-state constitutional theory, which is ultimately *epistemic* – tied to the uniqueness of the state-centred constitutional view of the world and of the conditions which make that world-view possible, and the critique offered by a typical state-centred constitutionalist such as Dieter Grimm who focuses only on the first-order normative or positive accomplishment of constitutionalism but nonetheless perceives the full form of such an accomplishment as *culturally* distinctive of and (probably) peculiar to the political form of the modern state (Loughlin 2009: 18, Grimm 2005).

banners as Global Administrative Law[12] and global constitutional law (Kumm 2009), would want to exclude or downgrade the significance of second–order publicness either because they do not consider that the kind of constitutive democratic publicness associated with the state-centred position *can* be plausibly understood as the source of all legal authority in the dense and multiform structure of transnational regulation, or because they believe that such a pedigree based conception of democratic publicness *should* in any case be held wholly or largely irrelevant to the question of the legitimate authority of transnational law. In focusing on the credentials of diversely situated arrangements of first-order norms they tend to understand publicness in terms akin to what Michael Walzer would call a 'reiterative universalism' (Walzer 2007: 187). That is to say, on the one hand, the qualities of publicness are seen to be intrinsic to public law as generally understood, while, on the other, the articulation of these common norms is not seen as a matter of simply 'reading off' the local version from some inert universal 'covering law' (Walzer 2007: 184), but as a continuous and progressive process of re-contextualization in which the universal is reshaped by the particular. According to one prominent scholar of Global Administrative Law, for example, the relevant universals can form around notions as general as the principles of legality, rationality and proportionality, together with respect for the Rule of Law and basic protection of human rights (Kingsbury 2009a: 31–4). Over time, these normative ideas, all of which are engaged in democratic output-oriented tasks of 'channelling, managing, shaping and constraining political power' (Kingsbury 2009a: 32) tend to circulate more widely and more readily. Gradually, 'as the layers of common normative practice thicken, they come to be argued for and adopted through a mixture of comparative study and a sense that they are (or are becoming) obligatory' (Kingsbury 2009a: 30). Meanwhile, a similarly cosmopolitan story is being told today about the development of constitutional law across state and post-state sites, centred upon the nurturing of universal constitutional commitments to principles of legality, subsidiarity, adequate participation and accountability, public reason and rights-protection (Kumm 2009: 52).

The reiterative universalists, therefore, believe in an authority system that is horizontal and normatively guided, whereas in the state-centred approach authority is understood to be vertical and lexically dictated. Democratic publicness, for the reiterative universalist, is about the trans-polity corroboration and vindication of best practice in polity sites that, in an increasing number of cases, lack a constitutive framework of democracy, whereas from the state-centred perspective it is first and foremost about continuing to insist on just that high modern constitutive pedigree

12 The Global Administrative Law project remains strongly associated with its founding institution, New York University. See, e.g., Kingsbury 2009a, 2009b. Kingsbury draws explicitly on Waldron's work (Waldron 2008) in these pieces. See also the similar project on public authority and international institutions based at the Max Planck Institute in Heidelberg. See e.g., Von Bogdandy, Dann and Goldmann 2008.

even where it is becoming remote from the relevant transnational contexts of the regulation of collective action. One or other of the twin democratic imperatives of publicness, input or output – either a constitutive collective self-authorization or an adopted commitment to an inclusive sense of public interest and responsibility in all legal contexts of collective action regardless of how removed they are from a constitutive frame – is given priority. Whichever side is emphasized however, the claim to publicness is arguably diminished and destabilized just because of the absence or neglect of the other.

This opposition helps to account for the attraction of a third approach, one that tries to give equal due to the importance of constitutive public authority and the shift of regulatory power away from the state. Such an outlook, often broadly based upon a Habermasian approach to public autonomy, insists that the deep pre-positive and proto-democratic structure of public authority that we tend to associate with the state need not, after all, be exclusively tied to the state. Rather, if we concentrate on its general properties rather than its conventional historical model, it is a structure that can also be found in other settings. These setting may include state-like bodies such as the EU, where at least some of the cultural and institutional preconditions of the reflexive construction of public autonomy, including the recent trace of documentary constitutionalism in the ultimately abortive Constitutional Treaty, may be present (Habermas 2001). But, on one view at least, perhaps most fully developed in the recent work of Nico Krisch, public autonomy, understood in the most general terms as the expression of a right to self-legislation can also imagined and fashioned – can provide the relevant 'scheme of intelligibility' – in other more modest and less state-like settings of transnational collective action. Such settings will be inhabited by actors who may be 'members' of multiple polities and who, therefore, do not owe exclusive or even predominant loyalty to any one particular polity (Krisch 2009, 2010). Within this model of pluralist public autonomy, according to Krisch, the weight of any particular collective claim to public autonomy will depend upon many factors; 'on the strength of its social grounding, of the participatory practices that support it as well as the plausibility of its attempt to balance inclusiveness and particularity' (Krisch 2009: 38–9). The last element in particular is vital. Public autonomy in a world of interpenetrated rather than mutually exclusive political domains, of non-holistic commitment to multiple segmentalized polities each with widely ramified decision effects, has to find a new balance between the (more broadly) *affected* and the (more narrowly) *affectively* engaged. There must be sufficient common commitment to form a sense of common 'publicness', but there must also be a recognition that insider and outsider are positions on a spectrum rather than categorical opposites, as well as an awareness that however the balance of affected interest and affective belonging is resolved in any one polity context must be assessed in the light of how it is resolved in all other overlapping contexts.

If we follow this approach, second order publicness may be revamped as a more mobile constitutive virtue of the law. And to the extent that original political authority can be conceived of in non-state settings, some of the burden of democratic publicness is removed from the second order input setting of the state, just as some of the burden is removed from the merely first-order and often predominantly output-orientated setting of the transnational. By this method, therefore, the test of the necessary publicness of law is one that tries to incorporate and remix aspects of all the main current strands of thinking – state-centred and reiterative universalists themes now joined and complemented by the possibility of original authority beyond the state.

## Conclusion: The Point of Departure

Yet, for all that it seems to offer a new horizon of possibility, and one to which this author has been attracted in his own work,[13] the conditional nature of the above formulation leaves an urgent political dilemma, and one that remains wrapped up in a deep conceptual question. Politically, to what extent *can* the emergence of non-state sites of governance ever adequately balance the loss of public authority by the states? In turn, this is as much a question of the limits of our categories for thinking about the 'political' and the 'legal' as it is an empirical question. For the underlying issue is whether the kind of collective autonomy we can imagine for the various generators of a new networked space of transnational collective decision, whether we are talking about the regulation of football or of Olympic sport, or the registration of internet names, or the upholding of regional human rights, or the development of a worldwide system for punishing crimes against humanity, or the protection of the rain forests, or the making of a transnational social market in Europe, bears a family resemblance to the kind of autonomy, originality and proto-democracy of collective authority we associate with the popular sovereignty of the modern state.

To the extent that it does bear such a family resemblance, it is because we believe the idea of publicness, with its strong links to democracy, to be sufficiently capacious and flexible and to identify and capture enough that is continuous between the high modern phase of statehood and the new phase of globalization, that it remains a useful master category for our legal foundations. To the extent that we believe the family resemblance to be lost, it is because we believe the conceptual mould of modern legal authority to be broken beyond repair, so requiring the very idea of law to be understood through a new scheme of intelligibility.[14]

---

13 See e.g., Walker 2002, 2008, 2009.

14 The division between an approach that utilizes and an approach that rejects ideas of 'publicness' can be very fine, so underlining the point that publicness is not just the paradigm case but also the limiting point of the modernist understanding of law. For example, Gunter Teubner develops a theory of law that seeks to transcend the distinction between public and private, but his depiction of constitutionalism as concerning the balance between the necessary autonomy and excessive jurisdictional scope and penetration of different functional sectors *inter se* in a differentiated global order is one which finds much

Whichever side of the divide we fall on, however, we cannot, or at least we cannot yet, escape the idea of law's necessary publicness. It provides an indispensable point of departure – in the sense of a starting point – for the key contemporary debate about the distinctiveness of our emerging ways of framing the domain of the legal in a globalizing world, in particular whether and how these ways are continuous with the received model of high modernity. Whether we may also anticipate a point of final departure *for* the idea of law's necessary publicness – in the sense of its valediction – depends on the practical outcome of that debate.

## References

Cane, P. 2005. The Anatomy of Private Law Theory: A 25th Anniversary Essay. *Oxford Journal of Legal Theory* 25, 203–17.

Gardner, J. 2010. Justification Under Authority. *Canadian Journal of Law and Jurisprudence*, 23, 71.

Geuss, R. 2003. *Public Goods, Private Goods*. Princeton: Princeton University Press.

Glenn, H.P. 2005. *On Common Laws*. Oxford: Oxford University Press.

Grimm, D. 2005. The Constitution in the Process of Denationalization. *Constellations*, 12, 447.

Habermas, J. 2001. Why Europe Needs a Constitution. *New Left Review* 11, 1–20.

*Human Rights Act* 1998. (c.42), London: HMSO.

Kingsbury, B. 2009a. The Concept of 'Law' in Global Administrative Law. *European Journal of International Law* 20, 23–57.

———. 2009b. International Law as Inter-public Law, in *Moral Universalism and Pluralism*, edited by H.S. Richardson and M.S. Williams. New York: New York University Press, 167–204.

Krisch, N. 2009. The Case for Pluralism in Postnational Law *LSE Legal Studies Working Papers*, 12/2009. Available at: http://papers.ssrn.com/sol3/papers.cfm?abstract_id=1418707.

———. 2010. *Beyond Constitutionalism: The Pluralist Structure of Postnational Law*. Oxford: Oxford University Press.

Kumm, M. 2009. The Cosmopolitan Turn in Constitutionalism: On the Relationship between Constitutionalism in and Beyond the State, in *Ruling the World?*, edited by J.L. Dunoff and J.P. Trachtman. Cambridge: Cambridge University Press, 258–325.

Loughlin, M. 2003. *The Idea of Public Law*. Oxford: Oxford University Press.

resonance in the work of Nico Krisch. See e.g., Teubner 2010. The contemporary range and detail of putatively post-public theories of law is, of course, a vast topic in itself, and one for another study.

———. 2008. Reflection on *The Idea of Public Law* in *Public Law and Politics: The Scope and Limits of Constitutionalism*, edited by E. Christodoulidis and S. Tierney. Aldershot: Ashgate, 47–65.
———. 2009. In Defence of *Staatslehre. Der Staat* 48(1), 1–28.
———. 2010a. *Foundations of Public Law*. Oxford: Oxford University Press.
———. 2010b. What is Constitutionalisation?, in *The Twilight of Constitutionalism*, edited by P. Dobner and M. Loughlin. Oxford: Oxford University Press, 2010, 47–69.
McHarg, A. 2006. Border Disputes: The Scope and Purposes of Judicial Review, in *Public Law in Scotland*, edited by A. McHarg and T. Mullen. Edinburgh: Avizandum, 219–40.
Oliver, D. 1999. *Common Values and the Public-Private Divide*. Butterworths: London.
Sen, A. 1999. Democracy as a Universal Value. *Journal of Democracy* 10, 3–17.
Teubner, G. 2010. Constitutionalising Polycontextuality. *Modern Law Review* 73 (forthcoming).
Thorburn, M. 2008. Justification, Powers and Authority. *Yale Law Journal* 117, 1070.
———. 2010. Reinventing the Night-Watchman State? *University of Toronto Law Journal* 60, 425–43.
van Hoecke, M. 2002. *Law as Communication* Oxford: Hart.
von Bogdandy, Dann, A.P. and Goldmann, M. 2008. Developing the Publicness of Public International Law: Towards a Legal Framework for Global Governance Activities. *German Law Journal* 9, 1375–400.
Waldron, J. 2008. Can There be a Democratic Jurisprudence?, in New York University Public Law and Legal Theory Working Papers, 35. Available at: http://papers.ssrn.com/sol3/papers.cfm?abstract_id=1280923 [accessed 5 December 2010].
Walker, N. 2002. The Idea of Constutional Pluralism. *Modern Law Review*, 317–59.
———. 2008. Beyond Boundary Disputes and Basic Grids: Mapping the Global Disorder of Normative Orders. *International Journal of Constitutional Law*, 6, 373–96.
———. 2009. Reframing EU Constitutionalism, in *Ruling the World?*, edited by J.L. Dunoff and J.P. Trachtman. Cambridge: Cambridge University Press, 149–77.
Wallace, R.J. 2008. Practical Reason. *Stanford Encyclopaedia of Philosophy*. Available at: http://plato.stanford.edu/entries/practical-reason/ [accessed 1 December 2010].
Walzer, M. 2007. Nations and Universe, in *Thinking Politically: Essays in Political Theory*, edited by David Miller. New Haven: Yale University Press, 183–218.

———. 2010. Constitutionalism and the Incompleteness of Democracy: An Iterative Relationship. *University of Edinburgh Law School Working Paper Series*, 2010/25. Available at: http://papers.ssrn.com/sol3/papers.cfm?abstract_id=1650016.

Wittgenstein, L. 1953. *Philosophical Investigations*. Oxford: Blackwell.

# PART I
# Constituted Publics

# Chapter 2
# Rediscovering 'The Public': The Curious Case of Benjamin Constant

Christopher McCorkindale

## Introduction

The title of this chapter makes an intentional play on that of F. Scott Fitzgerald's short story, *The Curious Case of Benjamin Button*. Fitzgerald's tale – in which the protagonist is born with the physical appearance and attributes of a 70-year-old man, and who ages in reverse until he dies an infant – was inspired by Mark Twain's remark that 'it was a pity that the best part of life came at the beginning, and the worst part at the end'. This chapter will focus on another Benjamin, the nineteenth-century French politician, political philosopher and novelist Benjamin Constant. The view of Constant's political philosophy which endures to this day is that espoused by Isaiah Berlin (1958: 11) and followed by Philip Pettit (1997: 18, 27, 271), each of whom reduce his political thought (1) to an anatomy of liberties *ancient* ('the liberty of belonging to a democratically self-governing community' (Pettit 1997: 18)) and *modern* ('being left to the rule of your own private will' (Pettit 1997: 18)), and (2), to the favouring of the latter (and the rejection of the former) as the conception of liberty most suited to the conditions of modern life. This is to say that modern man, (to paraphrase Hannah Arendt) much too busy in emerging private spheres to take political questions seriously, (Arendt 1951: 70) delegates those questions upwards, to a (presumably enlightened) political class, with the result that the public (participating) *in* law has become a public dispersed: atomized and protected in their private lives and civil liberties *by* law.

What follows will make a pitch for liberty back at the level of the political. More to the point, this chapter will suggest that Constant himself, *at the very moment that he renounced political liberty*, came to discover that private lives and individual freedoms were precariously held when their only guarantee was the benevolence of those in favour of whom that renunciation had been made. The security of the modern age then, the right of the moderns to peaceful enjoyment of their private rights and self-interests – what Ayn Rand has famously called the 'virtue of selfishness' (Rand 1964) – proved, in his analysis, to be little more than a mirage where the public had no freedom to express their *consent* to the grant and (perhaps more importantly) their *dissent* to the suspension of those laws. Constant's case is so curious – this chapter suggests – because, having announced himself as the modern *par excellence*, he began from that very moment to move, like Button, forward into the past – returning to the liberty of the ancients and the (re)constitution of the public realm as the remedy for the *ills* of modernity. In so doing he discovered, as Twain might have said, that the best part of liberty – that which 'submit[s] to all the citizens … the care and assessment of their most sacred interests, enlarges their spirit, ennobles their thoughts, and establishes among them a kind of intellectual equality which constitutes a people's glory and power' (Constant 1819: 327) – came at the beginning.

## Of Ancients and Moderns

This anatomy of liberty was drawn by Constant in his famous address, 'The Liberty of the Ancients Compared with that of the Moderns.' Delivered at the Athénée Royal, Paris, in 1819, here Constant drew a distinction – 'still rather new' at that time (Constant 1819: 309) – between *ancient* freedom as the freedom to engage *in* politics on the one hand, and a *modern* freedom *from* politics on the other. It was, at first anyway (and, as has been suggested here, this is an important qualification), Constant's thesis that ancient freedom is just that, ancient. It belongs irretrievably to the past, to the Athens which Aristotle knew, to the Sparta of Lycurgus, to Livy's Rome, but is no longer relevant in the modern world. Ancient liberty, he said, meant the freedom actively to participate, 'collectively, but directly', in the public realm: deliberating in the public square questions of war and peace, of alliances with foreign governments, voting on laws, calling those who occupied public office to account for their deeds and misdeeds, pronouncing judgments and so on. Whilst, however, in these ancient constitutions Constant saw an individual who was 'almost always sovereign in public affairs', the price which the citizen paid for that political freedom was his privacy. The free citizens of the free states of antiquity, he said, were no more than 'slave[s] in all [of their] private relations':

> All private actions were submitted to a severe surveillance. No importance was given to individual independence, neither in relation to opinions, nor to labour, nor above all, to religion…. In the domains which seem to us [moderns] the most useful, the authority of the social body interposed itself and obstructed the will of the individuals. (Constant 1819: 311)

In so far as Benjamin Constant understood it then, the freedom of the ancients *to* participate in the public square meant, consequently, no freedom *from* the burdens and the scrutiny of life in the public realm.

By way of contrast Constant saw that for the moderns it is not the sharing of social and political power with one's equals but rather 'the enjoyment of security in private pleasures' which is the aim: and so, 'they call liberty the guarantees accorded by institutions to these pleasures' (Constant 1819: 317). This is to say that the freedoms cherished by the moderns are those which protect the individual in the peaceful, private enjoyment of his self-interests, freed from the burdens of a public life. It means:

> ... the right to be subjected only to the laws, and to be neither arrested, detained, put to death or maltreated in any way by the arbitrary will of one or more individuals. It is the right of everyone to express their opinion, choose a profession and practice it, to dispose of property, and even to abuse it; to come and go without permission, and without having to account for their motives and undertakings. It is everyone's right to associate with other individuals, either to discuss their interests, or to profess the religion which they and their associates prefer, or even simply to occupy their days or hours in a way which is most compatible with their inclinations or whims. Finally, it is everyone's right to exercise some influence on the administration of the government, either by electing all or particular officials, or through representations, petitions, demands to which the authorities are more or less compelled to pay heed. (Constant 1819: 310–11)

Whereas the influence of the ancients on public affairs was direct, for the moderns their influence is only minimally felt, 'at fixed and rare intervals', and even then always only immediately to 'renounce it', by way of delegation to a public official through election (Constant 1819: 312). Accounting for the difference between ancient and modern *worlds*, Constant pointed to the sheer size of modern states (both in terms of territory and population) compared to the ancient city states, which made the direct participation of all impractical;[1] to the absence of slavery, an institution upon which the freedom of the classic republics had been built;[2]

1 As John Selden famously put it, representation was the primary form of political participation for the simple reason that 'the room will not hold all' (see John Selden (David Wilkins, ed.), *The Works of John Selden*, in three volumes, vol. 1, Clark, NJ, The Lawbook Exchange Ltd., 2006), p. 1747.

2 If his claim was dubious at the time – he held up the U.S. as an exemplar of the modern world, at a time when the decline of slavery in the northern states led to a 'second wave' of slave trading from north to south, where they were put to work on massive cotton, rice and tobacco plantations (see, for example, James Oliver Horton and Lois E. Horton *Slavery and the Making of America* (Oxford, Oxford University Press, 2005)) – there is little to suggest that the abolition of slavery (at least, as Constant understood it) has led to anything like the emancipation which he describes. James Tully, for example, has argued that dominant, even hegemonic understandings of constitutionalism obscure from view the full plurality of culturally diverse movements, who seek not only degrees of self-rule, but also a common ground into which that very diversity can be recognized. (James Tully *Strange Multiplicity: Constitutionalism in an Age of Diversity* (Cambridge, Cambridge University Press, 1995)). With a particular focus on American aboriginal peoples, Tully sees in the struggle for recognition 'one of the most dangerous and pressing problems of the present age' (Ch. 1, pp. 14–15). More still, whilst old political classes seek the (self-interested) preservation of their exalted status in the face of democratic challenge (Peter Oborne *The Triumph of the Political Class* (London, Simon & Schuster Ltd., 2007), we can see that the expansion of private interests has presented new sites of exploitation and slavery on a global scale. A recent report by the Hong Kong Christian Industrial Committee, for example, found that 'Western sports shoe companies have been relocating factories or seeking sub-contractors in Asia', not only 'where wages are lower', but also because 'systematic repression of labour movements promises a "docile" workforce'.

and – displaying his roots in the Scottish tradition of Hume and Smith[3] – to the growth of private spheres of industry and commerce which, he said, 'inspire in men a vivid love of individual independence ... [which] ... supplies their needs, [and] satisfies their desires, without the intervention of the authorities' (Constant 1819: 315).

The point of Constant's lecture, at least (and here is that qualification again) *at first*, was that whilst there was in his view, in a time long since past – in an ancient world – a political condition in which man was a "political animal" above all else, the condition of modern man, industrial man, commercial man, man of private enterprise, had consigned the collective concern for public affairs *to* that past: public freedom becoming at best an anachronistic curiosity, and – with Rousseau, Robespierre and the spectre of *la Terreur* fresh in his mind – at worst a dangerous threat to the private liberties of the individual (Constant 1819: 318–19).

What makes this anatomy of freedom so relevant here is two-fold. First, its enduring influence; secondly, the remarkable turn which Constant himself made, in the very same address, *back* to the liberty of ancients as the *remedy* for the ills of the modern individualism.

## Republicanism Revived?

As far as the impact of his work goes, whilst Constant may not have been entirely original in his thesis – surely owing a debt of gratitude to those giants of the Enlightenment who so inspired him during his formative years in Edinburgh – in modern literature his influence remains keenly felt, forming as it does the reference point for those who seek to work within, beyond or against that division of ancient (political/public) and modern (private) liberty. Above all, Isaiah Berlin has described Constant as being no less than 'the most eloquent of all defenders of freedom and privacy' (Berlin 1958: 11). Berlin's famous distinction between *negative* liberty (I am free 'to the degree to which no human being interferes with my activity' (Berlin 1958: 7)) and *positive* liberty (which, in the words of Charles Taylor, 'involves essentially the exercise of control over one's life' (Taylor 1991: 144)) clearly echoes not only the *distinction* drawn by Constant (ancient/positive; modern/negative) but also (at least, at first glance) the view that of the two it is negative freedom, freedom *from* interference, that is most suited to the condition of modern man. Just as Constant invoked the memory of *la Terreur* to discredit an ancient conception of (positive) liberty 'no longer valid', yet 'made fashionable' by philosophers such as Rousseau (Constant 1819: 318–19) so too Berlin, who made additions born of his own time and experience, Marx as well as Jean-Jacques,

(See Jack Eaton *Comparative Employment Relations: An Introduction* (Cambridge, Polity Press, 2000), Ch. 11, p. 167.)

3 At the age of 15, Constant was admitted to the University of Edinburgh where he had been exposed to the coal face of enlightenment thinking, describing the period as the most pleasant of his life (William W. Holdheim *Benjamin Constant* (London, Bowes & Bowes, 1961), Ch. 1, p.13).

Communist-era totalitarianism as well as the French Revolution. Moreover, whilst the distinction has come under serious and sustained attack in the field of philosophy,[4] it is undoubtedly the case that it continues to shape the terrain upon which contemporary battles about liberty, and the constitutions which define it, are fought. Before returning to Constant, allow me to follow this thought then to the conclusion that the distinction pervades even the attempt by Philip Pettit and Quentin Skinner to escape its dichotomy in search of a 'third' concept of liberty: freedom as non-domination.

*Pettit, Skinner and republican freedom as non-domination*

It is fair to say that over the course of the past decade or so, the concurrent work of Pettit and Skinner has brought about a revival, and indeed something of a reinvigoration, of republican ideas somewhere near the mainstream of political thought, historical inquiry, philosophy, and – the subject at hand – legal and constitutional theory. The force of this revival has sparked productive debates on at least two fronts. First, the interpretation of republicanism drawn by the pair has presented an internal challenge to republicans themselves. The tradition which Pettit defends, he tells us, 'is not the sort of tradition – ultimately, the populist tradition – that hails the democratic participation of the people as one of the highest forms of good', nor does it wax lyrical (as Pettit himself puts it) 'about the desirability of the close, homogenous society that popular participation is often taken to presuppose' (Pettit 1997: 8). In this respect, he seeks to recover the republican tradition from those, such as Charles Taylor and Michael Sandel, for whom (in his view) republicanism means above all else the positive/ancient freedom of the citizens to participate directly in the government of the polity. Identifying the German political thinker Hannah Arendt as the protagonist-in-chief of this 'populist' tale of republicanism, Pettit is clear that, as he sees it, democracy, and its institutional manifestations, are (if at all) of but *instrumental* importance to the health of the republic. 'Democratic participation may be essential to the republic', he concedes, 'but that is because it is necessary for promoting the enjoyment of freedom as non-domination, not because of its independent attractions: not because freedom, as a positive conception would suggest, is nothing more or less than the right of democratic participation' (Pettit 1997: 8).

This said, neither Pettit's nor Skinner's gaze is primarily aimed in this direction. As far as they are concerned, the (so-called) populists have already lost the

4 See, for example, Gerald MacCallum 'Positive and Negative Freedom', in Miller (ed.) (1991), for whom the simplicity of the ancient/positive, modern/negative dichotomy is misleading. For MacCallum, freedom is 'always *of* something (an agent or agents), *from* something, do, not to do, become or not become something; it is a triadic relationship' (100). Thus, MacCallum says, the freedom of an agent to act, for certain ends, opposed by certain constraints cannot be preconceived in the binary fashion of the straightforwardly negative or positive. Rather, negative or positive freedom can 'serve only to emphasise one or the other of two features of *every* case of the freedom of agents' (106).

argument with their liberal (*ergo* modern) counterparts. Secondly, then, theirs has been an attempt to demarcate a third sense of liberty, freedom as non-domination – a republican one in Pettit's mind, a neo-Roman one in Skinner's, though the two are (minor differences aside) more or less interchangeable – which, whilst eschewing the burdens of (ancient/positive) political liberty is at the same time different from, more demanding than and yet preferable to the dominant liberal paradigm of (negative/modern) freedom as non-interference (Skinner 2002b).

Skinner's attention is fixed on a period in English history – the 17th century, spanning the civil war and Glorious Revolution – when much in the way of opposition to a tyrannous king was framed by his opponents in parliament in the language of 'what is perhaps best described as the neo-roman element in early-modern political thought' (Skinner 1998: 11). The claims being made by James Harrington, John Milton, Marchamont Nedham and Algernon Sydney amongst others, were two-fold. First, they said, an individual could not be free unless he lived in a free state. Taking seriously the ancient metaphor of the body politic, a free state was defined by its capacity for self government:

> Just as individual human bodies are free, they argue, if and only if they are able to act or forebear from acting at will, so the bodies of nations and states are likewise free if and only if they are similarly unconstrained from using their powers according to their own wills in pursuit of their desired ends. (Skinner 1998: 25–6)

This could only be said to be the case, so it was put, where the actions of the body politic were determined by the will of its members as a whole. In order to achieve this, a number of constitutional implications followed: the laws which governed that state must only be made in accordance with the citizens' consent; each citizen must have equal opportunity to participate in the framing of those laws; the body of that people – 'too unwieldy to be assembled' (Harrington), and indeed prone to 'exorbitant and excessive' behaviour (Milton) even if they *could* be so assembled – was to be found in an elective assembly 'of the more virtuous and considering … chosen by the people to legislate on their behalf' (Skinner 1998: 32). Secondly, just as the individual who loses his liberty is made a slave, so too a nation or state which loses its freedom must be analyzed 'entirely in terms of what it means to fall into a condition of enslavement or servitude' (Skinner 1998: 36–7). Here we reach the crux of the neo-Roman argument, and the means by which Skinner distinguishes it both from the 'ancient' and the 'modern' understandings of liberty. Public servitude, said these stalwarts of the *Good Old Cause*, could be brought about in two ways. For one, a state will be rendered unfree where it is forcibly or coercively deprived of its capacity to act at will in pursuit of its own ends. So when Charles I entered the House of Commons to arrest five of its members, in a bid to prevent that national assembly from deliberating freely about public affairs, he could be said to be forcibly substituting his own will for that of the body politic – reducing England to a state of public servitude, and making himself an enemy to whom opposition was 'at once irresistible' (Skinner 1998: 48). More innovative, however, was the claim that a state could be rendered unfree even where, as a matter of fact, it is *not* governed tyrannically. 'Such a state', said Skinner, 'will nevertheless be counted as living in slavery if its capacity for action is in any way dependent upon the will of anyone other than the body of its own citizens' (Skinner 1998: 47–9). Hence the fierce opposition expressed by Milton not to the *exercize* of the King's 'negative voice' – his right to veto the legislative proposals put to him by the national assembly – but to the very *existence* of that right, which 'takes away the independence of parliament, making it subject to, and dependent on, the will of the king' (Skinner 1998: 52):

> Your rulers may choose not to exercise these powers, or may exercise them only with the tenderest regard for your individual liberties. So you may in practice continue to enjoy the full range of your civil rights. The very fact, however, that your rulers possess such arbitrary powers means that the continued enjoyment of your civil liberties remains at all times dependent on their goodwill. (Skinner 1998: 70)

In Pettit's language, adapting and updating this tradition, one can say that where such powers exist but are not, as a matter of fact, exercised, one may be said to be free from *interference*. One remains in a condition of servitude however by the power holder's capacity for *domination*. For Pettit, and in a clear parallel with Skinner's work, freedom from domination means 'precisely that no individuals have [arbitrary] power over you' (Pettit 1997: 25). Illustrating this point with the classic example of the relationship between master and slave, for Pettit the freedom of the slave is already compromised when the fact of non-interference by his master is secured at the cost of his own conscious act of self-censorhip; where the 'realm of possible futures' open to the slave is restricted by his second-guessing the behaviour which will curry favour with his master – be that by flattery or fawning (Pettit 2002: 348):

> It may just happen that my master is of a kindly and non-interfering disposition. Or it may just happen that I am cunning or fawning enough to be able to get away with doing whatever I like. I suffer domination to the extent that I have a master; I enjoy non-interference to the extent that that master fails to interfere. (Pettit 1997: 23)

The point, however, is that in the future the master may grow wearisome of such fawning, or wise to such cunning; may abruptly alter his disposition (for reasons internal or external), or may be succeeded by an altogether different character, more malevolent in nature. Where non-interference is secured only by such contingencies, the precariousness of that condition is clear. Where the fact of non-interference exists because of the absence of domination, however, the individual is protected against any interference that another may, at any time, intend.

Securing non-domination, in Pettit's analysis, requires a double movement: first, protection against *dominium*: the 'problems [of domination] which arise in people's dealings with one another'; and secondly, against *imperium*, where the state itself becomes an agent of domination. It is security against the latter, he says, which is tasked to our constitutions (Pettit 1997: 171). For Pettit, a constitution can secure non-domination only where it provides 'systematic possibilities for ordinary people to contest the doings of government.' By making decisions contestable, citizens can ensure that authority is exercized for public, rather than for private or sectional, interests (Pettit 1997: 183). Thus this conception of republicanism can be distinguished from liberty as non-interference because, contrary to that school of thought, interference (say, in the form of legislation) which *is* conducted in an environment of effective contestability cannot be said to be arbitrary, to induce unfreedom. In other words, just as there can be domination without interference, so too there can be interference without domination. At the same time, by focussing on contestability, Pettit draws the clearest distinction between his republican interpretation, and the populism (as he sees it) of Arendt et al. Non-domination, he says depends upon the citizens in some sense 'owning' and 'identifying' with the decisions being made. Consent, however, provides an unsatisfactory account of ownership in Pettit's mind. If, on the one hand, explicit individual consent is required for each decision, then non-domination becomes an inaccessible ideal. On the other hand, if implicit consent is enough, then non-domination becomes so accessible as to be meaningless: 'any decision which fails to drive me to the barricades will count as non-arbitrary.' Instead, then, Pettit suggests that by being able effectively to contest any decision which runs counter to our (individual/collective) interest we are able to own the decision: to ensure that it does reflect, or can be made to reflect those interests (Pettit 1997: 184–5). Because their conception rejects self-mastery – active participation and an actively given consent to the law – Pettit and Skinner's vision of republicanism is presented, like its liberal counterpart, as being one which furthers a *negative* conception of liberty: a freedom *from* domination by others. It is, however, one with a twist of positive liberty, to the extent only that something more than the absence of interference is needed: that being the existence of channels through which citizens might manifest their contestation to those laws which run counter to their interests (Pettit 1997: 85). It would seem then that theirs is not a 'third way' of understanding liberty at all, at least not in so much as the third way marks a wholly distinct alternative to that which has come before it. Rather, it is a 'way' which looks to broaden and enrich the meaning and consequences of negative liberty, the liberty of the moderns.

### *The domination of freedom as non-domination*

Republican freedom as non-domination, as it has been historicized by Skinner and theorized by Pettit has, over the course of the past decade or so, come itself to dominate modern republican discourse. A newcomer to republicanism who picked up a recent collection such as, say, Besson and Marti's *Legal Republicanism* (2009), or Maynor and Laborde's *Republicanism and Political Theory* (2008), could be forgiven for thinking that Pettit and Skinner's account of republicanism is the only show in town. Republicanism, however, is itself an ambiguous term – the most unintelligible in the English language, as John Adams famously said[5] – which offers a startling variety of (not always compatible) ideas on citizenship, constitutional form, institutional shape, international relations, trade, cosmopolitanism and much more. The dominant influence of just one such account, important though it may be, should not, therefore, be thought inevitable, a kind of republican 'end of history'. All of which begs the question: upon what contingency has this domination been brought about? The answer, as seen from this vantage point, has neatly been spelled out by Laborde and Maynor in the introduction to their 2008 collection. In order to be taken seriously by the mainstream, they say, republicans must themselves be recognized as taking seriously what they call 'the circumstances of liberal modernity – moral individualism, ethical pluralism, and an instrumental view of political life', and to fit (squeeze, even) old republican insights into them (Laborde & Maynor 2008: 1). By emphasizing that his republican account of freedom is (primarily) a negative one, Pettit is able to find a foothold in the liberal mainstream because, unlike others such as Arendt, Pocock and Rahe, his falls on the 'right' side of the ancient/modern (Constant) or positive/negative (Berlin) divide. This chapter will conclude, however, with the claim that, in striving to present a republicanism acceptable to 'the moderns' – one shorn of the spectre of revolution, tumult and terror – Pettit has conceded too much of the republican tradition at the altar of mainstream political theory. Furthermore, it seems to me that in doing so the republican account of freedom as non-domination struggles to escape the question of active consent, and to keep hidden from new friends the positive political liberty still at its core. Allow me to explain.

## *Recovering 'the public'*

Pettit suggests that, as a last resort for those frustrated by the outcome of their (unsuccessful) contestation, two options remain on the table. The first option is secession: that the '[dominated] group are allowed to secede from the state, establishing a separate territory, or at least a separate jurisdiction' (Pettit 1997: 199). The second, accepting that secession is not always viable or desirable, is that 'there should be room in any republican society for dissenting individuals and groups to claim a special treatment under the law' (Pettit 1997: 200). Whilst he admits that his investigations into what such accommodation might look like are embryonic at best, his chosen examples – the separate treatment afforded to indigenous populations in Canada and Australia, or to the Amish community – are, it seems, illuminating in two respects. First, because at this point – the point of dissent – it no longer makes sense to think of Pettit's republic as one based on contestability and not on consent. If the final expression of the citizens' contestation is dissent, a rejection of the principles by which they are governed and the creation

5 … in a letter to his confidante and some times adviser, Mercy Ottis Warren, dated 8th August, 1807.

of a new jurisdiction, presumably this must happen on the basis of consent, indeed, active consent, on the part of those dissenters; both to form together, to act-in-concert, as well as to constitute a new and separate political/constitutional entity. Secondly, by advocating dissent as a negatively constituted phenomenon (that is to say, as a freedom to escape from the dominant party) the creative force of conflict, which as we shall see lies at the core of Roman republican theory, is lost. Dissenters do not, in Pettit's account, confront the dominant rulers head on in a positive act of reconstitution between the parties. Rather they withdraw into their own communities, their own identities: each to their own private interests.

In more recent work, Quentin Skinner has sought to step back somewhat from the emphasis placed by Pettit and himself on the self-censoring slave as the archetypal dominated subject (Skinner 2008: 93). For Skinner, a focus on self-censorship is of but secondary importance to the main claim which (neo-Roman) republicans wish to make. Exponents of republican liberty as non-domination, he said, 'agree that anyone who reflects on their own servitude will probably come to *feel* unfree to act or forbear from acting in certain ways. But what actually *makes* them unfree is the mere fact of their living in subjection to arbitrary power' (Skinner 2008: 93–4). Now, it is true that this 'return to basics' by Skinner remains a few steps removed from the claim which is being made here – the claim that freedom *demands* the positive exercise of political liberty. It is possible to begin by saying, however, that by drawing back from the example of the self-censoring slave to the basic point that subjection to arbitrary power is the primary concern of those who value freedom as non-domination, Skinner offers the reminder that there are a number of possible scenarios in which domination might occur, including the predicament of one who is dominated without even coming to consciousness of that fact, or who may even be *indifferent* to her status as citizen, subject or slave. With this is mind, a return to his *Visions of Politics* (2002) is revealing:

> The Roman historians had entertained one further and yet more tragic thought about the effects of living in servitude. Provided that our loss of liberty is accompanied by a life of ease, they had argued, we may fall into such a state of corruption that we may cease even to wish for the more strenuous life of freedom and greatness. (Skinner 2002: 306)

So, Tacitus told how the French, once 'redoubted in war', had in time '[given] themselves over to peace and idleness', such that 'cowardice crept in, and shipwreck was made both of manhood and liberty together' (Skinner 2002: 306). The Romans, described by Arendt as 'perhaps the most political people we have known' (Arendt 1958: 7) fared little better – the nobility betraying their freedom when, upon Augustus's usurpation of power, they offered no resistance, 'so much [were they] more bettered in wealth, and advanced in honors'; preferring, as Sallust wrote, 'to live in subjection, than [to] command with Honour' (Skinner 2002: 306–7). From these sources, Skinner goes on to note the Englishman John Milton's late preoccupation with the idea of a people's willing subjection, particularly after the restoration of the monarchy in 1660. 'But what more oft in nations grown corrupt; And by their vices brought to servitude; Than to love bondage more than liberty; Bondage with ease than strenuous liberty' (Milton, in Skinner 2002: 306). With this brief but illuminating discussion, Skinner rests the theme. The point, however, is important and deeply rooted in the republican tradition so close to his (and to Pettit's) work. Domination may lead to interference, it may even lead to self-censorship; what Skinner calls the '*worst* betrayal of the birthright of freedom' (Skinner 2002: 306), however, is corruption not of the rulers but the ruled, the people themselves: not as the corruption of the *demos* was so often painted by the ancient authorities, in the form of *hyper*activity – in the form of licentiousness, avarice and anarchy – but rather in a deliberate withdrawal from the public realm into private pleasure, and a condition of *in*activity. Indeed, as we shall see, for Machiavelli, the opportunity for action was the very lifeblood of the Roman constitution.

## Rome Re-visited

According to Machiavelli, in every republic there were (generally speaking) two classes: an upper and a lower class, the nobility and the common people, the 'haves', as he called them, and the 'have-nots' (Machiavelli 1970: 115). What it was that the upper class 'had', and the lower class 'had not', was power, through the holding of political office. This being the case, Machiavelli posed himself the question: in whose hands, the 'haves' or the 'have-nots', is best placed the safeguarding of liberty. Answering the question, the Florentine addressed himself to the ambitions of each. Amongst the nobility, he said, there was 'a great desire to dominate.' That is to say, there was a desire to acquire more and more power. Amongst the common people, however, was simply 'the desire not to be dominated' (Machiavelli 1970: 116). For this reason, Machiavelli advised that it was in the hands of the common people that the safekeeping of liberty should be left:

> If the populace be made the guardians of liberty, it is reasonable to suppose that they will take more care of it, and … since it is impossible for them to usurp power, they will not permit others to do so. (Machiavelli 1970: 116)

Where Machiavelli distinguished himself from his peers, who equated discord with faction, and faction with unfreedom (Skinner 1981: 66), was his insistence that the (often violent) clashes between these classes was *constitutive of*, and certainly not the antithesis of, liberty, and thus the very dynamic of the republican constitution. Take, as a case in point, his praise for tumult in the streets of Rome.

> Look how people used to assemble and clamour against the senate, and how the senate decried the people, how men ran helter-skelter about the streets, how the shops were closed and how the plebs en masse would troop out of Rome – events which terrify, to say the least, anyone who read about them. (Machiavelli 1970: 116)

Unlike others who 'read about them', for Machiavelli these (seemingly anarchic) scenes were the very means by which the common people defended, indeed enhanced, their liberty. He was perfectly willing to accept that 'someone may object' to what looked, on the surface, like 'extraordinary and almost barbaric' acts. He was, however, unwilling to concede the point. No republic, he said, can be 'stigmatized in any way as disordered' in which tumult leads to the creation of good laws (Machiavelli 1970: 114). 'To me', he continued, 'those who condemn the quarrels between the nobles and the plebs, seem to be caviling at the very things that were the primary cause of Rome's retaining her freedom' (Machiavelli 1970: 113–14). Chastising those who 'pay more attention to the noise and clamour resulting from such commotions than to what resulted from them', for Machiavelli what *did* result from them was legislation favourable to liberty, his named example the creation of the tribunes. Charged with mediating between the plebs and the senate, and vested with such prerogatives as necessary to protect the former from arbitrary interference by the latter, the Roman tribunes were born of a conflict between constituted and constituent power:

> Hence if tumults led to the creation of the tribunes, tumults deserve the highest praise, since, besides giving the populace a share in the administration, they served as the guardian of Roman liberties. (Machiavelli 1970: 115)

From Machiavelli's observations, let us draw out three more: First, and agreeing with the line taken by Skinner and Pettit, we can say that the tradition which looks back to Rome in order to distinguish republican from liberal freedom identified amongst these Roman authorities a concern with non-domination. Indeed, the desire not to be dominated marked, in Machiavelli's view, the limits of the citizens' ambition. Second, however, these modern exponents of republican freedom as non-domination are not, on this author's reading of Machiavelli (nor, on Skinner's reading of Sallust and Tacitus), correct to identify the republican conception of non-domination as being a negatively constituted liberty; (merely) a freedom *from* domination. To be sure, Pettit takes great pains to demonstrate that freedom from interference is not a straightforwardly negative one, conceding that there *might* be a role for democratic participation compatible with his republican vision, even if such participation is instrumental in safeguarding liberty, rather than having any definitional connection to it (Pettit 1997: 51). This, however, underplays the relationship between non-domination and action. After all, active resistance, such as he saw in the tumults of Rome was not, for Machiavelli, *one* way in which non-domination could be achieved. Rather, the Florentine was clear in his assertion that '*all* legislation favourable to liberty is brought about by the clash between [the nobility and the common people]' (Machiavelli 1997: 113). Thus, where there is no such action, where the 'have-nots' do not resist the (inevitable, ever creeping) usurpation by those who 'have' and wish to acquire still more power, there will be *no* legislation favourable to liberty. Furthermore, in the *Annals* of Tacitus, in Sallust's *Conspiracy of Catiline*, as well as in Machiavelli's *Discourses*, those writers upon whose observations the neo-Roman tradition was built had made clear that, in their view, domination itself might lead, finally, to that very loss of virtue, specifically, the loss of a virtue of 'public mindedness', which reduces (by the promise of an easy way of life, of wealth, or security) active citizens to passive subjects. If Pettit is correct to say that freedom from domination 'is not a positive one' (Pettit 1997: 27), how are we to account for the claim by Tacitus that such cowardice makes a mockery not only of liberty, but (separately, on its own terms) 'manhood'; or the claim by Machiavelli that the tumults ensured not only the safeguarding of liberty, but (separately, on its own terms) the share of the common people in the administration of government? Third, if tumult did ensure the share of the common people in the administration of government, what can we say about the nature of that share? For Machiavelli, it was clear that the creative potential of tumult (the passage of good laws, the creation of the tribunes) testified to its being a share in the administration of the state. It would seem, however, that such share as the common people had was not a share in normal, everyday decision making. It was not, this is to say, a share in the administration of *ordinary* politics. Moreover, in Machiavelli's view, the common people demanded no such share. They wished *only* not to be dominated. Thus, their share in administration was limited to the *extraordinary* moments when those entrusted with political office attempted to take for themselves more (power) than they were due. The resistance of the people then, 'either [they] behaved in some such way as we have described or [they] refused to enlist for the wars, so that to placate [them], [they] had to some extent to be satisfied' (Machiavelli 1970: 114), at least as it was presented in the *Discourses*, occurred somewhere in between the ordinary exercise of everyday political power, and the revolutionary breaking down of old and building up of entirely new jurisdictions. Resistance or tumult marked what Kalyvas has called (though in reference to the work of others: Weber, Schmitt and Arendt) the politics of the extraordinary: when 'politics opens up to make room for conscious popular participation and extra-institutional, spontaneous collective intervention' (Kalyvas 2008: 7). Agreeing with Pettit that freedom from domination, as the Romans expressed it, was neither straightforwardly positive nor negative, this work suggests that Pettit goes too far to say that this conception of freedom is largely negative, with the positive twist that popular participation *might* be instrumental in achieving non-domination. Quite the opposite, it seems that courage (to step outside the life of ease, and to set aside one's private interests), and the public minded virtue of *zoon politikon*, was the *conditio sine qua non* of non-domination, demanding with it the self-constitution of a public space into which this confrontation, this moment of action, could assume reality: the tumults, and the consequent creation of the tribunes, evidence to Machiavelli that the 'city of Rome was one which provided such ways and means' (Machiavelli 1970: 114). If there was a negative twist to that freedom, then this was a freedom *from* the unwelcome intrusion upon, or closure of, that space, by the nobility. Returning now to Constant, the Frenchman – in a turn which must come as a surprise to the reader who has followed the anatomy of liberty which precedes it – put it quite brilliantly:

> [T]he holders of authority are only too anxious to encourage us to [surrender to them our right to share in political power]. They are so ready to spare us all sort of troubles, except those of obeying and paying! They will say to us: what, in the end, is the aim of your efforts, the motive of your labours, the object of all your hopes? Is it not happiness? Well, leave this happiness to us and we shall give it to you. (Constant 1819: 326)

His response was emphatic and stirring. 'No, Sirs', he said, 'we must not leave it to them. No matter how touching such a tender commitment may be, let us ask the authorities to keep within their limits' (Constant 1819: 326). It was Constant's fear that his contemporaries, the moderns, 'absorbed in the enjoyment of our private independence, and in the pursuit of our particular interests [might] surrender our right to share in political power too easily' (Constant 1819: 326). It would seem, in other words, that having *encouraged* us to retreat from the public realm, to enjoy security in our private liberty and to desert the rigors of the public realm, Constant discovered *at that precise moment* what was lost by doing so: the virtue of publicity.

## The Lost Treasure of Publicity

It is true that 'The Liberty of the Ancients' failed to pinpoint precisely what this loss might entail, beyond a general claim for political liberty, whatever that may be, however that may be exercised. For sure Constant made an Aristotelian appeal to *zoon politikon*: the claim that even the moderns find self-fulfilment only in the exercise of politics:

> Political liberty, by submitting to all the citizens, without exception, the care and assessment of their most sacred interests, enlarges their spirit, enobles their thoughts, and establishes among them a kind of intellectual equality which forms the glory and power of a people. (Constant 1819: 327)

Self-fulfilment however seems an unconvincing explanation for his sudden (re)turn to political liberty. After all, there was little spirit and certainly not much glory in his reflections back upon his own time in political office: 'a chance to fulfil a duty, which is the only way to lift the burden of doubt, memory, and unrest, the eternal lot of our wretched and transitory nature' (Constant, in Holmes 1984: 44). Rather, the somewhat banal textual explanation for the seemingly unfathomable contradiction built into Constant's speech betrays a more meaningful and altogether more interesting insight at the very point of his republican turn. As Stephen Holmes has said:

> The strikingly democratic conclusion to "Ancient and Modern Liberty" remains puzzling until we understand how the underlying logic of the argument of 1798 was adapted to meet the demands of Restoration politics. The lecture is a palimpsest. It is so complex because it was composed twice, the second version

> superimposed on the [barely edited] first after an interval of twenty years. By 1819, Constant's original fear of convulsive and compulsory patriotism had partly yielded to his hope that enhanced participation might advance liberal causes while keeping the ultras in check. (Holmes 1984: 43)

In the midst of this 20-year period, an unmistakable suspicion of politics, and retreat into the safety, security, and pleasures of the private realm, had suddenly been turned on its head: the tyranny of terror answered by no more than the tyranny of the emperor, Napoleon. What marks Constant as a relevant, and even critical thinker to this day is that he was able to locate the rise of that "usurper" in precisely the conditions of modernity which – in the first place – he had set out to praise. Amid the private happiness of multitudinous individuals in territorially expanded states, the public square had been deserted, and with it the citizen had lost his zeal for public duty. Only with the rise of Napoleon did Constant come to realize that what distinguished ancient and modern constitutions was not only their understanding of freedom, but the constitution of a *public* space within which *political* freedom could be exercised. Elsewhere, Constant had written:

> In the large associations of modern times, the freedom of the press, being the only means of publicity, is by this fact, whatever the form of government, the only protection of our rights. In Rome Collatinus could expose on the public square the body of Lucretia and the whole people was instructed of the outrage he had received.... But in our days the immensity of empires prevents this kind of protest. Partial injustices remain unknown to almost all the inhabitants of our vast regions. (Constant 1991: 82)

As Fontana has said, for Constant, '[p]ublicity, the transparency of actions of public authorities and institutions' was the soul of republican government ancient *and* modern (Fontana 1991: 81); the most meaningful check on arbitrary rule. Thus, he wrote:

> The coercive force needed to constrain a government to obey the laws is located in the constitution, in the penalties it pronounces against treacherous wielders of authority, in the rights it assures its citizens, and above all in the publicity it consecrates. (Constant, in Holmes 1984: 243)

Calling publicity 'a sacred right' Constant lamented the opportunism with which Napoleon had been able to navigate the obstacles and boundaries of civic privatism to establish his tyranny. Frenchmen could not, or would not, resist this tyrant because, deprived of publicity, they 'lived alone, ignorant of each other and in a painful sleep, interrupted by noises to which they contribute nothing. What results is a momentary annihilation of all opinion, all public suffrage' (Constant, in Holmes 1984: 247). Where the public was absent, to put it another way, there the seeds of tyranny were sewn. Thus, when Constant addressed the Athénée Royal, finally with the proposition that political liberty is *indispensable*, he was warning not only his audience but the French nation that when they need their civil liberties most they might just awake from their slumber to find them useless: 'to renounce [political liberty]', he warned us, ourselves, we: the moderns, 'would be a folly like that of a man who, because he only lives on the first floor, does not care if the house itself is built on sand' (Constant 1819: 326).

## Conclusion

This chapter seeks to recover the work of Benjamin Constant from those influential readings offered by Isaiah Berlin and Philip Pettit; arguing that there is much more to his political thought than an 'eloquent defence of freedom and privacy'. These accounts, which lay stress on Constant's praise for modern liberty as a freedom *from* the burdens and scrutiny of the public realm, each deny the relevance of political liberty as a positively constituted expression of consent to the law, and invoke Constant to that end. For they – and, as we have seen, with some considerable textual support for their position – Constant saw no public *in* law; only private individuals whose private interests were protected *by* laws, made *for* but *without* them. '[T]he true modern liberty', he said, 'is individual liberty' (Constant 1819: 327); and the greatest justification for the representative system – that in which the exercise of political rights is delegated to an elite few 'to do what [the people] can't or doesn't want to do itself' – was precisely that it allowed modern man more time to pursue his private endeavours (Constant 1819: 327).

Yet, the truly remarkable moment in Constant's work – that marked by a turn *back* to political freedom as the *only* guarantee of modern liberty – seems entirely to have been missed in those accounts. The rise of Napolean, and the futility of both civil liberty and representative institutions against the suppression of opposition at home, and wasteful militarism abroad, inspired from Constant a distinctly republican turn, one which called not for an elite few, but for 'all people – no exceptions' (Constant 1819: 326) to emerge from the private realm, to set aside their individual concerns, and reflexively to (re)constitute a space for the public in law. Placing Constant's thought firmly *within* the tradition of neo-republican or non-dominating freedom which Pettit sets out to praise, we can see what it is that is at stake here still for us, the moderns. In an 'age of rights', wherein political and judicial (as well as others, for example financial or economic) elites are all too keen to dissuade us from exercising fully our political rights (Bobbio 1996, Henkin 1996, Loughlin 2000), the danger is that we too might sleepwalk into tyranny; or worse still, that we already have and neither know nor care.

## References

Besson, S. and J.L. Marti. (2009). *Legal Republicanism: National and International Perspectives*, Oxford: Oxford University Press.

Bobbio, N. (1996) *The Age of Rights*, Cambridge: Polity Press.

Constant, B. (1819). 'The Liberty of the Ancients Compared with That of the Moderns', in B. Fontana (ed.) (2001) *Benjamin Constant: Political Writings*, Cambridge: Cambridge University Press., p. 307.

Ferguson, A. (1995). *An Essay on the History of Civil Society*, Cambridge: Cambridge University Press.

Frank, J. (2010). *Constituent Moments: Enacting the People in Post-revolutionary America*, Durham and London: Duke University Press.

Henkin, L. (1996). *Age of Rights*, New York: Columbia University Press.

Holdheim, W.H. (1961). *Benjamin Constant*, London: Bowes & Bowes.

Holmes, S. (1984). *Benjamin Constant and the Making of Modern Liberalism*, New Haven and London: Yale University Press.

Kalyvas, A. (2008). *Democracy and the Politics of the Extraordinary: Max Weber, Carl Schmitt and Hannah Arendt*, Cambridge: Cambridge University Press.

Laborde, C. and J. Maynor (eds). (2008). *Republicanism and Political Theory*, Oxford: Blackwell Publishing.

Loughlin, M. (2000). *Sword and Scales: An Examination of the Relationship between Law and Politics*, Oxfort: Hart Publishing.

Machiavelli, N. (1970). *The Discourses* (intro. by Bernard Crick), London: Penguin Books.

Pettit, P. (1997). *Republicanism: A Theory of Freedom and Government*, Oxford: Oxford University Press.

Polybius. (1979). *The Rise of the Roman Empire*, London: Penguin Books.

Rand, A. (1964). *The Virtue of Selfishness: A New Concept of Egoism*, New York: New American Library.

Skinner, Q. (1981). *Machiavelli*, Oxford: Oxford University Press.

———. (1998). *Liberty Before Liberalism*, Cambridge: Cambridge University Press.

———. (2002). I (in 3 vols.), Cambridge: Cambridge University Press.

———. (2008). *Hobbes and Republican Liberty*, Cambridge: Cambridge University Press.

# Chapter 3
# Democracy, Political Parties and the Will of the People

Andrew Maloney

The principle of popular sovereignty is intrinsic to contemporary notions of democracy. It envisages groups of 'free and equal' citizens uniting together to enact rules or laws which will advance or provide for the general welfare. However, the notion of a united and identifiable popular will as imagined by Rousseau (1762) is unrealistic given the size and complexity of modern societies and the corresponding existence of a diversity of interests and preferences. A more nuanced and realistic scenario entails the adoption of a collective decision procedure which recognizes the existence of substantive disagreement but provides a mechanism for at least its temporary resolution. The approach taken by most democracies is to extol the principle of majority rule as expressed through the mechanism of regular and competitive elections. It is this form of electoral accountability that ensures that the representatives elected and the subsequent rules and laws enacted reflect the *will of the people*. The existence of political parties is a necessary condition of such a process. Their myriad functions include the articulation and aggregation of collective preferences as well as acting as a conduit by which governments can both accede to power and be held accountable. Given the centrality of their role to the democratic process, it is commonly accepted that attempts to enforce legal prohibitions on the existence of specific parties should only be made under exceptional circumstances. (Venice Commission, 1999: Guidelines 1, 5 and 6)

It can be argued however that by defining 'the people' as a temporal and changeable majority, the principle of popular sovereignty potentially threatens the equal rights of those who find themselves in a temporal minority. Political parties while being a necessary component of the democratic process could, if achieving majority status, potentially act as a threat to the continuation of such a process.

> … [I]t is only a short step from proclaiming the sovereignty of the people to claiming the unlimited authority of its elected representatives, to proscribing opposition, and to denying individuals any rights other then those which the government with majority support deems fit. (Benn 1967)

A relatively recent example of a legal prohibition which encapsulates this potential dichotomy is the *Refah Partisi* case from Turkey. The legal dissolution of this party by Turkish authorities was upheld by the European Court of Human Rights on the grounds that its ideology and concomitant popularity posed a real threat to the equal rights of all Turkish citizens and the continuation of democratic governance. It is contended that the decisions reached in *Refah* violate the underlying assumptions of two contrasting yet complementary conceptions of democracy identified as 'electoral' and 'liberal' respectively. It is also argued, however, that neither conception of democracy can provide exclusively or entirely effectively for the representation of the 'will of the people'.

## Refah Partisi v Turkey

### *Background*

*Refah Partisi* or Welfare Party was an Islamic Political party founded in 1983. It regularly participated in subsequent national and local elections growing in popularity to a point where in 1995; it gained 158 out of 550 seats in the Turkish Grand National Assembly. In 1996, the party became the senior party in a coalition government and its chairman, Necmettin Erkaban, became Prime Minister of Turkey. The zeniths of the party's fortunes were short lived and both it and its leader were ousted from power in July 1997 in what was effectively a military coup (Kocak and Orucu, 2003: 415; Olbourne, 2003: 437; Harvey, 2004: 408).

Article 2 of the Constitution of the Republic of Turkey (1982) asserts that Turkey is a 'democratic, secular and social state.' Article 68 expressly prohibits political parties from activities contrary to the principles of 'a democratic and secular republic' and Article 69 states that parties become vulnerable to dissolution if adjudged to be 'centres' of such activities. After an application by the Chief Public Prosecutor in May 1997, the Turkish Constitutional Court formally dissolved *Refah* in January of the following year. The relevant judgement opined that Secularism constituted an indispensable condition of democracy in Turkey and as a result, *Refah*'s actions constituted a threat to Turkish democracy on three grounds. These were the advocacy of legal pluralism, the intention to introduce Islamic or Sharia law into the general law and the advocacy of the use of jihad or holy war to bring about their goals (Turkish Constitutional Court-Decision no. 1998/1). In response, the Party lodged an appeal to the European Court of Human Rights on the grounds that the dissolution amounted to a violation of their Article 11 right to freedom of association (Convention for the Protection of Human Rights and Fundamental Freedoms, 1950).

### *The Strasbourg judgements*

With respect to political systems, the Strasbourg Court has been unambiguous in its admiration for democracy. Relevant jurisprudence assumes democracy to be 'the only political model contemplated by the Convention and consequently the only one compatible with it'. It has also unequivocally placed political parties within the ambit of Article 11.

> … [P]olitical parties are a form of association, and that in view of the importance of democracy in the Convention system, there can be no doubt that political parties come within the scope of Article 11. (*United Communist Party v Turkey*, 1998: at 45; *Socialist Party v Turkey*, 1999: at 28)

During the *Refah* cases, the Strasbourg Court affirmed that 'drastic measures such as the dissolution of an entire political party '… may only be taken in the most serious cases'. However, it also argued that

> By the proposals for an overall societal model which they put before the electorate and by their capacity to implement these proposals once they come to power, political parties differ from other organizations which intervene in the political arena. (*Refah Partisi v Turkey*, Chamber, 2002; *Refah Partisi v Turkey*, Grand Chamber 2003 at 100)

Such reasoning, as Eva Brems (2006, 148–9) has argued, represents a qualitative shift in emphasis. Political parties as a necessary component of democratic governance deserve a high level of protection. However, because they have the potential to directly realize their aims in government, there may be more convincing arguments to prohibit them than other types of association. The application of similar logic allowed the Chamber to assert by a narrow 4–3 margin that the dissolution of *Refah* did not constitute a violation of the applicant's Article 11 rights, a judgement that was upheld unanimously by the Grand Chamber in a subsequent ruling (*Refah*, 2002 at 77; *Refah*, 2003 at 139).

These decisions were based on a number of factors. One was a proposal by the party to introduce a plurality of legal systems. This was interpreted by the Chamber as an infringement of both the neutral role of the state as a guarantor of rights and freedoms and of the principle of non-discrimination. Another was the refusal by the Party to condemn or discipline individual members who had publicly hinted at the acceptability of violent methods as part of an overall strategy (*Refah*, 2002 at 70 and 74). With specific regard to democracy, the Courts based their decision to uphold prohibition on two distinct but complementary lines of reasoning.

In its original decision, the Chamber claimed that as an Islamic Party, *Refah* held an allegiance to Sharia law which was incompatible with respect for the principles that underlay the Convention. Politically, Sharia as a religious 'dogma' was perceived as a threat to the Convention principle of political pluralism. With regard to other potential civil liberty issues, it was the Chamber's contention that Sharia 'clearly diverges' from the Convention in matters concerning criminal procedure and the role of women and that consequently 'it is difficult to declare one's respect for human rights while … supporting a regime based on Sharia.' This argument was reinforced by the Grand Chamber in its subsequent affirmation of the Chamber's decision (*Refah*, 2002: at 70, 74 and 72; *Refah*, 2003: at 123).

Having argued that *Refah*'s principles were inherently incompatible with the Convention, the Courts proceeded to argue that *Refah* constituted a practical as well as an ideological threat to democracy. In a combination of history and demography, the Chamber contended that the previous existence of a theocratic regime, the preponderance of Muslims within the country and the popularity of *Refah* at the time of dissolution made the establishment of a regime based on Sharia '... neither theoretical nor illusory but achievable' (Refah, 2002: at 65 and 77).

The Grand Chamber then went on to develop an argument heavily influenced by a theory known as Militant Democracy (Loewenstein, 1937). This theory emerged during the inter-war years as a response to the rise of Fascism and Communism and argues that in order to protect a system of democratic governance; States should take steps to restrict the political rights of anti-democratic forces. The influence of this theory on the Grand Chamber's subsequent decision is evidenced by its assertion that as democracy has been historically vulnerable to 'totalitarian movements organized in the form of political parties', democratic states should have the right to launch a pre-emptive strike against those they deem to pose a threat to democratic government. With specific reference to *Refah*, it argued (with the use of election results and opinion polls) that the party posed a real and identifiable threat to democracy and consequently, its dissolution was within Turkey's margin of appreciation[1] (*Refah* 2003: 99, 102, 107, 110).

While the aim of preserving a democratic system of governance is a worthy one, it is contended that the reasoning adopted in justifying *Refah*'s dissolution vitiates the commitment to popular sovereignty that it purports to uphold. In order to support this claim, it is necessary to examine the rationale for the Courts' decisions against the assumptions underlying the two competing conceptions of electoral and liberal democracy; those being a respective commitment to the principles of majority rule and equal respect.

## Electoral Democracy, Political Parties and Majority Rule

Democratic governance is often characterized as a universal aspiration and has even been described as a 'human right'(Mayerfield 2003). It is not, however, a uniform concept. The form that any specific democracy takes is dependent on a variety of factors including historical practices and socio-economic conditions. Despite the diverse nature of modern democracies, the one central and common factor to all is a commitment to the mechanism of elections.

### *The necessity of elections*

Proponents of an electoral view of democracy perceive the existence of an electoral mechanism as the most important attribute of a democracy. According to Richard Katz (1997), elections fulfil a number of functions within a democracy. Included amongst these are the installation of people to executive and legislative office and the provision of choice to individual voters in the selection of candidates

1 The margin of appreciation is a judicially developed doctrine that allows individual states a degree of latitude in their interpretation of Convention rights; see Smith 2007: 165.

for relevant posts. Two other inextricably linked roles that Katz attributes to the electoral process are the conferral of legitimacy upon office holders and the fostering of popular representation. The conferral of legitimacy is clearly based on the notion that officials are empowered by the public to act '*for them, or in their place*'. The centrality of this relationship is an essential component of democracy.

> Unless officials are representative in this minimal sense, the resulting government can make no claim to be democratic. Elections are the institutions by which the represented authorize their representatives to act for them, so no system can be democratic without elections. (Katz 1997: 100–106)

### *Political parties and elections*

Given that modern democracies are representative, the role of political parties in the electoral process is essential. One specific role is the aggregation of interests and preferences. Aggregation 'refers to a ... process by which parties bundle together the diverse demands of a variety of social groups'. Such a process is potentially troublesome as it may require a 'prioritization of demands' alongside attempts to maintain a unified coalition amongst different groups whose own priorities 'may be in tension with each other'(Webb 2002: 12). Despite the potential problems inherent in the aggregative process, it is essential if a specific party aspires to another role that parties play within democracies, that it be a conduit through which governments accede to power. With regard to the formation of governments, political parties offer individual voters both a selection of candidates and a set of policy proposals which they can contrast with other parties. In doing so, parties help to 'structure the voting choice' of the electorate (Epstein 1967:14) and help convert their aggregated preferences into the election of a government. Once a government has been formed, the final role of political parties is to ensure that the government remains accountable to the public. This is achieved in two ways. Firstly, the governing party's actions can be evaluated against the promises it made at election time. Secondly, a failure to match promises with action may result in a transformation of electoral preferences facilitated by the existence of competing parties with alternative proposals.

> ... [T]he government carries out the kind of policy programme with which the governing parties identified themselves at the previous election; their incentive for doing so lies in the need to face re-election and the prospect of having to retain the support of their electorates. (Ware 1996: 318)

### *Majority rule*

The subsequent claim to a 'democratic mandate' by elected governments is conventionally defended by the principle of majority rule in that either the policy being implemented or the party implementing it is preferred by a majority of voters (McDonald, Mendes and Budge 2004: 1–26). Given that the idea of equality of political influence is 'intimately connected to democracy' (Katz 1997: 100), the attraction of a principle of majority rule is evident. Firstly, it is issue neutral in that all voters' preferences are counted equally regardless of motive and secondly, the principle of anonymity means that the status of a person is irrelevant to the weight given to their preference (May 1952: 129). This principle is invoked regularly enough to make it the overriding basis on which governments' claim legitimacy for their actions. However, some of the reasoning used by the Strasbourg Courts in *Refah* constitutes a subversion of this principle.

### *Refah and majority rule*

As indicated earlier, the Court viewed *Refah*'s principles as a threat to both the principles underlying the Convention and to the Turkish principle of Secularism. When taken in conjunction with *Refah*'s increasing influence, it argued that the Turkish authorities had the right to interfere with *Refah*'s Article 11 rights.

> The Court accordingly considers that at the time of its dissolution Refah had the real potential to seize political power without being restricted by the compromises inherent in a coalition. If Refah had proposed a programme contrary to democratic principles, its monopoly of political power would have enabled it to establish the model of society envisaged in that programme. (Refah 2003: 110)

From the perspective of the principle of majority rule, this reasoning is troublesome. Firstly, by referring to *Refah*'s growing strength as a basis for prohibition, the Grand Chamber implies that a political party should be more vulnerable to prohibition or dissolution as its popularity increases. Such an idea is a clear violation of the idea of popular sovereignty. Not only does it undermine democratic accountability by removing a vehicle for the aggregation of preferences of a substantial part of the polity but it consequently sabotages the conception of equality of influence which is the basis for majority rule.[2]

> … [P]rohibition is a very restrictive measure, because it disregards the political choice of a large number of voters; it infringes not only the rights of party leaders, but of an increasing number of people. (Brems 2006: 178)

2 On July 30th 2008, the ruling AKP party escaped prohibition despite a 6–5 vote in favour as dissolution required at least 7 votes. The case against the AKP was similar to *Refah* in that the charges against the party were related to its attitude to Secularism. However, dissolution would have had arguably greater implications as it would have been targeted against a party with sole control of the government and a comfortable majority in Parliament. It seems that Strasbourg has been spared a particularly tricky decision. For a brief overview of the case, see Sarah Rainsford 'Narrow Escape leaves Turkey Divided' available at http://news.bbc.co.uk/1/hi/world/europe/7534342.stm.

Secondly, even if one were to accept the militantly democratic outlook of the Court, its own reasoning would negate the prohibition. By using the phrase 'If *Refah* had proposed a programme contrary to democratic principles' it implicitly accepted that *Refah* had *proposed* no such thing. In that respect, if one were to extend the logic applied by the Court in upholding the dissolution, there would be major repercussions for the continuing validity of majority rule throughout Europe.

> An extension of the ECHR's analysis would lead to the inference that any political party, with a monopoly of control, should be dissolved because its monopoly posed a threat to Turkey's democratic principles. (Schilling 2004: 514)

From this perspective, the dissolution of *Refah* can unquestionably be viewed as a violation of the electoral conception of democracy. This does not mean, however, that the assumptions underlying the electoral conception of democracy are flawless in their claim to represent the popular will. Firstly, by placing its entire emphasis on majority rule, it by definition places the interests of the majority ahead of those of the entire polity and opens up the possibility that the rights of those who are in the minority will be violated (Sartori 1987: 24, Donnelly 2003: 191). Examples of such violations have been documented by academics concerning countries such as Milosevic's Serbia and Putin's Russia where it is argued that the legitimizing instrument of elections co-exist with violations of the 'minimum criteria' of democracy such as rights of expression and association. These occur with such frequency that they 'create an uneven playing field between government and opposition' (Levitsky and Way 2002: 53).

Secondly, even in countries where the political rights of all are broadly protected, it is doubtful whether the electoral process accurately translates the preferences of the majority. To begin with, the absence of direct referenda makes it almost impossible to ascertain whether a particular policy has majority support at the time of implementation. Next, even if as is normally the case, majority rule is defined as allegiance to the 'highly aggregated alternatives offered by political parties' (Schmitter and Karl 1996: 52), recent research has shown that only rarely is a governing majority correspondent with the preferences of the majority of electors. For example, in the cases of countries with single member constituencies, governing majorities were produced by a plurality rather than a majority of voters by an almost six to one ratio. Alternatively, in countries with more proportional systems, while a governing majority was produced by the preferences of the majority of the electors in more than half the cases; this was overwhelmingly in the form of coalition government. As coalition governments are almost always produced by 'bargaining between parties' after the election, it is very likely that the subsequent governing majority is 'not one created by the voter's expressed preferences' (McDonald et al, 2004: 5–7, 10).

Electoral Democracy's claim to popular sovereignty can therefore be questioned on a couple of grounds. Not only is its claim to represent a majority of the polity at best dubious, the commitment to majority rule as an absolute principle poses a potential threat to the equal rights of all. Supporters of the *Refah* dissolution (Tardt 2005) have argued that the Strasbourg judgements can be interpreted as a legitimate attempt to stave off such a threat. It is contended, however, that such a view – while inspired by a notion of equal rights – grossly inflates the threat that *Refah* posed and in doing so undermines the principle of equal respect that serves as a basis for that very notion.

## Liberal Democracy, Political Parties and Equal Respect

Adherents of liberal democracy have long argued that an unfettered commitment to popular sovereignty represents a potential 'tyranny of the majority' over the liberty of the individual (De Tocqueville 1835, Mill 1859). In defense of such liberties, more contemporary liberal democrats have developed a principle which can be identified as 'equal respect' (Dworkin, 1978, Rawls 1999). This principle is utilized to argue that individual preferences should have a relatively equal moral worth and that it is the responsibility of the state to ensure that each individual has the right to express those preferences. It also contends that not only should individuals have equal opportunity to influence collective choice procedures but that they should be protected from the consequences of collective choices which have the potential to damage their liberty and autonomy. Such protections are more often than not expressed in the language of rights. Giovanni Sartori (1987) has argued that absolute majority rule can potentially lead to the emergence of a permanent majority which could entrench its power against the minority and thus remove the opportunity for minorities to convert into majorities and vice versa. Thus, popular sovereignty, according to this view, requires a limitation of majority rule by individual or minority rights.

> … [D]emocracy conceived as majority rule limited by minority rights corresponds to the people in full, that is, to the sum total of majority plus minority. It is precisely because the rule of the majority is restrained that all the people … are always included in the demos. (Sartori 1987: 32–3)

Therefore, in order to ensure all citizens are given a voice then the enforcement of collective preferences must be limited to allow for the continued participation of those who may find themselves in a minority. While the precise nature of these limitations is not clarified, at the very least they will require a commitment to political rights such as freedom of expression and association which are viewed by liberal democrats as being necessary to and contingent upon the continuation of democratic government.

> … [T]hat it is true that the rights of liberty have been from the beginning the necessary condition for the correct application of the rules of the democratic game, it is also true that the development of democracy has become successfully the principal instrument in the defence of the rights of liberty. (Bobbio 1985: 48)

Within such a paradigm, it is evident that political parties play a central role. Not only do they facilitate an aggregation of preferences during elections but they are central to the original and continuing articulation of those preferences. As early as the final years of the eighteenth century, James Madison (1787) argued that uneven levels of property ownership would lead to an inevitable difference of economic interest which would then be reflected in the formation of competing political factions. From a British perspective, the subsequent emergence in the nineteenth century of a two-party system which reflected the interests of both the aristocracy and the bourgeoisie and the subsequent challenge to it in the early years of the twentieth century by a party representing the interests of the industrial working class offers validation of Madison's foresight. The existence of political parties cannot, however, be solely attributed to the existence of economic inequality. The twentieth and early years of the twenty-first century have also seen the emergence of political parties throughout the democratic world whose overriding goals have been the articulation of social and political values which are primarily non-economic. Examples include parties whose main focus is the protection of the environment such as the *Greens*, those who wish greater self government for their nation or region such as the *Scottish National Party* and *Bloc Quebecois* in Canada, and those of a religious nature which include the *Christian Democrats* in Germany and *Refah* in Turkey. Parties such as these not only facilitate an articulation of preferences but also a potential transformation of preferences by offering a diverse range of policies from which the voting public can select. Given the importance of such a role, it is contended that just as the reasoning used by the Strasbourg Courts constitute a clear challenge to the electoral principle of majority rule, its attitude towards political Islam also represents a violation of the liberal notion of equal respect.

### *Refah and equal respect*

Firstly, the Chamber attributes to Sharia and consequently to political Islam a monolithic character by claiming that it is 'stable and invariable' and as such irreconcilable with 'principles such as pluralism in the political sphere' (*Refah* 2002: 72). This reasoning conveniently fails to take account of alternative interpretations of Islam[3] which are reconcilable with democracy and would potentially undermine Strasbourg's attempt to define Sharia as a 'fixed and homogenous concept' (Brems 2006: 157). Secondly, the Court, while conveniently ignoring the absence of any commitment by *Refah* to introduce a general system of Sharia law, perceived advocacy of individual policies such as permitting the wearing of the Islamic headscarf in school or the adjustment of working hour regulations to accommodate fasting during Ramadan as attempts to impose just such a system (Boyle, 2004: 7). It can be argued that the interpretation by the Court of such advocacies

3 See John L. Esposito and John O. Voll, *Islam and Democracy*, Oxford University Press, 1996.

as a threat to both secularism and democracy is suggestive of at best, an indifference to the Article 9 right to freedom of worship as applied to the majority Muslim population.

Next, if the Court was as committed to the principle of political pluralism as indicated above, then it should have viewed as worthy of protection the right of religious parties to argue in favour of policies reflecting their own world view. To conflate the promotion of potentially illiberal policies with a desire to destroy democracy as the Court does ignores the fact that such a fusion is not supported by the official policies of the party, by their actions when in power as the senior partner in a coalition government or by the methods and strategies used by the party in the public arena. Upholding the dissolution of *Refah* in the absence of any such evidence represents an unwarranted interference with the principle of equal respect (Refah 2003: at 55, *Refah* 2002: at 74).

> Illiberal Parties need not be anti-democratic. For example, a religious fundamentalist party that has the support of the electorate of a polity can remain essentially democratic both internally and externally, and yet systematically spread illiberalism. Even from the standpoint of militant democracy, however, illiberalism is not synonymous with anti-democratic, and hence prohibition of illiberal parties would not be as justified … as anti-democratic ones would be. (Rosenfeld 2006: 48)

Finally, when *Refah* is contrasted with other Turkish dissolution cases in which Strasbourg does find a violation of Article 11 rights,[4] a disparity is evident in the level of protection. For example, advocacies of self-determination for the Kurdish people in Turkey which were seen by the Turkish authorities as constituting 'threats to the indivisibility and national and territorial integrity of the State … [Were] not considered to be inconsistent with fundamental principles of democracy' yet in *Refah*, the challenge posed to Secularism by the advocacy of specific policies was viewed as such an inconsistency. This suggests that political advocacies of policies in line with Islamic doctrine are afforded less protection than those emanating from other ideologies (Kocak and Orucu 2003: 421). Therefore, in a similar vein to electoral democracy, it is opined that some of the main assumptions underlying liberal democracy are subverted by the judgements reached in *Refah*. However, another similarity between both conceptions is that liberal democracy's own claim to reflect the popular will is at least partially flawed.

As we have already seen, in pursuit of the goal of equal respect, liberal democracy attempts to ensure that all citizens are considered within a polity by placing certain limits on the collective decisions that an electorally-produced majority can enforce. These limitations on collective decision making are more often than not expressed in the language of rights. From a democratic perspective,

4 *United Communist Party v Turkey* (1998) 26 E.H.R.R. 121; *Socialist Party v Turkey* (1999) 27 E.H.R.R. 51; *Ozdep v Turkey* (2001) 31 E.H.R.R. 51; *Dep v Turkey* App. No. 25141/94 (2002); *People's Labour Party v Turkey* (2003) 36 E.H.R.R. 6.

such limitations can be viewed with suspicion. In a democratic society, there exists massive controversy as to which rights should be protected and how they should be interpreted. Examples of such controversies include those surrounding abortion and euthanasia in many countries and more specifically, the issue of gun control in the United States. While diversity of opinion on these matters constitutes a healthy reflection of a democratic society, the problem with liberal democracy is that it seeks to place decisions concerning such rights beyond the control of the populace and their elected representatives and into the hands of an unelected judiciary. The subsequent constitutionalization or legal entrenchment of such rights is suggestive of a consensus that, more often than not, does not exist.

> … [W]e cannot say … that the whole point of rights is to 'trump' or override majority decisions. For rights may be the very thing that the members of the society are disagreeing about, the very issue they are using majority voting to settle. (Waldron 1993)

In the specific context of Turkey, it is not only individual rights that are constitutionalized but the entire ideology of secularism. In its judgement, the Grand Chamber was able to assert that 'an attitude that fails to respect [Secularism] will not necessarily be protected under Article 9 of the Convention's protection of freedom of thought and religion'(Refah 2003: at 93). Again, such a statement can clearly be presented as a negation of the principle of pluralism, especially in a country where the majority of people are Muslims.

> If secularism … is an ideology, should it not, under European Court standards, compete within democratic society with other dispositions? Human Rights cannot trump what people regard as authentic meaning to such an extent that it imposes an ideology such as secularism. Yet this is precisely the position in Turkey, where Secularism has been imposed through the Constitution for generations…. (Boyle 2004: 15)

In Turkey, the imposition of the ideology of Secularism has acted as an obstacle to the implementation of popular preference. It is advanced that the dissolution of *Refah* exacerbated this by removing from the polity, a legitimate vehicle for the articulation and aggregation of those very same preferences. It is evident that in the specific case of *Refah Partisi*, the Strasbourg Courts in attempting to prevent a 'tyranny of the majority' allowed for the imposition of a liberal and secular tyranny of the minority over the political rights of Turkish citizens.

## Conclusion

Democracy cannot be understood without some conception of rights. As Martin Loughlin (2001) has argued, opportunities for political participation are closely tied to concepts such as freedom of expression and association 'and these must inevitably be expressed in the language of rights'. These rights when taken in conjunction facilitate both the aggregation and articulation of popular preference.

> … [D]emocracy is not essentially concerned with the aggregation of individual preferences through the mechanism of voting. Instead, it is designed to achieve the potential transformation of preferences of an active public realm which enhances opportunities for discussion and deliberation. Democracy is not just the will of a majority, but of a will that has been formed after wide ranging and free discussion. (Loughlin 2001: 42, 44)

With regard to the formation of a 'popular will', the Strasbourg Court argued that in order to secure the continued right of all Turkish citizens to participate in such a process, the Turkish authorities possessed both the right and responsibility to legally dissolve a temporarily popular vehicle for the articulation and aggregation of preference on the grounds that its ideology and popularity posed a dual threat to democratic governance. It is contended that in the specific case of *Refah*, such an argument is fundamentally flawed. By upholding the dissolution of a popular party without offering convincing evidence that it had challenged fundamental democratic norms, it sent a signal that political rights were to be interpreted as a bulwark against any collective choices which threaten a judicially determined liberal consensus rather than as a necessary constitutive factor to the formation of a popular will representative of the Turkish population at large. Modern democracy is not premised on an idealistic consensus as envisaged by Rousseau but on the existence of fundamental disagreement and the prospect of change as given expression by new candidates for public office and alternative legislative proposals. It is such disagreement which makes both competitive elections and political parties necessary. By endorsing the legal dissolution of *Refah*, the Court placed substantive limits on such change and effectively sacrificed the equal protection of a right fundamental to an articulation and aggregation of preferences necessary for the formation of a vibrant and diverse popular will. In doing so, rather than ensuring that the wishes of the entire Turkish polity be considered, the Court circumscribed the arena of legitimate political activity to those representative organs whose policies were not deemed as a threat to a constitutionally prescribed orthodoxy.

**References**

*Reference book*

The Concise Oxford Dictionary. 1991. 9th Edition,

*Books*

Bobbio, N. 1985. *Liberalismo et Democrazia.* Milan: Franco Agneli.
De Tocqueville, A. 1835 (2004). *Democracy in America.* New York: Library of America.
Donnelly, J. 2003. *Universal Human Rights in Theory and Practice.* 2nd Edition. Ithaca, NY: Cornell University Press.
Duncan, G. 1983. *Democratic Theory and Practice.* Cambridge: Cambridge University Press.
Epstein, L.D. 1967. *Political Parties in Western Democracies*. London: Pall Mall Press.
Esposito, J.L. and J.O. Voll. 1996. *Islam and Democracy.*Oxford: Oxford University Press.
Katz, R. 1997. *Democracy and Elections*. Oxford: Oxford University Press.
Mill, J.S. 1859 (2003). *On Liberty*. New Haven: Yale University Press.
Rawls, J. 1999. *A Theory of Justice*. Revised Edition. Oxford: Oxford University Press.
Rousseau, J.J. 1762. The Social Contract translated and edited by Gourevitch, V 1997. The Social Contract and Other Later Political Writings: Cambridge University Press.
Sartori, G. 1987. *The Theory of Democracy revisited.* Chatham, NJ: Chatham House.
Saward, M. 2003. *Democracy*. Cambridge: Polity Press.
Smith, R.K. 2007. *Textbook on International Human Rights*. 3rd Edition. Oxford: Oxford University Press.
Ware, A. 1996. *Political Parties and Party Systems*. Oxford: Oxford University Press.

*Book chapters*

Brems, E. 2006. Freedom of Association and the Question of Party Closures, in *Political Rights under Stress in 21st Century Europe,* edited by W.J.Sadurski. New York: Oxford University Press, 120–95.
Dworkin, R. 1978. Liberalism in *Public and Private Morality*, edited by S. Hampshire. Cambridge: Cambridge University Press, 113–52.
Karl, T.L. and P.C. Schmitter, 1996. What Democracy Is … Or Is Not, in L. Diamond and M.F. Plattner, *The Global Resurgence of Democracy*, 2nd edition. Baltimore, MD: John Hopkins University Press, 33–52.

Katz, R. 1986. Party Government: A Rationalistic Conception in *The Future of Party Government: Visions and Realities of Party Government*, edited by F.G Castles and R. Wildemann. The Hague: Walter de Gruyter, 31–71.

Loughlin, M. 2001. Rights, Democracy and Law, in *Sceptical Essays on Human Rights*, edited by T. Campbell, K.D. Ewing and A. Tomkins. Oxford: Oxford University Press, 41–60.

Madison, J. 1787. Federalist Paper X, The same subject continued: The Union as a safeguard against Domestic Faction and Insurrection, in *The Federalist Papers*, edited by Alexander Hamilton.Publius: 48–55.

Rosenfeld, M. 2006. A Pluralist Theory of Political Rights in Times of Stress, in *Political Rights under Stress in Twenty-First Century Europe*, edited by W.J. Sadurski. New York: Oxford University Press, 12–54.

Tardt, G. 2004. Political Parties' Right to Engage in Politics: Variations on a Theme of Democracy, in *Militant Democracy*, edited by A. Sajo. Utrecht: Eleven International, 81–112.

Webb, P. 2002. Political Parties, in *Political Parties in Advanced Industrial Democracies*, edited by D. Farrell, I. Holliday and P. Webb. Oxford: Oxford University Press, 1–16.

*Journal articles*

Boyle, K. 2004. Human Rights, Religion and Democracy: The Refah Party Case. *Essex Human Rights Law Review*, 1(1), 1–16.

Harvey, P. 2004. Militant Democracy and the European Convention on Human Rights. *European Law Review*, 29(3), 407–20.

Kocak, M. and E. Orucu. 2003. Dissolution of Political Parties in the Name of Democracy: Cases from Turkey and the European Court of Human Rights. *European Public Law*, 9(3), 399–424.

Levitsky, S. and L.A. Way. 2002. The Rise of Competitive Authoritarianism. *Journal of Democracy*, Vol. 13(2), 51–65.

Loewenstein, K. 1937a. Militant Democracy and Fundamental Rights Part I. *American Political Science Review*, 31(3), 417–32.

———. 1937b. Militant Democracy and Fundamental Rights Part II. *American Political Science Review*, 31(4), 638–58.

May, K. 1952 A Set of Independent, Necessary and Sufficient Conditions for Simple Majority Decision. *Econometrica*, 20(4), 680–84.

McDonald, M.D., S.M. Mendes and I. Budge. 2004. What are Elections for? Conferring the Median Mandate. *British Journal of Political Science*, 34, 1–26.

Olbourne, B. 2003. Refah Partisi (The Welfare Party v Turkey). *European Human Rights Law Review*, 4, 437–44.

Schilling, D. 2003–2004. Islamophobia and Turkey – Refah Partisi *v Turkey*. *Loyola L.A. International and Comparative Law Review*, 26, 501–15.

Waldron, J. 1993. A Right-based Critique of Constitutional Rights. *Oxford Journal of Legal Studies*, 13(1), 18–51.

Yturbe, C. 1997. On Norberto Bobbio's Theory of Democracy. *Political Theory*, 25(3), 377–400.

*Journal articles from an electronic source*

Benn, Stanley. 1967. Democracy. *Encyclopaedia of Philosophy* [online] www.ditext.com/benn/democracy.html [accessed March 16th 2010].

Mayerfield, J. 2003. Democracy and Other Human Rights. *American Political Science Association* [online] www.allacademic.com/meta/p63688_index.html [accessed March 20th 2009].

*News article*

Rainsford, S, 2008. Narrow Escape Leaves Turkey Divided. BBC News[online]. http//news.bbc.co.uk/1/hi/world/Europe/7534342.stm [accessed] August 2nd 2008.

*Legal instruments*

Constitution of the Republic of Turkey, 1982.

Convention for the Protection of Human Rights and Fundamental Freedoms in Europe (ECHR), 1950.

European Commission for Democracy through Law (The Venice Commission) – *Guidelines on Prohibition and Dissolution of Political Parties and Analogous Measures, CDL*-INF (2000)001 at www.venice.coe.int/docs/1999/CDL-INF (1999)015-e.asp.

*Cases*

***Turkey***

Turkish Constitutional Court – Decision No 1998/1.

***Council of Europe***

*Dep v Turkey* App. No 25141/94 (2002).

*Ozdep v Turkey* (2001) 31 E.H.R.R. 51.

*People's Labour Party v Turkey* (2003) 36 E.H.R.R. 6.

Refah Partisi *v Turkey* (Chamber) (2002) 35 E.H.R.R. 3.

Refah Partisi *v Turkey* Grand Chamber, (2003) 37 E.H.R.R. 1.

*Socialist Party v Turkey* (1999) 27 E.H.R.R. 51.

United Communist Party of Turkey (1998) 26 E.H.R.R. 121.

# Chapter 4
# Between Contract and Constitution: International Organizations and the Protection of Global Public Interests

Richard Collins

The (recent) history of international law is often narrated in terms of an as-yet-incomplete transition in the nature of the international legal order, from a transactional 'Westphalian' paradigm – e.g., Holland's (1898: 152) 'private law writ large' – towards a more communitarian model, aimed at the protection of global public interests (Simma 1994; Tomuschat 1998). This kind of progress narrative is by now a familiar account of the development of international law over the last two centuries (Miller and Bratspies 2008; Skouteris 2010), and manifests often in descriptions of paradigm shifts in the role and nature of international law: for example, a movement from a law of 'co-existence' to 'co-operation' (Friedmann 1964), or from 'sovereignty' towards 'international community' (Warbrick & Tierney 2006).

At the heart of this transition has been a process of 'institutionalization' brought about by the growing number and increasing authority of intergovernmental organizations (IGOs) throughout the twentieth and twenty-first centuries. International lawyers have, generally speaking, been enthusiastic proponents of this process of institutionalization, and have seen the growing autonomy of IGOs at the expense of state sovereignty as a reliable barometer of progress in the realization of an international rule of law. As Alvarez (2005: 585) notes,

> For many public international lawyers, the prospects for multilateral cooperation lie in the promise that IOs have become international legal persons to some extent independent of the states that have established them and that IO processes will encourage the consideration of 'community' interests and not merely the interests of self-interested states.

Nevertheless, much of this modernist faith is increasingly called into question in the post-Cold War era. An initial sense of liberal optimism at the beginning of the 1990s (Fukuyama 1992), fuelling hopes for the revitalization of the authority of IGOs previously hidebound by superpower rivalry and ideological divide (Franck 1990), has given way to an increasing perception of ideological bias, legitimacy deficits and a lack of accountability in many global institutions (Coicaud and Heiskanen 2001; Chimni 2004; Anghie 2004; Barnett and Finnemore 2004), not to mention anxieties over the potential normative and institutional conflicts arising as a result of the growing number of increasingly autonomous institutional actors in international law (Koskenniemi 2007: 12–13, Koskenniemi & Leino 2002: 558–60).

This chapter attempts to situate and explain this 'changing image' of international organizations (Klabbers 2001) in terms of a growing tension between the increasingly 'public', regulatory function of the international legal order and its underlying decentralized legal form – a tension which carries over to, and is reproduced within, the constitutional architecture of IGOs themselves. In particular, it is argued here that to the extent that international law has been explained according to this modernist, rule of law ideal, international lawyers have been unable to fully account for the protection of global public goods in international law, precisely because they fail to see this inherent structural tension as necessary to the legitimacy of the exercise of public authority in a decentralized legal order. As such, to the extent that the rule of law ideal has been seen as realizable only by overcoming decentralization, international lawyers have struggled to find alternative forms of legitimization, only helping to further perpetuate the anxieties recounted above. This chapter will conclude with some reflections on looking beyond this idealist vision, and rethinking the 'publicness' of international law by locating it in the space opened up between competing claims to legitimacy.

## Explaining International Law as Public Law

If such generalizations are permissible, we can describe modern international law as being underpinned by a broadly 'social' or 'sociological' doctrinal method, an approach which attempts to reconcile the law's political origins with its ability to normatively foreclose available political choices (Koskenniemi 1991: 4–7, 2005; Kennedy 1987). Most often this is expressed as a kind of 'modern' or 'modernist' positivism (Simma & Paulus 1998: 306–8; Miller & Bratspies 2008: 20–22), which essentially translates into an inevitable subjectivity in the sources of the law[1] – deriving law from the collective will of the system's constituents (states) – but recognizes thereafter that law must be woven into a systemic, 'institutional' fabric in order to preserve its objective autonomy as a restraint on interstate politics (Capps 2009: 127; Collins 2011). Essentially, it is this commitment to the autonomy of law which delineates mainstream, doctrinal approaches from more peripheral critiques and instrumental theories of international law (see e.g., Schachter 1983: 747; Warbrick 1991: 61).

This modern, 'institutional' approach can be traced back to a late-nineteenth century transition in international law, which sought to divorce the professional and academic study and practice of international law from its philosophical roots

1 Essentially, these are treaties, customary international law, general principles and the subsidiary sources included within Article 38(1) of the Statute of the International Court of Justice.

as an expression of enlightenment rationalism (Carty 1986: 8–13). Influenced by emerging principles of constitutional legitimacy, which had begun to transform the constitutional orders of European nation-states (Reus-Smit 1999; 129–31, 134–5), late nineteenth-century (largely European) jurists sought to make over the existing rudiments of multilateral diplomacy into a more ambitious, systemic, 'public' legal order, grounded at some level in the consent of sovereign states (Koskenniemi 2001: 11–97, 2009: 145–52).

This transformation did much to ingrain a 'discourse of institutional autonomy' in terms of the use of, and reliance upon, international law in the diplomatic practices of states (Reus-Smit 2004: 36–7), but for this reason it was also something of a 'paradoxical inheritance' (Kennedy 1997: 113). Deriving law from the actual practices (and *opinio juris*) of states makes the realization of a workable system of public order more realistic, yet also much more difficult; it stresses the autonomy of law (from politics; from morality) as its most important attribute, but raises difficult theoretical questions about the nature of this autonomy. In particular, insofar as modern doctrinal method seeks to reconcile the existence *and efficacy* of international law according to a Rule of Law ideal, drawn from domestic constitutional experience, it appears vulnerable to the critique of its irrelevance, instrumentality or indeterminacy in the absence of a centralized, sovereign authority, similar to that within the domestic state (e.g., Austin 1873: 188, 222).

Whilst international lawyers have been rightly critical of the limitations of the narrow, Austinian conception of law as command, or indeed, the more instrumental, neo-Hegelian alternative idea of law as sovereign *auto-limitation* (Verdross 1927: 262–86, Lauterpacht 1927: 43–50) – and indeed frequently point to both the reality and efficacy of international law in the relations between states (Franck 1995: 6) – in comparison to domestic legal orders international law is often seen to be constitutionally or structurally deficient in some way, failing to live up to the domestic ideal in many respects (Chesterman 2008; Beaulac 2009). Few 'mainstream' international lawyers have questioned the theoretical coherence of the 'rule of law' ideal by which they measure the efficacy (if not necessarily the reality) of international law in this respect (Collins 2011) – though some have indeed explicitly endorsed such a conceptual ideal after detailed theoretical enquiry (e.g., Kelsen 1953, Lauterpact 1932). Instead, most have resorted to one of two strategies to reconcile the decentralized structures of international law with this ideal.

One recurring strategy has been the ubiquitous domestic analogy which accepts the need for international law to fulfil the constitutional functions of legislation, adjudication and enforcement, but explains how such functions can be fulfilled in the absence of centralized authority (Koskenniemi 2005: 172–7). A classic example of this is Scelle's theory of '*dédoublement fonctionnel*', or 'role-splitting', which sought to explain how state officials exercised distinctly international executive, legislative or judicial capacities, when authorized to do so under the rules of the international legal order (Scelle 1934: 10–12).

On this basis Scelle was able to account for most international activity as part of a constitutional ordering of the international system (Scelle 1923: 124–41). Others have sought to explain mechanisms of 'self-help' in international law in terms of legal enforcement (Kelsen 1953: 31–4; Oppenheim 1920: 3–14), whilst others still have analogized multilateral treaties as a form of decentralized legislation (McNair 1930; Brierly 1944: 6). This kind of 'compensatory' discourse can be seen later also in Fitzmaurice's (1956) attempt to explain the role of the International Court of Justice (ICJ) in terms of legal enforcement, or Lauterpacht's (1958) emphasis on the quasi-legislative role of the Court in the absence of a centralized international legislature.

Whilst these views seem to rely on controversial assumptions related to external interpretations of state behaviour or institutional function (Koskenniemi 2005: 174–7), rather than any 'internal' element of legal self-understanding (Hart 1994: 88–91), more specifically, they also tend to be over-inclusive in their suggestion that e.g. reprisals, acts of self-help or the resort to war are necessarily concerned with the enforcement of legal rights as opposed to seeking to pursue more individualistic, political ends (*ibid.*: 232–3). Most fundamentally, whilst these kinds of 'functional' analogies might have once helped to underline the law's efficacy and reality against its critics, they have done so, arguably, at the price of continuing to perpetuate a sense of structural deficiency in the law (e.g., Brierly, 1963: 73). It was perhaps for this reason that Scelle (1948: 22) saw his scheme of '*dédoublement fonctionnel*' as a 'dangerous substitute' for a more perfect, hierarchical form of international organization, and that Oppenheim (1920: 11–12) hoped for a more efficacious enforcement regime with the development of more autonomous intergovernmental organizations such as the League of Nations.

As such, by far the most notable response to the autonomy problem has been to accept the conceptual model of domestic constitutional law as an ideal type, but reconcile the apparent structural deficiency of international law as resulting from the current under-development of its legal order – which is seen as evolving towards, but not yet fully realizing a more centralized constitutional architecture similar to the domestic state. This has allowed international lawyers to defend the reality of international law merely on the basis of the existence of an international society or community as such – *ubi societas ibi jus* (Koskenniemi 2005: 177–81) – whilst at the same time weaving into the law an implicit *telos* which sees the apparent structural deficiency as only reflecting the international community's intermittent stage of social development. On this basis, the difference between national and international legal orders is seen as a matter of degree (its level of centralization), rather than kind (Brierly 1963: 76; Lauterpacht 1932: 318). By highlighting the structural difference between legal orders in terms of international law's incompleteness, or 'primitive' nature (Campbell 1988: 193–5), the project of international law is set up in opposition to the status quo and in furtherance of the institutional conditions necessary to guarantee an international rule of law.

## Progress as 'Publicness' in the Institutionalization of International Law

It is little coincidence therefore that the twentieth century's 'move to institutions' (Kennedy 1987) has been implicated in this progressive vision of the growing force and strength of modern international law (Alvarez 2006: 324–6; 339). Even at The Hague Conferences at the turn of the twentieth century, many respected lawyers and diplomats interpreted the move to conference diplomacy and permanent arbitration as the embryonic beginnings of a global federal union (Holls 1900: 354–65; Schücking 1918: 18–42). Spurred on by the experience at The Hague, Oppenheim (1921: 20–21) hoped that the creation of the League and Permanent Court of International Justice (PCIJ) after the First World War would facilitate the 'constitutionalization' of the international system – an idea taken up with enthusiasm by some of the century's most famous jurists, such as Lauterpacht (1936: 34–5) and McNair (1934/1961: 734), who differentiated 'constitutional' treaties such as the League Covenant from other 'bilateral' agreements because of their broad ambition and public function.

Nevertheless, much of this constitutional analogy remained, again, at the level of function and substantive ambition rather than legal form – a point acknowledged explicitly by McNair himself (1934/1961: 740) – and summed up by Max Huber's cautious description of the Covenant as 'neither contractual ... nor constitutional' (cited in Zimmern 1936: 284). And even today, despite the normative and institutional advances associated with the move from League to United Nations (UN), few purport to directly analogize the latter (or its Charter) as a constitution for the international community as a whole (though see MacDonald 2005: 859–68; Fassbender 1998; 2009), but many continue to make strong comparisons on the basis of the distinctly public functions which the UN fulfils (Brownlie 1974: 26–7; White 2000: 94–5), or see such universal organizations as a kind of 'gap-filling' measure, attempting to enforce the normative will of the international community in the absence of centralized authority (Cassese 1986: 401–3).

At least at this level, therefore, there is considerable persuasive force in the proposition that IGOs have fundamentally transformed the character of international law; a transformation at least partly in accordance with the typical progress narrative described in the introduction. For instance, organizational *fora* such as the UN General Assembly play an increasingly important role in the processes of international law-making and application (Alvarez 2005; Charney 1993: 543–50), with UN-sponsored conferences adding to the centralization of the multilateral treaty-making process (Brölmann 2007: 101–12), or "democratizing" law-making by engaging non-state actors (Charnovitz 2006). Meanwhile, the post-Cold War dynamism of the UN Security Council has seen it take on a role not only, increasingly, in the enforcement of the law, but also 'quasi-legislative' and 'quasi-judicial' measures (White 2002: 15–16). In other fields, a proliferation of dispute settlement bodies has led to increasingly 'legalized' regimes and institutions (Goldstein et al. (eds.), 2001), particularly in bodies such as the World Trade Organization (WTO), leading some scholars to speak of a process of institutional 'constitutionalization' in this (Cass 2005), and various other IGOs (Klabbers 2004).

At the normative level, also, codification exercises undertaken by the UN's International Law Commission have resulted in treaty and customary recognition of so-called *peremptory norms* of international law, signally an emerging normative hierarchy (Shelton 2006; *cf.* Weil 1983), which in turn has been recognized, and tentatively progressed, by international courts and tribunals.[2] Meanwhile, the 'normative' output of the UN General Assembly is seen to have had a significant impact on traditional sources doctrine, with its resolutions acting as evidence of emerging customary international law (Roberts 2001), if not constituting in themselves a new, 'soft' form of international obligation, with significant persuasive force (Abbott & Snidal 2000; Boyle 2006). For many, these changes have led to a 'verticalization' in the sources of law, making it a much more dynamic force for the protection of community interests (see generally Delbrück (ed.) 1993).

Taken together, such changes have for the most part been embraced by international lawyers, signalling a welcome paradigm shift in the nature of the international legal order towards the more 'communitarian' ideal, previously outlined (Dugard 2007: 231; Tams 2003: 3; Orakhelashvili 2010). Even if the content of the purported community values and the meaning of 'community' itself are widely contested (Kritsiotis 2002), it is difficult to deny that states themselves have driven this change, as Simma and Paulus (1998: 276) put this, 'chanel[ling] the pursuit of most of their individual interests through multilateral institutions'.

At the same time, however, it is difficult also not to note a growing disconnect between the purported communitarian ambition and the institutional condition of international law, which – notwithstanding the developments revealed above – remains grounded within an inter-state, decentralized legal paradigm. As will be considered in the following section, it is this growing sense of dislocation which has led many international lawyers to call into question the assumption of a linear transition from private to public in the development of the law.

## Between Form and Function in the Transformation of Westphalian International Law

From the point of view of the 'mainstream' sociological method recounted above, we can appreciate how this dislocation begins to arise. The move towards a more public, communitarian paradigm in international law is said to arise from social need; that is, from the collective will of the international legal system's constituents (states), and is therefore effected in accordance with the tenets of Westphalian international law as traditionally understood. At the same time, however, what states have willed into existence are norms and institutional frameworks which

2 See e.g., *Military and Paramilitary Activities in and against Nicaragua* (*Nicaragua v United States*), Merits, Judgment of 27 June 1986, ICJ Rep. 1986, 14, 100–101.

appear in their scope, purpose and operation to increasingly challenge the coherence and legitimacy of Westphalian international law.

Rather than see an evolutionary transition from private to public, or sovereignty to community, it might be more enlightening therefore to consider Weiler's (2004) idea of a 'geological' layering in international law. Here, the development of the international legal order sees an increasingly regulatory, or 'governance' layer (developed through complex institutional regimes), atop a 'communitarian' layer (the product of a transition away from an individualist, or statist paradigm), itself atop an original base of Westphalian ('transactional') international law (Weiler 2004). This layering has not so much changed the nature of the law as complicated it, with the simultaneous existence of norms and structures the legitimacy of which derives from competing forms of political justification.

At the risk of oversimplifying Weiler's model, we can see how the competing paradigms sit uneasily with each other: the intergovernmentalism of the basal layer – the Westphalian legal form of international law – is what gives legitimacy and coherence to expressions of global public goods, but it is this intergovernmentalism which prevents a more efficient and effective means to protect those interests. In this respect, however, it may be too easy to portray this Westphalian layer as an outdated philosophical commitment to national interest and unrestrained sovereignty, and in that sense merely an older species of international law, occupying an uneasy space with a more dynamic, more communitarian and, indeed, more 'public' species of international law. However, it is perhaps more accurate to view this Westphalian base as the continuing structural condition, or *legal form* of the international legal order in the absence of agreement on one legitimate point of authority capable of legitimizing hierarchy in the law. This is a point better captured in Cassese's (1986: 32) metaphor, where he describes Westphalian international law 'like a human skeleton that can only be seen on an X-ray being covered by flesh and skin and clothes. Though momentarily concealed, it is still very much there, constituting the framework on which all the rest is based'. Looking at it this way, as the legal form upon which the more complex edifice of modern international law is constructed, does not in any way prejudice the nature, substance or function of the rules, structures or institutions of this constructed legal order, but it does help us come to terms with a growing tension between the law's decentralized legal form and the nature and extent of the interests it purports to protect.

We can imagine the implications of this *form-function* tension by placing competing legitimacy claims on two linked axes. International Law's legitimacy comes from the sense that it is *structured* on a horizontal axis, as a pluralistic order existing between sovereign-equal states in order to prevent imperialistic domination, but also, and increasingly (as a result of change in the substance of its normative concerns), to the extent that it penetrates state sovereignty on a vertical axis to protect and enforce community interests, e.g., issues of human rights and welfare that were traditionally conceived to lie within the domestic realm of states (Jouannet 2008). In the absence of any available theoretical justification for prioritizing the community interest over state will, or, in the absence of an alternative form of political agency capable of giving *a priori* legitimacy to the expression of community will at an institutional level, pushes on the vertical axis will necessarily therefore invoke counter-pulls on the horizontal axis.

At an institutional level, therefore, this makes the idea of IGOs representing global public interests somewhat problematic. On the one hand, whilst states have worked through IGOs to bring into being a more community-focussed international legal order, those same intergovernmental structures seem to undermine the full and effective realization of community ambition (Villalpando 2010: 409–10). In particular, processes of international law-making and enforcement seem still dogged by tedious and open-ended intergovernmental negotiation, or even paralyzed by the invocation of key national interests (Danilenko 1993: 11–15 & *passim*; Abi-Saab 1998: 256; Bianchi 2002: 268–9).

On the other hand, however, the anxiety also runs the other way. Where IGOs have developed a certain level of legal and political autonomy this, evermore so recently, has generated a significant amount of concern over the accountability of such exercises of global public power. For instance, the initial hope at the end of the Cold War that the UN Security Council would finally be made to 'work' (Franck 1990) only seemed to give way to concerns over its activism, precipitating calls for legal restraint (Sato 2001), whether through institutional reform (Fassbender 2004), or judicial review by the ICJ or other international courts (de Wet 2004, Orakhelashvili 2005). Similarly, increasing cynicism at the purported universality of the free trade and economic liberalization agendas of the WTO and global financial institutions has prompted calls for greater democratic representation and avenues for legal contestation (Stein 2001). Moreover, serious accusations of human rights abuses by UN peacekeepers, as well as alarming reports of institutional corruption have garnered enthusiasm for enhancing both internal forms of political accountability and external forms of legal control (Coicaud & Heiskanen 2001; Collins and White 2011).

From the perspective of many states themselves, this growing sense of legitimacy deficit has been accompanied by the realization that withdrawal from many organizations is simply not an option. As Alvarez (2006: 343) notes, for most states participation in IGOs is as much about guaranteeing as it is restricting or limiting their sovereignty – a clear sign of 'the very success of the Grotian consensus that led to their establishment, proliferation, and growing legal clout'.

## Re-Situating the Public in (Public) International Law?

As such, the modernist progress narrative which suggests a beneficent transition from sovereignty towards community has proved too naïve, too simplistic an explanatory device to come to terms with the shifts in authority, structure and power in an increasingly institutionalized – yet still decentralized – international legal order. It is hardly surprising therefore that recent calls for reform, control and legal restraint of IGOs have turned to alternative modes of legitimization and normative contestation, rather than simply revert back to political control through intergovernmental unanimity or consensus.

For instance, one recurring agenda has been the push to further nascent forms of transnational or supranational democracy (Held 2006: 275–81, 304–8), particularly through enhancing the participatory role and normative influence of NGOs and other non-state actors making up an embryonic 'global civil society' (Scholte 2004). For many others, however, the feasibility of direct political representation at the global level appears something of a chimera and, even if it were otherwise, there remains a great deal of scepticism as to the accountability or democratic credentials of NGOs or other non-state actors, capable of legitimizing such coercive forms of supra-state 'public' authority to begin with (Weiler 2004: 560–61; Somek 2008: 487–9).

Similar problems seem to haunt recent attempts to introduce a compensatory concept of 'constitutionalism' (Peters 2006; Klabbers, Peters & Ulfstein 2010), develop a less value-laden idea of 'global administrative law' (Krisch & Kingsbury 2006) or other normative frameworks for the exercise of political power beyond the state (von Bogdandy, Dann, & Goldmann 2008). Whilst it is beyond the scope of this chapter to give these emerging perspectives the full consideration they deserve, particularly considering that the underlying legitimacy concerns deserve serious attention, one has the feeling still that merely reconceptualizing the tension described here in terms of conformity with certain public law standards only raises further questions over the source determinant of the principles/values/norms themselves (Harlow 2006; Klabbers 2011), largely missing the *structural* nature of the legitimacy problem as described here.

Thus, to look for normative or ruled-based restraints *internally* within certain institutions or regimes, ignores the critical attack of structural bias in the operation of many IGOs in international law. For instance, if a WTO dispute settlement panel balances trade against human rights, environmental concerns or other global public interests, the controversial decision is merely shifted away from the membership in the plenary and given to a more limited body of decision makers, the normative preferences of which being, perhaps, one of the initial points of concern (Alston 2002; Howse 2002: 106–7). In fact, quite paradoxically, to 'constitutionalize' in this way may only be to enhance the authority of the institutional decision maker, contributing to normative clashes between competing regimes, and thus contributing to the deeper fragmentation (and perhaps systemic incoherence) of the international legal order as whole (Klabbers 2004: 23; Werner 2008: 350). Scholars' mixed reactions to the recent *Kadi* decision of the European Court of Justice,[3] which asserted the autonomy of the EU's (increasingly constitutional) legal order in the face of human rights concerns stemming from UN Security Council resolutions, seem to reinforce this concern to some degree (Cardwell, French & White 2009: 235–9).

3 Case C-402/05, *Kadi v. Council and Commission* [2008] ECR I-6351.

On the other hand, the *Kadi* case does raise increasingly important questions about the possibility of holding IGOs to account *externally* under the existing rules of the broader international legal order. It is hardly surprising that in light of the kinds of concerns raised in this chapter a number of prominent international bodies, jurists and academics have recently devoted considerable effort and time to developing a framework for the international legal responsibility of international organizations.[4] Yet this development in itself seems to miss an important structural point which relates to the very nature of organizations. Much of this developing framework has tended to treat IGOs as one-dimensional actors within the international legal order, ignoring the way in which states work through organizations to participate in, restructure and develop that same legal order (Brölmann 2007: 5–6, 262–7). Looked at from this perspective, the problem is not so much the actions of the organization as an autonomous entity which are of concern, but rather how its independent legal personality might actually serve to shield states from accountability for abuses of precisely the kind of human rights norms which the institutionalization of international relations has done much to advance and protect (d'Aspremont 2007) – as, indeed, the recent *Behrami* decision before the European Court of Human Rights seems to have suggested (Collins and White 2011).[5]

Ultimately, much of this attempt to develop a rule-based approach to control the activities of IGOs ignores the fact that, being constituted within the international legal order, the interstate agreements which give rise to IGOs will only reproduce the same tensions described here within the life of the organization itself. Though some organizations might appear more constitutional than contractual – just compare the UN, WHO or the EU with NATO, for example – no organization (or organization's constitutive instrument, for that matter) can be viewed entirely in contractual or constitutional terms (White 2006: 14–23). Where institutional autonomy manifests, it does so internally in terms of a dynamic of competing authority claims between the states and the institution, which spills over externally into an uneasy push and pull of legitimacy claims between competing legal actors, rather than in terms of a relationship of legal subordination to a higher normative authority. At a *formal level*, autonomy manifests in international law in terms of the independent legal personality of organizations, but this places the organization alongside states within the international legal order, rather than constituting

4 See e.g., International Law Association, 'Accountability of International Organisations' (Final Report of Committee on Accountability of International Organizations, Berlin Conference, 2004), available at: http://www.ila-hq.org/download.cfm/docid/6B708C25-4D6D-42E2-8385DADA752815E8 (last accessed 1 July 2010); and the 'Report of the International Law Commission on the Work of its Sixty-First Session, 4 May to 5 June and 6 July to 7 August 2009', UN Doc. A/64/10, 2009, Chp. IV, paras. 31–51; available at: http://untreaty.un.org/ilc/reports/2009/2009report.htm (last accessed 1 July 2010).

5 *Behrami and Behrami v France* and *Saramati v France, Germany and Norway* (2007) 45 EHRR SE10.

it above them in a relationship of hierarchical subordination (Bederman 1996; Brölmann 2007).

As such, applying public law standards internally ignores the fact that states remain in control in a way, and not merely to a degree, which would be impossible for legal subjects within the constituted order of a state. The justifications for the exercise of authority manifest themselves in a different way. Similarly, at the external level, the continued level of direction and control exerted by member states makes the organization a partly transparent entity, through which states participate within, and – as we saw above – potentially themselves breach the rules of, the international legal order as a whole. Ultimately, it is this institutional condition which 'help[s to] explain why we can both chide the WTO for doing too much and for doing too little ... why we can criticize the UN for both having expanded beyond its proper mandate, and for not doing enough to redeem the world' (Klabbers 2005: 86).

### When the Shoe Doesn't Fit? Some Final Thoughts

This might sound like a negative, even somewhat nihilistic conclusion to reach, but this is not really the point being made here. It is not at all the intention here to undermine the possibility or reality of IGOs fulfilling distinctly 'public' functions in international law, even if the method and means by which they do so at the international level is somewhat more complex than at the domestic level. In fact, it is precisely this complexity which opens up space for the potential expression of a truly global public interest.

To explain, Klabbers (2005: 285–6) usefully situates the schizophrenic identity of IGOs by analogizing this in terms of the distinction drawn by Michael Oakeshott (1975) between the ideas of *societas* and *universitas*, recently reinvigorated in Martin Loughlin's (2003) theory of public law. Unlike the rule of law paradigm, these are not ideal-types, but analytical constructs which allow us to understand the contours of a tension in different forms of political association (Loughlin 2003: 18–19; Klabbers 2005: 286): the idea of *universitas* being an 'enterprise' association, or a coming together for a common purpose; *societas* suggesting a more limited form of association built upon bonds of civility, or of legality – a commitment to be bound formally by rules, rather than being bound towards any pre-defined ends (Oakeshott 1975: 201–3).

If we can situate this tension in forms of organization outside of the state form – as indeed, Oakeshott seems to suggest[6] – then, on the one hand, this requires us to take seriously the necessary interaction between these two forms in the life of an IGO (Klabbers 2005: 291). On the other hand, however, it also potentially sheds light on the mutually constitutive role of law and politics in *all forms of* institutionalized human association aimed at the realization of public goods.

6 Oakeshott (1975: 200) claimed that the tension between these concepts allowed us to distinguish between and make intelligible 'the many-in-one human associations'.

In this way, we might still be able to account for key structural differences between international and domestic legal orders, whilst at the same time moving beyond the rule of law ideal in both forms of political association. As Loughlin explains this, the interplay between the concepts of *societas* and *universitas* creates an entirely artificial, fictive unity which we embody with legal personality – a *persona ficta*, to borrow Oakeshott's terminology (1975: 204). This fictive unity – whether state or IGO – allows us to imagine a sense of common identity, common purpose and, perhaps, universal interest, as distinct from a mere aggregation of separate, competing wills (Loughlin 2003: 50–60). The point of this, the advantage of this fictional *and functional* embodiment of a community will is exactly its artificial character: its provisional, contingent flexibility. Because it is fictive, impersonal *and fundamentally reliant on political will*, the idea of common purpose it embodies, whether in legal rules or otherwise, is always provisional and negotiable, underlying the still important legitimizing role of the constitutive base of authority.

For the purpose of the current study this suggests, first of all, that the increasingly *functional* public role fulfilled by IGOs in international law allows for a level of collective action under conditions of inherent political plurality, a plurality reflected in the legal form of the decentralized international legal order. It also, however, suggests that we might need to reorient our understanding of the relationship of law and politics to some degree, and in that sense call into question the rule of law ideal by which we measure the efficacy of international law. As Loughlin (2003: 28) astutely observes,

> We are unable to make progress in understanding public law [and by my own implication, public international law also] by devising some ideal construct of law – whether as a model of rules or a model of rights – and then seeking to reinterpret the world in accordance with its precepts. From a positive perspective it is important that we keep these competing rationalities open to investigation and accommodation.

As such, rather than seeing law's 'publicness' solely in terms of its ability to restrain political action, it might be better understood in the constitutive role of harnessing, bounding, guiding, but ultimately guaranteeing the exercise of, coordinated political power towards common ends (Kratochwil 2000: 39–40; Loughlin and Walker 2007: 1–3). This alone will not resolve issues of concern as to the accountability and legal responsibility of increasingly autonomous IGOs in international law, but it may help dispel the myth that these concerns can be fully assuaged merely through institutional design.

**References**

Abbott, K.W. and D. Snidal. Hard and Soft Law in International Governance (2000) 54 *International Organization* 21.

Abi-Saab, G. Whither the International Community? (1998) 9 *European Journal of International Law* 248.

Alston, P. Resisting the Merger and Acquisition of Human Rights by Trade Law: A Reply to Petersmann (2002) 13 *European Journal of International Law* 815.

Alvarez, J.E. *International Organizations as Law-Makers* (Oxford: Oxford University Press, 2005).

———. International Organizations: Then and Now (2006) 100 *American Journal of International Law* 324.

Anghie, A. International Financial Institutions in C. Reus-Smit (ed.), *The Politics of International Law* (Oxford: Oxford University Press, 2004), pp. 217–37.

Austin, J. *Lectures on Jurisprudence or the Philosophy of Positive Law*, 4th edn., revised and edited by R. Campbell (London: John Murray, 1873).

Barnett, M. and M. Finnemore. *Rules for the World: International Organizations in Global Politics* (Ithaca, NY: Cornell University Press, 2004).

Beaulac, S. The Rule of Law in International Law Today in G. Palombella and N. Walker (eds.), *Relocating the Rule of Law* (Oxford: Hart, 2009), p. 197.

Besson, S. and J. Tasioulas. Introduction in S. Besson and J. Tasioulas (eds.), *The Philosophy of International Law* (Oxford: Oxford University Press, 2010), p. 1.

Bianchi, A. Ad-Hocism and the Rule of Law (2002) 13 *European Journal of International Law* 263.

Boyle, A. Soft Law in International Law-Making in M.D. Evans (ed.), *International Law*, 2nd edn. (Oxford: Oxford University Press: 2006), p. 141.

Brierly, J.L. *The Outlook for International Law* (Oxford: Clarendon Press, 1944).

———. *The Law of Nations*, 6th edn. (Oxford: Clarendon Press, 1963).

Brölmann, C. *The Institutional Veil in Public International Law: International Organizations and the Law of Treaties* (Oxford: Hart, 2007).

Brownlie, I. The United Nations as a Form of Government, in J.E.S. Fawcett and R. Higgins (eds.), *International Organization* (1974), p. 26.

Campbell, A. International Law and Primitive Law (1988) 8 *Oxford Journal of Legal Studies* 169.

Capps, P. *Human Dignity and the Foundations of International Law* (Oxford: Hart, 2009).

Cardwell, P., D. French and N.D. White. Case Comment: *Yassin Abdullah Kadi and Al Barakaat International Foundation v Council and Commission* (Joined Cases C-402/05P and C-415/05P) Judgment of 3 September 2008 (2009) 58 *International and Comparative Law Quarterly* 229.

Carty, A. *The Decay of International Law: A Reappraisal of the Limits of Legal Imagination in International Affairs* (Manchester: Manchester University Press, 1986).

Cass, D.Z. *The Constitutionalization of the World Trade Organization* (Oxford: Oxford University Press, 2005).

Cassese, A. *International Law in a Divided World* (Oxford: Clarendon Press, 1986).

Charney, J.I. Universal International Law (1993) 87 *American Journal of International Law* 529.

Charnovitz, S. Nongovernmental Organizations and International Law (2006) 100 *American Journal of International Law* 348.

Chesterman, S. An International Rule of Law? (2008) 56 *American Journal of International Law* 331.

Chimni, B.S. International Institutions Today: An Imperial Global State in the Making (2004) 15 *European Journal of International Law* 1.

Coicaud, J.-M. and V. Heiskanen (eds.). *The Legitimacy of International Organizations* (Tokyo: United Nations University Press, 2001).

Collins, R. Modernist-Positivism and the Problem of Institutional Autonomy in International Law in R. Collins and N.D. White (eds.), *International Organizations and the Idea of Autonomy: Institutional Independence in the International Legal Order* (London: Routledge, 2011), p. 22.

Collins, R. and N.D. White. International Organizations and the Idea of Autonomy: Introduction and Overview in R. Collins and N.D. White (eds.), *International Organizations and the Idea of Autonomy: Institutional Independence in the International Legal Order* (London: Routledge, 2011), p. 1.

Danilenko, G.M. *Law-making in the International Community* (Dordrecht, Martinus Nijhoff Publishers, 1993).

d'Aspremont, J. Abuse of the Legal Personality of International Organizations and the Responsibility of Member States (2007) 4 *International Organizations Law Review* 91.

de Wet, E. *The Chapter VII Powers of the United Nations Security Council* (Oxford: Hart, 2004).

Dugard, J. The Future of International Law: A Human Rights Perspective (2007) 20 *Leiden Journal of International Law* 729.

Fassbender, B. The United Nations Charter as Constitution of the International Community (1998) 36 *Columbia Journal of Transnational Law* 529.

———. Pressure for Security Council Reform in D. Malone (ed.), *The UN Security Council: from the Cold War to the 21st Century* (Boulder: Lynne Rienner, 2004), 341.

———. *The United Nations Charter as the Constitution of the International Community* (Leiden: Martinus Nijhoff, 2009).

Fitzmaurice, G.G. The Foundations of the Authority of International law and the Problem of Enforcement (1956) 19 *Modern Law Review* 1.

Franck, T. United Nations Based Prospects for a New Global Order (1990) 22 *New York University Journal of International Law and Politics* 601.

———. *Fairness in International Law and Institutions* (Oxford: Clarendon Press, 1995).

Friedmann, W. *The Changing Structure of International Law* (London: Stevens & Sons, 1964).
Fukuyama, F. *The End of History and the Last Man* (New York: Avon Books, 1992).
Goldstein, J. *et al.* (eds.). *Legalization and World Politics* (Cambridge, MA; London: MIT Press, 2001).
Harlow, C. Global Administrative Law: The Quest for Principles and Values (2006) 17 *European Journal of International Law* 187.
Hart, H.L.A. *The Concept of Law*, 2nd edn. (Oxford: Oxford University Press, 1994).
Held, D. *Models of Democracy*, 3rd edn. (Cambridge: Polity Press, 2006).
Holland, T.E. *Studies in International Law* (Oxford: Clarendon Press, 1898).
Holls, F.W. *The Peace Conference at the Hague, and its Bearing on International Law and Policy* (New York: MacMillan, 1900).
Howse, R. From Politics to Technocracy – and Back Again: The Fate of the Multilateral Trading Regime (2002) 96 *American Journal of International Law* 94.
Jouannet, E. What is the Use of International Law? International Law as a Twenty-first Century Guardian of Welfare (2008) 28 *Michigan Journal of International Law* 815.
Kelsen, H. Théorie du Droit International Public (1953-III) 84 *Recueil des Cours* 1.
Kennedy, D. The Move to Institutions (1987) 8 *Cardozo Law Review* 841.
———. International Law and the Nineteenth Century: History of an Illusion (1997) 17 *Quinnipiac Law Review* 99.
Kingsbury, B. Legal Positivism as Normative Politics: International Society, Balance of Power and Lassa Oppenheim's Positive International Law (2002) 13 *European Journal of International Law* 401.
Klabbers, J. The Changing Image of International Institutions in J-M. Coicaud and V. Heiskanen (eds.), *The Legitimacy of International Organizations* (Tokyo: United Nations University Press, 2001), p. 221.
———. Constitutionalism Lite (2004) 1 *International Organizations Law Review* 31.
———. Two Concepts of International Organization (2005) 2 *International Organizations Law Review* 277.
———. Autonomy, Constitutionalism, and Virtue in International Institutional Law in R. Collins and N.D. White (eds.), *International Organizations and the Idea of Autonomy: Institutional Independence in the International Legal Order* (London: Routledge, 2011), p. 120.
Klabbers, J.A. Peters and G. Ulfstein. *The Constitutionalization of International Law* (Cambridge: Cambridge University Press, 2010).
Koskenniemi, M. Theory: Implications for the Practitioner in P. Allott *et al.*, *Theory and International Law: An Introduction* (London: British Institute of International and Comparative Law, 1991), p. 1.

———. *The Gentle Civilizer of Nations: The Rise and Fall of International Law 1870–1960* (Cambridge: Cambridge University Press, 2001).
———. *From Apology to Utopia: the Structure of International Legal Argument* (Cambridge: Cambridge University Press, 2005).
———. Constitutionalism as Mindset: Reflections on Kantian Themes about International Law and Globalization (2007) 8 *Theoretical Inquiries in Law* 9.
Koskenniemi, M. and P. Leino. Fragmentation of International Law? Postmodern Anxieties (2002) *Leiden Journal of International Law* 55.
Kratochwil, F.V. How Do Norms Matter? in M. Byers (ed.), *The Role of Law in International Politics* (Oxford: Oxford University Press, 2000), p. 35.
Krisch, N. and B. Kingsbury. Introduction: Global Governance and Global Administrative Law in the International Legal Order (2006) 17 *European Journal of International Law* 1.
Kritsiotis, D. Imagining the International Community (2002) 13 *European Journal of International Law* 961.
Lauterpacht, H. *Private Law Sources and Analogies of International Law (with Special Reference to International Arbitration)* (London: Longmans, 1927).
———. The Nature of International Law and General Jurisprudence (1932) 37 *Economica* 301.
———. The Covenant as the Higher Law (1936) 17 *British Yearbook of International Law* 54.
———. *The Development of International Law by the International Court*, 2nd edn. (London: Stevens & Sons, 1958).
Loughlin, M. *The Idea of Public Law* (Oxford: Oxford University Press, 2003).
Loughlin, M. and N. Walker. Introduction in M. Loughlin & N. Walker (eds.), *The Paradox of Constitutionalism: Constituent Power and Constitutional Form* (Oxford: Oxford University Press, 2007), p. 1.
Macdonald, R. St. J., The International Community as a Legal Community in R. St. J. Macdonald and D.M. Johnston (eds.), *Towards World Constitutionalism: Issues in the Legal Ordering of the World Community* (Leiden: Martinus Nijhoff, 2005), p. 853.
McNair, A.D. The Functions and Differing Legal Character of Treaties (1930) 11 *British Yearbook of International Law* 100.
———. International Legislation (1934) 19 *Iowa Law Review* 177, reprinted in A.D. McNair, *The Law of Treaties* (1961).
Miller, R.A. and R.M. Bratspies (eds.). *Progress in International Law* (Leiden: Martinus Nijhoff, 2008).
Oakeshott, M. *On Human Conduct* (Oxford: Oxford University Press, 1975).
Oppenheim, L. *International Law: A Treatise, Vol. 1*, 3rd edn. (London: Longmans, Green & Co., 1920).
———. *Future of International Law* (Oxford: Clarendon Press, 1921).
Orakhelashvili, A. The Impact of Peremptory Norms on Interpretation and Application of the UN Security Council Resolutions (2005) 16 *European Journal of International Law* 59.

———. Peremptory Norms as an Aspect of Constitutionalisation in the International Legal System in S. Muller and M. Frishman (eds.) *The Dynamics of Constitutionalism in the Age of Globalization* (The Hague: Hague Academy Press, 2010), p. 153.

Peters, A. Compensatory Constitutionalism: The Function and Potential of Fundamental International Norms and Structures (2006) 19 *Leiden Journal of International Law* 559.

Reus-Smit, C. *The Moral Purpose of the State: Culture, Social Identity, and Institutional Rationality in International Relations* (Princeton, NJ: Princeton University Press, 1999).

———. The Politics of International Law in C. Reus-Smit (ed.), *The Politics of International Law* (Cambridge: Cambridge University Press, 2004), p. 14.

Roberts, A.E. Traditional and Modern Approaches to Customary International Law: A Reconciliation (2001) 95 *American Journal of International Law* 757.

Sato, T. The Legitimacy of Security Council activities under Chapter VII of the UN Charter after the End of the Cold War in J-M Coicaud & V. Heiskanen (eds.), *The Legitimacy of International Organizations* (Tokyo: United Nations University Press, 2001), p. 309.

Scelle, G. Essai de Systématique de Droit International (Plan d'un Cours de Droit International Public) (1923) 30 *Revue Générale de Droit International Public* 116.

———. *Précis de Droit des Gens: Principes et Systématique. Pt.2, Droit Constitutionnel International* (Paris: Sirey, 1934).

Schachter, O. The Nature and Process of Legal Development in International Society in R. St. J. Macdonald and D.M. Johnston (eds.), *The Structure and Process of International Law: Essays in Legal Philosophy, Doctrine, and Theory* (The Hague: Martinus Nijhoff, 1983), p. 745.

Scholte, J.A. Civil Society and Democratically Accountable Global Governance (2004) 39 *Government and Opposition* 211.

Schücking, W. *The International Union of the Hague Conferences*, translation by Charles G. Fenwick (Oxford: Oxford University Press, 1918).

Shelton, D. International Law and 'Relative Normativity' in M. Evans (ed.), *International Law*, 2nd edn. (Oxford: Oxford University Press, 2006), p. 159.

Simma, B. From Bilateralism to Community Interest in International Law (1994–VI) 250 *Recueil des Cours* 221.

Simma, B. and A. Paulus. The 'International Community: Facing the Challenge of Globalization (1998) 9 *European Journal of International Law* 266.

Skouteris, T. *The Notion of Progress in International Law Discourse* (The Hague: TMC Asser Press, 2010).

Somek, A. The Owl of Minerva: Constitutional Discourse Before its Conclusion (2008) 71 *Modern Law Review* 473.

Stein, E. International Integration and Democracy: No Love at First Sight (2001) 95 *American Journal of International Law* 489.

Tams, C. *The Enforcement of Obligations* Erga Omnes *in International Law* (Cambridge: Cambridge University Press, 2005).

Tomuschat, C. International Law: Ensuring the Survival of Mankind on the Eve of a New Century, General Course on Public International Law (1999) 281 *Recueil des Cours* 9.

Verdross, A. Le Fondement du Droit International (1927-I) 16 *Recueil des Cours* 247.

Villalpando, S. The Legal Dimension of the International Community: How Community Interests are Protected in International Law (2010) 21 *European Journal of International Law* 387.

Von Bogdandy, A.P. Dann and M. Goldmann. Developing the Publicness of Public International Law: Towards a Legal Framework for Global Governance Activities (2008) 9 *German Law Journal* 1375.

Warbrick, C. The Theory of International Law: Is There an English Contribution? in P. Allott *et al.*, *Theory and International Law: An Introduction* (London: BIICL, 1991), p. 61.

Warbrick, C. and S. Tierney (eds.). *Towards an 'International Legal Community'? The Sovereignty of States and the Sovereignty of International Law* (London: BIICL, 2006).

Weil, P. Towards Normative Relativity in International Law? (1983) 77 *American Journal of International Law* 413.

Weiler, J.H.H. The Geology of International Law – Governance, Democracy and Legitimacy (2004) 64 *Zeitschrift für Ausländisches Öffentliches Recht und Völkerrecht* 547.

Werner, W.G. The Never-Ending Closure: Constitutionalism and International Law in N. Tsagourias (ed.), *Transnational Constitutionalism: International and European Perspectives* (Cambridge: Cambridge University Press, 2007), p. 329.

White, N.D. The United Nations System: Conference, Contract or Constitutional Order? (2000) 4 *Singapore Journal of International and Comparative Law* 281.

———. *The United Nations System: Toward International Justice* (London: Lynne Rienner Publishers, 2002).

———. *The Law of International Organizations*, 2nd ed., (Manchester: Manchester University Press, 2006).

Zimmern, A. *The League of Nations and the Rule of Law 1918 – 1935* (London: MacMillan, 1936).

# PART II
# Unconstituted Publics

# Chapter 5
# 'Unconstituted Publics'?

Scott Veitch

## Some Observations and Questions

The title of this collection – *The Public in Law* – invites a number of possible readings, many of which are engaged with in the other chapters. Just a few of these will be highlighted here before some questions to be explored further in this chapter are briefly raised.

Together the terms public and law have a familiar legal presence. 'Public law' is that which conventionally deals on the one hand with relations concerning the arrangement, capacities and functioning of the institutional organizations of government and their interrelation, and on the other the relationship of these institutions to citizens. As well as positive laws dealing with these relations, public law is also, as Loughlin (2010) suggests, concerned with something more fundamental: the very constitution of political society, the conditions according to which a community constitutes legitimate authority. In both senses, public law is traditionally contrasted with private law, which deals with legal relations amongst citizens and other legal persons in their private, familial, economic, and (in the case of government institutions) non-governing capacities, and rests on the twin pillars of property law and the law of obligations.[1] The distinction, familiar enough already to first year law students, is acknowledged to be in several respects far from watertight.[2]

'Public' may also refer to *the* public, as a noun: the public as a body of people. The public 'in law' here concerns the manner in which 'the public' appears in the representational categories of the law; it refers to how a non-legally constituted body of the people appears in the eyes of the law. The matter of who makes up any particular public is not pre-given, but is fluid and contingent. The public may refer to a huge range of different sizes of population for example: the public may be of a village, or of a state, or even 'the global public'. Or it may be identified by reference to a particular function, such as a profession, or constituency. A nice ambivalence exists, in English usage at least, where 'the public' can be referred to in the singular or the plural: for example, 'the public *is* ...' – as if it were one,

1 See, for example, Thomson (2006: Chapter 1)

2 Compare, for example, Emile Durkheim (1984: 28): 'All law is private, in the sense that always and everywhere individuals are concerned and are its actors. Above all, however, all law is public, in the sense that it is a social function, and all individuals are, although in different respects, functionaries of society.'

a unified body – or 'the public *are* …' – acknowledging that the public are always and only many, a multitude.

These various publics may have many attributes and capabilities: there is, for example, the public interest and public opinion; publics can have funds and holidays – public funds, public holidays – and they may use the funds to buy things, taking things into public ownership. They may even have – they often especially *do* have – enemies, who are, curiously enough, often given numbers: public enemy number one, number two, etc. And then there are public houses, public parks, various forms of public transport, public conveniences and so on.

'Public' as an adjective is used to describe the *quality* of being open or general. Making something public means making it potentially available or accessible to all. Or it can mean bringing something out of its hiding place into the light, putting it on display. In this sense, with respect to law, the 'public in law' has a more nuanced, though no less significant meaning: it can express that aspect of law which is its 'publicness'; law's *public quality*. The nature of law, part of its essence, it is claimed, requires it to be 'public'. This is perhaps best understood by comparing it with its opposite, which in this instance is not so much 'private' law, as 'secret' law, which is arguably no law at all. It is in this sense that Lon Fuller argued that promulgation was one of the eight essential criteria of legality. In fact, for him, it was the only one whose existence was a matter of duty and not merely aspiration: if law is understood as the subjection of human conduct to the governance of rules, then it is necessary that law is made publicly available – published, publicized (the Latin root is the same) – since unknowable law is no law at all. It is this that helps ground the 'reciprocity between government and citizen with respect to the observance of rules' (Fuller 1969).

This public quality also means belonging to the people – of whatever group might be represented as the collective – as a generality. What this means has been the subject of great contestation. Where this generality refers to the state and its citizens, then there is, according to one tradition of political philosophy, a further specificity in terms of the mode of action and justification appropriate to it, namely *public reason*. According to John Rawls, 'in a democratic society public reason is the reason of equal citizens who, as a collective body, exercize final political and coercive power over one another in enacting laws and in amending their constitution'. It is 'public', he suggests, in three ways:

> as the reason of citizens as such, it is the reason of the public; its subject is the good of the public and matters of fundamental justice; and its nature and content is public, being given by the ideals and principles expressed by society's conception of political justice, and conducted open to view on that basis.

That public reason is to be 'so understood and honoured' is 'not a matter of law'; not a matter, that is, of an imposed duty, but rather an aspiration to an 'ideal conception of citizenship for a constitutional democratic regime' (Rawls 1993: 213–14).

Contrarily, it was precisely the specificity attributed to this kind of understanding of public reason that attracted the critique of the young Marx. The claim that 'every member of the nation is an *equal* participant in national sovereignty' meant endorsing the limitations of political equality at the cost of allowing free reign to 'non-political', 'non-public' reasons in their fullness:

> The state abolishes, in its own way, distinctions of birth, social rank, education, occupation, when it declares that birth, social rank, education, occupation, are non-political distinctions. ... Nevertheless, the state allows private property, education, occupation, to act in *their* way – *i.e.*, as private property, as education, as occupation, and to exert the influence of their *special* nature. Far from abolishing these real distinctions, the state only exists on the presupposition of their existence; it feels itself to be a political state and asserts its universality only in opposition to these elements of its being. (Marx 1982/1843: 45)

Later, this chapter will return to the set of issues raised by this.

This contribution will ask a number of questions about the nature of the public and of the public in law that these introductory observations provoke. In particular: Is 'the public' anything other than a projection of an institution? Could what stands as 'the public' be known otherwise than as a figure or place or grouping conjured up by the need or desire of a specific political, legal or media project? If it could not, is the notion of an 'unconstituted public' – a public unbound, so to speak – a contradiction in terms? And why does it matter? That is, what is at stake in addressing such questions? Secondly, is there something distinctive, unique, sui generis – something qualitatively underived and underivable – about the 'public' in law? And again, what is at stake in assessing whether there is or is not such a quality?

This chapter will suggest that different senses of 'the public' *are* constituted by a range of institutional logics, and that these co-exist in ways that do not add up to a coherent or singular overarching notion. In this sense, 'the public' in its different guises functions as a mode of classification available to be deployed for particular ends, and hence as an important regulative signifier. *And yet*, the 'public' – as noun and as adjective – also arguably retains an ongoing imaginative presence; it provides a horizon whose unreachable quality operates as a figure of inexhaustible potential, especially around contestations of what an 'unconstituted' public might promise or threaten. It is this ongoing, energizing dynamic with respect to constituted and unconstituted publics that the chapter considers briefly in closing.

## The Potential of the Public Sphere

On one view the question 'How do we know what 'the public' – any public – is?' is an epistemological one. But it is one that also appears tied to questions of purpose. As already noted, publics can vary according to many different factors, but identifying a particular public seems linked to whatever end or goal is deemed appropriate to it. This is not to say that a particular public or its recognition is to be conceived in purely instrumental terms; rather it is to note that its existence is tied primarily to a hermeneutical understanding and not a purely categorical one. It is important to recognize this because it is that hermeneutical dimension which also, crucially when it comes to the public, points to a second order dimension, one which brings with it more significance than the mere *content* expressed in actors' self-understanding. In this respect it might be argued that the designation of something as public, or a public, contains a number of dualities that explain both its centripetal and centrifugal – or if you prefer, its organizing and disruptive – capabilities.

We can fruitfully consider this in the context of society's so-called 'public sphere'. In its Arendtian understanding, the public sphere is traced back to its Attic roots, and stands constructed as the brightly lit stage on which citizens engage one another directly in public debate. Here 'public-spiritedness' demands participation in the goods of the *common* realm, constituting a non-instrumentalized display the practice of which is its own end and not those of any particular or private self-interest. In stark contrast to this, the contemporary 'public sphere' is often seen to be replete with power interests, powerful forms – none more so than those associated with the distortions of the 'popular' media – which have seen the public sphere become a place where interest groups seek out recognition, advantage and, if they have to, engage in compromise. In this sphere, particular groups or interests may clothe their claims as representations of the general public – its needs, interests, benefits, goods – when it comes to all sorts of activities: entertainment, health, environmental practices, revenue-raising, and so on. Here a familiar criticism is offered that what is claimed to be in the public interest in fact represents the needs, interests etc of only a few. Business, professional, parliamentary, media, and other expert groupings may all be accused of engaging in this form of practice. Such more or less tightly institutionalized forms of activity may make claims to represent their constituents on the public stage, or may, in claiming to act in the interests of the general public as a whole, classify and promote their projects and agendas as the best understanding of the public sphere itself.

Today, this latter form seems far more sociologically plausible than the Arendtian seems attainable. Our question here nonetheless is to ask whether that is all that can be said of the public sphere: does it remain always and only a projection of interests, susceptible to capture and hijack by power lobbies, or do there exist further capabilities that are not exhausted by those projections and susceptibilities? To explore the latter possibility – through an inversion of the familiar critiques just noted – there are three potentialities that can be considered. These are drawn from part of the work of Jurgen Habermas (1996), an important theorist of the public sphere, though they by no means capture all or even most of what he has to say on the topic. The potentialities are identified in turn as those associated with latency, dependency, and the mode of actualization in the public sphere.

According to Habermas,

> Public opinion can be manipulated but neither publicly bought nor publicly blackmailed. This is due to the fact that a public sphere cannot be 'manufactured' as one pleases. Before it can be captured by actors with strategic intent, the public sphere together with its public must have developed as a structure that stands on its own and reproduces itself *out of itself*. (1996: 364, original emphasis)

Although the public sphere is not a system, there is in this description nonetheless something of an autopoietic quality to it with respect to its formation and continuation. The crucial temporal dimension signals a priority – '*Before* it can be captured …' – that has also therefore a qualitative aspect: the public and the public sphere do not emerge as an agglomeration of private realms or a tally of private interests. Significantly, for Habermas, it is this mode of formation and reproduction of the public sphere that 'remains latent in the constituted public sphere – and takes effect again only in moments when the public sphere is mobilized' (ibid). In other words, even where it is sociologically the case that the public sphere is open to domination by particular interests, it nonetheless provides a site for the appearance of a potentiality that can be drawn on to reject, recast, and progress *against* private intrusions into the public. Without this latency, of a potentially renewable 'public', there can only ever be the competition and compromises of particular interests.

This can be evidenced further by the potential associated with a specific *dependency*, which may also remain latent but which also seems core to the operation of the public sphere. For Habermas, '… the endogenous mobilization of public sphere activates an otherwise latent dependency built into the internal structure of every public sphere, a dependency also present in the normative self-understanding of the mass media: the players in the arena owe their influence to the approval of those in the gallery' (382). (The Arendtian overtones of stage, actors and audience resonate clearly in Habermas's depiction of the public sphere in this respect.) Hence even where there may be, for example, an overbearing sense of the money-driven saturation of media content, there is never any guarantee that approval cannot be withheld, that the audience may begin to boo and walk out. If not exactly a mutuality, then this latent dependency – in part induced by the need for power itself to *appear*, in whatever guise – and the potential it carries, is nonetheless again not reducible to private competition as such.

The third potentiality rests in the mode of actualization of action in the public sphere. It is here that the duality with respect to the hermeneutic understanding of the public sphere that was adverted to earlier appears at its most explicit. For the engagement in the public sphere has a second-order meaning, going beyond that associated with its content, and any conflict or resolution of that content. As Habermas notes, 'Whatever the manifest content of their public utterances, the performative meaning of such public discourse at the same time actualizes the function of an undistorted political public sphere as such'. With respect to politics, for example, this 'dual orientation' of actors' public political engagement can 'directly influence the political system', but – and this appears to be the decisive point – 'at the same time [the actors] are also reflexively concerned with revitalizing and enlarging civil society and the public sphere as well as with confirming their own identities and capacities to act' (369–70). It is precisely this reflexivity that embodies the distinctively 'public' quality of the public sphere. At once self-referential and dually oriented with respect to the mode of actualization, the public sphere invites a reciprocity that the competition of strategically geared self-interest, unless postulated in some mystic concept like the invisible hand, does not. On this account, public-oriented, public sphere activities and groupings, and the mode of challenging and the changes they can make, do have a distinctive quality. For this reason they have been characterized as the 'carriers of the potentials of cultural modernity'.[3]

These three potentialities significantly challenge the view that the public sphere is reducible to the play of private interests. For if the latter *were* true, then it also follows that no common or communal project could be invoked or would be possible. There would be nothing beyond self-interest, nothing whose aspiration could be other than self-seeking, nothing to be thought (of) 'in common'. Indeed it is precisely this mind-set and these practices of competitive self-interest that the potentialities of the public sphere might work to disturb.

Under current conditions however these claims are not free from further challenge. There are two major sources of vulnerability that can be noted, and these will be the subject of the remainder of the chapter. The first is described by Habermas himself, and results from a perhaps surprising source. That is, while the quality of publicness has its own claimed distinctiveness, it is threatened not only by intrusions of private interest and power (along the lines already noted), but is, conversely, susceptible to the collapse or even weakening of the *non*-public sphere. In certain circumstances, Habermas argues,

> a panoptic state not only directly controls the bureaucratically desiccated public sphere, it also undermines the private basis of this public sphere. Administrative intrusions and constant supervision corrode the communicative structure of everyday contacts in families and schools, neighbourhoods and local municipalities. ... Communicative rationality is thus destroyed *simultaneously* in both public and private contexts of communication. (369, original emphasis)

The public here, in other words, is vulnerable not only from attacks specific to it, but also to a diminution in the capabilities of actors and activities in non-public realms. The sources of this are readily identifiable with (and this is the irony) nominally public state or administrative intrusions. (Habermas associates these features explicitly with 'totalitarian societies of bureaucratic socialism'.) But *pace* Habermas they are not limited to such public origins. Those aspects of power that would operate through positive or productive modes, rather than in a deductive manner (of the state bureaucratic kind), may extend this vulnerability.

3 Habermas (1996: 370). Habermas is here quoting Cohen and Arato's interpretation of himself, appropriately enough perhaps, given the context of self-referentiality.

Hence identifiable disciplinary or bio-political forms (of the kind analyzed by Foucault and others) that utilize the creative working of power formations, succeed through their constant involvement in shaping the 'communicative structure of everyday contacts'. As these also occur in non-totalitarian societies, the 'private basis of the public sphere' may be vulnerable not only to public sphere intrusions but also to a range of power practices that cut across public/private dimensions and leave both more susceptible than the optimum constitutional democratic account would present.

The second vulnerability is different, and in an important sense more radical. Here the danger arises not so much from the collapse of the public and private – from whichever side it originated – but from the nature of the separation of the two. As this problem is manifested quite clearly in the legal realm, this will form the basis of the final section.

## The Public In and Out of Law

Let us return to this via the quote from Marx above. Marx had posed the question of whether it was the case that, if there was an equal and universal non-property based right to vote in state elections, 'the masses have won a victory over the property owners and financial wealth'? (Marx op. cit., quoting Hamilton). His answer was that in one sense they have, namely at the level of political equality and emancipation in the state. But, he continued, the latter by no means exhausted what emancipation or equality meant as such. In a capitalist society, the influence of wealth and property continued under conditions of political equality at the level of the state. But this influence was not mere happenstance, not just a contingent fact. Rather – and this was the crucial point – political equality *relied on* the existence, and separation, of private interests. For Marx 'the political annulment of private property not only fails to abolish private property but even presupposes it' (ibid.). The nature of property relations therefore conditioned what was available to be understood *as* political emancipation: without the particularity of private property, there could be *no* experience of the 'universality' of political equality. Just as a slave-based economy set the underlying conditions for the meaning and experience of the imperial state, or the feudal governing order corresponded to the mode and relations of feudal production, so too with the bourgeois state. That contemporary political equality might have been an improvement on previous forms of state rule in no way changed the fact either that a lineage of exploitation continued nor that the relation between material and political form was not broken but remained intact albeit in a different form. 'What you see clearly in the case of ancient property, what you admit in the case of feudal property, you are of course forbidden to admit in the case of your own bourgeois form of property', wrote Marx and Engels (1982/1848: 234). What made this harder to see was the very universal equality that was postulated – and in reality *experienced* – at the level of the state. But this latter form itself *depended on* the material reality of inequality and exploitation rooted in alienated labour and capitalist production. The state was a detour to emancipation, but emancipation got stuck there, as far as it could go since the state, its law, and its underlying 'non-political' ground, determined and limited what could count as emancipation.

This points us towards the more profound vulnerability of the 'public' in the sense of a generality or a universality. The concern here is not that it is captured by private interests, nor that it is a particular interest that is falsely universalized. Rather it is that where 'the public' registers or acts in an organized way, then it too is forced to work through an institutionalized detour. The public sphere, Habermas noted, was not a system but it was still structured. This may provide benefits. But it may provide its own blindspots – things 'you are of course forbidden to admit'.

Let us consider then the most prominent manifestation of the organization and guaranteeing of the public today, namely its legal underpinning. The capitalist society Marx described has mutated, but it has not gone away. Part of that mutation in the post-industrial west has involved what Loughlin describes as the dual movement of the politicization of law and the legalization of politics which is the hallmark of the 'age of rights' (Loughlin 2000). The public of these societies – regional, national, European, whatever – is increasingly constituted in or as a legal society, and secured in legalized manner. Again, as Habermas observes: 'Today legal norms are what is left from a crumbled cement of society … Law stands as a substitute for the failures of other integrative mechanisms – markets and administrations, or values, norms, and face-to-face communications' (Habermas 1999: 937). Where this is so, the public of rights and dignities which is achieved comes with a new kind of ambivalence. For it is at one and the same time an extraordinarily highly regulated society in this sense: the tracks along which freedom can be enacted are already laid.

And hence the danger to 'the public'. It lies not in its particular content – striated as that may be by powerful interests – but in its form. In the juridical security established, the thinking that it has reached, in the democratic constitutionalism of a market society, its highest form is expressed through law as the best, perhaps only, institutional arrangement for reaching common goods through communicative rationality and transparency. The experience of this *as* the public experience relies not just on a separated and entrenched legally constituted civil society (as Marx had put it) and all that still goes with it in a capitalist society, but increasingly on an anxious awareness that this is the *only* available means to secure the ends of public emancipation and common good. The legal form is crucial, and it has real effects. Hence an 'unruly public' is no longer to be considered a political force or public movement that might 'carry the potential of modernity', but is rather something to be feared, like Hobbes's state of nature. Where the public is the legally underwritten public – one that is genuinely of us all, as universal human rights bearers – who would gainsay this? Who indeed?, for it is precisely this fear, this simultaneously confident and nervous experience ('Who might take away what we have?') that becomes the norm.

The danger, the vulnerability of the idea of 'the public', lies then in an immense failure of the imagination. Where the public 'in law' sets terms of engagement then there may be, like family 'in-laws', good things to be said about them. But sometimes these other 'in-laws', as is well known, generate frustrations, misunderstandings, and often ultimately, more or less satisfactory bust-ups. But being told that with the 'public in law' all the means of possible resolution are already there and given signifies that the regulatory forms have already been settled and possible outcomes determined. As Legrand puts the point succinctly in the context of European legal integration, 'for every problem, there appears to be a solution and the solution is almost always law' (Legrand 2006: 14). Whatever lies beyond such rationality can only be the irrational.

But as we have suggested, the 'public' has been thought of as so much more than this. The dualities that make up the *potential* of the public sphere – latency, dependency, and the mode of actualization – invoke the possibilities of an 'unconstituted public' as an expression of or figure for the carrier of movements that progress through unprepared ways and unexpected dissonances. Where these movements are limited – where dissonance must refer itself to what Isaiah Berlin described as the 'approbation of the official auditor' – then 'the public' loses that unruly energy and potential. It is precisely this that is at stake in thinking about the public and the public in law today.

A 'public unbound' is not about organizing or organized power, but wrests free of these realities and is imaginative; it is an unstructured dialogue or even no dialogue at all. It is the potential, the possibility, the freedom that at some important level 'you are of course forbidden to admit' … nothing.

If this sense of the public is not only imaginative but imaginary does that matter? Of course it does. This is part of its vulnerability. But then again, that alone is its power.

## References

Durkheim, E. 1984. *The Division of Labour in Society* (transl. W.D. Halls), London: Macmillan.
Fuller, L. 1969. *The Morality of Law* (2nd ed.) New Haven: Yale University Press.
Habermas, J. 1996. *Between Facts and Norms* (transl. W. Rehg), Cambridge, MA: MIT Press.
———. 1999. Between Facts and Norms: An Author's Reflections 76 *Denver University Law Review* 937.
Legrand, P. 2006. Antivonbar 1:1 *Journal of Comparative Law*, 14.
Loughlin, M. 2000. *Sword and Scales*, Oxford: Hart.
———. 2010. *Foundations of Public Law*, Oxford: Oxford University Press.
Marx, K. 1982/1843. On the Jewish Question in D. McLellan ed., *Karl Marx: Selected Writings*, Oxford: Oxford University Press.
Marx, K. and F. Engels. 1982/1848. The Communist Manifesto in D. McLellan ed., *Karl Marx: Selected Writings*, Oxford: Oxford University Press.
Rawls, J. 1993. *Political Liberalism*, New York: Columbia University Press.
Thomson, J. 2006. *Scots Private Law*, Edinburgh: Greens.

# Chapter 6
# A Dilemma for the Civil Disobedient: Pleading 'Guilty' or 'Not Guilty' in the Court Room?

Piero Moraro

## Introduction

This chapter centres on a crucial moment of the relation between a citizen and the law of her political community, namely the case of disagreement and dissent. It will focus on the practice of Civil Disobedience (CD), and the aim is to highlight how the fact that the latter implies an open defiance of the letter of the law need not entail a disapproval of its role within the life of a democratic society. More specifically, my claim will be that, under certain circumstances, it is exactly by resorting to an illegal behaviour that citizens can fulfil their duties as political agents, and show their commitment to the values underlying the life of their political community.

For the purposes of this argument, the conception of CD that will be refered to is as 'a public, non-violent, conscientious yet political act, contrary to law, usually done with the aim of bringing about a change in the law or policies of the government' (Rawls 1999: 320). It is generally agreed that one of the elements that differentiate a civil disobedient from a plain law-breaker is that the former does act illegally, but in her case 'fidelity to law is expressed [...] by the willingness to accept the legal consequences of [her own] conduct' (Rawls 1999: 321). That is to say, one of the main elements of CD is, according to this view, that the citizen, who resorts to breaching the law, willingly submits to the sanctions that will follow the violation of the particular legal enactment. This includes the idea that, when appearing at the criminal trial after the act of CD, a civil disobedient should plead guilty, and undergo the legal punishment.

The intention is to focus specifically on how this willingness to accept the legal consequences for an act of CD should be understood: that is to say, the goal is to analyze in more detail what is implied by the concept that a civil disobedient should possess such a disposition. Clarifying this aspect will reveal a crucial aspect of the relationship between civil disobedients and the law: that the decision to challenge the prosecution in court, by pleading 'not guilty', rather than a lack of fidelity to the law, might reveal the defendant's respect for law's authority.

The idea behind these considerations may by summarized by the following claim:

> In a case of CD, there is a presumption that the defendant should plead not-guilty when faced with the legal charges.

Note that this claim is stronger than the idea that it is sometimes permissible to plead not-guilty in a case of CD. According to the view defended below, it should be presumed that, as civil disobedients, defendants will plead not guilty: this need not rule out cases where the guilty plea might be more appropriate to the communicative aims of CD, under the circumstances.

This chapter will be *exclusively* interested in *the disposition of the civil disobedient* towards the law. That is to say, the discussion should not be seen as suggesting what kind of verdict the *judge* should issue in cases of CD. Although this article will have something to say regarding what kind of legal appeals should be available to a civil disobedient, that need not lead to the conclusion that the judge should also accept them. The target of this analysis is to show how an attitude of respect for the law is displayed during a trial for CD by the defendant: therefore this work will leave aside the (undoubtedly very important) question of how the state should treat a civil disobedient who pleads not guilty.

## CD on Trial: The Problem

The discussion will begin with the claim that the main feature of CD lies in its *communicative nature* (Rawls 1999: 321; Brownlee 2004): the breach of the law that characterizes CD should be intended as a form of speech act that seeks to draw public attention to a particular law or policy. CD represents the citizens' attempt to *persuade* the majority in power that a law or policy needs to be reconsidered. The view to be defended in this chapter is that the communicative aims of the civil disobedients often carry *from the street to the court room*. Hence, the claim will be made here that the trial constitutes a central part of an act of CD.

Appearing at the trial to answer the charge of wrongdoing should be seen, therefore, as an inherent part of the communicative aims underlying the choice to do CD. Highlighting this aspect is important, in order to address a conception of CD that forbids challenging the prosecution's charges during the trial. According to this conception, a civil disobedient should not deny the accusation of criminal wrongdoing. If there is a requirement for civil disobedients to accept the legal consequences of their illegal behaviour, it should follow that they should enter a *guilty plea* when faced with the charges (Cohen 1971). In adherence to a long-established conception of 'passive' resistance, a civil disobedient should appear at the trial, if at all, to bear witness to the injustice she is denouncing through the act of disobedience, without arguing against the prosecutor's charges, nor contesting the court's decision. This supports the idea that an act of CD should *rule out* the attempt to justify one's behaviour, i.e., to argue that the act should not be punished:

according to this view, it would go beyond the aims of CD to try to convince the judge and the jury that the illegal act was not a *crime*. Aiming to justify one's act of disobedience would contradict the requirement to accept punishment, and would go beyond the communicative aims of CD.

Against this position, this chapter seeks to endorse an analogy between the communicative nature of CD, on the one hand, and a conception of the criminal trial as a 'communicative enterprise' that aims for rational *persuasion* of the participants.[1] The criminal trial is the place where the communicative process between the state and the citizens can develop to a full extent: through a process of *reciprocal* reason-giving, the state calls the defendant to account for her allegedly illegal behaviour, and the defendant has a chance to explain the reasons for her conduct.

As for CD, what underlies the criminal trial is a demand for rational *persuasion* among the agents taking part in it. This, as this chapter will argue, reveals that civil disobedients have strong reasons to *defend* themselves, at the trial, against the charges of wrongdoing. These reasons arise out of the attitude of respect for the law and, ultimately, of the duty to respect fellow citizens as autonomous agents. When such defence fails, for example when the judge or jury issue a verdict of guilty in spite of the disobedient's not-guilty plea, she still has an obligation to accept the punishment following from that verdict. In many cases, arguing against being punished is part of the communicative nature of CD and shows, as will be argued, an attitude of respect for the law.

## The Criminal Trial as a 'Communicative Process'

Article 10 of the Universal Declaration of Human Rights states that everyone 'is entitled in full equality to a *fair* and public hearing by an independent and impartial tribunal, in the determination of his rights and obligations and of any criminal charge against him'. It is useful, for the present discussion, to point out some elements that make a trial a 'fair' one. Hildebrandt (2006: 25) highlights six aspects that are central to the idea of a fair trial. According to her summary, a fair trial requires 1) an impartial and independent judge, 2) a public trial, 3) a presumption of innocence, namely that the defendant will not be punished until proven guilty and that the onus is on the prosecutor to prove the guilt, 4) an equality of arms between prosecution and defence, 5) that the judgment will be based on evidence presented in court, and 6) that the proceedings will be based on a right of confrontation. What follows from claiming that there is a human right to a fair trial is that these elements represent constitutional guarantees that an individual, who appears at the trial, possesses and can enforce against the state (Duff *et al*: 51).

---

1 This analogy was first proposed by Kimberley Brownlee (2007), who however focuses on the institution of *punishment*, rather than on the criminal trial. Like Brownlee, I will build largely on Antony Duff's idea of responsibility as 'answerability', with particular reference to Duff (1986), and Duff *et al*., (2007).

According to Duff (1986), the criminal trail has its moral correspondent in the process of *blame*, which he describes as a way to call someone to *account for* alleged wrongdoing (Duff 1986, 2001). In the view he defends, 'blame' is not something that we merely do *to* an individual e.g., to have her change behaviour. Seeing 'blame' under this light can be highly misleading, according to Duff, for it emphasizes the 'goal', namely the change in the behaviour of the blamed person, over the way in which this change is achieved. Blaming someone is a way to engage that person in a moral argument: it is, therefore, something that we do *with* the blamed person. When we blame someone, we tell her that we think she acted wrongly, and why we think so: in doing this, we *call her to respond* to our charge. Such response could be either an admission of guilt and acceptance of our criticism, or a denial of the charge and a defence of her own conduct:

> I may try to show him that his conduct was at odds with moral values which he himself accepts; or to persuade him of the significance and relevance of values by which he was previously unmoved. If he comes to accept my judgment on his past conduct, he must also agree that he should act differently in the future, if the occasion arises. Thus, in persuading him to accept my criticism of his past conduct I also persuade him to modify his future conduct. (Duff 1986: 48)

The element to emphasize in this account is that it fosters treating others as individuals who can be *persuaded*, through *rational* argument, of the reason why they are being blamed. We blame someone to bring her to acknowledge her wrongdoing and to finally accept that she deserves punishment. That is why – if we managed to change the conduct of the blamed person, but only because she may want to avoid some inconvenience – our blaming her would have failed. On the other hand, if we did not manage to persuade her to change conduct, while making her respond seriously to our blaming, we would have reached significant success (Duff 1986: 48–9).

In engaging the other person in this way, we treat her as a *responsible* agent: as one who can offer reasons to account for her behaviour to those who accuse her of wrongdoing. Being 'responsible', under this perspective, implies being 'answerable', being ready to answer for what one is responsible for (Duff 2005). What characterizes the criminal trial, under the communicative theory discussed here, is this same purpose to call the defendant, as a fellow citizen, to answer to the charges moved against her. The purpose and meaning of the *trial* closely resemble that of *blaming*: underlying both, there is the respect for the accused/blamed person as a responsible agent, who is called to answer the accusation. Most importantly, both blaming and the criminal trial seek to lead the subject to understand the reasons why she is accused/blamed: hence, one of the 'proper ends' of the criminal trial is to persuade the defendant, in cases of a verdict of 'Guilty', that what she did was wrong and deserves punishment (Duff 1986: 129). That is why, when this persuasion is not pursued, the value of the trial as a communicative enterprise might be compromised.

The right to a fair trial, under this perspective, ultimately reflects a *right to be blamed*, that is to say, a right 'to be treated, respected and cared for as a moral agent' (Duff 1986: 70). When we blame someone for something, we seek to involve her in a discussion, with the aim of persuading her that what she did was *wrong*: we therefore acknowledge her status as a rational being that can be persuaded (though not forced) to see her behaviour as blameworthy. We also acknowledge, as we will see below, that she has a right to reply to our accusation and to *persuade us* that we are wrong in blaming her. The point to stress is that calling one to account is a way to show respect for her.

Against this background, we can grasp what lies behind the claim that the criminal trial should aim for the defendant's *assent* to the verdict (Duff 1986: 116; Duff *et al.*, 2007: 127–30). Rather than simply imposing the verdict on the defendant, with the aim to change her future conduct, the prosecution and the judge should aim to persuade her of the reasons why she is guilty as charged. It is important to see the analogy between this conception of the trial and the notion of CD as a communicative act. For a successful act of CD, it is *necessary* that the addressee of the message acknowledge the disobedients' request. To this extent, a case where the civil disobedients managed to convince the majority in power to change a seriously unjust law, yet that change occurred out of the majority's fear of further acts of disruption, would have failed as a form of communication. In spite of achieving the target of social change, this would have been an *unsuccessful case of CD*. On the other hand, if after serious debate within the community, e.g., on the media, in public spaces, *at the criminal trial*, the majority decided to reject the disobedients' call for reconsideration, the act of CD would have fulfilled its communicative aim.

As part of 'calling to account', the trial offers the defendant the chance to explain her alleged law-breaking behaviour, and to contest (or, eventually, accept) the charges moved by the prosecutor. This emphasis on the defendant's right to be heard, to be persuaded, and *to persuade*, shows that the communication at the trial runs 'in both directions' (Duff *et al.*, 2007: 96). That is, it is not only the defendant who is called upon by the state to answer the charges: *the defendant also calls the state to account for the accusation*, requiring that the state answer for the accusation. The defendant has a right both to persuade and to be *persuaded* by the prosecutor. This is what it means to acknowledge the defendant's status as a rational individual, capable to understand why she is being blamed and to act accordingly. By calling the defendant to appear at the trial, the state is demanding that she account for her behaviour.

## Responsibility *and* Liability

The criminal trial aims to involve a defendant in a process of rational persuasion, to lead her to see why her behaviour deserves condemnation. How can this process of persuasion be achieved *at the criminal trial*? For a guilty verdict to be issued, it is necessary not only that the prosecutor shows that the defendant committed the act of which she is accused: the prosecutor has also to prove that the act constitutes a *criminal wrong* that, therefore, deserves punishment. This suggests that the fact that someone has in fact committed the act she is being charged with, is not sufficient to make that person *guilty*. One of the aims of the trial is to prove someone's *responsibility* for committing a crime. However, even when responsibility is proved, the assessment of guilt requires further establishing *criminal liability* (Duff 2005: 88). Responsibility is necessary, not sufficient, to establish the defendant's guilt: a defendant could admit responsibility while, at the same time, denying that she is liable for that very act (Duff *et al.*, 2007: 130–31). Hence, a defendant who is accused of having done X may admit that she did X: yet, she can challenge the court arguing that X was, under the particular circumstances in which she acted, not wrong. She could then offer a reply to the accusation, one that – she would argue – exculpates her and thus blocks 'the transition from responsibility to liability' (Duff *et al.*, 2007: 130; Gardner 2007: 122). The case of self-defence offers an example of this distinction: although the agent is *responsible* for the death of the victim, the fact that she was acting in self-defence may make her not *liable* to criminal punishment.

This applies also to the case of CD. Activists who appear in court often appeal to the defence of necessity, to argue that what they did was *justified* under the circumstances, and that, for that reason, they should not be punished. An example of this is offered by the case of the 'Pit stop Ploughshares', five catholic activists who, in July 2005, were put on trial in Dublin: two years before, in February 2003, during the build-up to the military operation 'Shock and Awe' on Iraqi soil, they had disarmed a U.S. warplane parked for a pit-stop at Shannon airport. After attacking the nose cone and windows of the plane with hammers and paint, the protesters had remained there, praying, offering no resistance when arrested. At the trial, they admitted that they had forced their way into the hangar and had attacked the plane (thus acknowledging *responsibility* for violation of private property); yet, they claimed that their actions were legally justifiable, since they were trying to protect lives and property in Iraq, which the U.S. had invaded the month after their act of CD. They therefore denied *liability* for that action.[2] The contention was that their act was not 'wrong' and was not against their obligation to the protection and promotion of individual autonomy (hence, their moral obligation to the law).[3]

The intention in the remainder of this chapter is to consider what, according to some views, appears to be wrong with offering legal defences at the trial for CD. As has already been suggested here, some have argued that appealing to legal defences to *justify* one's illegal conduct may not be compatible with the behaviour of a virtuous civil disobedient. In light of the above discussion, concerning the criminal trial as a 'two-way process' of communication between the state and the defendants,

2 Retrieved at: http://www.indymedia.ie/article/77455. The court accepted the defense of necessity and the activists were acquitted.

3 By appealing to the defense of 'justification', the defendants claim they were *justified* in acting as they did. A different case is that of 'excuse', where they claim that they acted as charged but should be 'excused' nonetheless.

this chapter will argue for the compatibility between pleading 'not guilty' and being a civil disobedient, one who possesses and displays an attitude of respect for the law. Civil disobedients go to the trial with the intention to *persuade* the court, and their fellow citizens, that their act of CD is still consistent with the commitment to the liberal principles the legal system is designed to protect, and to promote.

## The Civil Disobedient at the Trial

Hence, this argument will now focus on the behaviour of a civil disobedient who appears at the criminal trial. My aim is to consider what kind of plea she should offer when asked to account for her behaviour. By analyzing these options, this chapter will seek to identify the different claims they imply regarding one's own liability. My discussion will focus only on the 'guilty' and the 'not guilty' plea, although there are other alternative that might be available (standing mute, pleading in mitigation), which will not be considered here, due to space constraints.

The civil disobedient could plead 'guilty': by doing so, she admits *both* responsibility ('Yes, I did trespass on military property') and liability ('Yes, I did commit a criminal action'). In that case, the judge might decide to sentence her, without further inquiry.[4] The civil disobedient, on the other hand, could decide to plead *not guilty*. As mentioned already, this could mean either of two things: a denial of responsibility, of having committed the action as alleged by the prosecutor; or an admission of responsibility, accompanied by a denial of liability ('Yes, I did X, but X does not represent a criminal action'). If the prosecution proves the commission of the offence (i.e., proves responsibility), the onus then lies on the defendant either to offer evidence of a defence (only then does the prosecution have the burden of disproving it), or even sometimes to prove the defence – though on the balance of probabilities rather than beyond reasonable doubt.

## On Pleading Guilty

This discussion will now go more into the merits, or demerits, of these choices for a civil disobedient. According to Kirkpatrick (2008: 15), what distinguishes 'civil' from 'uncivil' disobedience is that, in the former, agents comply with the power-conferring rules stating who is in charge of interpreting, adjudicating, and enforcing the law. They also breach the law openly and deliberately, that is to say, with no attempt to hide what there are doing, nor to conceal their identities. In light of these considerations, it may be argued that, when called to account for their

4 '[Y]et the judges, upon probable circumstances, that such confession may proceed from fear, menace or duress, or from weakness or ignorance, may refuse to record some confession and suffer the party to plead not guilty', 2 Hawk. 466, cited in Hampton (1982), p. 184.

law-breaking behaviour, civil disobedients should plead guilty, admitting that they did violate a legal directive and are therefore, liable to be punished. Attempts to do otherwise, for example pleading *not guilty* and challenging the prosecution to prove the fact that the protesters breached a law, would be in stark contrast with the underlying assumptions at the core of the choice to do CD:

> Three aspects of civil disobedience counsel that its practitioners should accept the legal consequences of their acts. First, civil disobedience pursues a civil society within the confines of the social contract. Second, it seeks social reform through persuasion. Third, it requires its practitioners, as moral political actors, to be morally consistent. Attempting to avert punishment ... may undermine the justification for civil disobedience. ... (Bauer & Eckerstrom 1987: 1189)

Critics point out that seeking for a justification for CD does not display the appropriate disposition towards the law that citizens of a flourishing community should possess. In fact, a conscientious act of disobedience should acknowledge that a violation of the law, even when accomplished out of a concern for the common good, will be subject to punishment (McEwen 1991). If one was to think otherwise, she would fail to show due consideration for the state's authority to compel obedience. This, in turn, would signal a deficiency in her character as a civil disobedient.

According to this view, then, challenging the accusation of wrongdoing would contradict the disposition of a sincere civil disobedient towards the law. A sincere act of CD resorts to deliberate violation of a legal enactment, to raise concerns about a particular law or policy. Regardless of whether or not she succeeds in having the policy at hand reconsidered, the civil disobedient should make no claim regarding the inappropriateness of state's decision to punish her for the law-breaking behaviour.

Thus, for example, Gandhi thought it was not the protesters' business to assess the legal status of their own act of CD: that was the task of the judiciary only.[5] Although there could be *moral* ground to justify what the protesters did, this should not lead to any argument for the existence of a *legal* justification for the act of CD. Denying this idea would overlook the fact that CD 'is a method of protest that posits that while the obligation of conscience transcends all duty to the state, the criminal activity performed pursuant to that duty to conscience is not immune from punishment' (McEwen 1991: 987). There should be neither room nor need,

5 'I am here, therefore, to invite and submit cheerfully to the highest penalty that can be inflicted upon me for what in law is deliberate crime, and what appears to me to be the highest duty of a citizen. The only course open to you, the Judge and the assessors, is either to resign your post and thus disassociate yourselves from evil, if you feel that the law your are called upon to administer is an evil, and that in reality I am innocent, or to inflict on me the severest penalty, if you believe that the system and the law you are assisting to administer are good for the people of this country, and that my activity is, therefore, injurious to the common weal.' Trial of Mahatma Gandhi, Ahmedabad, India, 18th March 1922. In Homer (1956), pp. 205–6.

therefore, to argue in defence of CD: being punished should be seen as part of doing CD. Pleading 'not guilty', hence challenging the prosecutor to prove the disobedients' criminal liability, is not what CD aims for. Seeking a justification differs from the aims of CD.

From this standpoint, pleading *guilty* should be central to the character of a civil disobedient. There is an idea of expressing 'the highest respect for law' which risks being lost when protesters seek for a justification. While appealing to the latter implies the pursuit of an acquittal, CD should express the agent's willingness to face the consequences of her own actions.

Under this perspective, CD represents a breach of law that aims to communicate a message, and that terminates with the arrest. Once the act has been committed, conscientious disobedients should not seek to achieve anything else in terms of acquittal: they may appear in court to take on the legal consequences for the illegal act, as a sign of consistency with the endorsement of the overall political system. Appearing at the trial would be their way to bear witness to their commitment to the cause for which they are protesting. Yet, civil disobedients should seek nothing from the trial itself, apart from *being there*: insofar as CD is pursued to draw public attention on a public issue, there is no reason to deny that it implies, nonetheless, a breach of the law, as such subject to legal punishment.

If, however, we focus on the shared communicative nature of CD and of the criminal trial, we might start questioning this idea. In fact, the emphasis on *persuasion* may give support to the idea that CD, as a communicative act, might not terminate when the police arrest the protesters. Rather, we should conceive of CD as carrying 'from the streets' into the courtroom: the trial would then represent a central moment of communication for a civil disobedient. A polity that fosters citizens' participation in the public life, and their commitment to the values of a democratic community, should encourage and welcome individuals who 'actively' contribute to the debate about the common good. Such contribution should not lead the individual to surrender herself to the court's judgment without offering reasons for her behaviour. Quite the contrary: good citizens should be keen to explain the reasons behind their act of CD, and to reaffirm their commitment to the rule of law. As we saw above, the trial calls the civil disobedients to account for their alleged wrong

However, there is a more important issue that should make us wary of the claim that a civil disobedient should plead guilty. The two following sub-claims will be defended in order to explain how this is so:

1. an ex-ante willingness to be punished might fail to acknowledge the power of the law to bind morally its subjects;
2. an admission of 'guilty' is an admission of failing to treat others with the respect due to their status as autonomous agents.

## On Pleading Not Guilty

This chapter contends that civil disobedients have a duty to *expose* themselves to the risk of punishment, but not to *seek* punishment, nor to submit to it by pleading guilty without contesting the accusation.[6] According to the position defended here, an *ex ante* acceptance of punishment might fail to show respect for law's binding authority over its subjects (Levine 2004). This analysis therefore criticizes the very idea that accepting punishment (in the 'broad' sense) displays an agent's attitude of respect for the law: quite the contrary, it might be that the *ex ante* disposition to submit to punishment would fail to grant the appropriate respect to law in a crucial way.

What does it mean to have respect for the authority of law? It means accepting that law has the power to influence individual behaviour by giving reasons for action: the fact that the law says 'Do not X' is a (pro tanto) binding reason for an agent to avoid X-ing (Edmundson 2007). It is a claim for compliance from its subjects; a claim whose legitimacy citizens have internalized, thus seeing law's instructions not as coercive impositions of power, but as directives aimed at the common good (Hart 1994, p. 90). It is from this standpoint that we can say that a citizen *respects* the law. This form of respect plays a central role in the account of civic virtue defended in this work. It entails a willingness to take the law 'seriously', that is, to understand what claims the law makes and why it makes them. Citizens take the law seriously when they see that 'the existence of a legal rule directing one to φ is always a non-trivial reason to φ' (Edmundson 2007: 9).

Given this notion of respect, we should be wary of the idea that an *ex ante* acceptance of punishment is necessary in order to display the *appropriate* respect for the law. Consider a different case of rule following, that of a game, e.g., football. Imagine a football player who deliberately commits a series of infractions during the match: she touches the ball with the hand to help herself towards scoring a goal, she tackles her opponent very violently, she feigns pain to falsely accuse the opponent of irregular tackles. This person just plays like this, in the hope of getting away with it: however, she is well aware that she is violating the rules of the game and, in fact, always accepts the punishment from the referee, without arguing whether or not she really deserves that red card. She is willing to accept the punishment, for she knows that she acted irregularly. There seems to be something *intrinsically wrong* in this individual as a football player: in spite of the fact that she 'respects' the referee's authority to punish her, it would be very hard to say that this player is displaying the character of the good player, who *abides* by the rules of football. It would be quite inappropriate to show her to young players, as an example to follow.[7] Along the same line, we

6 A similar position is defended in Boyle (1988).

7 Nonetheless, the history of football is full of cases like this. During this year's Football World Cup, Ghana was going to score at the very last minute against Uruguay, and to qualify for the semi-finals. However, Uruguay's midfield Suarez deliberately stopped the ball with the hand, hence preventing Ghana's victory. It should go without saying that

can imagine a daughter who disobeys her father's command to stay at home on a particular night: the girl openly defies the father's order by walking out of the house. However, on returning home she accepts being punished by her father for the act of disobedience. Barring particular circumstances, we should be wary of saying that the girl, in accepting the punishment imposed on her by her father, is thereby showing respect for the latter's authority. It seems even less plausible to say that by undergoing the punishment, that girl is displaying the character of 'a good daughter'. The point is that her open disobedience lacked the appropriate degree of respect she should owe her parents. Both in this case, and in that of the football player, something is missing in the relationship between the subject (the player, the daughter) and the *authority* (the rules of the game, the parent).[8] What, in my view, is missing is the obligation-generating weight that the norm (in these cases, the game's rules and father's order) is supposed to have. *Pro tanto*, this should have priority over whatever happens *after* that norm has been disregarded:

> [W]hile seeking to evade punishment – whether by stealth, violence or necessity defence arguments – implicitly accepts the obligatory force of the law, breaking the law and accepting the punishment, with plans to break it again, simply instantiates the belief that the law has no moral force. (Levine 2004: 375)

What this chapter tries to demonstrate is that being willing to accept the punishment *before* the act of disobedience (the *ex ante* willingness to be punished discussed above) does not give proper consideration to the fact that the law claims the authority to obligate its subjects to obey. An ex ante acceptance of punishment might not give support to the agent's disobedience: in some cases, it would rather display the agent's failure to treat the law with the due respect, that is, to take the law seriously.

Thus, the criticism against a not-guilty plea for CD might be misleading. A civil disobedient who tries to defend herself against the charges of wrongdoing, by arguing that she should not be punished, and that her action was *not against the law*, may be displaying a proper attitude of respect for law, as opposed to one who admits her guilt. Pleading 'not guilty' for CD would not defy the authority of the law: rather, it may reaffirm it. Someone who does CD and is *unwilling* to be declared 'guilty', recognizes the moral power of the law to bind individual conduct, in a way that may possibly be stronger than the Gandhi-like civil disobedient: the

---

Suarez did not act as a good football player should – although he did not argue when the referee sent him off, and regardless of the fact that his compatriots saw him as the country's saviour. An even clearer case was that of Manchester United player Eric Cantona, who remains famous for having jumped off the field during a match to kick Matthew Simmons, a supporter of the opponent team. Again, his 'acceptance' of the punishment does not seem to contribute to a positive assessment of his character as game player. See Greenfield & Osborn (2001), pp. 149–50.

8 See Raz (1979), pp. 13, 21, for the distinction between '*being* an authority' and '*having* an authority'.

attempt to justify one's behaviour, through the legal means offered by the trial, demonstrates the disobedients' commitment to taking the law seriously.

Furthermore, we need to highlight *the reasons why a civil disobedient aims to avoid a guilty verdict*. These do not refer to a desire to escape the pain that punishment would inflict on the disobedient. There is a deeper motivation for rejecting the label 'guilty'. As Higgins 2004 has argued, we ought to respect the law because we ought to respect other people: the failure to acknowledge the authority of law is a failure to acknowledge others' right to organize their activity based on the reasonable expectation that we will comply, as they do, with the rule of law. Where the law is well-functioning, people can organize their expectations around its directives. Citizens 'construct their daily lives around the scaffolding of laws. Disrespect for law destabilizes this structure' (Higgins 2004: 66). The criminal act represents a denial of the respect owed to other person: being declared guilty, or labelling oneself 'guilty', amounts to admitting one's own disrespect for the law and, thus, for other persons. This, in turn, is a betrayal of the liberal values that the civil disobedients, on the other hand, intend to preserve.

It follows that a civil disobedient, as distinguished from a criminal, seeks to eschew the verdict of 'guilty' not (only) to avoid the legal sanctions that accompany such verdict, but because she wants to be a citizen who *respects* the law. She does not want to be judged 'criminal', in the same way in which a player who respects the rules of the game does not want to be called a 'cheater'. The behaviour she adopted when doing CD flows from her commitment to respecting individual autonomy; if she was to declare herself *guilty*, she would contradict her intention to act in abidance with the values of a democratic community. This is why a virtuous civil disobedient should seek to persuade the prosecutors, and the community, that she did what she did out of respect for autonomy and, therefore, for the law. The fact that CD implies the breach of a particular law should support the idea 'that the acts we all have in mind as acts of civil disobedience really are violations of the law of the pertinent jurisdiction properly understood. But it may turn out that on a more sophisticated and enlightened view of the law they are not' (Dworkin 1985: 115).

The argument offered here is an attempt to understand this relationship in light of a 'more sophisticated and enlightened view of the law'. This view enables us to see what reasons citizens have to *respect* the law, as the institution that protects and promotes individual autonomy. The authority of law does not derive from its being a mere command imposed over its subjects: law derives its power from its relation to human well being. Thus, the value of the law lies in the value of the autonomy it protects and promotes. This need not support the idea that '*lex iniusta non est lex*': the obligation to obey the law extends to those directives that are not unreasonably unjust (Edmundson 2004). However, the perspective presented in this work is committed, once more, to the idea that the relationship between the citizen and the law should go beyond that of merely a subject faced with a *system of rules*:

> [Positivism] holds that a legal obligation exists when (and only when) an established *rule* of law imposes such an obligation. [...] [Against this view], we may want to say that an obligation exists whenever the case supporting such an obligation, in terms of binding legal *principles* of different sorts, is stronger than then case against it. (Dworkin 1977: 64–5)

A civil disobedient should then plead 'not guilty', to persuade her fellow citizens that she did not defy her political obligation: she could rightly claim that her act, though against what the law says, was not against what the law is meant to implement, that is, not against the duty to respect other persons as autonomous agents. This is where the main difference between an action of CD and a *criminal* action lies. The breach of the law, in the former case, may represent the way virtuous citizens 'acquit rather than ... challenge their duty as citizens' (Dworkin 1985: 105).

> There is a *statistical presumption* that [illegal acts] are, in any given case, wrong. But that is *not to say that it is their character as illegal acts that makes them wrong* or contributes in any degree to their wrongness. Rather their illegality is a characteristic contingently linked to the other properties that truly make them wrong; so that its presence may be a more or less reliable index or clue to the presence of wrongness, not its ground or basis. (Feinberg 1994: 173. Added emphasis)

The aim of this chapter was to highlight the fact that active participation in the life of a democratic community is not synonymous with uncritical obedience to the law. If there is any value in the idea that being a citizen is 'something that we do, not something (such as a power, for example) that we possess or use or watch or think about' (Barber 2003: 123), then we can appreciate how some cases of 'illegal' behaviour are compatible with the requirements of citizenship. From the perspective adopted in this chapter, an act of CD might constitute the right action to do, for an individual *qua* citizen, under the particular circumstances: as such, it might deserve praise, not punishment.

**References**


Barber, B. 2003. *Strong Democracy: Participatory Politics for a New Age*, 20th Anniversary ed., Berkeley: University of California Press.

Bauer, S.M., and P.J. Eckerstrom. The State Made Me Do it: Applicability of the Necessity Defence to CD, *Stanford Law Review*, vol. 39, no. 5, May, pp. 173–1200.

Boyle, F.A. 1988. *Defending Civil Resistance Under International Law*, pp. 7–30.

Brownlee, K. 2004. Features of a Paradigm Case of Civil Disobedience. *Res Publica*, vol. 10, no. 4, 337–51.

———. 2006. The Communicative Aspects of Civil Disobedience and Lawful Punishment. *Criminal Law and Philosophy*, vol. 1, no. 2, pp. 179–92.

Cohen, C. *Civil Disobedience: Conscience, Tactics and the Law*, Columbia University Press.

Duff *et al.* 2006. *The Trial on Trial*, vol. 2, Oxford: Hart Publishing.

———. 2007. *The Trial on Trial*, vol. 3, Oxford: Hart Publishing.

Duff, R.A. 1986. *Trials and Punishments*, Cambridge: Cambridge Studies in Philosophy.

———. 2001. *Punishment, Communication and Community*, Oxford: Oxford University Press.

———. 2005. Answering for Crime, *Proceedings of the Aristotelian Society*, 106, pp. 87–113.

Dworkin, R. 1977. Is Law a System of Rules?, reprinted in Dworkin, R., (ed.), *The Philosophy of Law*, Oxford: Oxford University Press.

———. 1985. *A Matter of Principle*, Oxford: Oxford University Press.

Edmundson, W. 2004. State of the Art: the Duty to Obey the Law, *Legal Theory*, 10, pp. 215–59.

———. 2006. The Virtue of Law-Abidance, *Philosopher's Imprint*, vol. 6, no. 4, pp. 1–21.

Feinberg, J., *Freedom and Fulfilment: Philosophical Essays*, Princeton: Princeton University Press.

Gardner, J. 2007. *Offences and Defences*, Oxford: Oxford University Press.

Greenfield, S., and G. Osborn. 2001. *Regulating Football: Commodification, Consumption and the Law*, Pluto Press.

Hampton, C. 1982. *Criminal Procedure*, 1982, London: Maxwell.

Hart, H.L.A. 1994. *The Concept of Law*, 2nd edition, Oxford: Oxford University Press.

Higgins, R.C.A. 2004. *The Moral Limits of Law*, Oxford: Oxford University Press.

Hildebrandt, M. 2006. Trail and 'Fair Trial': From Peer to Subject to Citizen, in *Duff et al.*

Homer, A.J. (ed.). 1956. *The Gandhi Reader: A Sourcebook on His Life and Writing*, Indiana University Press, pp. 205–6.

Kirkpatrick, J. *Uncivil Disobedience: Studies in Violence and Democratic Policies*, Princeton: Princeton University Press.
Levine, M.S. 2004. Punishment and Willingness to Pay, *Gonzaga Law Review*, 40, pp. 329–77.
McEwen, Stephen J., Jr. 1991. The Protester: A Sentencing Dilemma, *Notre Dame Journal of law, Ethics & Public Policy*, vol. V, no. 4, pp. 992–3.
Rawls, J. 1999. *A Theory of Justice*, Cambridge, MA: Harvard University Press.
Raz, J. 1979. *The Authority of Law*, Oxford: Clarendon Press.

# Chapter 7
# Justifying Civil Disobedience With Reference to EU Public Consensus[1]

Haris Psarras

## Introduction

The European Union (EU) has developed into a laboratory for the unification of people from European countries under a multilevel public authority. So understood, the EU experiment consists in the emergence of a fresh public consensus model through a state-driven initiative aiming to establish a supra-state, multilevel governance structure. The idea that serves as point of departure for this paper is that the new consensus model cannot escape having an impact on the way one perceives and justifies cases of civil disobedience in the EU context.

Thanks to its conscientious character, civil disobedience is probably the noblest form of dissent. It can best reveal occasional tensions between officials' decision-making and the public consensus that officials' decisions are meant to serve. With that in mind, the paper discusses the influence that EU fresh public consensus has on the justifiability of civil disobedience. Furthermore, it uses the decision of the European Court of Justice (ECJ) on the case C-274/99P, *Connolly v Commission*, as a platform to investigate both the challenges that civil disobedience in the EU context brings with it and an alternative perspective on its judicial treatment.

The paper is comprised of four sections. The first considers civil disobedience as citizens' values-oriented disrespect not towards authorities' legitimacy, but rather towards particular instances of officials' decision-making. It suggests that, since civil disobedience scrutinizes officials' practice of public consensus with reference to principles that public consensus aspires to, any fresh consensus model invites rearticulation of the justification conditions of civil disobedience. The second section claims that EU public consensus, as it emerges through EU multilevel governance, urges rejection of the traditional judicial approach to civil disobedience that exemplifies the hierarchical conception of responsibility. The third section reads the case C-274/99P as involving an act of justifiable civil disobedience and then claims that the ECJ failed to acknowledge such justifiability due to its adherence to the hierarchical conception. The fourth section advocates

1 My research is funded by the Hellenic State Scholarships Foundation (I.K.Y.), to whom I am grateful for their generous support. I would also like to thank the participants of the University of Glasgow Colloquium *Unruly Peoples and the Legal Public* for their insightful comments on an early draft of this paper in June 2010.

an alternative conception of civil dissenters' responsibility that better suits the originality of EU governance and consensus.

## Civil Disobedience: Enlightened Scrutiny of the Practice of Public Consensus

This paper will begin by defending the idea that civil disobedience is the form of dissent that best spotlights occasional tensions between principles embedded in public consensus and their practice by officials. The discovery of the link between public consensus and civil disobedience will help show first, why changes in the former should be taken into account by justifications of the latter; second, why in constitutional regimes the legitimacy of civil disobedience can be affirmed not only by political activists but also by the judiciary.

This analysis reflects Rawls' conception of civil disobedience.[2] Among the features of civil disobedience that this conception emphasizes are first, its political character and second, the fact that civilly disobedient citizens recognize authorities' legitimacy and challenge no more than officials' particular decisions (Rawls 1972: 363–8). In Rawls' words (1972: 366), civil disobedience 'expresses disobedience to law within the limits of fidelity to law'. There is no paradox here. Civil disobedience is a case of disobedience to law, understood as rules issued by officials, but is still loyal to the law, understood as the constitutional legitimacy of authorities and the principles to which officials' decision-making aspires (e.g., Rawls 1972: 363). The target of civil disobedience is not the consensus that backs up the law. In this sense, civil disobedience highlights a difference between the legitimacy of political institutions and the everyday exercise of institutional decision-making power by officials; it affirms the former, yet, when it comes to controversial measures, challenges the latter.

Rawls (1972: 365) also considers civil disobedience as a political act in the sense that 'it is [...] guided and justified [...] by the principles of justice which regulate the constitution and social institutions generally'. This understanding of the political character of civil disobedience reveals the link between civil disobedience and public consensus. It is not only that dissenters take authorities as legitimately established, but also that they disobey officials' decisions in the name of the core of public consensus; in the name of principles that back up authorities'

2 The focus of this paper is the Rawlsian account. Rawls considers civil disobedience within the framework of a nearly just political order, focusing on its justification with reference to the principles of justice underlying such a political order. In that respect, his analysis suits the particularity of civil disobedience actions that take place within the EU context and which, in particular, make an appeal to EU public consensus. For the same reasons, other plausible approaches are excluded here, such as those extolled by Joseph Raz (1979: 272–5) for whom, in the first place, there is no right to civil disobedience in a liberal state, or Kent Greenawalt (1987: 232) who accounts even for acts of civil disobedience that 'lack a justification derived from the existing political order'.

legitimacy and that officials are meant to practice through decision-making. Civil disobedience is then a response to occasional tensions between public consensus and its practice by officials; disobedience to rules or policies issued by consensus-backed authorities' officials that justifies itself through an appeal to the values and decision-making patterns that such consensus consists in.

These remarks allow consideration of the impact that the emergence of a new public consensus model can have on the justifiability of civil disobedience. As long as civil disobedience appeals to constitutive principles of public consensus, changes in the latter should be reflected in justifications that honour civil disobedience as a political act within the limits of law. The Rawlsian conception also suggests that the judicial treatment of civil disobedience does not necessarily result in its rejection as unlawful. In constitutional polities, in which public consensus enjoys constitutional status and its practice is under judicial control, the justifiability of civil disobedience is to be assessed by the courts and can be affirmed through judicial decisions. As Rawls (1972: 365) suggests, 'in a constitutional regime, the courts may finally side with the dissenters and declare the law or policy objected to unconstitutional'. At first glance, it might seem incongruous to classify as civil disobedience even the infringement of rules that after being infringed were judicially deemed constitutionally unacceptable. Yet the fact that a court might recognize dissenters' adherence to the constitution does not qualify them as less disobedient in the first place, since the genuineness of their dissent lies in their eagerness to defend their cause, even in case the courts eventually treat it as lawbreaking.

Once the judicial legitimization of civil disobedience is allowed for, it is possible to both escape treating its justifiability as foreign to judicial reasoning and to honour civil disobedience as a vehicle for the renovation of institutional politics. Later, this paper will say more about potential positive judicial responses to civil disobedience, but first this paper will consider how EU multilevel governance has modified public consensus and the justifiability of civil disobedience at the EU level.

## The Impact of EU Multilevel Governance on EU Public Consensus and Civil Disobedience Justifiability: The Hierarchical Conception of Civil Dissenters' Responsibility under Challenge

The EU brings with it a new, multilevel model of governance (e.g., Scott and Trubek 2002: 5–6, Lebessis and Paterson 2001). This section will briefly discuss the originality of EU multilevel governance; then it will focus on its bearing on EU public consensus and the challenges that such fresh consensus sets to what is considered here as the traditional judicial approach to civil disobedience. Most institutional novelties in the EU are due to its multinational and supra-state character. The EU model draws inspiration from institutional patterns that developed within the political sphere of the nation-state, but transcends them in an effort to bring the exercise of authority in tune with the complexities of a technocratic, postnational, globalized world.

Multilevel governance is first reflected in the pluralistic constitutional setting of the EU. The European polity does not subscribe to the founding ideals of either a sovereign state or an international organization. Its ultimate aim is the establishment of a public authority that, instead of being state-centred – as it is the case with sovereign nations – or state-driven – as it happens with international organizations – consolidates itself at a supra-state level. In the nation-state context, hierarchically stratified state authorities have traditionally been taken as the major apparatus of demos, conceived as a culturally coherent and politically self-contained community. On the contrary, in the EU both state authorities and non-state actors work together to become the vehicle for a transition towards a horizontal rather than vertical network of interdependent legal orders and communities (e.g., Walker 2002: 337).

The multilevel character is also discoverable in the EU institutional setting. The institutionalization of the European polity is performed with a high degree of openness that renders the lines between the legislative, executive and judicial branches of government less discernible (e.g., De Burca 2003: 816). The fragmentation of the tripartite distinction of state functions initiates a model of governance that is more alert to policy effectiveness and more open to auxiliary institutional agents (committees, agencies) that contribute their expertise in given areas (e.g., Chiti 2000, Pedler and Schaefer 1996). Another sign of institutional flexibility is ECJ's judicial lawmaking activity. In this respect, the EU experiment advocates a model of institutional agency that undermines the claim to incontestability and the rigid legal categories that institutionalization traditionally brings with it.[3]

The fresh institutional design also causes crevices to the static hierarchies of member states' pyramidal model of decision-making. EU governance substitutes a developing mosaic of interconnected local, regional, national and supranational policy-makers for the highly centralized and strictly stratified government mechanism that flourished in the state context. The culmination of EU multilevel governance is probably the improvement of policymaking through dialogue with civil society (Art. 11 TEU)[4] and the closure of the gap between authorities and citizens according to what de Burca (2003: 815) describes as 'a more participatory and contestatory conception of democracy'.

The change of governance paradigm within the EU can be accredited with generating a new public consensus model, tailored to the needs and potential of multilevel governance, as described above. The new EU public consensus is pluralistic, open-ended and responsive to active citizenship. The legal traditions

3 On the rigidity of institutionalization, see Christodoulidis 2003: 413.

4 TEU stands for the consolidated version of the Treaty on European Union as last amended by the Treaty of Lisbon.

that contribute to its pool are considered as complementary to each other. Its institutional background is adaptable to the changing needs of an ongoing polity.

Given that changes in public consensus should be reflected in the justifiability of civil disobedience,[5] there emerges the question of in what respect EU's fresh public consensus invites officials, particularly judges, to modify their perception of civil disobedience and the justification conditions that apply to it. To answer the puzzle, it is necessary to consider that within the EU consensus model, officials' authority to implement EU principles is decisively emancipated from the strict hierarchical patterns that are found in a state-based government structure.

The EU model encourages 'non-state actors at subnational and transnational level' to challenge officials' practices through EU inter-institutional checks and balances (Bellamy and Castiglione 2003: 20) and takes account of the needs of civil society, as expressed in citizen-led initiatives (Art. 11(4) TEU). What is of interest here is that the traditional judicial approach to civil disobedience (the one that developed within the state context) was inspired by an uncompromising respect for the very hierarchical structure of public authority that has been steadily losing ground in the supra-state EU framework. What is labeled here as a traditional judicial approach to civil disobedience (henceforth, traditional approach) is exemplified by the courts' unwillingness to acknowledge that in some cases civilly disobedient citizens' interpretations of constitutional principles may be better than competing interpretations that underlie rules or policies issued by officials who enjoy discretion in the matter in question.

This paper claims neither that what is taken as the traditional approach has invariably been followed by the judiciary in the state context nor that there is any necessary conceptual link between such an adjudicative practice and the state-based institutional paradigm. For instance, in constitutional democracies, courts do generally treat the law as a practice of principles rather than just as the fruit of hierarchical decision-making anyway. Having said that, the traditional approach is still a convenient label for what has been a probably implicit (yet widespread) judicial doctrine about civil disobedience in numerous constitutional states.

The core idea of the traditional approach is that civil dissenters are responsible for lawbreaking, if their interpretation of the constitutional principles they seek to defend through disobeying particular rules or policies is neither instantiated in officials' decisions nor detectable in the way courts have so far interpreted them. The traditional approach, so understood, rejects any solely principles-based defense of civil disobedience.[6] It does not leave room for dissenters to defend before the court their own understanding of public consensus, if such understanding has not been previously espoused by the relevant responsible officials. Since it classifies as unlawful any act of dissent that justifies itself through direct appeal to public consensus principles, the traditional approach can be taken to exemplify the

5 See section 1 above.

6 Note though that the justification of civil disobedience, as conceived by Rawls, is primarily principles-based. (See section 1 above.)

so-called hierarchical conception of responsibility, as it applies in the field of civil disobedience. The said conception is one of the five conceptions of responsibility that according to Bovens (1998: 148), are pertinent to complex organizations.

The hierarchical conception, when used in the context of civil dissenters' responsibility (henceforth, hierarchical conception),[7] treats as illegitimate non-officials' or hierarchically inferior officials' disobedience to rules or policies issued by officials or hierarchically superior officials respectively. The hierarchical conception has been considered as too narrow to accommodate the ongoing flattening of the pyramidal structure of authority, particularly so when it comes to the EU context (e.g., van Gerven 2005: 215–16). Given the changes that multilevel governance brought in EU public consensus, the hierarchical conception proves to be not only narrow, but also obsolete. The pluralistic constitutional agenda, the polycentric institutional structure and the promotion of a rather bottom-up policymaking, as discussed earlier in this section, render strict hierarchical patterns unsuitable for the EU model of governance. In this respect, when it comes to cases of civil disobedience, the traditional approach and the hierarchical conception that it rests upon fail to reflect the novelty of EU public consensus.

## Connolly Case: a Case of Justifiable Civil Disobedience

Any attempt to revive the hierarchical conception in the judicial treatment of civil disobedience at the EU level would be in discordance with the constitutional and institutional openness of the EU. Yet the hierarchical conception proved to be deeply rooted in judges' perspective on civilly disobedient acts. It was even the ECJ that sought recourse to the black-and-white rationale of the hierarchical conception to find an easy, yet dubious way out of the puzzle to which a case of civil disobedience towards EU officials gave rise. This is the decision on the case C-274/99P, *Bernard Connolly v Commission* [2001], ECR I-1611 (henceforth, the Connolly case); its importance has already been recognized and discussed (e.g., Türk 2009: 139–40, van Gerven 2005: 218–19, Blanquet 2002: 1423–41). This paper will now consider the Connolly case as involving a justifiable civilly disobedient act and will then suggest that the ECJ failed to acknowledge the justifiability of the said act, because it followed the traditional approach and apprehended the case through the prism of the hierarchical conception.

Bernard Connolly, a senior Commission civil servant, while on leave on personal grounds in 1995, published a book entitled *The Rotten Heart of Europe – The Dirty War for Europe's Money*, without the permission of the appointing

7 The term 'conception of civil dissenters' responsibility', as used in this paper, does not encapsulate any straightforward juridical recipe for assessing responsibility in cases of civil disobedience. It rather refers to certain investigatory reflexes of judges to cases of civil disobedience; to internalized assumptions about civil dissenters' responsibility that judges are not necessarily fully conscious of, but tend to activate, while they attempt to orient themselves within the highly dilemmatic context of civil disobedience.

authority that Art. 17(2) of the old Staff Regulations (henceforth, SR) provided for. The book reflected a personal opinion that conflicted with the Commission policy. According to the Commission 'Mr Connolly ... seriously prejudiced the interests of the Communities and ... damaged the image and reputation of the institution' (Joined Cases T-34/96 and T-163/96, *Connolly* v *Commission* [1999] ECR-SC I-A-87 and II-463, para. 19). Apart from criticizing the Commission policy in the process of European integration in the economic and monetary field, Connolly's book also reflected the professional experience Connolly had gained while carrying out his duties at the Commission. In that respect, the case raised issues of trust that were considered as amounting to a breach of Connolly's duties of good faith and loyalty to the institution. Following proceedings, Connolly was removed from his post for the infringement of Art. 11, 12 and 17(2) of the SR. After the Court of First Instance (CFI) dismissed his action for annulment of the opinion of the Disciplinary Board of 7.12.1995 and of the decision of the appointing authority of 16.01.1996, Connolly turned to the ECJ to appeal the CFI judgement.[8]

To acknowledge the civil disobedience aspect of Connolly case, one should take two points into account. First, Connolly, who did not request permission to publish his book and was therefore held responsible for breaking Art. 17(2) (under which, officials shall not publish any matter dealing with the work of the Communities without permission), 'could not have failed to be aware that he would be refused permission on the same grounds as those on which permission had previously been refused in respect of articles in which he had already outlined the ideas that form the core of the ... book' (T-34/96 – T-163/96, para. 19, C-274/99P, para. 5). Second, Connolly claimed that the interpretation of the SR 'on which the Disciplinary Board's opinion and the [CFI] contested decision [were] based [was] contrary to the principle of freedom of expression laid down in Article 10 of the European Convention on Human Rights [henceforth, ECHR], in that it [led], inherently, to the prohibition of any publication'; 'constraints on freedom of expression are permissible only in the exceptional cases listed in Article 10(2) of the ECHR', he added (C- 274/99P, para. 18).

With that in mind, this paper considers Connolly's decision to publish his book without requesting permission as a civilly disobedient act.[9] The fact that Connolly had previously been refused permission with regard to articles that he later included in his book suggests that he did not ask for permission for the publication of the book itself, not because he ignored that the Commission required from him to do so, but rather because he chose to disregard the Commission policy. In that respect, Connolly's act is deliberate and can qualify as an act of genuine disobedience. Furthermore, it amounts to an act of *civil* disobedience, since it

8 Note that since 2005, it is the European Union Civil Service Tribunal that adjudicates at first instance disputes between the EU and its civil service.

9 Van Gerven, too (2005: 218), remarks on the civil disobedience aspect of the Connolly case; He actually classifies it as a case of civil disloyalty, while discussing civil disobedience as being in direct opposition to the hierarchical conception.

was performed in the name of freedom of expression, a right that is protected under the ECHR and enjoys the status of a general principle of law within the EU (e.g., Art. 6(3) TEU;[10] Case 4/73, *J. Nold, Kohlen- und Baustoffgrosshandlung* v *Commission* [1974] ECR 491, para. 13; T-83/96, *van der Wal v Commission* [1998] ECR II-545, para. 46). To the extent that Connolly's conduct was inspired by his devotion to the promotion of freedom of expression, it was, as Rawls (1972: 365) would put it, 'guided and justified' by one of the principles that regulate the EU constitutional framework.

This work also suggests that Connolly's act is one of *justifiable* civil disobedience. This idea deserves further clarification. It can be argued that all acts of civil disobedience are justifiable to the extent that they are performed in the name of constitutionally endorsed values. Indeed, if the issue is moral justifiability, then any act that, according to the Rawlsian conception, amounts to civil disobedience should count as justifiable. And the concept of justifiability, when used with reference to civil disobedience, does traditionally refer to justifiability in moral terms (e.g., Farrell 1977). Yet, what is of interest here is what one can label as legal justifiability; that is, the conditions under which a civil dissenter's reading of the constitutional principles she defends through her protest, proves to be an arguably correct interpretation of the law on the issue; an interpretation whose endorsement or rejection deserves sophisticated judicial consideration. In such case judges are expected to carefully scrutinize whether the rule that was breached does actually honour what it is meant to serve, that is the legal principles governing the issue in question.

The importance of legal justifiability is best conceived, if one considers that only citizens that engage in legally justifiable civil disobedience, have a good chance to see the judiciary taking their reasoning seriously and possibly even siding with them. Not all acts of morally justified civil disobedience qualify as legally justifiable too, no matter the fact that they might all resist severe injustices. Moreover, not all legally justifiable acts of civil disobedience succeed in receiving a positive response from the judiciary. The judicial recognition of a civilly disobedient act as legally justifiable obtains, once the court treats dissenter's interpretation of the principles in question as plausible and starts investigating whether this interpretation is more appropriate than the one that underlies the rule that was infringed. This does not mean that judges' balance of reasons will necessarily deem dissenter's conduct lawful, and the rule she protested against incompatible with a principled approach to the law applicable in the case. A legally justifiable civilly disobedient act does eventually count as legally justified,

10 Before the amendment of the Treaty on European Union by the Treaty of Lisbon, Art. 6(2) qualified fundamental rights, as guaranteed by the ECHR, 'as general principles of Community law'. After the Treaty of Lisbon entered into force, Art. 6(3) qualifies them 'as general principles of the Union's law' and Art. 6(1) provides that the Charter of Fundamental Rights of the European Union shall have the same legal value as the Treaties. (The freedom of expression and information is provided for in Art. 11 of the Charter.)

if the principled interpretation which it seeks justification through, is not just an arguably correct, but the most appropriate interpretation of the law on the issue.

There is no straightforward technique for judges to apply in their quest for the legal justifiability of civil disobedience. Rawls (1972: 387) concedes that '[c]ourts should take into account the civilly disobedient nature of the protester's act, and the fact that it is justifiable' so that they 'reduce and in some cases suspend the legal sanction'. Yet Rawls does not offer any clear-cut answer on how the justifiability of civil disobedience is to be assessed. The puzzle is to be solved before the court on a case-by-case basis. Some of aspects that it is advisable to take into account for a reflective decision-making in such cases are: 1) the closeness of the link between the rule that was disregarded and the principle (or principles) that guide the disobedience. (If the rule is taken to be in breach of the principle, as happens in direct civil disobedience, then the dissent is more likely to enjoy legal justifiability than in the case of indirect civil disobedience, where the rule that has been broken is different from the one that the civilly disobedient citizen wishes to protest against; in the latter case, the infringement of a random rule is a means to protest government's policy, not a moral complaint against the rule itself.)[11] 2) any previous judicial decisions in similar cases as well as any debates and controversies among legal experts, politicians or agents of civil society that might had earlier questioned the rule that was infringed; 3) the place of the relevant principle in the constitutional tradition and the way it has been interpreted so far.

The legal justifiability of Connolly's disobedience cannot be comfortably dismissed. Connolly disobeyed a policy of the Commission that consisted in interpreting Art. 17(2) of the SR as requiring officials to request permission for a publication even in cases where no conditions or restrictions on freedom of expression would be allowed under Art. 10(2) ECHR. Connolly justified his disobedience by appealing to the principle of freedom of expression whose central role in EU law has been acknowledged by the TEU and ECJ decisions, as discussed earlier in this paper. In that respect, it should be noted that in an earlier case, the ECJ had made clear that Community officials too, fully enjoy freedom of expression, since 'the duty of allegiance to the Communities imposed on [them] in the Staff Regulations cannot be interpreted in such a way as to conflict with freedom of expression' (C-100/88, *Oyowe and Traore v Commission* [1989] ECR 4285, para. 16).

Yet the ECJ failed to affirm the legal justifiability of Connolly's dissent. This paper does not claim that this failure is instantiated in the fact that the Court eventually endorsed the disciplinary decision that had removed Connolly from his post. (The ECJ judgement would not necessarily have been different, if the ECJ had acknowledged Connolly's dissent as justifiable, since the recognition of legal justifiability does not inescapably lead to suspension of sanctions.) The ECJ can be said to have ignored the legal justifiability of Connolly's disobedience, because it

11 For the distinction between direct and indirect civil disobedience, see Rawls (1972: 364–5) and Cohen (1969: 224–6).

did not even engage in a substantive assessment of the principled interpretation of law in which Connolly's appeal to freedom of expression was grounded .

Connolly's argument can be summarized as the claim that an EU official who does not request permission to publish a controversial book does not actually infringe her duty of loyalty to the Communities in the name of freedom of expression, but just assigns to that duty the place it deserves in the light of and with full respect to the said freedom. According to Connolly, the duty of loyalty does not clash with freedom of expression; it just exists within its limits. The ECJ argued that Connolly alleged that Art. 17(2) of the SR does not pursue a legitimate aim (C-274/99P, para. 51). Yet Connolly did actually object not to Art. 17(2) itself, but to the way the Disciplinary Board interpreted it (C-274/99P, para. 18). Instead of opting for a principled understanding of the duty of loyalty and aligning itself with Connolly in that such a duty exists only within the framework of freedom of expression, the ECJ conceived the said duty and freedom as two equally legitimate considerations that may occasionally clash against each other (C-274/99P, para. 44–5); the inevitable conclusion of that argument was that the Community Courts could not decide but on whether the Commission struck a fair balance between the two (C-274/99P, para. 48). Thus, in Connolly case, the ECJ considered a fundamental right as having equal status to and being in potential conflict with a hierarchical duty. Yet, as the ECJ itself had earlier asserted (C-100/88, para. 16), there is in fact no room for disharmony here, since the normative status of the former is a priori higher than that of the latter.

The reason why the ECJ rejected Connolly's correct interpretation of freedom of expression is that it (the ECJ) proceeded along the lines of the hierarchical conception. According to this conception, a civil dissenter's principles-based justification of her dissent should be disregarded, in the case that it differs from the understanding of the very same principles that has been espoused by officials or, in case the dissenter is an official herself, by her hierarchical superiors. And it is probably only within the context of such a controversial conception that one would not be taken aback to read ECJ's casuistic assertion that institutions 'charged with the responsibility of carrying out tasks in the public interest' enjoy a *right* (to carry their tasks effectively) that can justify 'specific restrictions on the exercise of the right of freedom of expression' in terms of Art. 10(2) ECHR (C-274/99P, para. 46).

The ECJ failed to resist the hierarchical conception and the traditional approach to civil disobedience it brings with it. In doing so, it missed a good chance to acknowledge that the justifiability of civil disobedience should not be read exclusively through the eyes of officials – (they would hardly be favourably disposed towards disapproval of their policies anyway) – as well as that EU fresh governance paradigm and consensus facilitate alternative approaches to citizens' noble dissent.

## Towards the Civic Conception of Civil Dissenters' Responsibility

This section briefly explores a conception of civil dissenters' responsibility that better suits EU public consensus and can hence be offered as an alternative to the anachronistic hierarchical conception. To first briefly summarize the argument so far, it has been settled that civilly disobedient citizens seek justification for their acts through appealing to public consensus understood as the set of principles that underlie the constitution of their political community. It was then suggested that major changes in public consensus do inevitably invite the judiciary to revise the way it qualified cases of civil disobedience as legitimate or illegitimate before such changes occur. This paper also defended the idea that the EU institutional experiment has considerably modified the model of public consensus that had solidified itself within the nation-state, since EU multilevel governance deeply challenged the rigid hierarchical structures of official decision-making in the form they had generally been practised in the state context. In that respect, this paper took EU public consensus as offering a chance to cast doubt upon the excessive cautiousness with which the judiciary has traditionally treated civil disobedience. The hesitation by the judiciary in justifying civil disobedience is often due to the hierarchical conception of civil dissenters' responsibility; a conception that no matter its inability to feel the pulse of EU public consensus, was followed by the ECJ in a case of civil disobedience, Connolly case.

To advocate a competent alternative conception of civil dissenters' responsibility within the EU context, it is important to first realize in what respect the hierarchical conception, as reflected in the ECJ decision on Connolly case, was proved defective. The ECJ discussed two opposed rationales on how an alleged conflict between freedom of expression and EU civil servants' duty of loyalty should be solved: one underlying the arguments of the Commission and one defended by Connolly. The former suggested that a balance should be struck between freedom of expression and the duty of loyalty. The latter claimed that the clash between the two was actually illusory, since the duty of loyalty should be understood as applying only within the limits of freedom of expression. It is the latter rationale that best suited the special importance assigned to fundamental rights by both the Treaty on EU[12] and past decisions of the ECJ. Yet and no matter the fact that the ECJ did once again stress its devotion to freedom of expression (C-274/99P, para. 43) it ultimately chose to vindicate the reasoning of the Commission (C-274/99P, para. 48). If the ECJ adopted Connolly's perspective, it would find itself assessing the justifiability of a civilly disobedient act according to standards not only foreign to, but also in conflict with the official policy of the Commission on issues of loyalty, as it was instantiated in the disciplinary measures against Connolly.

Now one can reasonably ask what the problem is if a court's consideration of the justifiability of a civilly disobedient act reflects the dissenter's perspective and

12 See note 10 above.

is at odds with the treatment of the act by the officials who issued or safeguard the rules or policies that were infringed. The answer, not less reasonable than the question itself, is that there is no problem, to the extent that the perspective of the dissenter can allow for a principled interpretation of the law on the issue. Yet the supporters of the hierarchical conception find this answer unsatisfactory. To their mind, civil disobedience can be deemed legally justifiable only on the ground of interpretations that have already been instantiated in relevant officials' rules or policies. It is in that respect that the hierarchical conception fails to take into account the complexities of civil disobedience. If the hierarchical conception acknowledged the puzzle about legal justifiability, it would not reject any readings of a civil disobedience case without having first assessed their potential to lead to a principled approach to the law on the issue, and on the sole ground that they were put forward by the civil dissenter (and not by the officials she disobeyed).

Having in mind the unconscionable rigidity of the hierarchical conception and its paralyzing impact on the impartial treatment of cases of civil disobedience, one can better consider what standards an alternative conception of civil dissenters' responsibility should satisfy; the substitute to the hierarchical conception should be modelled after the aspirations that the hierarchical conception failed to meet. As for the investigation into the legal justifiability of civilly disobedient acts, the alternative conception should be flexible enough so that it neither endorses nor excludes lines of reasoning on the basis of whether they are defended by officials or by the dissenter. This is to ensure that any justifications of a civil disobedience act, when discussed in court, will be tested in terms of whether they can proffer a coherent legal interpretation, no matter whether they echo the treatment of the case by officials involved in it or more generally by relevant governmental policies. Otherwise hardly any room will be practically left for the judicial vindication of legally justifiable acts of civil disobedience, which means that in most cases the fair treatment of civil dissenters will remain an unfulfilled desideratum.

Particularly when it comes to civil disobedience in the EU context, performed in the name of principles embedded in EU public consensus, there is a need for a conception of responsibility that will also be in tune with the impact that the multilevel governance paradigm has on the way officials, on the one hand and active citizens, on the other, are expected to engage in the practice of principles within EU discontinuous institutional environment. The crevices in the pyramidal structure of authority and the intensification of the participation of civil society in policy formation that EU scheme of governance resulted in, invite the consideration that European citizens might sometimes be in a better position to promote the principles of the European polity than EU officials. Active citizenship may not have been granted any open-ended authorization to intervene in EU institutional politics, but from the teleological perspective that is inherent in the European unification process the service that a certain initiative renders to EU principles is more important than the qualification of such initiative as officially authorized or unauthorized. Since the relationship between EU multiple institutional orders is 'heterarchical rather than hierarchical' (Walker 2002: 337), lawfulness is less a matter of compliance with the given patterns of a pyramidal authority and more a matter of diffuse, principles-based control over a rather horizontal network of synchronized authorities. Furthermore, the extensive judicialization of public decision-making encourages both officials and citizens to scrutinize whether state and supra-state bodies are sufficiently committed to the promotion of the principles of European integration, conceived as a law-governed ongoing process. Under these conditions, legally justifiable civil disobedience can better unfold its innovative impact on institutional practices.

With that in mind, one realizes that as for cases of civil disobedience within the EU context a workable alternative to the hierarchical conception should be able to account for the constructive role that active citizenship can play in consolidating the everyday practice of EU public consensus. In his analysis of the Connolly case, van Gerven (2005: 217) discusses Connolly's behaviour as potentially justifiable under the so-called civic conception of responsibility. Van Gerven's understanding of the civic conception as 'loyalty to citizens and civic values' is that coined by Bovens (1998: 149). 'In this conception … [d]isobedience is allowed only when it can be justified by an appeal to general, public interests. One could think, for example, of interests such as the preservation of the rule of law, the enhancement of democratic control, …' (Bovens 1998: 163).

Bovens's civic conception of responsibility prioritizes active citizenship over hierarchical authority. In that respect, it does indeed have enough room to accommodate civil disobedience's potential to defend principled readings of law that have not yet gained the acclaim of officials. If adopted at the adjudication on cases of civil disobedience, the civic conception will stimulate the openness of the judiciary towards the fair assessment of acts of dissent that claim to be performed 'within the limits of fidelity to law' (Rawls 1972: 366) and, when appropriate, will even facilitate their full judicial legitimization.

Of course, it should be noted that Bovens's account of the civic conception has not particularly been formulated to serve as a conception of civil dissenters' responsibility. On the contrary, its field of application is vast. It can apply to responsibility attribution in any complex organization, no matter whether this is authority-based or managerial; no matter whether the hierarchical superiors in question act as employers or as officials. Therefore, for Bovens's account to be applicable to the justifiability of civil disobedience, one should first adjust it to the particularities of the complex relation between vision-driven civil dissenters and rule-abiding officials.

One of the reasons why civil disobedience counts as a quite particular instance of non-compliance is that both civil dissenters and the officials they disobey seek justification for the legitimacy of their acts or decisions respectively, through appealing to the same pool of principles: public consensus. In that respect, the objective of the civic conception of civil dissenters' responsibility could not be to defend civil society as any kind of top political value. When civil disobedience is performed in defense of active citizenship, this is because active citizenship enjoys the status of a public consensus principle. The objective of the civic conception, when being applied to civil disobedience, should be to ascertain that both officials' and civil dissenters' conflicting perspectives on what public consensus demands will be treated on equal grounds by the judiciary.

Thanks to EU high degree of judicialization and multilevel checks and balances, it is both institutional and non-institutional actors (e.g., officials and citizens respectively) that enjoy a functional role in fostering EU public consensus. Given the dynamic of such institutional environment, claims raised in the context of the civic conception such as 'that certain forms of disobedience to orders issued by one's direct superiors are acceptable as a way of achieving [civic values]' or that 'loyalty to one's superiors is only provisional [with] the loyalty to the public interest and to the democratic process [being] the ultimate obligations' (Bovens 1998: 164) can gain more ground. Thus, one can qualify the civic conception of civil dissenters' responsibility within the EU context as proceeding on the assumption that in case a citizen infringes a rule or policy, she is not automatically deprived of her role as potentially legitimate advocate of public consensus principles. Or in other words that the courts should take citizens' attempts to defend EU public consensus through occasionally infringing officials' decisions as seriously as they take officials' attempts to serve such consensus through issuing measures that occasionally end up generating widespread controversy and attracting dissent.

As for the Connolly case, the civic conception would require from the ECJ not necessarily to deem Connolly's behaviour as an instance of legally justified dissent, but certainly to consider on equal terms Connolly's and Commission's views on the balance between freedom of expression and the duty to loyalty; hence to decisively reduce the margin of appreciation that Commission claimed to enjoy on the issue. This would allow the Court to assess the sanction imposed on Connolly, not in terms of the balance that the Commission struck between two allegedly conflicting principles, but in terms of the normative status that freedom of expression and the value of loyalty enjoy as constitutive elements of a coherent consensus.

## Conclusion

The fragmentation of the hierarchical structure of authority that EU multilevel governance brings with it invites the judiciary to adopt an inclusionary approach to EU public consensus; to read it not only through the eyes of EU or member-states' officials, but also through a perspective that can honour the noble expectations of those civilly disobedient citizens who consider themselves bound by a supra-state law and community of principles.

This of course does not mean that all readings of EU consensus enjoy the same degree of legitimacy and should have an equal say in the decision-making process. Some of them should gain priority over other. Yet their approval is to be made on the basis of the service they offer to a coherent and efficient practice of EU principles. And this suggests that the question of whether they were put forward by officials exercising discretion or by active citizens expressing dissent is irrelevant and misleading when it comes to their classification as legitimate or illegitimate. The institutional innovations of the EU should then make civil dissenters happy. Within the European governance paradigm, judges can hardly find excuses to close their ears to readings of EU public consensus that cast a doubt on how officials expect the European people to practice it.

## References

Bellamy, R. and D. Castiglione. 2003. Legitimizing the Euro-'Polity' and its 'Regime': The Normative Turn in EU Studies. *European Journal of Political Theory*, 2(1), 7–34.

Blanquet, M. 2002. Case C-274/99P, *Connolly* v. *Commission*, Judgment of the Court of 6 March 2001, [2001] ECR I-1611. *Common Market Law Review*, 39(6), 1423–41.

Bovens, M. 1998. *The Quest for Responsibility: Accountability and Citizenship in Complex Organisations.* Cambridge: Cambridge University Press.

Chiti, E. 2000. The Emergence of a Community Administration: The Case of European Agencies. *Common Market Law Review*, 37(2), 309–43.

Christodoulidis, E. 2003. Constitutional Irresolution: Law and the Framing of Civil Society. *European Law Journal*, 9(4), 401–32.

Cohen, M. 1969. Civil Disobedience in a Constitutional Democracy. *The Massachusetts Review*, 10(2), 211–26.

de Burca, G. 2003. The Constitutional Challenge of New Governance in the European Union. *European Law Review*, 28(6), 814–39.

Farrell, D.M. 1977. Paying the Penalty: Justifiable Civil Disobedience and the Problem of Punishment. *Philosophy and Public Affairs*, 6(2), 165–84.

Greenawalt, K. 1987. *Conflicts of Law and Morality*. Oxford: Clarendon Press.

Lebessis, N. and J. Paterson. 2001. Developing New Modes of Governance, in *Governance in the European Union*, edited by O. De Schutter, N. Lebessis and J. Paterson. Luxemburg: Office for Official Publications of the European Communities, 259–94.

Pedler, R.H. and G.F. Schaefer. 1996. Preface, in *Shaping European Law and Policy: The Role of Committees and Comitology in the Political Process*, edited by R.H. Pedler and G.F. Schaefer. Maastricht: European Institute of Public Administration, ix–xi.

Rawls, J. 1972. *A Theory of Justice*. Oxford: Clarendon Press.

Raz, J. 1979. *The Authority of Law: Essays on Law and Morality*. Oxford: Clarendon Press.

Scott, J. and D.M. Trubek. 2002. Mind the Gap: Law and New Approaches to Governance in the EU. *European Law Journal*, 8(1), 1–18.

Türk, A.H. 2009. *Judicial Review in EU Law*. Cheltenham: Edward Elgar Publishing Ltd.

van Gerven, W. 2005. *The European Union – A Polity of States and Peoples*. Oxford and Portland, Oregon: Hart Publishing.

Walker, N. 2002. The Idea of Constitutional Pluralism. *Modern Law Review*, 65(3), 317–59.

# PART III
# Excluded Publics

# Chapter 8
# Excluded Publics – Included Privates: The Janus Headed Nature of the Liberal Public-Private Divide

Daniel Augenstein[1]

## Introduction

The justification of the liberal public-private divide rests on two distinct claims that are often lumped together: first, that the distinction between a 'public sphere' and a 'private sphere' is a meaningful way to cognize and structure modern pluralistic societies; and secondly, that there is a meaningful way to distinguish what is or ought to be 'public' from what is or ought to be 'private'. Both claims are of course interrelated: to posit something in the private sphere excludes it from the public sphere and such exclusion will appear arbitrary if it cannot be defended on the basis of a convincing delimitation of 'public' and 'private'.

Accordingly, critics of the liberal public-private divide tend to reject the distinction between the public sphere and the private sphere because it rests on a partisan understanding of public and private. While sharing the premise of this argument, the present author is hesitant to subscribe to its conclusion. The proper response to concerns that the liberal public sphere continues to be populated by the proverbial white heterosexual Christian male is not to dismantle the public/private sphere distinction, but to contest majoritarian conceptions of the public that underpin it, and to vindicate a robust private sphere that protects minorities from majoritarian assault.

On this view, the critical role of the liberal private sphere is to secure minorities a vested interest in society by allocating them a protected space for the development and expression of values that have not (yet) been recognized by majoritarian traditions and cultures. Perhaps needless to reiterate, propositions of the like are routinely discredited on the ground that they allegedly foster the formation of 'secluded communities' that become insulated from the critique of society. More often than not, such allegations build on a comfortable yet incongruous equation of 'society' with 'majority' that nourishes the furore of one (dominant) part of society that another (subordinate) part of society resists the assimilation to cultural norms and practices that, in effect or intention, denigrate and exclude them.

---

1 I am grateful to the participants of the Tilburg Philosophy of Law Colloquium for their helpful comments and suggestions.

Be that as it may, the aim of this chapter is not to suggest that the liberal public-private divide could or should create a non-permeable and incontestable 'wall of separation' between majoritarian publics and minoritarian privates. On the contrary, the institutionalization of the liberal private sphere avouches the membership of minorities *in* the nation-state as a prerequisite for their identification and critical engagement *with* the nation-state. On this account, the distinction between the public sphere and the private sphere provides the framework for negotiating the 'public' and the 'private' between national majorities and religious minorities as members of the same national community. This discloses the 'Janus-headed nature' of the liberal public-private divide that the present chapter defends as default position: the exclusion qua public from the public sphere contains a simultaneous inclusion qua private in the private sphere that is premised upon the inclusion of the excluded in the polity as a whole.

## The Chimera of the Neutral-as-Secular Public Sphere

On a liberal reading, the public-private divide appears both constitutive of and constituted by liberal neutrality. The public-private divide is constitutive of liberal neutrality in that the division of society into a public sphere and a private sphere demarcates the realm in which liberal neutrality is properly thought to apply. Liberal neutrality thus presupposes the existence of a public sphere as separated from other social spheres defined as private. Yet the liberal public-private divide is also constituted by liberal neutrality in that the distinction between the 'public' and the 'private' that underpins it is itself justified in terms of liberal neutrality. In this latter sense, the liberal public-private divide is vindicated by virtue of a neutral distinction between public and private.

Perhaps the most prominent distinction between 'public' and 'private' that underpins the distinction between the public sphere and the private sphere is that between 'the secular' and 'the religious'. Historically, the evolution of the public-as-secular and the concomitant privatization of religious difference contributed to putting an end to the Christian bloodshed in Europe. This may in part explain the contemporary fear of some that religion might 'smuggle' itself back into the public sphere and endanger the 'citadel of the secular state' (Sajó 2008). It may also explain the paramount importance of liberal neutrality in attempts to justify its enduring exclusion. A secular understanding of the public, or so the argument goes, is justified by virtue of liberal neutrality because it secures a neutral public sphere in which citizens, stripped of their religious differences, can encounter each other as equals.

This justification of the secular public sphere from liberal neutrality, while superficially attractive, is not conclusive because the distinction between the public sphere and the private sphere that is constitutive of liberal neutrality cannot be constituted by way of a neutral distinction between the (secular) public and the (religious) private. Crudely put, liberal neutrality can only apply to the public sphere after a non-neutral distinction between public and private has been put into place: the secular public sphere can only be neutral between *different* religions if and to the extent that *all* religions have already been demarcated as private.

Consider by way of example the French tradition of *laïcité* that represents the perhaps purest and most principled form of separation between the secular public sphere and the religious private sphere. The French nation-state assimilates the *citoyen* to its re*public*an identity, while leaving her free to pursue her religious beliefs as a private individual. This separation of citizens' public and private 'selves' is legally entrenched through *laïque* state neutrality that purports to react with institutional blindness to the fact of religious and cultural diversity. As Poulter (1997: 50) says:

> The principle of secularity *(laïcité)* is applied with particular fervour in France because the notion of modern citizenship as a status quite separate from distinctive ethnic identities and religious differences has become firmly entrenched in the public mind ever since the days of the Revolution, as corollary of the classical republican principles of equality and fraternity.

The principle of *laïcité* that commits French public schools to a strictly secular education was challenged in 1989 when three school girls insisted on wearing headscarves in class. The headmaster suspended the girls, claiming to apply a well-established French rule prohibiting religious symbols in state schools. In the same year, the Conseil d'État gave a legal opinion holding that while the wearing of religious symbols in public schools was not by itself incompatible with the principle of *laïcité*, it could be restricted through ministerial decree in case it (among others) perturbed the school order and the peaceful running of schools (Avis no. 346893). Over the following years, the Conseil d'État reversed a number of school decisions suspending or excluding students who had refused to remove their headscarves. In Kehrouaa, for example, the court struck down a school regulation on the basis that it was too general and indiscriminate, thus violating the students' freedom of religion. In Mlle Saglamer, the court stressed that penalties for wearing a headscarf could only be applied if it was established that the behaviour of the pupil amounted to an act of pressure or proselytism or interfered with the public order in school. In Aoukili, by contrast, it upheld the exclusion of students in the more specific context of physical education activities.

In 1994 François Bayrou, the then Minister of National Education, issued a circular in which he urged the heads of educational institutions to ban ostentatious religious symbols, triggering further debate about the principle of secular neutrality in French public education. In 2004, the French parliament eventually passed a law prohibiting the wearing of any signs manifesting a religious affiliation in public schools.[2] Most recently, attempts have been made to extend the ban of

2 Loi no 2004–225 du 15 mars 2004 encadrant, en application du principe de laïcité, le port de signes manifestant une appartenance religieuse dans les écoles, collèges et lycées public.

certain religious symbols from public schools to the public sphere as a whole. In September 2010, the French Senate overwhelmingly approved a bill that would make it illegal to wear garments such as the niqab or the burka (both forms of a full-faced veil) anywhere in public. The bill still has to pass the scrutiny of the French Conseil Constitutionnel and, pending a successful application, of the European Court of Human Rights (ECtHR).

At first sight, the French ban of religious symbols from the public sphere seems to keep with the liberal promise of state neutrality. After all, limits on the exercise of religion are justified by virtue of securing a neutral-as-secular public sphere and guaranteeing the equal protection of religious freedom in the private sphere. However, such an argument overlooks that the normative ideal of a *laïque* public sphere is the result of a historical process informed by the interrelation of Christianity and secularization (Asad 2003). The justification of the secular public from liberal neutrality is flawed because *laïcité* stems from, and remains embedded in, a French national culture infused with secular and Christian values. As Hervieu-Léger (2006: 51) notes,

> it is impossible to appreciate the discussion of many questions in French public life which have nothing strictly to do with religion (from food quality to the ethical regulation of science, the management of hierarchical relationships in business, the future of rural society, societal expectations of the state, and demands for workers' rights) without being aware of the extent to which French culture is impregnated with Catholic values.

Mutatis mutandis: it is convenient for French secularized Christians and Christian secularists to endorse the privatization of religious faith that underpins the liberal public-private divide because they conceived it in the first place. The conception of a secular public does not require them to change their dress, appearance, behaviour, or habits concerning the role of religion in public life. Hence today the awkward alliance against the headscarf between French left-wing secular Republicanism and right-wing Christian Catholicism:

> The Right and the Left can define the prohibition on Islamic headscarves in the classroom as a defence of either French Christian or French secular culture, because the two are not at all mutually exclusive. Current Western Christian religious practice defines that women and men bare their heads in public, non-sacred buildings, and that convention – the absence of a religious marker – has been accepted as a secular practise. But the absence is also a marker, and for other religious traditions with other religious practices, going bareheaded may be seen as an overtly Christian practice, or at the least one in weak disguise, especially if that practice is legislated in a dominantly Christian country. (Moruzzi 1994: 664)

This problem of the non-neutrality of secular neutrality is everything but new. If, John Locke had argued in his Epistola de Tolerantia of 1689,[3]

> such were the state of things, that the interest of the commonwealth required all slaughter of beasts should be forborne for some while, in order to the increasing of the stock of cattle, that had been destroyed by some extraordinary murrain; who sees not that the magistrate, in such a case, may forbid all his subjects to kill any calves for any use whatsoever? Only it is to be observed, that in this case the law is not made about religion, but about political matter; nor is the sacrifice, but the slaughter of calves thereby prohibited. (Locke 1991: 37)

However, while the farmer who cannot kill his calf until the stock has been sufficiently increased will merely suffer a temporal economic disadvantage, the religious believer, when not engaging in the rituals required by her faith, will risk her salvation. And it is difficult to see why Locke's proposal should seem equally congenial to both of them. That the law is not made *about* religion is simply not sufficient to establish its neutrality *in relation to* religion. Placed in the contemporary context of the headscarf controversy it is, as Modood (1998: 393) remarks, surely a contradiction to require both that the secular state should be neutral between religions and that the secular state should require certain religions with specific public ambitions to give them up.

One way to address this critique is to maintain that the secular public sphere is (at least) neutral in the sense that it does not aim at discriminating between different religions, and/or that it is (at least) neutral in the sense that does not draw on religious justifications. However, such models of formal or reason-based equality that would cognize Locke's problem as a form of merely 'indirect' discrimination hide as much as they reveal. They cannot determine whether secular neutrality requires religions to be treated equally in a positive sense (all religions in the public sphere), or equally in a negative sense (all religions out of the public sphere). But surely, this is precisely what is at stake in the contest between 'public' and 'private' religions – which leads right back to the primordial problem of defining what should count as 'public' and 'private' for the purpose of the liberal public-private divide.

## Our Modern Atheists

As is well known, Locke's defence of religious toleration was not particularly tolerant after all, despite his claim to have drawn a bright-line distinction between the 'business of civil government' and the 'business of religion'. Having established that the power of the Magistrate was confined to protecting the 'civil order of the Commonwealth', Locke was quick to identify certain (religious) doctrines that nevertheless came under his jurisdiction because they posed a threat to that

3 The *Epistola de Tolerantia* was first published anonymously in Latin in 1689. Citations refer to the original English translation by William Popple, as reprinted in Locke (1991).

very order. Having argued that 'Mahometans' should not be excluded from the civil rights of the Commonwealth *because of their religion*, Locke (1991: 46–7) maintained that a Church

> can have no right to be tolerated by the magistrate, which is constituted upon such a bottom, that all those who enter into it, do thereby, ipso facto, deliver themselves up to the protection and service of another prince. It is ridiculous for anyone to profess himself to be a Mahometan only in religion, but in everything else a faithful subject to a Christian magistrate, whilst at the same time he acknowledges himself bound to yield blind obedience to the Mufti of Constantinople; who himself is entirely obedient to the Ottoman emperor.

More bluntly put, the Magistrate must use his 'rods and axes' against his Catholic subjects because their obedience to the Pope undermines his political authority.[4] The same goes for those 'who deny the being of God' because 'promises, covenants, and oaths, which are the bonds of human society, can have no hold upon an atheist' (Locke 1991: 47). Importantly, Locke does not simply say that some Catholics and atheists may pose a threat to public order – he claims that this is always and necessarily the case because the threat lies *in the very nature of being* a Catholic or atheist. Moreover, Locke does not merely propose to curtail their rights to express their religious (non-)beliefs. Rather, Catholics and atheists must be denied the civil rights of the Commonwealth *altogether* because they have placed themselves outside the civil order and the bonds of human society: 'the taking away of God, though but even in thought, dissolves everything' (Locke 1991: 47).

Why bother? After all, few people today would still subscribe to the Lockean premise that Catholics undermine the political authority of the secular state, and even fewer people are likely to believe that atheists are immoral and cannot be trusted. Locke's argument is tailored to a Christian society in a Christian state, and is therefore unlikely to raise much excitement in a contemporary audience (Dunn 1990). Nevertheless, there may still be some dystopian lessons to be learnt from the way Locke disqualifies certain (religious) doctrines from membership in the liberal society – for liberal societies in which Locke's rhetorical 'Mahometans' have come to claim a real presence.

Already two decades ago, Brian Barry (1990: 57) alerted us that we are likely headed for 'a new Dark Age' that betrays the Enlightenment hope that the cessation of persecution and censorship would lead to the triumph of liberal attitudes. On the one hand, 'there is little chance of selling neutrality to non-liberals, which means that non-liberals will continue to hold views about the proper role of state action that run counter to liberal policy prescriptions'. On the other hand, the 'prospects of survival' of liberal institutions depends on 'there being in the population a large proportion of people with a liberal outlook' (Barry 1990: 56). More recently, John Finnis (2009) has found new evidence in support of the Dark Age thesis in the

4 Jeremy Waldron (2002: 221) thinks that Locke should be read literally here, charging Muslims rather than Catholics – which would serve my argument just as well.

jurisprudence of the European Court of Human Rights. According to Finnis, the Chamber and the Grand Chamber Judgment of the Strasbourg court in Şahin show that the British House of Lords in Begum did not say what it really wanted to say.

What the majority of judges did say in Begum was that the decision of Denbigh High School to prohibit Shabina Begum attending school dressed in a *jilbab* (a long loose-fit overgarment) did not interfere with her right to express her religious beliefs (Art. 9(1) ECHR) because she could choose to 'compromise and, if necessarily sacrifice' the expression of her beliefs, or to move to another school whose uniform policy would accommodate her religious dress requirements (Begum 2006: 50, 54). Moreover, all judges concurred that assuming there had been an interference with Article 9(1) ECHR, it would have been be justified in the light of Article 9(2) ECHR because the school uniform policy pursued the legitimate aim of protecting the rights and freedoms of others by promoting social cohesion and religious harmony among opposing groups. Finnis is right to complain about such 'conceptual slackness of human rights-law-in-action' (Finnis (2009: 433). Delimiting freedom of religion at the interference stage relieves the school from the onus of justifying its uniform policy altogether. At the justification stage, the judges' focus on the legitimate aim of the policy, combined with a good deal of deference to the school authorities, waters down the school's burden of proving that Begum's exclusion was 'necessary in a democratic society', thus responding to a 'pressing social need'.

What Finnis thinks the House of Lords really wanted to say is what Finnis himself thinks (2009: 440):

> Confronted by the grave warnings thus issuing from courts of great pan-European authority, citizens of countries whose Muslim population is increasingly very rapidly by immigration and a relatively high birth rate may ask themselves whether it is prudent, or just to the children and grandchildren of everyone in their country, to permit any further migratory increase in that population, or even to accept the presence of immigrant, non-citizen Muslims without deliberating seriously about a possible reversal – humane and financially compensated for and incentivized – of the inflow.

Now clearly, their Lordships could not have said what Finnis thinks they wanted to say after Lord Bingham had found it 'important to stress at the outset that this case concerns a particular pupil in a particular school in a particular place at a particular time. … The House is not, and could not be, invited to rule whether Islamic dress, or any feature of Islamic dress, should or should not be permitted in the schools of this country' (Begum 2006: 2). So let's focus on the 'grave warnings' issued by the European Court of Human Rights.

According to Finnis (2009), the outcome of Şahin was predictable after the ECtHR had upheld the ban of the Turkish Refah Party, among others, because Refah Partisi had advocated and intended to introduce Islamic law in Turkey. Leyla Şahin, by contrast, only wanted to continue her university education wearing a headscarf. Istanbul University suspended her, a decision that the ECtHR eventually upheld in a split Grand Chamber Judgement. Before the Strasbourg court, the Turkish government did not submit, let alone substantiate, that Ms Şahin was connected to extremist political movements, or that she had ever tried to impose her religious views on others.[5] Which is why the Chamber judges contended themselves with accepting the Turkish Government's view that the headscarf ban was justified as a general 'preventive' measure (Şahin 2004: 96). The Grand Chamber, after cursorily observing that 'the impugned interference primarily pursued the legitimate aim of protecting the rights and freedoms of others and of protecting public order', considered that it could not 'apply the criterion of proportionality in a way that would make the notion of an institution's "internal rules" devoid of purpose' (Şahin 2005: 99). In a similar vein, the ECtHR's earlier Dahlab decision had dismissed the application of a Swiss primary school teacher against the headscarf ban as manifestly ill-founded, despite the uncontested fact that Ms Dahlab had been wearing a headscarf for more than five years without causing any obvious disturbance or complaints, and that she had never tried to influence or proselytize her students.

Whatever 'warnings' the Strasbourg judges may have wanted to convey, they would be based on very tangible evidence. Judge Tulkens' lone dissent in Şahin rings true: 'only indisputable facts and reasons whose legitimacy is beyond doubt – not mere worries or fears – are capable of … justifying interference with a right guaranteed by the Convention' (Şahin 2005, Dissenting Opinion of Judge Tulkens: 5). The problem with Finnis' interpretation is that it conflates the Court deferring to the views of the Turkish authorities with the Court endorsing these views. Indeed, the ECtHR's justification for employing a wide margin of appreciation is a far cry from Finnis' contention that the Court could indulge his own view, namely that the 'intimidatory pressures for conformity which are the main ground for the headscarf ban in Turkey and the *jilbab* ban in Denbigh High School are often … early precursors of jihad' (Finnis 2009: 439):

> Where questions concerning the relationship between State and religions are at stake, on which opinion in a democratic society may reasonably differ widely, the role of the national decision-making body must be given special importance. This will notably be the case when it comes to regulating the wearing of religious symbols in educational institutions, in respect of which the approaches in Europe are diverse. Rules in this sphere will consequently vary from one country to another according to national traditions and the requirements imposed by the need to protect the rights and freedoms of others and to maintain public order. (Şahin 2005: 108–9)

5 The applicant, by contrast, accepted the importance of upholding the principle of secularism and the neutrality of Turkish universities, but maintained that her wearing a headscarf had not caused any disruption, disturbance or threat to the public order. In her view, the headscarf did not threaten republican values or the rights of others, nor could it be regarded as inherently incompatible with the principle of secularism and the neutrality of education, see Şahin (2004) at paras. 83–8.

As if to rebut Finnis's interpretation, the ECtHR has adopted a more cautious approach in its recent headscarf jurisprudence (Dogru 2008; Kervanci 2008). Referring to the case-law of the French Conseil d'État,[6] the Court clarifies that the wearing of headscarves is 'not inherently incompatible with the principle of secularism in [French] schools' (Dogru 2008: 70), justifying its decision to uphold the ban on grounds of health and safety considerations specific to physical education classes.

According to Dunn (1990: 19), Locke's fear of atheism could be deemed 'a sort of spiritual equivalent to AIDS in the most hysterical and contemporary understandings' (1990: 19). The atheist's denial of the existence of God reduces the law of nature to the conflictive interests of individuals who, left to their own fallible devices, have no reason to trust each other and hence no capacity to form a peaceful and stable society. Jeremy Waldron (2001: 221) has defended Locke's exclusion of 'Mahometans' against liberal critique by arguing that Locke could concede the possibility that not all Muslims yielded blind political obedience to the Ottoman emperor. One question is whether Locke and his contemporaries believed that for a 'Mahometan' to profess himself a faithful subject of the Magistrate could be anything but 'ridiculous' pretence. Another question is whether we, that is, liberal majorities upon whom the 'prospects of survival' of liberal institutions depend (Barry 1990: 56), have once again come to believe the same. If so, Locke is very alive and liberalism is, in Dunn's words, 'well and truly dead'.

## Excluded Publics – Included Privates

In section 2 it is argued that the distinction between the public sphere and the private sphere that is constitutive of liberal neutrality cannot be constituted by way of a neutral distinction between the (secular) public and the (religious) private because liberal neutrality presupposes, rather than justifies, an equation of 'public' and 'secular' and 'religious' and 'private' respectively. Once the liberal veil of ignorance is lifted, two further justifications for decreeing public religions as private for the purpose of the liberal public-private divide surface: *laïcité* as promotion of individual autonomy that lies at the heart of a perfectionist morality; and *laïcité* as a communitarian ideal that fosters a civic sense of loyalty to a particular historical community (Laborde 2003).

For those who defend the equation of 'secular' and 'public' on grounds of individual autonomy, the ban of religious symbols from the public sphere is justified because it liberates Muslim women from heteronymous social structures that persist in the private sphere – a position enthusiastically endorsed by President Sarkozy when advocating the French burka ban: 'The burka is not a religious sign. It is a sign of the subjugation, of the submission, of women. … We cannot accept in our country women imprisoned behind bars, cut off from social life, deprived of identity' (cited in Carvajal 2009). The blemish of this heroic posture is that it

6 See above, section 2.

becomes self-defeating once placed in the context of the liberal public-private divide: we foster the inclusion of Muslim women by excluding them from the 'autonomous' public sphere and forcing them back into the 'heteronymous' private sphere that deprives them of their 'identity'. Its hypocrisy becomes apparent upon reflection on who is putting whom 'behind bars' here: the identity and autonomy of Sarkozy's 'subjugated' Muslims and Finnis's 'politicized' Muslims are promoted on the back of their denial. The wearing of the headscarf is reduced from an expression of *religious* identity to, respectively, a *cultural* badge of oppression or a *political* harbinger of a hostile theocratic takeover. This provides the pretext for categorically denying that Muslim women could embrace the headscarf as an autonomous choice, that is, as a self-conscious expression of their struggle to define their place as female Muslims in the secularized Christian nation-state. What gets lost in the relentless crusade of secular autonomy against sacred heteronomy is, as Balibar remarks, the tragic character of a situation in which Muslim women 'become the stake of a merciless struggle for prestige between two male powers which try to control them, one on behalf of patriarchal authority wrapped up in religion, the other on behalf of national authority wrapped up in secularism' (Balibar 2004: 359).

This leaves us with the third and final tenet of the secular public, a communitarian notion of civic loyalty that strives to resurrect a 'traditional Catholic-inspired sociability' (Laborde 2003: 170) in new national clothes. On this view, the ban of religious symbols from the secular public sphere is justified because it inculcates a robust national identity capable of transcending particular religious and cultural loyalties. Bereft of its neutralist pretensions the conversion of believers into citizens works through the imposition of majoritarian national traditions and cultures on religious minorities. During the parliamentary debates of the 1994 French law prohibiting the wearing of any signs manifesting a religious affiliation in public schools, a member of the Assemblée Nationale used his '*bon sens paysan*' to provide us with a contemporary interpretation of the traditional French way of transforming (Catholic) 'peasants into Frenchmen': 'Islam has settled rather recently in our country. Its faith is absolutely respectable. But its adherents, as everybody else, must adapt to our values and traditions, not the other way around.'[7]

Ultimately, the 'neutrality' and 'autonomy' justifications for excluding public religions from the public sphere collapse into this kind of national majoritarianism that betrays the liberal promise not just to assimilate but to transcend religious diversity. National majorities posit the distinction between the secular public sphere and the religious private sphere in order to populate the former and relegate religious minorities to the latter. It is *our* national *and* secular *and* Christian conception of 'public' that directs the neutrality principle towards the exclusion of (certain) religions from the public sphere, as it is *our* national *and* secular *and* Christian

7 *Journal Officiel de la République Française*, Année 2004. – No 17 [2] A.N. (C.R.), at 1463; 'L'islam est d'implantation relativement récente chez nous. Sa croyance est parfaitement respectable. Mais, comme pour toutes les autres, c'est aux tenants de cette religion de s'adapter à nos valeurs et traditions et non l'inverse.'

conception of 'private' that reduces the political subject behind the veil to a false dichotomy between secular autonomy and sacred heteronomy. The nationalist stitch of the liberal public-private divide debunks integration as both assimilation and segregation: we want them to integrate, but we do not really want to integrate them.

So why not do away with the liberal public-private divide altogether? Because, as suggested in section three, this would exacerbate rather than mitigate the effects of what John Stuart Mill (1859) so perceptively described as the tendency of society 'to fetter the development, and, if possible, prevent the formation, of any individuality not in harmony with its ways, and compel all characters to fashion themselves upon the model of its own'. Dismantling the liberal distinction between the public sphere and the private sphere does not neutralize majoritarian conceptions of 'the public' but allows them to colonize society as a whole, thus bereaving religious minorities of their last refuge.

In the worst case scenario, this leads to a reinstatement of the liberal distinction between the 'secular public' and the 'religious private' as a totalistic distinction between 'national members' and 'Muslim non-members' of the polity as a whole. Which boils down to nothing less – or more – than the revocation of the liberal quid pro quo by national majorities: religious minorities are assimilated to the secularized Christian public sphere at the promise that the expression of their religious beliefs will be respected and protected in the religious private sphere.

In an earlier contribution to the debate, John Finnis (2007: 443) advocated the indefinite detention of (Muslim) non-citizens awaiting deportation on grounds of a Kelsenian notion of the 'legal system's subsiding unity through time [that] cannot be explained without foundational reference to the group whose legal system it is'. According to Finnis, the primordial legal distinction between nationals and aliens breathes life into the national community because it endows the 'indispensible framework for articulating, expressing, ratifying, and demanding … integration in and assimilation to this nation-state rather than some other' (Finnis 2007: 444). However, as Finnis himself realizes, the conferral of citizenship as a legal status does not vouch for membership in the national community. The deeper challenge to constitutional order, he concludes (2007: 444), is

> posed by nationals who regard their nationality as a form of alienage because … they believe their true Nation lies altogether beyond – but is ordained to have dominion over – the bounds and territories, and the constitutional principles and rights, that frame and structure our nation's common good.

Locke could not have put it any better. It is ultimately a concern with national membership, not legal citizenship, which motivates Finnis' proposal to prevent any further Muslim migration and reverse the inflow of Muslim immigrants. That we are (sometimes[8]) legally prevented from deporting Muslim nationals is

8 Under the amended UK Immigration, Asylum and Nationality Act 2006, British citizens who hold a double nationality can be deprived of their citizenship if the Secretary of State is satisfied that the deprivation is 'conductive to the public good'.

just a tedious detail in the real debate about whether Muslims can be nationals at all. It is in this latter debate that one wonders whether Finnis's proposals are likely to generate the 'level of trust and common sympathies' necessary 'to outweigh competing bonds of kin, castle, religion or ethnicity' (Finnis 2007: 445). And it is because we once again have this debate that liberals should more than ever vindicate the distinction between the public sphere and the private sphere.

If the distinction between nationals and aliens is a prerequisite for the subsiding unity of the legal system, the distinction between the public sphere and the private sphere is under contemporary conditions of religious and cultural pluralism a prerequisite for the subsiding unity of the national community to which the legal system refers. It provides the framework for articulating and ratifying not only what it means to *belong to* the nation-state but also what it means to belong to *the nation-state*. The exclusion qua public from the public sphere contains a simultaneous inclusion qua private in the private sphere that is premised upon the inclusion of the excluded in national community as a whole. My point is not simply that the exclusion of religious minorities from the public sphere entails their inclusion in the private sphere. It is, more fundamentally, that their coinstantaneous exclusion from the public sphere and inclusion in the private sphere entails the recognition of their enduring membership in a national community in which belonging is not conditional on religious faith or national fate. On this reading, the distinction between the public sphere and the private sphere as constitutive of liberal neutrality is a prerequisite for contesting the distinction between public and private as constituted by liberal neutrality. The liberal public-private divide tames the aggressive reanimation of religious and national ideologies that reduce the distinction between majoritarian publics and minoritarian privates to a primordial opposition of friend and foe, thus purchasing national solidarity at the price of stigmatizing 'an enemy within' (Raz 1998: 201).

With historical hindsight, Locke was wrong in thinking that Catholics could not be(come) loyal citizens because they had sworn allegiance to the Pope, but he was right in pinpointing the source of the malaise that still haunts the European nation-states: 'it is not the diversity of opinion, which cannot be avoided, but the refusal of toleration to those that are of different opinions, which might have been granted, that has produced all the bustles and wars, that have been in the Christian world upon account of religion' (Locke 1991: 52). Barry, Finnis & Co. may or may not be right in heralding a new 'Dark Age', but they are certainly wrong in diagnosing the nature of the threat. Where national majorities unilaterally impose their traditions and cultures on religious minorities under the weak disguises of defending secular state neutrality and defeating sacred heteronomy, backed up with the threat of removal from the polity, they jeopardize the very being and becoming of a national community. Under such conditions, liberals indeed cannot afford the 'luxury of unilateral disarmament' (Barry 1990: 57).

## References

Ashad, D. 2003. *Formations of the Secular.* Stanford: Stanford University Press.

Balibar, E. 2004. Dissonances within *Laïcité. Constellations* 11(3), 353–60.

Barry, B. 1990. How Not to Defend Liberal Institutions, *in Liberalism and the Good*, edited by R.B. Douglass, G.M. Mara and H.S. Richardson. London: Routledge, 44–58.

Carvajal, D. 2009. Sarkozy Backs Drive to Eliminate the Burq. *The New York Times* [Online] Available at: http://www.nytimes.com/2009/06/23/world/europe/23france.html [last accessed: 8 December 2010].

Conseil d'État, Avis no. 346893 (27 November 1989), English summary in [1990] *Public Law* 434–5.

Conseil d'État, Kherouaa, Kachour, Balo, Kizic, no. 130394 (2 November 1992).

Conseil d'État, Aoukili, no. 159981 (10 March 1995).

Conseil d'État, Mlle Saglamer, no. 169522 (27 November 1996).

Dunn, J. 1990. *Interpreting Political Responsibility*. Cambridge: Cambridge University Press.

ECtHR, *Dahlab v. Switzerland*, Application no. 42393/98 (Decision of 15 February 2001).

ECtHR, *Refah Partisi and Others v Turkey*, Application nos. 41340/98, 41342/98, 41343/98 and 41344/98 (Third Section, Judgement of 31 July 2001).

ECtHR, *Refah Partisi and Others v Turkey*, Application nos. 41340/98, 41342/98, 41343/98 and 41344/98 (Grand Chamber, Judgement of 13 February 2003).

ECtHR, *Leyla Şahin v. Turkey*, Application no. 44774/98 (Fourth Section, Judgement of 29 June 2004).

ECtHR, *Leyla Şahin v. Turkey*, Application no. 44774/98 (Grand Chamber, Judgement of 10 November 2005).

ECtHR, *Dogru v France*, Application no. 27058/05 (Fifth Section, Judgement of 4 December 2008).

ECtHR, *Kervanci v. France*, Application no. 31645/04 (Fifth Section, Judgement of 4 December 2008).

Finnis, J. 2007. Nationality, Alienage and Constitutional Principle. 123 *Law Quarterly Review* 123(Jul), 417–45.

Finnis, J. 2009. Endorsing Discrimination Between Faiths: A Case of Extreme Speech?, in *Extreme Speech and Democracy*, edited by in I. Hare and J. Weinstein. Oxford: Oxford University Press, 430–41.

Hervieu-Léger, D. 2006. *The Role of Religion in Establishing Social Cohesion, in Conditions of European Solidarity*. Vol. II: *Religion in the New Europe*, edited by K. Michalski. Budapest: Central European University Press, 45–61.

House of Lords, *Regina (SB) v Governors of Denbigh High School* [2006] UKHL 15 (Begum).

Laborde, C. 2003. Toleration and *Laïcité*, in *The Culture of Toleration in Diverse Societies*, edited by C. McKinnon and D. Castiglione. Manchester: Manchester University Press, 161–78.

Locke, J. 1991. A Letter Concerning Toleration, in *A Letter Concerning Toleration in Focus*, edited by S. Mendus and J. Horton. London: Routledge, 9–90.

Mill, J.S. 1859. On Liberty: Introductory. [Online]. Available at: http://www.bartleby.com/130/1.html [last accessed: 8 December 2010].

Modood, T. 1998. Anti-Essentialism, Multiculturalism and the 'Recognition' of Religious Groups. *Journal of Political Philosophy* 6(4), 378–99.

Raz, J. 1998. Multiculturalism. *Ratio Juris* 11(3), 193–205.

Sajó, A. 2008. Preliminaries to a Concept of Constitutional Secularism. *International Journal of Constitutional Law* 6(3–4), 605–29.

Waldron, J. 2001. *God, Locke and Equality*. Cambridge: Cambridge University Press.

# Chapter 9
# The Prisoner's Right to Vote: The Creation of an Abnormal and Excluded Public

Vanessa De Greef

## Introduction

No sooner has a prisoner arrived in prison that he or she realizes that keeping his fundamental rights is not always obvious. Is he or she still be part of the public? Does he or she still count? Are we attending the birth and the spread out of a particular public, the public of prisoners?

Contact with the outside world is essential for prisoners and fulfils many functions in prison (e.g., Van Zyl Smit and Snacken 2009: 213). However prisoners can see their voting rights suspended. Even though there are many 'constitutional democracies' where prisoners retain their voting rights,[1] there is no consensus on this matter from an international perspective (e.g., Blais, Massicotte, Yoshinaka 2001: 41–62).[2] Besides, one must be aware that the effectiveness of the right to vote for prisoners – even in preventive detention where prisoners could not be legally deprived of their right to vote – is rarely practiced.

Recently, the European Court of Human Rights (ECtHR) decided to monitor in a more assiduous way how states organize free elections and to set aside the possibility to use implicit limitations to the right to vote (e.g., ECtHR, Case of *Mathieu-Mohin and Clerfayt c. Belgium*, No. 9267/81, 2nd March 1987, Case of *Hirst v. The United Kingdom* (Grand Chamber), No. 74025/01, 6th September 2005 and Case of *Frodl v. Austria*, No. 20201/04, 8th April 2010). Making the Convention a 'vivid instrument' and constructing a democratic European order, the Court gives a progressive interpretation to article 3 of the First Protocol to European Convention of Human Right (Natale 2006: 941–2).

---

1 For instance, all prisoners keep their right to vote in Denmark, Ireland, Island, Switzerland, Croatia, Bosnia, Sweden, Finland, Slovenia, Spain, Poland, Macedonia, Cyprus, Latvia, Lithuania, Ukraine and in the Netherlands.

2 In Europe, '13 countries prevent sentenced prisoners from voting, while a further ten restrict the rights of some sentenced prisoners to vote' (Van Zyl Smit and Snacken 2009: 253). A few countries even ban prisoners from voting for a period following the end of incarceration (e.g., Dhami 2005: 236, Campbell 2008: 1).

But what we could not deny is that 'until recently, large classes of people, prisoners among them, were excluded from the franchise. The assumption that they were not fit or "worthy" of voting – whether by reason of class, race, gender or conduct – played a large role in this exclusion' (Chief Justice, expressing the majority opinion in *Sauvé v. Canada*, SCC 68, [2002] 3 S.C.R. 519, para. 43).

Indeed law itself can play an important role in exclusion. This article will illustrate that it participates to the creation of a public of prisoners who are characterized by negative identities. The purpose of this study is two-fold. First, it aims at understanding how law contributes to the construction of a public of prisoners and secondly, to demonstrate that the 'normal public', the public who should have the capacity to vote, does not – in fact – exist.

Disenfranchisement implies that an individual loses his badge of dignity and personhood and that he does not count anymore (*Sachs J., August v. Electoral Commission* (South Africa), 1999, para. 17, cited in Lardy 2002: 524). He is now a 'pseudo-citizen'; he does not matter (Cholbi 2002: 558). According to Lardy, using disenfranchisement as a punishment treats prisoners as *former* members of the community who are thus no longer subject to the moral authority of the political community (Lardy 2002: 527).

Why should prisoners agree to these legal norms if they are not considered as citizens?

This paper will first show reasons invoked for disenfranchisement and how these lead to the fabrication and the maintaining of a distinct public, the prisoners' public. Second, this paper will analyze the construction of negative identities and see how Dewey's and Habermas's theories cope with these identities. This will illustrate that prisoners do not actually form a public but also that the normal public, wanted by law, does not exist. Finally, this paper will explain that the prisoners' right to vote can result in a 'win-win' operation for society and the relevant individuals. But it will not be sufficient to express the voice of 'the people').

## Criteria for the Creation of a Prisoners' Public

Beyond legal rules and their effectiveness, legitimacy lies at the heart of this debate. This section addresses the reasons for banning a type of public from voting. The legitimacy of government's reasons are doubtful when the arguments invoked do not resist a reasoned analysis.

First, reasons for disenfranchisement will be canvassed, so as to decypher how a public of prisoners emerges. Then, the impact of negative identities reflection – as experienced by prisoners – will be examined. The creation of a public of prisoners could have serious consequences for prisoners.

*Creating a public: the search for criteria*

At least seven arguments have been raised to justify the disenfranchisement of prisoners:

First, legal tradition and history remind us of the notion of 'civil death' (Cholbi 2002: 543–4). The original purpose of civic death, 'the strongest condemnation by state and society', was to expose offenders to humiliation and stigmatization (Orr, cited in Jago and Marriott 2007: 3). Nowadays, being civilly dead is replaced by the idea of breaching the social contract: a person is excluded from society when he or she did not respect the social contract. Considered to have failed to put aside his own interest for the sake of the public good, the convicted prisoner lacks civic virtue (e.g., Jago and Marriott 2007: 3). This argument was invoked by the UK government in the ECtHR Case *Hirst v United Kingdom*. It implies that prisoners are rational human beings who choose criminal activity and are conscious of all the legal consequences of their actions (e.g., Dhami 2005: 239). This could refer to the *criminology of the other* that outlines that criminal actions are voluntary (e.g., Garland 2001: 185).

Secondly, retribution and forfeiture[3] are invoked. These could make some sense for someone who precisely violated electoral law (e.g., Eudes 2006: 582).[4] However, it does not seem legitimate for all crimes. For Cholbi (2002: 545–6), this argument presupposes that crimes are political acts which necessarily threaten public order. But proponents of retribution fail to acknowledge that most crimes are directed at persons and their property and not the state as such; few criminals commit crimes with the aim of political revolution.

On the contrary, if committing a crime is not always a political act, defining what is a crime *is* a political act. There is not a unique vision of deviance: behaviours considered as crimes differ according to periods and societies. Thus contents, limits and control of deviance are 'stakes in a power game'[5] (Peyre 1979: 50).

Thirdly, electoral integrity is defended. The purity of the ballot box is an interesting argument. Prisoners are labelled as deviant and abnormal (e.g., Jago and Marriott 2007: 5). Deviants are presumed to be immoral; they are seen to have a character defect (e.g., Goffman 1975: 13). Whether people outside of prisons are – automatically – examples of morality can be doubted. It would be a strange shortcut to make the presumption that people are virtuous when they are not in prison. It is important to recall that voting 'is a basic right, one that

3 Some authors distinguished these two notions because forfeiture constitutes a distinct civil penalty accompanying a conviction (Lardy 2002: 530). Nevertheless, we found that they were closely related and that similar arguments were invoked for both.

4 In Germany, disenfranchisement concerns individuals who commit serious offences which may undermine the state or which constitute tampering with elections (e.g., Van Zyl Smit and Snacken 2009: 253). See also the ECtHR Case *Hirst v. United Kingdom* and Case *Frodl v. Austria* where the Court outlined the 'direct link between the facts on which a conviction is based and the sanction of disenfranchisement'.

5 Personal translation.

does not depend on possessing some requisite degree of virtue' (Cholbi 2002: 556). Some also wonder why those who breach civil law obligations and those who are convincted without a prison sentence retain their voting rights if one follows the logic suggested (e.g., Lardy 2002: 530). Finally, some pursue this argument and assess the prisoners' incompetence to vote because of the mental incapacity related to the offence they committed or related to their learning of deviant behaviours (e.g., Lardy 2002: 530). The mental incapacity invoked here and the deviant behaviours are again defined by certain power-holders, which makes this qualification particularly relative. This argument will turn against those who invoke it because mental incapacity could have some unpredicted consequences. Indeed, in the process of rehabilitation, maintaining adult roles are important: treating individuals as incapable is likely to render (re)integration far more difficult (e.g., Van Zyl Smit and Snacken 2009: 254).

Fourth, deterrence is invoked as a justification for disenfranchisement. While the deterrence argument may be questioned with regards to imprisonment altogether, it is particularly weak with regards to the potential loss of voting rights. Does one think of loosing one's right to vote when committing an offence (e.g., Jago and Marriott 2007: 3)?[6]

Fifth, rehabilitation is sometimes used to suspend the prisoners' right to vote. There is a certain hidden logic behind this vision: by being excluded from voting, the prisoner remembers his or her past criminal acts and he or she is more likely to commit himself to being rehabilitated (e.g., Cholbi 2002: 558). For some analysts, however, exclusion does not facilitate rehabilitation and even if the causes of criminal behaviour are unclear, social isolation and a sense of powerlessness play a substantial role in these causes (e.g., Cholbi 2002: 558). Worse, disenfranchisement may also 'foster further criminal behaviour' (Dhami 2005: 239).

Sixth, administrative inconvenience is invoked. It mostly relates to the difficulty of organizing the right to vote in prisons. This argument must be considered and the financial means must be taken into account. Some go further and defend the restriction of certain rights in prisons because of the need for discipline and control (e.g., Jago and Marriott 2007: 3).[7] Others held that the votes of prisoners may be determinative of the election result – overall if the prisoners are registered to vote in the district of the prison and not in their home constituency (e.g., Lardy 2002: 532–3).

Seventh, and related to this last argument, it is argued that prisoners could misuse the vote to promote 'soft on crime policies' (Jago and Marriott 2007: 5). Some authors have demonstrated that this reasoning implies that prisoners constitute an organized group that wants to use the ballot for a common purpose which is contrary to the common good (e.g., Brenner and Caste 2003: 237). Moreover, this

---

6 Indeed prisons are the best places to learn how to make new offences and when you are free, committing offences is easier when society excludes you more than ever (e.g., De Greef 2007).

7 The authors invoked an argument made by Lord Steyn in *R. v. Home Secretary ex parte Simms* [2000] 2 AC 115.

argument means that legal rules would exclude a group based on the way they would vote (e.g., Dhami 2005: 240). This argument also assumes that prisoners will vote *en bloc* (e.g., Lardy 2002: 534). Is this fear not an evidence that those in power assume that prisoners form a public?

### *The emergence of a public of prisoners*

These reasons for banning prisoners from voting hide an underlying motivation: the fabrication and the maintaining of a distinct and dangerous public constituted by prisoners (e.g., Dilts 2006: 28).

Clearly prisoners are all seen to lack civic virtue, they commit political acts against the State, they are deviant, abnormal, they have a character defect, a mental incapacity and they vote en bloc – because of their common purpose – to implement 'soft on crime policies'.

Prison's success is indeed 'the fabrication of a distinct class of dangerous person: the delinquent' (Dilts 2006: 7). Can we really distinguish a 'public' of prisoners?

Such a public is fallacious because it is created by 'the Other' and not by prisoners themselves. The reasons invoked above to ban voting rights refer to some characteristics that constitute the relevant public. The notion of 'the public' is obviously not clear. For Brugidou (2008: 14), a public will depend on forms of 'collective coordination' that have three distinct dimensions: the sharing of an identity, an agreement on a problem diagnosis and a commitment in a collective action. While prisoners may face difficulty in engaging in collective action, they are sometimes subsumed under with a common identity and they could share a common diagnosis of various problems.

For John Dewey, we must distinguish a passive public from an active one. In a passive sense, the public consists in a group of people 'whose liberty of action is at risk because of indirect effects of activities at which they do not participate' (Zask 2001: 65). Forbidden to vote, their freedom of action is limited and prisoners could belong to a passive public. In an active sense, the public will re-establish this freedom with a coherent and organized set of activities: this public will identify its interests and finally, seek to protect these interests through representatives (e.g., Zask 2001: 65). Though some imagine prisoners become an active public in the sense of Dewey – for instance they would vote en bloc for a common purpose –, we will see in the next part below that not everyone is able to access this effective public. At best, then, prisoners would constitute a 'passive public'.

*The damage associated with the creation of an unclean public*

Tragically, the construction of a public of prisoners is, in a sense, working.[8] And law helps to achieve this aim when a ban on voting exists or when the voting's rights remain theoretical. It seems that 'disenfranchisement, like the prison, is clearly not simply punitive, but a technology producing the kind of subject that requires disenfranchisement' (Dilts 2006: 23).

According to labelling theory, the label attributed to a convicted person after the offence has a direct influence on a second offence. Inserting more deeply an individual into a delinquents' group and isolating him from the non-delinquents' group leads him to adopt a delinquent status: his social position and his identity are modified because of his relation with authorities (e.g., Lassalle 1979: 175). Negative identities are thus arduous to clean off: they are part of the mental development of the subject (e.g., Le Blanc 2007: 180).

These identities play several functions. First, society stigmatizes those that it excludes; these strangers are necessary for the groups' sustenance as judgments about normality become largely admitted (e.g., Le Blanc 2007: 179–80). Secondly, focussing on a category of outcasts enables turning a blind eye to illegalities committed by others.[9]

Regarding the right to vote, society and especially those who make laws (or statutes) create a legal process through electoral legislation to construct or to strengthen a certain type of public. We transform these anticipations into requests. Prison produces attributes such as 'deviant', 'delinquent', 'criminal'. These qualifications can constitute a stigma (e.g., Goffman 1975: 13).[10] Treating persons with such stigma as 'non totally human', 'we, the normal people' inflict on them certain types of discrimination 'whereby we effectively reduce, even if it is often unconsciously, these persons' chances' (Goffman 1975: 15).[11] Such stigmatized persons can have different reactions: they sometimes tries to improve their condition to reduce the effect of these stigma. Alternatively, they can resolve themselves to fatalism.[12] In case of voting rights, it is difficult to see how prisoners could reduce the stigma except by trying, as Mr Hirst,[13] to ask the judicial power –

8 This article does not canvass the possibilities for prisoners to fight against these constructions.

9 As Foucault showed with the fabrication of the delinquent, 'it enables the organization of other illegalities, aids in the control of the margins of society, controls lesser forms of disorder, aids in colonization of the periphery, and allows the illegality of dominant groups' (Dilts 2006: 20).

10 Relations will have to be taken into consideration to create this stigma.

11 Personal translation.

12 On that matter, see the following study: Deblander, F. 2002. *Le papier sale: le casier judiciaire en Belgique, instrument de la stigmatisation?* Thesis for La Faculté des Sciences Politiques et Sociales de l'Université Catholique de Louvain (Belgium).

13 Mr Hirst was prevented from voting in Britain and brought a case to the European Court of Human Rights (ECtHR Case *Hirst v United Kingdom*).

when the legislative power is not responding – to disapprove a legal rule. But this initiative shows that prisoners could belong to an active public. While excluded from one public – the voting citizens' public – they can nevertheless be included in another public – the citizens' public with access to some form of justice.

Some probably wonder whether a stigma actually arises from disenfranchisement. The answer is positive: disenfranchisement has an impact in one's identity construction and 'labels individuals as "second class" citizens' (Dhami 2005: 243). An American survey showed that 'disenfranchisement was stigmatizing and a sign of social isolation, even if individuals did not exercise their right to vote in the past' (Dhami 2005: 243). There is a need to feel 'like full citizens' (Dhami 2005: 243, Touraut 2005: 13–14.).

Analysing the reasons for disenfranchisement helps to understand how prisoners are seen as a public, even if that notion is polysemic and fluid. This public construction is followed by consequences: on the one hand, the labelled person could suffer from stigma and could assume the roles given by society; on the other hand, society used these negative identities in order to have them take on several functions.

## The Hopefully Impossible Normal Public

This part will analyze to what extent public theorists like Dewey and Habermas break away with negative identities and define a public or a public sphere that includes prisoners. Beyond the right to vote, the possible participation in the public or belonging to a public sphere is essential for anyone and arguably even more for excluded persons. Secondly, this paper will seek to demonstrate that neither a prisoners public, nor a normal public, actually exist, however presumed by law.

### *Prisoners in the public?*

Some public opinion theories underline how theorists try to associate more and more people together in a same public or in a same public sphere. How do these theories affect prisoners' negative identities? Conversely, how are they affected by those negative identities? Beyond the right to vote, prisoners must – during and after their incarceration – have the possibility to debate with other citizens about political affairs and to express their opinion. Indeed, they form a part of the 'global public'.

For Fraser (2001: 132), Habermas idealized the bourgeois public sphere and failed to analyze other rival and non-liberal public spheres. Some groups are indeed excluded from the official public sphere and try to create a counter civil society (e.g., Fraser 2001: 132). According to Fraser (2001: 133), exclusions and conflicts become decorative details for Habermas, the public sphere is a utopian ideal or means a new domination mode. Fraser (2001: 134) particularly wants to question some of Habermas's hypotheses when he suggests that people should partake in public debate as if they were equals or when he disapproves the multiplicity of publics.

In fact, Habermas tried to answer to this critic and to consider how excluded publics could access to this public sphere. By its exclusion from power, 'the people' has, for Habermas (1997: VI–IX), a place in this public sphere and could transform this sphere with its discourse. But some questions remain: how can the excluded persons fight against dominant publics, why can they not form a public by themselves and integrate in a second step a more global public sphere (e.g., Fraser 2001: 139–41)?

For prisoners, the problem is reversed: they are already seen as a public.[14] The deeper question is to know when they could be part of this public sphere. Is the right to vote not a starting point to help them participate – now and later – into this sphere? Moreover, would being part of this sphere erase their negative and common identities? Indeed, even when some excluded publics were authorized to participate to the public sphere, this participation could be restricted in practice. But also, and as well as the act of voting, being part of this public sphere does not require to take decisions; being part of this sphere makes prisoners still belonging to 'weak publics' (e.g., Fraser 2001: 147).

Considering a multiplicity of publics, it is essential for a person that he or she can belong to several publics, even if they all participate to a more global sphere. First, this adherence to several publics will allow persons to develop themselves and to avoid suffering from one public identity, particularly when this identity is negative. Secondly, it is essential to consider a more global public to which all the different publics can belong to be sure they will be able to fight against dominant publics or the power itself. Consequently, all the different publics must be fluent and permeable – and not unique nor homogeneous – to constitute this global public.

For his part, in *The Public and Its Problems*, Dewey (2003: 155) sought to discover the means of gathering a multiform, dispersed and mobile public. He tried to see how the public will be able to recognize itself, to define itself and to express its interests. To find the conditions that will enable this shapeless public to work democratically, Dewey (2003: 156) outlines 'the nature of the democratic idea from the aspect of its generic social signification' and explains how individuals and group members must act together and how their interest must relate to common goods. As each individual is a member of several groups, these groups must interact fully and with flexibility together to aim at this aspect of the democratic idea (Dewey 2003: 156). However, not everyone is able to be part of several groups. The 'good citizen' could be a fully integrated person and will find his or her conduct enriched when being part of several groups: answers of different groups reinforce each other and groups will finally agree on common values (Dewey 2003: 156). But if someone is not this 'good citizen', he or she can forget this ideal. For Dewey (2003: 156), thieves' gang members can connect their interests with their gang but this gang 'cannot interact in a flexible way with other groups; it can only act when isolating itself'.

14 However they didn't decide to become this public. The way prisoners could form a public – by their own decision – will necessitate further research.

Without any social and economic considerations of the reasons that drive people to steal, the thief is condemned to belong to a unique public that cannot go beyond his self-interest. In this sense, society's closing is so intense and the possibility to be integrated could be so difficult that the prisoner could be limited to his or her self interest.[15] But this fatalism leads to placing the prisoner in a unique type of public forever.

For Dewey, the good citizen is able to put aside self-interest. By contrast to this theory, elite democratic theorists see citizens as too focused on their narrow self-interest and justify – even if the rationality of the logic is not evident – why elites should have central decision-making roles in politics. According to them the elite is the only one who is able to deny his or her self-interest (e.g., Clawson and Oxley 2008: 160). But Clawson and Oxley (2008: 160) showed that self-interest does not really influence citizens' policy attitudes except when the effects of a policy are 'visible, tangible, large and certain'. They take for instance the homeowner who is in favour of property tax cuts, the smoker who is opposed to cigarette taxes and the gun owner who is less supportive of gun restriction than people who do not own guns (Clawson and Oxley 2008: 160). Consequently, it seems reductive and improper to see in the thief or in the prisoner someone who is not able to be interested in common goods. On the contrary, common goods would probably resolve or reduce thefts. Therefore, the argument invoked by Dewey – that the thieves' public cannot interact with other groups – does not resist a reasoned analysis.

A reason invoked by the disenfranchisement supporters is prisoners' mental incapacity. Neither Dewey nor Lippman believe in an omnipotent citizen (e.g., Brugidou 2008: 22). But this citizen will be saved because he or she will take part in a public that will produce a collective knowledge about an issue that partakes in his or her development (e.g., Brugidou 2008: 22). Then if the citizen does not have to wear every quality to take part to an active public, we wonder why the prisoners could not be part of it.[16]

In sum, it appears that the prisoners' negative identities remain in Dewey's public and they are not truly resolved in Habermas's public sphere.

### *Deconstruction of the public of prisoners and legal construction of a normal public*

As the foregoing shows, some theories let prisoners' negative identities prevail. The purpose of the last part of this paper is twofold. First, it aims at deconstructing the idea of a unique public of prisoners and, secondly, it seeks to show that a normal public, supported by law, does not exist.

15 Criminal records are partly responsible for this (e.g., De Greef 2007: 66).

16 Many studies have demonstrated substantial differences in political knowledge across demographic groups (e.g., Clawson and Oxley 2008: 198-203). The next part of this paper argues that we cannot presume that all prisoners lack political knowledge.

Touraut has tried to classify different categories of prisoners[17] according to their relationship with citizenship.[18] Some could be sceptical about such a categorization. Indeed it is paradoxical that categories are useful to show that people – in this case, prisoners – are not homogeneous. This French study showed how prisoners live differently in the prison. It also showed that they do not have a common will to attain a precise goal and that they entertain distinct relationships with norms. In other words, this categorization is helpful to understand that prisoners do not form a single public.

On a related front, who is this perfect person some prisoners would love to be and some would hate to become? By the exclusion of some types of public, law seems to allow the access to a so-called democracy only by a 'normal public', a public that is pure, civic, mentally capable, beautiful – in the past, the present and the future – and who strictly follows norms. Normal persons would probably live in horrible sadness. The normal man, if he was real, dreams of a unique norm that governs his life (e.g., Le Blanc, 2007: 63). This man denies conflicts between norms even if he should consider that 'the conflict is thus not between the normal and the abnormal because there is no sense to get out of norms but between a majority norm and a minority norm'[19] (Le Blanc 2007: 10). Searching for a normal person is as absurd as searching for an abnormal one in the figure of the prisoner. 'The normal man is not the ordinary man'[20] says Le Blanc (2007: 29). 'If this man was real, this normal man would be rare among pathologic men' (e.g., Le Blanc 2007: 29–33).

If legal norms try to limit the electorate to normal people, it is a wrong reckoning: these people do not exist and will never exist.

## Come Together Right Now? Including Publics for Democracy

This paper tried to demonstrate how law was able to restrict the right to vote to certain groups or certain publics. Reasons invoked for disenfranchisement are

17 Touraut distinguished between different types of prisoners: the first category relates to prisoners who have a strong link with citizenship, who are interested in political questions. The second type concerns prisoners who reject the normative model of life in society; they are not interested in political questions because politics are source of domination and pretence of democracy. The third category refers to prisoners who have never voted because they did not feel recognized by the society. But they express a will to start a new life, to get interested by political questions and to live according to society's norms. The fourth and last category defined by Touraut concerns prisoners who were integrated and who now feel excluded. These prisoners are engaged in a process of decitizenship. See Touraut 2005: 6–15.

18 The question of citizenship leads to asking if the notion of 'public' would overlap the notion of 'citizenship' which is as large as the first notion. The common denominators between citizenship and the public will necessitate further research.

19 Personal translation.

20 Personal translation.

not really convincing but they have had the effect of implicitly recognizing the existence of a public of prisoners. Disenfranchisement has an impact on identity construction and it will not be easy to dispose of negative identity. In a more general manner, public theorists did not want or did not think how to include prisoners in a more global public. However, prisoners cannot be restricted to a unique public and the normal public does not exist.

For some, law can be considered as 'means' to guarantee individuals participation and to channel it in a way that the environment will be richer and less opaque for individuals (e.g., Zask 2003: 23). But if law is sometimes perceived as an instrument to defend weak people, it can in reality exclude them.

However, prisoners and societies both have the possibility to make a so-called 'win-win' operation. Cholbi (2002: 559) outlines that:

> Allowing felons to vote would encourage them to participate in civic affairs, with beneficial results: criminals will strengthen their ties to their communities … enhance their ability to deliberate about long-term policies that affect more than their own self-interest. … [D]enying felons the vote can only serve to stigmatize felons and to exacerbate factors known to contribute to criminal behaviour.

For prisoners, the right to vote has its significance in terms of symbolically holding a part of political power (e.g., Touraut 2005: 3) but more particularly, this right strengthens their participation and is a sign of their citizenship. Citizenship is a source of social ties and produces 'collective identification modes' (Touraut 2005: 3).

For society, this kind of exclusion harms democracy itself more than the individual that democracy strives to punish (Supreme Court of Israël, *Hilla Alrai v. Minister of Interior et al.*, cited in Eudes 2006: 583).

Beyond these benefits, the democratization of education is a means to stimulate and to develop public opinion.[21] Access to higher education will promote the involvement of people, prisoners or not prisoners, in political affairs (e.g., Hoffman-Lange (2008: 61). Also, training in prison is essential to compensate the higher education failures.

Demanding voting rights for prisoners will not be sufficient. Elite democratic theorists are of the view that the public is only capable of voting and that elites are more supportive of the civil rights and liberties of marginalized and/or unpopular groups (e.g., Clawson and Oxley 2008: 8). Clawson and Oxley (2008: 344) find the right words to explain this theory: 'from this perspective, the goal of democracy is system stability rather than the development of good citizens'. On the contrary, we should give these groups the possibility to change the system.

These persons or groups must be able to enter into different publics they choose themselves and to defend different interests and different norms that perhaps would get into conflict. The unique norm does not exist, nor the normal man.

21 Also to develop a critical thinking about prejudices related to justice (e.g., Cartuyvels and Van Campenhoudt 2004: 42) To see how information must be given, see Indermaur and Hough 2002: 198–214.

Identity is partly a social product (e.g., Goffman 1973) and it is essential that 'the continuity of this relational self implies that the autobiography of the self is continuously re-written in confrontation with the flow of new events that shape one's perception of self, world and others' (Hildebrandt 2006: 8).

But today society and especially those who govern us do not help the self to be re-written or the prisoner to start a new life, as social or economic realities can have a paralysing effect. A utopian idea could be that all different publics could participate all together in the society they all want. But before realizing this ideal, it will probably be necessary to assemble all the 'weak publics' who share common interests in an intermediary public sphere. However that may be, all these different publics would have to be fluent and permeable – and not unique nor homogeneous – to constitute a global public that will enable the different publics to fit together and become stronger.

## References

Blais, A., L. Massicotte and A. Yoshinaka. 2001. Deciding Who Has the Right to Vote: A Comparative Analysis of Elections Laws. *Electoral Studies*, 20, 41–62.

Brenner, S. and N.J. Caste. 2003. Granting the Suffrage to Felons in Prison. *Journal of Social Philosophy*, 34(2), 228–43.

Brugidou, M. 2008. *L'opinion et ses publics. Une approche pragmatiste de l'opinion publique*. Paris: Presses de la Fondation Nationale des Sciences Politiques.

Campbell, D. 2008. Give Prisoners Right to Vote, says UN. *The Guardian* [Online, 19 September]. Available at: http://www.guardian.co.uk/society/2008/sep/19/prisonsandprobation.civilliberties [accessed: 1 April 2009].

Cartuyvels, Y. and L. Van Campenhoudt. 2004. Comment étudier les attentes des citoyens à l'égard de la justice?', in *Public Opinion and the Administration of Justice, Proceedings of the international colloquium held in Leuven, Belgium, 25–27 September 2003*, edited by S. Parmentier, G. Vervaeke, R. Doutrelepont and G. Kellens. Brussels: *Politeia*, 33–49.

Cholbi, M.J. 2002. A Felon's Right to Vote. *Law and Philosophy*, 21(4/5), 543–65.

Clawson, R.A. and Z.M. Oxley. 2008. *Public Opinion. Democratic Ideals, Democratic Practice*. Washington: CQ Press.

De Greef, V. 2007. Et si on vous marquait au fer rouge? ou l'acceptation d'une vision unique de la deviance. *Report on Criminal records for* La Ligue des droits de l'Homme [Online]. Available at: http://www.liguedh.be/web/Comm_Justice_Doc.asp [accessed: 1 April 2009].

Dewey, J. 2003. *Le Public et ses problèmes*. Trad. J. Zask. Pau/Paris: Publications de l'Université de Pau/Farrago/Editions Léo Scheer.

Dhami, M.K. 2005. Prisoner Disenfranchisement Policy: A Threat to Democracy? *Analyses of Social Issues and Public Policy*, 5 (1), 235–47.

Dilts, A.T. Foucault and Felon Disenfranchisement, Draft prepared for presentation at the Annual Meeting of the Midwest Political Science Association, Chicago, Illinois, 20–23 April. Available at: http://www.allacademic.com/meta/p_mla_apa_research_citation/0/9/7/6/9/p97690_index.html [accessed: 25 March 2009].

Eudes, M. 2006. Vers l'abolition des dernières restrictions au droit de vote. Etudes des frontières du corps électoral. *Revue trimestrielle des droits de l'homme*, 67, 575–95.

Fraser, N. (trad. M. Valenta). 2001. Repenser la sphère publique: une contribution à la critique de la démocratie telle qu'elle existe réellement, in *L'opinion publique. Perspectives anglo-saxonnes*, edited by L. Blondiaux, D. Reynie and N. La Balme. Paris: CNRS Editions, coll. Hermès, 31, 109–42.

Garland, D. 2001. *The Culture of Control*. Chicago/Oxford: University of Chicago Press/Oxford University Press.

Goffman, E. 1973. *La mise en scène de la vie quotidienne*. Paris: Les Editions de Minuit.

———. 1975. *Stigmate*. Paris: Les éditions de Minuit.

Habermas, J. 1997. *L'espace public*. Paris: Editions Payot et Rivages.

Hildebrandt, M. 2006. Privacy and Identity, in *Privacy and the Criminal Law*, edited by E. Claes, A. Duff and S. Gutwirth. Antwerp-Oxford: Intersentia, 43–58.

Hoffman-Lange, U. 2008. Studying Elite vs Mass Opinion, in *The Sage Handbook of Public Opinion Research*, edited by W. Donsbach and M.W. Tragott. Los Angeles/London/New Delhi/Singapore: Sage Publications, 53–63.

Indermaur, D. and M. Hough. 2002. Strategies for Changing Public Attitudes to Punishment, in *Changing Attitudes to Punishment*, edited by J. Roberts and M. Hough. Cullompton: Willan Publishing, 198–214.

Jago, R. and J. Marriott. 2007. Citizenship or Civic Death? Extending the Franchise to Convicted Prisoners. *Web Journal of Current Legal Issues* [Online], 5. Available at: http://webjcli.ncl.ac.uk/2007/issue5/jago5.html [accessed: 2 July 2010].

Lardy, H. 2002. Prisoner Disenfranchisement: Constitutional Rights and Wrongs. *Public Law*, 524–46.

Lassalle, J.-Y. 1979. L'application de la loi pénale par les organes de justice, in *La théorie de la stigmatisation et la réalité criminologique*, 18ème Congrès Français de Criminologie (18–20 Oct. 1979, Aix-en-Provence). Aix-en-Provence: Presses universitaires d'Aix-Marseille.

Le Blanc, G. 2007. *Les maladies de l'homme normal*. Paris: Editions Vrin.

Natale, V. 2006. Le droit à des élections libres ou la construction d'un véritable ordre démocratique européen, *Revue trimestrielle des droits de l'homme* 17 (68), 939–72.

Peyre, V. 1979. La déviance et la délinquance dans le contexte de la sociologie de la déviance, déviance secondaire et carrière criminelle, in *La théorie de la stigmatisation et la réalité criminologique*, 18ème Congrès Français de Criminologie (18–20 Oct. 1979, Aix-en-Provence). Aix-en-Provence: Presses universitaires d'Aix-Marseille, 47–60.

Touraut, C. 2005. Etude dynamique des rapports à la citoyenneté d'acteurs incarcérés. *Champ pénal/ Penal field*, nouvelle revue internationale de criminologie [Online], 2. Available at: http://champpenal.revues.org/453 [accessed: 2 July 2010].

Van Zyl, D. and S. Snacken. 2009. *Principles of European Prison Law and Policy*. New York: Oxford University Press.

Zask, J. 2001. Pourquoi un public en démocratie: Dewey versus Lippman, in *L' opinion publique. Perspectives anglo-saxonnes*, edited by L. Blondiaux, D. Reynie and N. La Balme. Paris: CNRS Editions, coll. Hermès, 31, 63–6.

Zask, J. 2003. La politique comme expérimentation, Introduction of the book by J. Dewey: *Le Public et ses problèmes*, Trad. J. Zask. Pau/Paris: Publications de l'Université de Pau/Farrago/Editions Léo Scheer. 7–44.

# Chapter 10
# Subjects to Citizens: 'Native' Enfranchisement in Reconstituting the Imperial Public of the British Empire, c. 1887–1914

Coel Kirkby

At the end of the long nineteenth century, a new federation spanning the seas was very nearly born. Imperial federalists in Britain and her colonies sought to re-found the Empire as a world-state unified by its 'Englishness'. They saw this idea of a 'Greater Britain' as a solution to clamouring democrats at home, surging nationalists in the colonies, and an overburdened navy holding it all together (Bell 2007). This new idea took concrete shape in a series of Colonial (later renamed Imperial) Conferences that brought together the leading statesmen of the colonies to debate Imperial policies and closer political union. They also functioned to constitute an elite body above the British and colonial parliaments to give institutional shape, if ever so briefly, to an imagined Imperial state.

This chapter sketches a constitutional history of the British Empire over three decades that takes seriously the idea of an imagined public sustained by law. By weaving together elite constitutional debates in the London conferences with laws governing the 'native' franchise in two settler colonies, Canada and the Cape, this paper suggests that the latter's increasingly racialized basis undermined the nascent Imperial public and hastened its demise. As the elites introduced the idea of 'Greater Britain' to forge an Imperial council to supersede Westminster and the colonial legislatures, it was reflected at the edges of Empire in colonial laws governing 'natives' with the aim to transform them into civilized subjects imbued with moral virtue and an understanding of property. This ideal was supplanted by the rise of nationalism rooted in new colonial identities that contrasted 'white' with 'black'. When 'white' superseded 'British' or 'English' as the principal marker of inclusion in the public, the 'natives' could, and indeed *must*, be segregated politically and spatially.[1] This excluded 'natives' from both the old Imperial public and the new white publics of the newly-styled Dominions. As colonial leaders began to press their claims as nations against Britain after 1900, there was no space left for natives as equal subjects within the greater, imagined Imperial public.

1 Needless to say, women were entirely excluded from the Imperial public (with the single exception of Queen Victoria).

## Native Subjects of Greater Britain

'I am an Englishman', declared Sir Alexander Campbell, Lieutenant-Governor of Ontario (PP 1887a: 468). His statement neatly captured the feeling of most other Imperial representatives from 35 Crown colonies – from Cyprus to Hong Kong, and Jamaica to the Gambia – attending Queen Victoria's Golden Jubilee in 1887, alongside Members of Parliament, European nobility, and over 50 foreign heads of state. A few days later, after the festivities subsided, Sir Henry Holland, Secretary of State for the Colonies, convened the first Colonial Conference with representatives of the settler colonies.[2] Holland welcomed the delegates by stressing that this conference with the 'Mother Country and the Colonies' was 'of importance in itself' since it was the first time Imperial and colonial leaders had ever met together (PP 1887b: 7–8). To the colonial delegates, Holland's words stressed their novel and hopeful feeling of being Englishmen leading the Empire to a new, more glorious chapter in its progressing history.

Most delegates accepted Charles Dilke's claim in *Greater Britain* that, 'the power of English laws and English principles of government is not merely an English question – its continuance is essential to the freedom of mankind' (1868: 407). Over a decade later, John Seeley (1883) defined 'Greater Britain' as Britain and the settler colonies in his defence of Imperial expansion. This polity was a robust world-state unified by (i) community of race, (ii) community of religion, (iii) community of interest; 'a global political space occupied by millions of people united by a common history and common institutions' (Bell 2007: 110). If, as Seeley's contemporaries agreed, Greater Britain was populated by a single race, two immediate problems arose. First, did this single racial polity comprise a single nation, or multiple ones? Second, how could this imagined polity accommodate its non-English, European peoples, namely the Scots, Welsh, Irish, French-Canadians and Afrikaners?

By expansion England into Greater Britain, the idea of 'Britishness' as a political identity began to supercede, though not replace, that of 'Englishness' (Armitage 2000: 24–60). Unlike its continental neighbours (the Hapsburg Empire excepted), Britain had not created a single state claiming to manifest a national consciousness. At the 1887 conference, delegates used the terms 'England' and 'Britain' interchangeably and often preferred the former when speaking of the Imperial government. Campbell's self-definition as 'English', however, had excluded the two major non-English yet European populations in the settler colonies: the French-Canadians in Canada, and Afrikaners in the Cape and Natal colonies. The only non-English representative present, Jan Hofmeyr, an Afrikaner from the Cape, defined himself, not an Englishman, but a 'British citizen'

2 The 11 colonies in 1887 by seniority were: Newfoundland, Canada, New South Wales, Tasmania, Cape of Good Hope, South Australia, New Zealand, Victoria, Queensland, Western Australia and Natal. By 1914, the colonies were Newfoundland, Canada, New Zealand, Australia and South Africa.

(PP 1887a: 468). This was significant coming from the man who had founded a political party, the *Afrikaner Bond*, to challenge English control of Cape politics. But whatever their other identities, the Conference delegates all saw themselves as belonging to a single, transcendent 'British' polity.

Despite this peculiar usage, colonial elites in the 1880s did not doubt that they belonged to any political entity other than the British Empire. Richard Jebb (1911: p. 12), a later observer, recalled that the colonies, even 'mature' Canada, saw themselves as 'vassals invited to confer with their overlords, who would graciously listen to their representations'. These British elites could exercise their will through their local legislatures; yet, while sometimes pushing against Imperial policy, they continued to accede to the principle, reiterated by the Colonial Secretary, that a colony might have 'to forego some object which it may have desired to attain' for 'the general good of the Empire' (PP 1887: 7). Conscious of their perceived mistakes with the American colonies, Imperial officials trusted colonial elites to use a measure of self-control to restrain themselves in the exercise of their 'self-governing' powers.

The first Colonial Conference of 1887 was also striking for its silences. When the colonial delegates used 'English' or 'British', it was usually in contrast to other European people or Americans. Yet they barely mentioned the nearly 300 million non-European subjects ruled at the time. This silence is explained in part by the late Victorian political convention that the self-governing colonies represented their indigenous peoples through their legislative bodies. In Canada, the *Indian Act* of 1876 provided for the Governor in Council to 'enfranchise' any 'sober and industrious' Indian man at his request. In 1885, the *Electoral Franchise Act* extended the federal vote to all Indians (in the older provinces) who met rural property qualifications. Similarly, the 'coloured' (referring to all non-European) men of the Cape Colony had been enfranchised for several decades, though it was subject to a minimal financial or property bar (Constitutional Ordinance no. 29 1852; Parliamentary Voters' Registration Act 1887). While native men in Canada and the Cape suffered civil 'disabilities' (as they were then called), they could and did participate in the public realm upon proving three key elements of their civilized character: self-control, Christianity and respect for property. In this light, it is not so strange that the colonial delegates could believe that they spoke as representatives for those, admittedly few, 'civilized natives' who had been granted the privilege and responsibility of the franchise.

In 1894, the leaders of the self-governing colonies met again, this time in the Canadian capital of Ottawa. For the Australian and New Zealand delegates, their journey began many weeks earlier aboard a steamer to Vancouver, and then by train across the American continent on the newly completed Canadian Pacific Railway. As Sir Henry de Villiers, then Chief Justice of the Cape Colony, exclaimed: 'It is the first occasion upon which representatives from every part of the British Empire have met together, not in London, but in one of the Colonies', to talk about Imperial matters (PP 1894: 43). If the idea of Greater Britain had not resulted in concrete institutions since 1887, these men still believed that the Empire appeared to be fusing into what Joseph Chamberlain, the future Colonial Secretary, would herald a few years later as, 'Greater Britain beyond the seas', united by, 'the knowledge of the English tongue and the English love of liberty and law' (PP 1897: 6–7). For the new Imperial Federalists, 'sentiment' and not history was the glue of Greater Britain. The ancient 'rights of Englishmen' were no longer the particular heritage of Englishmen, but rather extended to all the English-speaking people of Greater Britain. English race, language, laws and traditions thus served as the 'sentimental' bond of the British Empire.

Stressing 'Englishness' as the sentimental bond of a new Imperial federalism, however, alienated French-Canadian and Afrikaner subjects. The Colonial Conference reports were peppered with statements by speakers trying, with little success, to resolve this tension. Lord Jersey, for instance, referred to Sir Wilfred Laurier, the new Canadian Prime Minister, as, 'a gentleman of the French-speaking race, educated and trained, as he observed, on French systems – who expressed in the warmest terms the loyalty and gratitude to the British Crown of that important portion of the Canadian population' (Jebb 1911: 189). While distinct in race, laws and language, Lord Jersey argued, Laurier was British nonetheless by virtue of his (and his peoples') loyalty to the Crown expressed as a shared sentiment of values. Yet this contradicted Chamberlain's definition based on the English language, institutions and law, which placed non-English federalists like Bourassa and Hofmeyer in a political no-man's land, 'outside the fold but within the Empire' (Jebb 1911: 290).

If French-Canadians and Afrikaners were 'outside the fold', then indigenous populations were even further removed during the 1890s. The virtues of English institutions and laws, transmitted through its tongue, were not beyond the reach of 'civilized natives' until this old idea of integrating individuals gave way to an attempt to isolate and only then gradually advance entire communities. In Canada, new amendments to the *Indian Act* first increased the discretionary powers of the Superintendent-General of Indian Affairs to determine who was, and who was not, an 'Indian,' (1887) and then set the rules for which non-tribal members could live on an Indian reserve (1894). The government then repealed the 1885 franchise law, which effectively disenfranchised all but a tiny handful of Indians (*Franchise Act* 1898; PP 1900). The Cape Parliament also reduced the number of enfranchised natives by first raising the franchise property test (*Franchise and Ballot Act* 1898) and then denied the franchise to all natives in the newly annexed Transkeian territories by defining their property as 'communal' tenure (*Glen Grey Act* 1894). These colonial laws ironed the creases of the Imperial polity by reorienting the franchise along arbitrary racial lines of 'white' and 'native', and thus drastically reducing the number of enfranchised native men.

The colonial premiers next met with Chamberlain, the new Colonial Secretary, in 1897 during Queen Victoria's Diamond Jubilee. They were sworn in on arrival as 'Right Honourable' members of the Privy Council, a largely ceremonial act since the premiers would never participate in the Council. But it symbolised an idea, pushed by the colonial leaders, for recognition as 'nations' equal in status, if not stature, to the United Kingdom (PP 1897: 8). Moreover, the 1897 Conference affirmed the precedent, established in 1894, to pass formal (though non-binding) resolutions by majority vote. This change from consensus to plurality again reinforced the idea that each colony was equal in status to the United Kingdom. As Imperial unification 'evolved', as all delegates then assumed it would, it would increasingly be along the principle of equal 'nations'.

Two years later the Imperial army attacked the 'Boers' of the two independent Afrikaner republics of South African Republic ('Transvaal') and Orange Free State. The two camps first battled a rhetorical war over whether the Transvaal would grant *uitlanders* (mostly English settlers, literally 'outlanders') representation in the *Volksraad* legislature. Jan Hofmeyr, that self-proclaimed 'British citizen', was among the many Cape Afrikaners who travelled to the Transvaal capital of Pretoria to petition for limited voting rights for *uitlanders*. Whether by accident or design, the talks failed and war was declared. Imperial troops immediately suppressed presumed Cape Afrikaner rebels, who became the first European community within the Empire to suffer at the hands of its armed forces since the rebellious subjects in the 13 American colonies over a century earlier. The (all-women) Fawcett Commission report (PP 1902a) documented the 'concentration camps', as they were called, holding 30,000 Afrikaner women and children (and many more natives besides) who would die there in appalling conditions. These camps, organized on racial lines, deeply marked the collective memories of Afrikaners, as well as stirring up the worst fears of the distant French-Canadians.

## Native Citizens of New Dominions

The first post-war Colonial Conference took place in 1902 to coincide with the coronation of Edward VII. In his opening speech to the colonial Premiers, a triumphant Chamberlain lauded colonial 'loyalty' to the British Empire (PP 1902b: 4). He thus sought to calm colonial fears – especially in Canada and the South African colonies – of an Imperial federation united by the threat of force. Instead, if the colonies so chose, they could strengthen the sentimental bond with military, trade and political ties. Chamberlain further exploited this post-war moment by stressing the value of the Imperial armed forces by a classical Greek allusion, exclaiming the 'weary Titan staggers under the too vast orb of its fate. We have borne the burden for many years. We think it is time that our children should assist us' (PP 1902b).

Chamberlain's 'weary Titan' speech was intended, in part, to counter a particular challenge from the Canadian Premier. Before the 1902 Conference, Laurier had to defend his government against an attack by Henri Bourassa, an M.P. from Laurier's own party, who feared the indefinite military and financial obligations of Empire (1903: 38). Bourassa was also troubled that he and his fellow French Canadians were asked to support the Empire in crushing the nascent Afrikaner republics. Laurier reiterated his response to Bourassa in the 1902 conference: 'If you want our aid, call us to your councils.' By his 'weary Titan' retort, Chamberlain implied that the British government would only share the political decision-making powers of Imperial rule when the colonies showed they were ready to share the military and financial burdens. By referring to the colonies as 'children' in his appeal, Chamberlain stressed their subordinate status relative to the Imperial government. This is especially striking since he spoke of the colonies as 'nations' at all other times during the Conference (PP 1902b: 5). Until the colonies took up the burdens of Empire, they would remain subordinate to the 'Mother Country'.

As the idea of nationhood took hold in Imperial debates, colonial bureaucrats were strengthening their control over native populations within their territories. In Canada, a revised *Indian Act* bill (1901: 77) would have given the Department of Indian Affairs sole discretion to decide whether an Indian was qualified for enfranchisement. The South African Native Affairs Commission surveyed the legal situation of 'natives' in these colonies from 1903 to 1905. Their report noted that enfranchised Cape 'natives' represented about 15 percent of the over 135,000 eligible voters in 1903 (PP 1905: 67). In order to avoid the problem of nearly one million potential 'native' voters 'weakening in any way the unchallenged supremacy and authority of the ruling race', the Commission recommended, 'separate voting,' by 'natives' for a fixed number of representatives in the colonial legislatures (PP 1905: 68–9). If adopted, Africans in the Cape would have lost their right to vote directly with European voters for 'white' representatives, and thus been further separated from the public space.

In the early years of the twentieth century, Imperial federalists believed a unified Empire was inevitable given the Afrikaners' defeat, naval hegemony and a global 'electric girdle' of near-instant communication. Alfred Lyttelton, who briefly succeeded Chamberlain as Colonial Secretary before the Liberal's landslide election victory in 1906, supported his predecessor's idea of a permanent 'Imperial Commission' meeting at regular intervals to work out details of past conference resolutions and reach agreement on outstanding issues before the regular meetings of a new, quasi-legislative Imperial Council. It would also seek to 'harmonize' legislation across the Empire. Imperial federalists all advocated some form of institutionalized pan-colonial participation in governing the Empire. Moreover, Alfred Milner, a leading federalist, was busy reconstructing the South African colonies as a unified and loyal Dominion (Worsfold 1913).

When the Colonial Conference convened again in 1907, Alfred Deakin, the Australian Prime Minister, pushed for what he called an 'Imperial Council'. His choice of words was unfortunate, however, since it recalled the unified Imperial government advocated by Lyttelton and the Imperial federalists. Lord Elgin, the new Colonial Secretary (and born in Montreal) did not support the Lyttelton proposal. When Deakin reiterated that he only used the term 'Council' to capture the permanence of the conference without changing its constitution, Laurier interjected that, 'if the basis of the union which now binds the British Empire remains as it is now, a proper and always permanent recognition of the principle that every community knows best what does for itself, then we cannot go wrong'

(PP 1907a: 6). Jameson, the Cape Colony Premier, sought to clarify Deakin's point, and thus reassure Laurier, by distinguishing between the 'Council' as, first, a link between quadrennial conferences, and, second, a link between the governments themselves (thus partly replacing the Colonial Office). While Deakin argued for the body to perform both functions, Jameson limited its role to a secretarial link. But Laurier and Botha, the Transvaal's Premier, along with Lord Elgin (though for quite different reasons), remained implacably against any change that appeared to constitute an Imperial council threatening the principle of self-government.

Almost all Premiers wanted control over a proposed Secretariat to be appointed and paid by themselves, not Britain. This modest cost, they believed, would ensure that it remained free from Colonial Office manipulation. Yet they relented, at Laurier's insistence, and retained the status quo of the Colonial Office acting as conference administrator. Laurier also insisted that decisions of the secretarial body must be based on the consent of all members rather than a majority vote. Lord Elgin had thus succeeded in keeping the administration of the Conference under control of his Colonial Office and in thwarting a new, independent secretariat under the Imperial and colonial control. But Deakin and his allies did wring several important changes to the Conference structure over Lord Elgin's objections. Laurier agreed with them to rename the meetings 'Imperial Conferences' to recognize the equal status of the colonies and the British government. An even greater victory was to have the British Prime Minister sit as president of the Conferences with the Colonial Secretary and colonial Premiers as *ex officio* members (PP 1907a: 11). As Deakin put it, the new arrangements would indicate, 'a meeting of Governments with Governments' (PP 1907a: 9).

Laurier, with Deakin and Ward, then sought to underline their equality in status by introducing the term 'Dominion" to distinguish their 'young nations' from India and the Crown dependencies since 'we have passed the state when the term "Colony" could be applied to Canada, New Zealand, and Australia' (PP 1907c: 81). While Canada had styled itself a 'Dominion' since Confederation in 1867, the term's new use was intended to stress the equal status both among the self-governing colonies, and between them and the British government. Lord Elgin wanted to preserve the Imperial government's superior status, and thus drew a distinction between the United Kingdom and the colonies as a collective. Since all these governments were part of the King's 'Dominions', Elgin suggested distinguishing between the colonial Dominions, and the Dominion of the British Isles and Ireland. The colonial leaders agreed to compromise by referring to the self-governing colonies as, 'the Governments of the self-governing Dominions beyond the seas' (PP 1907c: 89). Laurier then pushed to use 'His Majesty's Government' to refer to each colonial government since they were all the King's governments. But Elgin insisted on reserving that term for the sole use of the British government.

The Conference delegates also discussed a draft naturalization bill then before the UK Parliament. While the colonies wanted a uniform law on naturalization across the Empire, not all leaders were happy with the draft bill (PP 1907a: 26).

Premier Botha, supported by Deakin, objected that, 'naturalization under an Imperial statute of persons of non-European descent should not affect their status under the law in force in any self-government colony' (PP 1907b: 56). In other words, the colonial premiers wanted to distinguish between British subject status and national citizen status. Any individual could become a British subject by adhering to the procedural requirements of the revised Imperial statute, but this would no longer guarantee them equal civil rights across the Empire.[3] By agreeing to these changes, the British government acknowledged a disjunction between 'Imperial' and 'national' political identities in the Empire for the first time.

Two other exchanges highlight this new Imperial-national distinction. In a conference session on commercial relations, Winston Churchill, the Colonial Undersecretary, noted that some colonies wanted to hold votes on duties applied within the Empire. He then threatened that the British government would respond by removing control over duties from the informal authority of the Colonial Office to the less sympathetic authority of Parliament. This move, Churchill argued, would undermine colonial self-government, the 'root principle' of Empire (PP 1907b: 47). This principle was also at stake in a proposed resolution by Deakin to create an Imperial Court of Appeal.[4] This reform would unite the House of Lords, which heard appeals from the UK, and the Judicial Committee of the Privy Council, which heard appeals from the Dominions, Crown colonies and India. Deakin listed several complaints against the Judicial Committee, such as the House of Lords had better judges and gave useful dissenting judgments, but above all he wanted recognition of equal status between Britain and the Dominions. The quest for a single court of final appeal for all the Empire was thus not entirely at odds with a colonial push for greater 'national' self-governing powers. Imperial equality, for the colonial delegates, meant less the idea of equal status as subjects, and more that of self-governing Dominions enjoying equal status with the UK.

In the secret closed door meetings of the 1907 Conference, talks were held between Imperial officials and the Cape, Natal and Transvaal representatives to work out the details of a united African colony. Two years later the British Parliament passed the *South Africa Act* of 1909 creating the Union of South Africa, the newest Dominion. While the constitution limited the franchise to 'European male adults', it also contained a special provision in article 35(1) that no electoral law, 'shall disqualify any person in the province of the Cape of Good Hope [...] by reason of his race or colour only'. The section remained only at the insistence of Cape liberals, like Merriman and even Hofmeyer, and an Imperial government uncomfortable with disenfranchising all non-white subjects.

3 Non-European British subjects had never enjoyed equal civil rights with their fellow European subjects despite rhetoric of equality at each Conference. Nevertheless, they could and did appeal to the principle of equality to press for the civil rights like the franchise (Karatani 2003: 74–6).

4 Chamberlain had first introduced this idea during the 1897 Colonial Conference (*PP* 1907a: 26–8).

The constitution only referred to 'natives' once more, and even then only indirectly. The 'Governor-General in Council' was given power in article 47 over the 'control and administration of native affairs and of matters specially or differentially affecting Asiatics'. With the exception of the 'Cape native clause', the 1909 Act thus constituted a new 'European' (effectively 'white') polity whose very text excluded 'natives'.

In 1911, barely a year after King Edward VII proclaimed the Union, the Premiers of the self-governing colonies met again in London at the inaugural 'Imperial Conference', as the Colonial Conference was renamed. Prime Minister Asquith, speaking as the Conference president, claimed that the British Empire, 'does not draw its unifying and cohesive force solely from identity of race or of language' (PP 1911: 23). The Empire, he argued, had, 'reached in [its] evolution', a unique stage in history, for two reasons:

> The first is the reign of Law: wherever the King's writ runs, it is the symbol and messenger not of an arbitrary authority, but of rights shared by every citizen, and capable of being asserted and made effective by the tribunals of the land. The second is the combination of local autonomy – absolute, unfettered, complete – with loyalty to a common head, co-operation, spontaneous and unforced, for common interests and purposes .... (PP 1911: 22)

For Asquith, the rule of law and self-government formed the 'the political instinct of our race' (PP 1911: 23). By stressing 'local autonomy', he adapted older ideas of Imperial federalism to accommodate the new reality of five self-governing Dominions formed out of 11 dependent colonies two decades earlier. Asquith reflected a subtle change in describing 'Englishness', the 'sentimental' bond of Empire, less in terms of a shared language, laws and institutions, and more in terms of race.

Premier Joseph Ward of New Zealand described the Empire as, 'a family group of free nations, England is the first among the free nations, and, consequently, changes during the last three-quarters of a century, in my opinion, demand that the old relation of "mother to infants" should cease' (PP 1911: 46, 48). Since the Dominions were nations equal in status, not stature, to 'England', Ward suggested first, 'creating parliaments for the different nationalities in the [United] Kingdom', and then an Imperial Parliament in London with proportional representation from each self-governing nation within the Empire. Thus Ward sought to synthesize, and then institutionalize, the older idea of Imperial federation and the newer one of Dominions as equal 'nations'.[5] The other Premiers accepted neither Asquith nor Ward's ideas. Louis Botha, like Laurier and Andrew Fisher, the Australian Premier, was wary of an Imperial Council since he believed that, 'the self-governing powers of the various parts of the Empire must necessarily be encroached upon' (PP 1911: 70). Yet even Botha believed that, in time, such a pan-Imperial body

5 As Laurier reflected later, 'At each imperial conference some colonial leader was put forward by the imperialists to champion their cause' (Skelton 1965: 342).

would evolve out of these Imperial Conferences. Laurier did not see the need to drastically reform the Colonial Office and instead preferred the current practice of informal dealings.

While Ward's idea of an Imperial Parliament proved unpopular, the Dominion leaders were more united in pressing to finally establish a unified Imperial Court of Appeal. Batchelor, the Australian Premier, advanced the main argument for the Court by again stressing the 'anomalous position' of having two courts of final appeal in an Empire of equal nations (PP 1911: 215). Recognizing British official resistance to a single court, Malan, a South African minister, suggested a single court of appeal to be unified in name but bifurcated in practice (PP 1911: 232). The common name would capture the Imperial unity between nations of equal status. By retaining two divisions, however, appeals from the United Kingdom and those from elsewhere in the Empire would remain distinct. Questions of efficiency and pragmatism aside, Malan reminded his fellow delegates that the 'sentimental' bonds of Empire were as important as those of commerce or arms. The Dominions were no longer vassals of the British government, but rather equals united by the King as their common sovereign. The form of Imperial institutions, as much as their practice, needed to express this idea.

A unified Imperial Court of Appeal seemed to imply a unified Imperial legal system. Dr. Findlay argued for Australian and other Dominion judges to sit on the Court, which would help create a 'uniformity of law', resulting in 'closer Imperial unity' (PP 1911: 238). But no Dominion leader supported Imperial uniformity when it came to naturalization laws. Batchelor stated their shared view that, 'every self-governing Dominion must determine for itself whom it admits to its citizenship' (PP 1911: 250). Naturalization, Laurier concurred, 'is one of the incidental powers of sovereignty', limited to a Dominion's territory, and was delegated to the Dominions through the British government's grant of constitutional self-government (PP 1911: 252). Laurier tempered this powerful word by arguing for the principle that once a British subject anywhere, one became a British subject everywhere. Malan agreed and added that, 'you do not necessarily give him all the rights of a British subject in all parts of the Empire' (PP 1911: 255). Whatever restrictions Laurier, Malan and the other Premiers envisioned, it clearly undermined the older idea of British subjects potentially holding equal political rights (often honoured in the breach) throughout the Empire.

The new British man ('*civis Britannicus*', Laurier calls him) was now subject to two 'sovereign' publics: Imperial and Dominion. Malan introduced an idea he called 'segregation', which would bifurcate the national public of each Dominion to assign each race its own exclusive space. If 'white' and 'coloured' were distinct in racial and political status, then their intermingling would only complicate South Africa's delicate project of a 'white' national public uniting English and Afrikaner people. The idea of the equality of Imperial subjects became submersed in the segregated hierarchy – white versus black / coloured / native – of the new national polities in the Dominions.

The Canadian and South African legislatures translated this new national idea into laws segregating their respective races. The *Indian Act* was amended (1911: 46) to permit all companies, municipalities and other authorities with the statutory power necessary to expropriate reserve land needed for 'public works'. The Indian Superintendent could recommend to the Governor-in-Council that he request a judge to determine if it was, 'expedient, having regard to the interests of the public and of the Indians of the bands for whose use the reserve is held', to remove the Indians from their reserve (and, in practice, away from white settlements). This crucial section was the first law to contrast the 'public' interest with the Indians' interest, which implied that Indians were somehow outside the new 'white' public space. When a judge found it 'expedient', he might order the forced removal of Indians from the geographic space of the 'white' polity. The South African Parliament legislated the *Native Lands Act* in 1913 that created a commission to delineate reserves for Africans, as well as prohibiting land sales across the 'colour line'. Fully realized, the law would create 'white' and 'native' spaces, which would be mirrored in segregated political structures. Sol Plaatje (1916: 21) captured the shock of fellow 'natives' in his homeland: 'Awaking on Friday morning, June 20, 1913, the South African Native found himself, not actually a slave, but a pariah in the land of his birth.' Indeed, Plaatje's shock could apply to native men across the Empire who were now outside both the Imperial and national publics.

## Conclusion

In the three decades leading up to 1914, 'natives' in Canada and the Cape Colony were transformed through law from Imperial subjects to national citizens. The Imperial elites constantly negotiated and re-negotiated the constitution of Empire. While the brief rise of Imperial federalism promised to re-constitute the Empire on the lines of an expanded 'English sentiment', it ultimately gave way to colonial nationalisms. The Imperial public occupied by civilized men was then fractured into several colonial publics occupied by white citizens with limited loyalties to the Crown. This changing self-conception in turn informed the colonial bureaucrats who legislated their native populations into a segregated space outside both Imperial and national publics. Tracing the barbarous borders of British Empire enables us to see how law has shaped our inherited publics of today, which take for granted a contingent, imagined line encircling those inside from the barbarians beyond.

## References

*Parliamentary papers*

Colonial Conference, 1894: Report by the Right Hon. the Earl of Jersey, G.C.M.G., on the colonial conference at Ottawa, with the proceedings of the conference and certain correspondence. 1894. (C. 7553), London: HMSO.
Fawcett, M.G. Report on the Concentration Camps in South Africa by the Committee of Ladies appointed by the Secretary of State for War, containing reports on the Camps in Natal, the Orange River Colony, and the Transvaal. 1902a. (Cd. 893), London: HMSO.
Imperial Conference (Minutes of Proceedings). No. 7. (Dominions: Colonies: Conference). 1911. (Cd. 5745), London: HMSO.
Memorandum on Legal Status of British N. American Indians in Canada. 1900. (Cd. 427), London: HMSO.
Minutes of Proceedings of the Colonial Conference. 1907c. (Cd. 3523), London: HMSO.
Papers relating to a Conference between the Secretary of State for the Colonies and the Prime Ministers of Self-Governing Colonies, June to August 1902. 1902b. (Cd. 1299), London: HMSO.
Proceedings of the Colonial Conference, vol. I. 1887a. (C. 5091), London: HMSO.
Proceedings of the Colonial Conference, vol. II. 1887b. (C. 5091-I), London: HMSO.
Proceedings of a conference between the Secretary of State for the colonies and the premiers of the self-governing colonies, at the colonial office, London, June and July 1897. 1897. (C. 8596), London: HMSO.
Published Proceedings and Precis of the Colonial Conference, 15th to 26th April 1907. 1907a. (Cd. 3404), London: HMSO.
Published Proceedings and Precis of the Colonial Conference, 30th April to 14th May 1907b. 1907b. (Cd. 3406), London: HMSO.
Report of the South African Native Affairs Commission. 1903–1905. 1905. (Cd. 2399), London: HMSO.

*Legislation*

Electoral Franchise Act 1885 (c. 40). Ottawa.
Franchise Act 1898 (c. 14). Ottawa.
Franchise Act 1898 (c. 61). Ottawa.
Franchise and Ballot Act 1892 (no. 9). Cape Town.
Glen Grey Act 1894 (no. 25). Cape Town.
Indian Act 1876 (c. 18). Ottawa.
Indian Act 1887 (c. 33). Ottawa.
Indian Act 1894 (c. 32). Ottawa.
Indian Act 1901 (bill). Ottawa.
Indian Act 1911 (c. 14). Ottawa.

Judicial Committee Amendment Act 1908 (c. 8). London.
Native Lands Act 1913 (no. 27). Cape Town.
Parliamentary Voters' Registration Act 1887 (no. 14). Cape Town.
South Africa Act 1909 (c. 9). London.

*Manuscripts*

Armitage, D. 2000. *The Ideological Origins of the British Empire*. Cambridge: Cambridge University Press.

Bell, D. 2007. *The Idea of Greater Britain: Empire and the Future of World Order, 1860–1900*. Princeton: Princeton University Press.

Bourassa, H. 1903. *Les Canadiens-Français et l'Empire Britannique*. Québec: Imp. S.A. Demers.

Chamberlain, J. 1897. *Foreign and Colonial Speeches*. London: Routledge.

Dilke, C.W. 1868. *Greater Britain: A Record of Travel in English-Speaking Countries, During 1866–7*. London: Macmillan.

Herbst, J.F. 1930. The Administration of Native Affairs in South Africa. *African Affairs*, 29, 478–89.

Jebb, R. 1911. *The Imperial Conference: A History and Study*. Vol. I. London: Longmans, Green and Co.

Karatani, R. 2003. *Defining British Citizenship: Empire, Commonwealth and Modern Britain*. London: Frank Cass.

Leslie, J. and R. Macguire. 1979. *The Historical Development of the Indian Act*. 2nd ed. Ottawa: Treaties and Historical Research Centre, Corporate Policy, Department of Indian and Northern Affairs Canada.

Mackenzie, J. 1888. Austral Africa: Extension of British Influence in Trans-colonial Territories, in Proceedings at a Meeting of the London Chamber of Commerce, Assembled on 14 May, 1888, to hear an address from Mr. John Mackenzie (London), 30.

Mantena, K. 2010. *Alibis of Empire: Henry Maine and the Ends of Liberal Imperialism*. Princeton: Princeton University Press.

Milner, A. 1909. *Imperial Unity. Speeches Delivered in Canada in the Autumn of 1908*. London.

Plaatje, S.T. 1916. *Native Life in South Africa, Before and Since the European War and the Boer Rebellion*. London: P.S. King.

Seeley, J.R. 1883. *The Expansion of England: Two Courses in Lectures*. London: Macmillan.

Skelton, O.D. 1965. *The Life and Letters of Sir Wilfred Laurier*. Vol. II. Toronto: McClelland and Stewart.

Worsfold, W.B. 1913. *The Reconstruction of the New Colonies Under Lord Milner*. London: K. Paul, Trench, Trubner.

# PART IV
# Public/Private

# Chapter 11
# The Public/Private Dichotomy and the Unity of Capitalist (Re-)production

Gregor Clunie

Much political and legal theory is animated by an understanding of the public sphere as a space or moment which exists independently of and prior to the private. The 'public' is regarded as containing – or otherwise facilitating the production of – democratically generated imperatives which may be deployed to structure or limit the activities of political and economic actors. According to this account, the 'private' appears as a secondary, derivative realm which is framed and constituted by the public. Neil Walker, in the article which introduces this volume, develops a sophisticated and updated version of this position. The following discussion will appeal to the analytical tools of Marxist political economy in order to investigate the operative relevance of the public/private dichotomy from the perspective of capital accumulation. The latter is in capitalist society a privileged vantage point, since in a system of generalized commodity production and exchange, the imperative of the self-valorization of value systematically subordinates the goal of the satisfaction of human needs. In such a system, capital appears as a totalizing subject, a 'self-moving substance' of individual circuits and the organizing principle of society as a whole (Smith 2009: 180, 189). The argument will proceed with an assessment of the organic interconnection of capitalist production and social reproduction, with the aim of developing the understanding that in accordance with the intensive development of capitalism, the commodity form comes progressively to structure both production and reproduction. It will be further contended that as the commodity form penetrates relations of economic production and concomitant processes of social reproduction, similarly the legal form as its juridical reflex is coherent across the fields of private and public law. From this perspective, it is revealed that all law is fundamentally of a bourgeois character, its deep structure and logic being that of the commodity form, whilst the dichotomy between public and private appears as a first order distinction operating to facilitate and rationalize the reproduction of the social conditions which ground capital accumulation. This analysis is based upon – and will attempt to develop – a particular understanding of the dialectical relation of states and capitals, both domestically and in the world market. This latter, global level is the one at which abstract labour, value, money and capital are ultimately defined (Smith 2009: 190). Consequently, it will be necessary to touch on how forces of competitive accumulation operating in the global economy give rise to a process of uneven and combined development, the latter producing patterns of territoriality which re-structure the relation between states and capitals at the domestic level.

If the validity of this analysis is upheld, there are serious implications for the transformative potential of public law and its strategic operationalization in political projects. If law's inner logic mirrors that which structures the system of generalized commodity production and exchange through which social wealth in capitalist society is produced and distributed, it follows logically that legal mechanisms will be of limited utility in rectifying the social contradictions which emerge out of this process. 'The public' which appears in law will be recognized as formally structured by the logic of commodity exchange, whilst being in substance restrained by its subordination to the maintenance of conditions facilitative of capital accumulation. In addition to these substantive points, this paper seeks to argue for and attempts to demonstrate, albeit imperfectly, a particular methodological approach. It is the view here that Marxist political economy provides the sharpest set of analytical tools with which to interrogate contemporary economic and political processes. In the present connection, the detailed account of capitalist property and production relations supplied by Marx's *Capital* allows the development of an understanding of the interrelation of capitalist production and social reproduction. Marx's project also provides a set of abstract tendencies of capitalist development which form the starting point for an analysis of concrete historical trends. More broadly, the historical materialist method facilitates the situation of the legal within the fluid and contradictory totality of social relations. In this view, law may only be properly understood in the historical context of its material development as a sub-set of social relations unfolding as part of a dialectically integrated whole. Of course, to do justice to this position is extremely difficult, for in rising from the total to the particular it is necessary to survey an extremely wide range of social phenomena (Lefebvre 1976: 68).

## Capitalist Production and Social Reproduction

It is vital to understand the state not as external to and constitutive of economic relations, but rather as an important moment in the very process of commodity production and circulation. The coercive power of the state apparatus is presupposed at every stage of the circulation of capital, from the purchase of labour-power and means of production, through the regulation of the production process to the sale of the commodities produced on the market. Viewed historically, the state serves as a crucial mechanism in the inauguration of the capitalist mode of production, being a coercive lever in the process of social upheaval understood in terms of 'primitive accumulation', a function effected through an extensive and intensive expansion of its repressive apparatus. Subsequently, the state has an enduring role to play in the reproduction of social conditions facilitative of capital accumulation, these conditions being informed by the coercive effects of the operation of the law of value in the world market. At this point, a degree of analytical confusion can arise insofar as the *state* mediates the 'vertical' antagonism between capital and labour, whilst simultaneously forming part of the *state system* which articulates the 'horizontal' competitive interaction of capitals at the international level. The latter process of competitive accumulation gives rise to a tendency towards the dynamic technological and sociological development of the production process, this entailing a continual adjustment of the quantity and quality of the required objective and subjective factors of production. Historically, the state has played a central role in ensuring the availability of sufficient labour-powers possessing the degree of physical and mental dexterity appropriate to the extant level of development of the productive process. The coercive power of the state has also been projected internationally to ensure control over economic territory, facilitating access to raw material inputs and markets for surplus realization. In addition to technological innovation, the process of competitive accumulation also instantiates a tendency towards the concentration and centralization of capital which leads progressively to uneven and combined development in the geography of the global capitalist system. As a result, national economies become oriented towards the fulfilment of particular functions within an international division of labour articulated through the interrelation of heterogeneous regional contexts. Specifically, the antagonism between industry and agriculture is played out at a global level, as advanced industrial economies seek an agrarian 'economic supplement' by the military and financial subjugation of countries with predominantly agrarian economies (Bukharin 2003: 108). In the context of the global dominance of finance capital and its international institutionalization in the interests of dominant state-capital blocs, the economic and geopolitical competitiveness of different state-capital formations informs the policy options that are available to state managers with regard to the regulation of economic production and social reproduction within their territory. At this stage, in order to pre-empt a familiar criticism, it must be recognised that the requirements of capitalist production do not mechanistically generate appropriate social forms, this translation being mediated by a political process through which are articulated conflicting class interests. Indeed, as Kevin Doogan has recognized, the labour market is itself an inefficient mechanism for the transmission of the requirements of production, insofar as it is structured by embedded class relations inflected with historical and cultural contingencies which change within a generational time-frame (Doogan 2009). However, it would be a mistake of a similar magnitude to attempt to understand politics in abstraction from the cleavage between capital and labour, which is not confined nor is confinable within relations of production as narrowly conceived, rather inevitably coming to structure the social and political environment in its totality. This is captured from one perspective by Tony Smith when he contends that 'the choices of state officials … are made within structural constraints systematically rewarding behaviour furthering the accumulation of total social capital and penalizing all other modes of action' (2009: 242). Further, at a more visceral level, the subordination of social and political demands to the imperatives of capitalist economy is especially apparent in the context of the current global financial and economic crisis.

Society exists as an ensemble of social relations through which is articulated a process of economic production, this presupposing and interpenetrating with relations of social reproduction. In the form of society characterized by generalized commodity production, i.e., capitalist society, social wealth appears as an immense collection of commodities (Marx 1990: 125), while social relations assume the form of exchange relations between commodity owners. The commodity form thus comes to structure not only relations of production as narrowly conceived, but also concomitant processes of social reproduction. The continuation of surplus value production, and consequently of capital accumulation (its reproduction on an expanded scale), requires the availability of an adequate stock of labour-powers possessing the degree of physical and mental skill and dexterity appropriate to the level of technological development of the production process. Recalling the analysis of Marx in volume two of *Capital*, the circuit of money capital, which most starkly reveals the valorization of value, money-making and accumulation as the driving motive of capitalist production, may be represented by the formula M–C$<^{L}_{mp}$..P..C'–M'. Here, *M* is capital value in the functional form of money capital, *C* represents value wrapped in the material shell of the commodity, *L* and *mp* stand for labour power and means of production – the subjective and objective factors of the production process –, the sum of the two forming productive capital *P*. The circuit of money capital interacts with the individual consumption of the worker insofar as M–L is for her L–M (or C–M), the first phase of the circulation which mediates her consumption: L–M–C, where C is the means of subsistence (Marx 1992: chapters 1–4). The second phase, M–C of the circuit by which the worker reproduces herself is thus not contained within the circuit describing the motion of the individual industrial capital in relation to which her labour is employed. However, such consumption, insofar as it is essential to her physical regeneration and consequently her existence on the market as exploitable material for the capitalist, is an essential precondition for even the simple reproduction of that capital – indeed its very existence *as capital*, understood as value in motion. Further and in logical consequence, the motion of the sum of individual capitals, or total social capital is conditional upon the reproduction of labour powers in general. From the perspective of capital accumulation, social reproduction appears as an evanescent (or fractally related) process accounting for the renewal of the production input *L*.

The availability of adequate stocks of labour is not the only precondition for capital accumulation, as is immediately evident from the summary analysis above. Indeed, labour-power (*L*) becomes capital in the hands of the buyer only as a component part of productive capital (*P*). Thus, the production process requires that the capitalist has access to means of production (*mp)* – comprising raw materials, energy, machines, buildings, etc., – of an appropriate nature and quantity to facilitate the production of surplus value through the consumption of labour-power. The means of production will often themselves be products of the movement of other individual capitals, revealing the intertwinement of the metamorphoses of individual capitals in the totality of social production (Marx 1992: 178). Furthermore, the entire enterprise will be futile if there exists not the market for the sale of the commodities produced by the capitalist, this exchange being the mechanism for the realization of the value embodied therein. In the exposition of these basic prerequisites for capitalist production, we may recognize that they each presuppose a number of other social and environmental conditions. For instance, the availability of labour-powers depends on the wage-labour relation being the most convenient way for the worker to gain access to the means of subsistence, while the realization of surplus value through the sale of the commodities produced presupposes adequate protection against the expropriation of such commodities by way other than exchange, i.e., theft.

The social conditions facilitative of capital accumulation are, from a historical perspective, quite contingent. One need only recall the tragic ordeal of the earnest entrepreneur Mr Peel to recognize the difficulties of carrying on capitalist production in the absence of the political and legal environment necessary to institute and reproduce the requisite relations of production (Marx 1990: 931–3). The social foundations for the interaction in the marketplace of capital and labour, figures which arise neither naturally nor a-historically, are lain by a process of 'primitive accumulation'. This entails the forcible expropriation of the mass of the population from the means of production and their created dependency upon money wages. While primitive accumulation follows different modalities and chronologies in different countries, it is possible – using the classic example of the agricultural revolution in England – to identify as central dynamics the creation of new forms of property rights, the extinguishment of customary rights and perquisites, the legal regulation of the wage-labour relation and a restructuring of welfare provision (Marx 1990, Overton 1996, Hobsbawm 1962, Thompson 1975, 1991, Doogan 2009). The transition from feudal to capitalist modes of production is facilitated by the operation of the state, as the concentrated and organized force of society. Thus, state power is employed 'to hasten, as in a hothouse, the process of transformation of the feudal mode of production into the capitalist mode, and to shorten the transition' (Marx 1990: 915–16). In the English case, the enclosure of six million acres of common land between 1760–1830, a substantial factor in the created dependency of the agricultural population upon money wages, was officially sanctioned by acts of Parliament – something Marx has described as a 'parliamentary coup d'état' (Marx 1990: 886). Of course, this is conditional upon a political process by which the emerging bourgeoisie progressively enlists the state apparatus in its service, whilst also necessitating an intensive and extensive transformation of that apparatus as appropriate to the social tasks it is required to undertake. In England, this rebalancing of political forces was prefigured by the royal defeat occasioned by the English Revolution of 1640–1660 and the consolidation of that defeat in the Glorious Revolution of 1688 (Stone 1985, Hill 1991). The extension and deployment of the state's repressive apparatus is exemplified by the experience of the Black Act of 1723, which created 50 new capital offences and 'signalled the onset of the flood-tide of eighteenth-century retributive justice'

(Thompson 1975: 206, 223). The Black Act, amended by subsequent enactments and evolving through a process of creeping judicial interpretation, became a malleable instrument of repression used to punish by example those displaying malice to the gentry and thereby strengthened the resources of stability in a time of popular disaffection. Moreover, the 1723 Act must be seen as part of a broader process whereby the independent livelihoods of the rural poor, based upon the survival of pre-capitalist use-rights over land, were eroded by legal (as well as economic) forces. As Edward Thompson remarks, the foresters were seeing 'the very roof beams which housed their practical economy..being eaten away' as successive legal decisions 'signalled that lawyers had become converted to the notions of absolute property ownership, and that … the law abhorred the messy complexities of use-right' (Thompson 1975: 240–41). Further, the institution of the labour market required more than created dependency through a redefinition of traditional rights and perquisites as criminal offences, it being necessary to domesticate the worker into the regime of wage-labour, and to regulate the conditions of labour – including such matters as the length of the working day and the level of wages – in such a manner as to facilitate capital accumulation. Thus it is possible to witness in the English case a succession of enactments which regulated wage-labour in such a manner as to create and reproduce conditions of exploitation, something recognized by Adam Smith in his observation that 'Whenever the legislature attempts to regulate the differences between masters and their workmen, its counsellors are always the masters' (Smith 1814: 142). One of the most notable statutes is the Master and Servant Law of 1823, which instituted a profound asymmetry in the rights and obligations of employers and workers, providing for instance that a breach of contract on the part of a master constituted a civil offence, while the violation of an agreement by an employee was a criminal offence subject to retribution of up to three months imprisonment with hard labour. There is evidence to suggest that some 10,000 prosecutions per year occurred under the 1823 Act (Doogan 2009: 106).

Once the rule of capital has been established, the state plays an enduring role in the institution and reproduction of the social conditions necessary for accumulation. While this entails a variety of activities, we will maintain our focus on the reproduction of labour-powers. The latter, being directly related to the welfare of the population and falling within the ambit of the 'public' sector as opposed to the 'private' economy within the ontological framework of the liberal dichotomy, is especially relevant in our present connection. We can through historical analysis chart the continual evolution of state functions and responsibilities in response to the productive requirements of the developing forces of production (Doogan 2009: 110). At this point it is crucial to recall that the driving force behind the technological development of the production process is the coercive pressure of competitive accumulation. Given that the value of a commodity is based upon the socially necessary labour time required to produce it, the innovating capitalist who increases productivity through the introduction of new machinery or a revised social organization of labour produces commodities with a social value higher than their individual value. She thus secures an ephemeral competitive advantage, since she may increase her profit margin and/or undercut her competitors by selling the commodities produced below their social value. Since the magnitude of the surplus realized is a factor determining the size of the fund available for reinvestment in production on an expanded scale, competing capitalists are then forced to similarly increase the productivity of their own enterprises, lest they be faced with a diminishing rate of profit, shrinking consumer bases and ultimately the threat of being forced out of business. The cumulative effect of the process is to generalize the gains in productivity made by the first capitalist, pulling the social value of her commodities down to their individual value, whilst altering the typical value ratio between constant capital (means of production) and variable capital (labour power) in the sector – a tendency Marx referred to as a rising 'organic composition' of capital. The technological dynamism entailed by this process of competitive accumulation and the consequent revision of the conditions of labour require a continual adaption of the physical and intellectual abilities of labour powers. While this may be facilitated to some degree by individual capitals themselves, their limited sectoral and temporal outlooks often limit the extent to which they may take actions which are rational from the perspective of total social capital. For example, the industrial practices in Britain of the late eighteenth and early nineteenth centuries led to the premature exhaustion and untimely death of factory workers, threatening to undermine the reproduction of labour-powers at the present level of productivity. In this context, the factory legislation of 1853–1860, which achieved a remarkable physical and moral regeneration of labour-powers (Marx 1990: 406–8) could be understood as the state acting to mediate the myopic actions of individual capitals in the interests of total social capital. Indeed, as Doogan has commented, the period from the early 1830s to the 1880s saw the emergence of a body of legislation marking a shift from orthodox economic liberalism towards social and national protectionism, the government increasingly intervening to mitigate the worst social effects of nascent industrial capitalism. Thus the state 'assumed overall responsibility for the reproduction of the next generation of labour' (Doogan 2009: 108).

The physical maintenance of the workforce is crucial not only to ensure the future supply of waged labour necessary to facilitate reproduction of capital on an expanded scale, but may also be of import in relation to the military articulation of a state's imperialist pretensions, particularly where the extant military paradigm is especially labour-intensive. Thus, following the experiences of the Boer War and First World War, changes in government healthcare policy significantly improved levels of medical fitness by the beginning of World War II (Doogan 2009: 110, Timmins 1996). Here, then, one can witness the intersection of the State's responsibilities in reproducing in a domestic context social conditions facilitative of capitalist production and the labour implications of the military action required internationally to gain and maintain control over economic territory. Moving from healthcare to education, the industrial revolution necessitated a dramatic turnaround in the responsibilities of the state at all levels, demonstrated by the fact that while in 1818 only 7 per cent of children attended day school, by 1880 schooling had been made compulsory for all five- to ten-year-olds. Further, following the emergence of a skills gap between the British workforce and those of other Western European countries including Germany, state funding for higher education was introduced (Doogan 2009, 109–10).

A period of particular import in relation to the development of state responsibility for social reproduction is that of the 'golden age' of Western capitalism, beginning in the aftermath of the Second World War and continuing until the 1960s in the US and the 1970s in Western Europe and Japan (Harman 2009). This was a period of economic growth of unprecedented longevity and consistency, something explicable at least in part by the mass devaluation of capital effected by the destruction of the war and the operation of the 'permanent arms economy', the latter functioning to offset the rising organic composition of capital (Harman 2009: chapter 7, Callinicos 2010, Kidron 1970). An economic environment characterized by a high rate of profit and the relative productivity of capital in the US and Western Europe provided the necessary objective conditions for concessions to labour in the form of welfare policies and social security schemes which together represented a 'socialization' of labour costs. Of course, these developments were not automatic, being rather driven by the subjective articulation of the demands of labour in a favourable context of historically low levels of unemployment and at times acute labour shortage (Harman 2009: 172–5). In order to perform the function of nourishing the suddenly finite number of labour-powers in a context of scarcity driven by expanding production, the state apparatus underwent a profound reorganization in its re-configuration as the 'welfare' state. Unsurprisingly, this period also marked the high point of the reformist political and ideological project of social democracy, which sought in contradistinction to its demographically and geographically limited material basis, to provide a universal solution to the social impact of capitalist economy. The boom, however, did not continue beyond 1973, when the crisis which erupted in the advanced capitalist countries and a large part of the third world marked the return of traditional economic cycles of boom and bust. Chris Harman seeks to understand the end of the golden age in terms of the victory of the dynamic of market competition over that of inter-imperialist military competition. The uneven global distribution of arms expenditure allowed economies with relatively low levels of expenditure to invest proportionately more in industry and achieve faster rates of growth than the militarized economies of the US, Russia and (to a lesser degree) the UK and France. These latter countries were consequently forced to scale back their military expenditure in view of economic competition from the increasingly productive economies of Japan and Germany. In this way, the permanent arms economy ceased to operate as an escape valve for the accumulating pressure of the global economy (Harman 2009: 191–201).

Following the crises of the 70s, there emerged the political and economic project of neo-liberalism which, driven by the 'Dollar-Wall Street Regime', sought to promote policies favourable to the interests of US investment banks and transnational corporations. This relied on US dominance of the international financial architecture and was prefigured by the harsh monetary discipline imposed on the world economy by the 'Volcker shock' of 1979 (Callinicos 2009: 191, Gowan 1999). The social impact of these developments has been experienced extremely unevenly, with processes of welfare re-commodification and retrenchment proceeding with widely varying speed and intensity in different regional contexts. Thus, welfare regimes in Western Europe were seen to be relatively resilient (Doogan 2009: 119–22), whilst in many peripheral economies there were experienced profound social changes which often appeared as wanton destruction. Crucial to understanding the complexities of the neoliberal project is to recognize that it is driven by a bi-linear attempt to redistribute the costs of the emergent crisis: firstly from capital to labour and secondly; from the powerful state-capital formations comprising the core of the global economy to the weaker peripheral economies. With regard to the latter, the international financial system can be seen as the transmission mechanism by which the effects of a crisis of over-accumulation and profitability are spatially displaced and diffused from the core to the periphery, like the concentric rippling of a puddle in the rain. Further, the resilience of welfare provision in one form or another demonstrates that such services do not represent pure loss for capital, but are rather indispensible to the extraction of surplus-value insofar as the latter is dependent upon the reproduction of labour-powers. To bring our historiography up to date, the emergence from behind the veil of financialization of a chronic crisis of over-accumulation and profitability in the global financial and economic crisis precipitated by the US sub-prime mortgage crash of 2008 has generated a generalized politics of 'austerity'. This entails a policy package which seeks to redistribute to labour the costs of its own reproduction and to increase the rate of exploitation by disciplining the wage-labour relation through strategic retrenchment of welfare provision. Moreover, in a UK context David Cameron's 'big society' appears little more than a thinly veiled attempt to squeeze increasing amounts of unpaid labour from the pores of society, further reducing the proportion of the costs of social reproduction borne by capital. Once again, we must be careful to avoid implementing a crudely economic-functionalist understanding of state action, since the specific reforms mentioned must be recognized as the outcome of a process of political contestation. However, logically, the range of policy options available to the capitalist state are informed by the necessity of maintaining social conditions facilitative of capital accumulation, whilst the environment in which political contestation occurs is profoundly structured by the capital relation.

The crucial point which must emerge from this discussion is that the process of capitalist production presupposes and is interconnected with processes of social reproduction. The continuation of capital accumulation is dependent upon the reproduction of labour powers at a level of productivity informed in different local contexts by the international division of social labour. The global organization of capitalist production into a plurality of different capitals which are structurally connected to states also gives rise to a competitive dynamic which requires that the organization of social reproduction be rational and cost-effective from the perspective of surplus-value generation. For instance, if a capital in state A is able to access labour-powers of a particular productivity at a price *to it* which is below that at which labour-powers may be obtained in state B, then the state A-based capital will have a competitive advantage over capitals based in state B. In this regard, premiums extracted from capital by taxation to cover costs of reproduction – such as National Insurance in the UK – can be considered as augmenting expenditure on wages, or variable capital (v), thus impacting the rate of exploitation: s/v, where *s* represents surplus value. However, it would be a mistake to infer from this that the interests of total social capital necessarily lie in a neoliberal agenda entailing the reduction of corporate taxation to a minimum and the privatization of public services, since the latter may detrimentally affect general profit rates by another mechanism. While the privatization of healthcare and educational provision may hold prospects of substantial profits for capitals operating in relevant sectors, such enterprises do not lend themselves to decentralized organization, such that there will exist a tendency for these fields to become quickly dominated by a small number of very large capitals. The latter may ultimately use their monopoly power to effect a redistribution of surplus from other sectors, impacting upon the general rate of profit and the ability of capitals elsewhere in the economy to compete internationally. By way of example, it is certainly open to argument that the premiums extracted by healthcare providers in the US erect a ceiling for the rate of exploitation for industrial capital, under which conditions for instance, the Detriot-based General Motors may be out-competed by Japanese automobile manufacture. Ultimately, the centralization and rationalization of social reproduction entailed by its administration by the state apparatus may in certain circumstances represent the most efficient mode from the perspective of total social capital. Further, it may be contended that the public/private dichotomy grounds the organizational framework within which public bodies may facilitate the reproduction of social conditions which, despite being essential to the valorization circuits of individual capitals, lie outwith both such circuits and the organizational capacities of the individual capitals concerned.

Beyond the requirements that labour-powers be reproduced with the requisite skills determined by the spatial and temporal location of production and that such reproduction is effected in a manner that facilitates the maintenance of an internationally competitive rate of exploitation, there remain of course a multitude of organizational methods by which labour could be appropriately reproduced. These economic considerations thus form only a framework within which there rages continual political contestation over the financing and delivery of social services, key issues being the distribution of cost between surplus value (s) and variable capital (v) and the extent to which provision is linked directly to employment. Note however that the interconnection between capitalist production and social reproduction under capital is not exhausted by the requirements of the former operating as a substantive limit to the organization of the latter. Additionally, the *form* of social relation which accompanies capitalist production, i.e., the relation of commodity exchange, comes inevitably to profoundly structure reproductive processes as it structures social relations in their entirety.

## The Commodity-Form Theory of Law and the Public/Private Dichotomy

The bourgeois epoch is not the first in which society has been fragmented into classes, the consumption of the ruling class being fuelled by the extraction of surplus labour from a subordinate social grouping. However, under capitalism such exploitation assumes a specific form, surplus labour appearing as surplus *value* generated by the consumption of labour-power mediated by the mechanism of the wage-labour relation. In contrast to economic systems founded upon enslavement or indenture of a direct, personal nature, the wage-labourer remains formally free insofar as she sells not herself, but her capacity to labour for a limited period, while the person of her employer is subject to periodic change. Coercion, as the pivot between economics and politics, also undergoes a reorganization under capitalism, insofar as the use of force is progressively divested from the person directly implicated in the extraction of surplus labour, such power being congealed instead in the body of an institutionalized collective public authority. Capitalist society might be described then as class society *par excellence* insofar as labour is exploited *as a class* by capital organized collectively and operating coercively through the mechanism of constituted public authority. This is of course not to make a crude or conspiratorial assessment of the influence of the agency of capital over parliamentary politics, but rather to recognize that under capitalism, society is *capitalist* society inasmuch as social relations in their totality are structured by the logics of commodity production and exchange and subordinated in substance to the maintenance of this specific form of organization of social production.

Whilst the most fundamental form of regulation of social relations in capitalist society is economic, being grounded in the coercive effects of a class-inflected organization of the means of production, this is supported by regulatory mechanisms of a political and legal nature. The latter attains in bourgeois society a particular significance, the legal form here achieving its most universal and consummate articulation. For Pashukanis this is no mere coincidence, since the deep grammar of the legal form, entailing a specific *legal* modulation of social relations, forms a logical unity with the relations of commodity production and exchange which characterize capitalist society. Now, of course, commodities were produced in pre-capitalist societies, yet it is only in bourgeois society that commodity production becomes *generalized* – that use-values are increasingly produced primarily for exchange, and progressively, the entirety of social wealth passes through the mechanism of commodity circulation (Marx 1990). It is under these conditions that the legal form obtains universal significance and legal ideology can obtain a firm grip on human consciousness. Given that the core of Pashukanis's jurisprudence is laid out in his *Law and Marxism* (1983) and has been usefully interpreted by Arthur (1977) and Miéville (2006) amongst others, here it will be necessary only to highlight a few important points which will facilitate progress in our present connection. Pashukanis argued that there is an 'indissoluble internal connection' between the categories of the economy based on the commodity and on money, and the legal form itself. This connection is borne out by the category of the legal subject, which can be regarded as 'the indispensible and unavoidable complement of the commodity'. The legal subject, as the 'abstract bearer of all possible legal claims', can be compared directly with, and indeed recognized as the juridical reflection of, the commodity owner, as an 'abstract, impersonal subject of rights in things' (Pashukanis 1983: 14, 42). The definition and attribution of legal personality, being the mechanism by which individuals are represented or instantiated in the legal process is a crucial aspect of the broader process of juridification. The latter can be understood in terms of the assimilation of social relations to a set of standard forms, providing for the observation and regulation of those relations by specified corporate social organizations which are empowered to modulate those relations by the deployment of defined coercive actions. The place to begin in attempting to understand the consequences of such regulation for social development is an analysis of the manner in which those forms of modulation facilitate the production and distribution of use-values and, by extension whether they presuppose a particular method of effecting the latter.

The juridical *persona* is a mask which constitutes the legal subject, simultaneously signifying her existence and mystifying the contours of the face beneath. One of the primary logics which informs the operation of legal personality is abstraction, insofar as the complex material and social context which grounds the relation between individuals is reduced to the rational interaction of legal persons who are considered (from the perspective of the legal) to be free and equal. Whilst the legal person is in general an abstract bearer of subjective rights, crucially in the context of the present discussion there do exist certain operative distinctions between legal persons, not least that which differentiates 'public' and 'private' persons. Organizations designated as 'public' are, in general terms, legally constituted corporate social entities which emerge from constitutionally structured political processes, charged with the performance of more or less loosely defined 'public' functions. They can be thus seen as mediating the actions of private persons in such a manner that their individual, narrowly focused actions can be accommodated to the maintenance of the operative socio-economic order, the latter grounding the power and maintenance of the state apparatus. The distinction between public and private persons grounds the derivative dichotomy between public and private law, the two spheres being distinguished primarily by the extent to which the interests of legally constituted 'public' persons are implicated – such that they are permitted certain freedoms of action – within that realm. Upon a detailed analysis, the public/private boundary is revealed as porous, whilst it may also be seen to shift in location when mapped across different legal disciplines, which are themselves internally and inconsistently demarcated. Similarly, the categories of 'public' and 'private' personality are not watertight, there being many organizations which straddle the boundary or are otherwise difficult to locate relative to it. This volume in part seeks to make sense of the operation of the notion of 'the public' across the legal system as a whole.

This argument would contend that a particularly privileged perspective from which to understand the operation of the legal public/private dichotomy is the perspective of capital accumulation, informed by the dialectic of state and world market in the context of the coercive operation of the law of value in the global economy. Whilst this is not the only manner in which the public/private divide can be cognized, it is of particular resonance given that in a system of generalized commodity production and exchange, the imperative of the self-valorization of value systematically subordinates the goal of the satisfaction of human needs. Capitalism is driven by accumulation for accumulation's sake, production for production's sake, whilst social reproduction assumes organizational and procedural forms which are oriented towards the achievement of optimal conditions for accumulation. In this regard it is useful to recall Tony Smith's criticism of the 'humanist social ontology' underlying much political economy when he asserts that it 'fails to grasp the inversion whereby humanly created social forms generate an inhuman subject whose end ('self-valorization') comes to have precedence over human ends' (Smith 2009: 178). A similar critique could apply to constitutional and administrative law scholarship which presupposes that the institutional and procedural articulation of political authority is primarily informed by humanist-functional imperatives. Drawing again from Smith, it might be said that constitutional law scholarship 'fail[s] to comprehend how the property and production relations of capitalism define a social order in which valorization, not human flourishing, is the ultimate end of social life'. Under a system of generalized commodity production, capital appears as a totalizing subject, a 'self-moving substance' of individual circuits and the organizing principle of society as a whole (Smith 2009: 180, 189). This entails the real (as opposed to formal) subsumption of labour by capital, effecting a restructure not only of the activities of labour within the narrow spatiality and temporality of employment, but of the existence and reproduction of labour in its entirety. The 'capital fetishism' which inevitably accompanies this process of inversion veils the subordination of human needs to valorization, transforming capital from a contingent, evanescent product of a particular organization of property and production relations into the driving force behind social development and the satisfaction of human wants. Capital is thus understood not as congealed past labour parasitically exploiting the creative energies of living social labour, but as the well-spring of social wealth and productive human endeavour. When the recognition that in a capitalist social order valorization becomes the immanent end of social interaction is coupled with an understanding that the legal form unfolds in harmony with the development of generalized commodity production, it is possible to begin to understand that the legal system in its entirety is deeply structured by the logic of capitalist accumulation. In this context, the public/private dichotomy is revealed as a first order distinction which facilitates and rationalizes the development of organizational forms which support accumulation in a context of global competition. Specifically, as we have discussed in some detail here, it allows for the rational and efficient organization of social reproduction on a large scale.

The public/private divide operates to sever the fluid and contradictory totality of social relations into two spheres within which legally constituted 'public' organizations are given different degrees of influence and the legal regulation of social relations differs in quality and intensity. Far from being an unmarked space in which collectively and democratically generated imperatives are imposed upon a bounded (and derivative) private realm, the public sphere rather displays the birthmarks of its origin in the genesis of the public/private dichotomy, being deeply structured by the logic of the commodity form. This may appear counter-intuitive to the legal thinker who regards legal relations as deriving from overarching legal norms and civil society as a product of the will of an institutionally-grounded sovereign power. Following Pashukanis, it is necessary to turn these conceptions on their head, recognizing that the norm cannot exist but in the concrete multiplicity of legal relations, these being the fabric through which the norm is woven, whilst appreciating that the state, far from producing civil society, rather grows out of it, whilst the latter in turn rests upon a foundation of economic relations (Pashukanis 1983: 85–8).

Given an historically grounded understanding of the development of the legal form which recognizes its intertwinement with the generalization of commodity production and exchange, the logical unity of private and public law follows necessarily. If in capitalist society valorization becomes the overriding goal in view of which social relations are structured, whilst valorization requires concrete labour employed in a particular locality to pass the test of social utility overseen by the operation of the law of value in the world market, then public bodies must act in such a way as to facilitate the maintenance of a rate of exploitation which is internationally competitive. In this context, it would appear that the burden of proof shifts to representatives of those schools of thought which insist upon a substantive independence of the public sphere to show how the latter maintains its insulation from the central dynamics of capital accumulation. This being said, it will be useful here to invoke some evidence to reinforce this paper's analytically generated conclusion regarding the logical unity of private and public law. Firstly, the structural cohesion of private and public law is apparent at a fairly superficial institutional and procedural level. In the UK, the superior civil courts exercise jurisdiction over all justiciable disputes, irrespective of whether they concern private citizens or public authorities. Further, in England the practice is to avoid a hard and fast demarcation between public and private law in the determination of procedural matters, whilst in Scotland the structure of remedies does not require a distinction to be drawn between public and private law (*Stair Memorial Encyclopaedia*, Administrative Law Reissue, section 5). Public bodies are a subspecies of a broader category of legal persons, which Pashukanis has taught the field to understand as the juridical reflex of the commodity owner. Constancy of form is also apparent at a basic doctrinal level, the rule of law requiring equality before the law of all legal persons whether designated as 'public' or 'private', while logics of private interaction inform theoretical understandings of constitutional and administrative regimes; note for instance the ubiquity of the 'social contract' metaphor. More profoundly, the centrality of human rights discourse and the institutionalization of the latter in regional and international regimes reflects a structuring of the public sphere and articulation of questions of the distribution of social wealth in accordance with the conflict of egoistically generated private interests. This structural framing of profound political questions already presupposes the type of 'asocial sociality' formed by the interaction of dissociated private producers (Smith 2009). Thus, the citizen is in a position formally analogous to that of the commodity owner, her bundle of rights against a legally constituted public authority being the mirror of the owner's rights in her commodity in respect to all those who may make competing claims. The structural rigidity of public law is further revealed in contexts which do not lend themselves comfortably to the form of regulation presupposed by this structure. For instance, anti-discrimination legislation, as a form of public, administrative law approaches the problem of the inequality of remuneration received by male and female workers by treating women as a series of abstract individuals, each possessing the formal right to equal pay. This attempt to formalize the marginalized group as equal is founded upon the 'subsumption of a particular category – women – into a formal, abstract, juridical one, and to *insist upon its abstract equality*' (Miéville 2006: 111). Insofar as this form of administration displays a fidelity to the legal form by attempting to emulate or approximate the latter's abstraction, it will necessarily be limited in its substantive efficacy.

One criticism of the account developed here might be that it fails to recognize that the legal subjects which animate public law are not merely isolated individuals, but corporate entities such as associations, trades unions, utilities and public corporations. However, as China Miéville has convincingly argued, such a shift in legal subjectivity does not represent a change in the basic ontological structure of law, but rather 'a shift in the atoms of the juridical relationship *on the basis of the commodity relationship under changing conditions of mass industrialisation and the commodification of labour-power itself*'. Just as Marx recognized that the legalization of capital and labour as collectives results from the very nature of labour-power as a commodity, the developments in legal subjectivity in accordance with the changing conditions of late capitalism must be understood as a development of the legal form on the basis of that form itself (Miéville 2006: 101–13). Indeed, as Tony Smith has recognized, the definition of what constitutes a corporate 'person' and the forms of legally permissible interactions which can be undertaken by those persons must be regularly revised by state judicial apparatuses in light of the shifting organizational forms adopted by capital as a result of the tendencies towards concentration and centralization, especially in a global context where these trends are articulated in cross-border mergers and acquisitions, joint ventures and subcontracting arrangements (Smith 2009: 237). Similarly, public institutions charged with the maintenance of social conditions facilitative of capital accumulation may assume varying organizational forms in different economic and political contexts. These adaptations are driven by factors including the tendency for the commodification of new areas of social life ('accumulation by dispossession') to increase in importance in the context of crises of over-accumulation in other sectors, and the necessity for states to intervene in research and development programmes and networks of knowledge production in order to create 'innovation systems' in sectors with potentially high rates of profitability. The changing organizational forms assumed by capital emerge out of the commodity form as the shifts in legal subjectivity represent an evolution of the legal form on the basis of that form itself.

## 'The Public in Law'

It has been attempted to illustrate the interpenetration of relations of production and reproduction in capitalist society, arguing that the commodity form comes to structure the emergent totality. This discussion has further argued that this unity is mirrored by the formal coherence of public and private law, the distinction between the two forming the juridical framework for the establishment of organizational forms which both maintain the existence of capital as a plurality of capitals and provide for the rational reproduction of the social conditions of accumulation. Consequently, the space provided by the 'public' in law is revealed as formally structured by the logic of commodity exchange, whilst being in substance restrained by its subordination to the maintenance of conditions facilitative of capital accumulation. Public and private law form the poles of a first-order distinction which is subsumed within the 'legal' as a formally coherent mother category, the logic of which is the logic of the commodity form. These conclusions place in a different perspective Neil Walker's aim of establishing the second-order 'publicness' of law, whilst revealing the futility of the broader ideological tug-of-war between the civilists and publicists for mastery over the jurisprudential universe. This analysis has established not the second-order 'publicness' of law, but rather a second-order *bourgeois*ness. It is possible to thus conclude either that Walker is wrong, or perhaps more frighteningly, that he is *right*. For as has been discovered, in a profound sense, the subject which animates capitalist society is not the human being, but capital itself, whilst the corresponding public is not a corporate association of human beings, but total social capital. The only manner in which it is possible to reverse the dialectical inversion by which the human being was supplanted by an alien pseudo-subject as the organizing principle of society as a whole is by effecting a profound restructuring of the mode by which society produces its means of subsistence, such that it ceases to simultaneously reproduce the antagonistically related estates of capital and labour. Legal mechanisms are not sufficient to procure such a revolutionary transformation, insofar as 'it is totally impossible to reconstitute society on the basis of what is merely an embellished shadow of it' (Marx 2000: 215). This is not to underestimate the importance of the legal reforms which in limited historical and geographical contexts have assuaged some of the worst social consequences of capitalist development. Rather it is to recognize that the momentum and energy crystallized in such enactments is not of *legal* origin, being born rather of the conflict of antagonistically related classes. Law is a mechanism which mediates social relations which return ultimately to economic and political dynamics as their centre of gravity.

## References

Arthur, C. 1977. Towards a materialist theory of law. *Critique*, 7(1), 31–46.
Bukharin, N. 2003. *Imperialism and World Economy*. London: Bookmarks.
Callinicos, A. 2009. *Imperialism and Global Political Economy*. Cambridge: Polity.
Doogan, K. 2009. *New Capitalism? The Transformation of Work*. Cambridge: Polity.
Gowan, P. 1999. *The Global Gamble: Washington's Faustian Bid for World Dominance*. London: Verso.
Harman, C. 2009. *Zombie Capitalism: Global Crisis and the Relevance of Marx*. London: Bookmarks.
Hill, C. 1991. *The World Turned Upside Down: Radical Ideas During the English Revolution*. London: Penguin.
Hobsbawm, E. 1962. *The Age of Revolution: Europe, 1789–1848*. London: Weidenfeld & Nicholson.
Kidron, M. 1970. *Western Capitalism Since the War*. London: Penguin.
Lefebvre, H. 1976. *The Survival of Capitalism: Reproduction of the Relations of Production*, translated by F. Bryant. London: Allison and Busby.
Marx, K. 1990. *Capital: A Critique of Political Economy*. Vol. 1. London: Penguin.
———. 1992. *Capital: A Critique of Political Economy*. Vol. 2. London: Penguin.
———. 2000. *Karl Marx: Selected Writings*. D. McLellan ed. 2nd edn. Oxford: Oxford University Press.
Miéville, C. 2004. *Between Equal Rights: a Marxist Theory of International Law*. Leiden: Brill.
Overton, M. 1996. *Agricultural Revolution in England: the Transformation of the Agrarian Economy 1500–1850*. Cambridge: Cambridge University Press.
Pashukanis, E. 1980. *Selected Writings on Marxism and Law*, edited by P. Beirne & R. Sharlet. London: Academic Press.
———. 1983. *Law and Marxism: A General Theory*. London: Pluto Press.
Smith, A. 1814. *An Inquiry into the Nature and Causes of the Wealth of Nations*. Edinburgh.
Smith, T. 2009. *Globalization: A Systematic Marxist Account*. Chicago: Haymarket.
*Stair Memorial Encyclopaedia* [Online: LexisNexis Butterworths]. Available at: www.lexisnexis.com/uk/legal [accessed: 15 March 2011].
Stone, L. 1985. 'The bourgeois revolution of seventeenth-century England revisited'. *Past and Present*, 109, 44–54.
Timmins, N. 1996. *The Five Giants: A Biography of the Welfare State*. London: Fontana Press.
Thompson, E. 1975. *Whigs and Hunters: the Origin of the Black Act*. London: Penguin.
———. 1991. *Customs in Common*. London: Merlin Press.

# Chapter 12
# The Public Nature of Private Law?

Claudio Michelon

Theories of the public domain have often struggled to provide a credible account of private law. Private law, as the law of the private domain, is often seen as the foil to public law and the public domain. However, private law is still law and, as this paper shall argue, that carries an inescapable public element with it. Any non-purely-instrumentalist conception of law would have to accept that law stands for more than the interests of a discreet part of the relevant social group (even those of a 'majority' in that group). In doing so, it would have to accept that, despite appearances to the contrary, law deserves respect as an embodiment of the mutual interest of the members of that group in the flourishing of one another. This conception of the political nature of law is bound to be controversial and what is meant by it here shall be clarified (and qualified) below. This public aspect of private law seems at odds with the idea of the private domain. As a matter of fact, the private domain, in its canonical liberal interpretation, stands in opposition to the idea of the 'public', as it refers to a space where one is free from the obligation to take into consideration anyone else's needs (let alone their flourishing).

The phrase 'private law' might then appear to be an oxymoron. However, that impression lies on an incorrect conception of what private law is about and of why it is worth preserving in a certain form (or so this argument shall claim). Through law, the private domain might be construed as a meaningful space of interaction. That is not to say that private law teaches people to care for one another. It might or might not do so in certain contexts, but the claim here does not rely on this empirical thesis. The point that this paper tries to make in what follows is conceptual and it has implications for the questions of what private law stands for and of what form it should take.

In the last century, private law's self-understanding, the narrative in which it finds its meaning, has been a constant source of existential anxiety for the best private lawyers. One of the central objectives in arguing for the public nature of private law in this paper is to outline an alternative narrative under which the many important changes undergone by private law in the twentieth century across most Western legal systems could be seen as the unfolding of an idea, rather than as an encroachment of foreign ideas on the main body of 'real' private law.

In order to make this point in section three it is necessary to first deploy two strands of argument that will prove useful there. First, it is necessary to explain what is meant by the claim that law is always grounded on the connectedness between members of a particular political group (in the next section).

Secondly, it is necessary to outline in more detail the conceptual structure that underlies the liberal understanding of the private sphere, which this paper will attempt to do in the section following the next.

## Law's Claim to Connectedness

This discussion will begin with an explanation of in which sense law is bound up with an anti-individualist conception of the political. There are two irreconcilable ways of understanding the meaning of political institutions, including the law. On the one hand, there is a liberal way to understand such institutions, according to which they are conceived as tools to purge private vice collectively, either by effectively building better people (e.g., Hurka 1996: 147ff)[1] or by providing mechanisms that make private vice work for the benefit of public good (as does Rawls, 1971). In stark contrast to that, there is a conception of political institutions as a mediating place between the need for concrete decisions to be made in particular situations and the 'transcendent' (for need of a better word), never fully graspable, meaning of those decisions.

Institutions mediate between 'transcendence' and immanence in the sense that they offer mechanisms that help answer the question about what should be done in concrete cases, while still pointing to an ultimate meaning that lies beyond them. For the liberal's adversary, political institutions create a space in which political (not merely academic) discussion on the ultimate meaning of communal life – that is, the questions about what constitutes justice in that community, what are the mutual duties between citizens, and so on – is made possible because it is relatively insulated from the pressures of deciding what to do here and now. Moreover, it makes political *action* possible because it partially insulates it from the fundamental discussion about the meaning of communal life. Hence, the meaning of communal life is the energy that moves the machine, the all-pervasive force that makes the political enterprise make sense, the underpinning of all political argument, while, at the same time, being relatively insulated from institutional practice and, in that sense, lying beyond it.

Liberals deny that meaning lies beyond the political institution and believe that politics resolves itself within political institutions, as a study of their cunning (generating virtue from vice, or public good from private vice, or some other such combination). The adversaries of liberalism are anthropologically pessimist and believe that no institution would be able to accomplish such task. For them, political institutions are not constantly changing because they are moving

1 Liberal Perfectionists can claim to be the heirs of a tradition that stretches as far back as Plato's Republic and has its *locus classicus* in Aristotle's politics, 1131b24–1132b12. However, modern perfectionists are prey to a confidence in their own ability to build appropriate institutions that never victimized Aristotle, who was not blind to the essential contestability of political concepts.

(or trying to move) towards a perfected version of themselves, but because they will always fall short of fully capturing what, lying beyond, animates them.

Carl Schmitt has offered the best account of this mediating role of the juridical form. The juridical form mediates between the concrete decision in concrete political communities and the ideal (of truth, justice or, as Schmitt sometimes put it, the idea of law). As he wrote in *Political Theology*:

> The age-old Aristotelian opposites of deliberation and action begin with two distinct forms; whereas deliberation is approachable through legal form, action is approachable only by a technical formation. The legal form is governed by the legal idea and by the necessity of applying a legal thought to a factual situation, which means that it is governed by the self-evolving law in the widest sense. Because the legal idea cannot realize itself, it needs a particular organization and form before it can be translated into reality. (Schmitt 2005: 28)

Schmitt never ceased to praise Hobbes' insight that 'auctoritas non veritas facit legem'(Schmitt 2005: 33), but that is not to say that truth (that is, truth about the ultimate meaning of communal life) was irrelevant in the justification of law. A claim to act on the true conception of the meaning of communal life is made by all factions in society who put forward a particular political agenda and, hence, a claim to truth cannot differentiate one proposed policy or legal regulation from another in and off itself. As Schmitt was well aware, the politically important question is, of course, *who decides*.

However, that should not obscure the fact that the *political* decision presents itself as an interpretation of truth, not the imposition of a societal faction's interests. That is at the core of Schmitt's critique of parliamentary democracy. Parliaments can only be proper political institutions if they are true spaces of deliberation. When they become bargaining stalls, parliaments lose their specific politicity and become subject to the nemesis of the political, to wit: pure economic rationality (1985: 4ff and, for the tyranny of economic rationality, see 2008: 26).

It is that commitment to truth about the meaning of communal life that is assumed as a condition of all legal and political discourses. Political authority is, of course, not conditional on the actual truth of the particular conception of the meaning of communal life held by the sovereign. But the fact that the *political* authority (as distinct from a powerful robber) must present itself as defending a conception of communal life has important implications. A claim to political authority and the law that relates to it always points towards something that cannot quite be realized in the world, to a form of connectedness that lies beyond itself. Fleshing out what that connection might mean is a daunting task and, as was explained above, this is a fundamental reason why political institutions are needed.

Thus, a claim to political supremacy always implies that the authority claims to take into account in his or her decision-making the best interest of the whole of the political group (and not only one of its factions). The basic reason why the best interest of each and every member of the political body has to be taken into account is the fact that the authority acknowledges a significant connectedness between them. This is the reason why the distinction friend–enemy is so important. By establishing the frontier between friend and enemy, the authority establishes a community between the members of a particular group and, in doing so, makes everyone's flourishing a relevant aspect of everyone else's.

What that means is that all members of a particular political community have an interest in the flourishing of everyone else, whether they acknowledge it or not. From this perspective, one's politically relevant social network goes beyond the group of people one loves and even the group of people one knows. It includes people one has never met and people one will never meet. This lack of acquaintance does not detract from the fact that the realization of all members of the relevant community is conceptually connected to everyone else's realization.

Notice the gulf between that political conception of connectedness and a purely moral conception of connectedness, such as the one put forward by liberal perfectionists. The latter is dependent on a substantive theory of what is in the best interest of all members of the community and, for that reason, has more difficulty in accommodating the essential contestability of political concepts. A political conception of connectedness, although by no means empty, acknowledges that feature of political concepts and conceives political institutions as mediating between conflicting versions of the substantive connection and the actual communal decision.

Indeed, within this conception of political connectedness there is a lot of scope for disagreement. There might be disagreement as to what the relevant community is or should be; as to whether self-destructive choices made by an individual can limit the impact of his or her failure to achieve his or her full potential on another's own self-realization; as to the appropriate division of social labour in relation to the help different classes of individuals might need; as to whether or not this help can be claimed as a right against others, and so on.

Yet law, as a political institution, is always an expression of that sort of political connectedness and it is ultimately always accountable to it.

To be sure, this is not uncontroversial. This 'claim to connectedness' is in stark opposition not only to liberal individualism, but also to all other forms of pure legal instrumentalism. For political instrumentalists, law is a social arrangement whose point is its capability of bringing about certain states of affairs which are evaluated by self-standing standards. Liberalism's peculiarity is to think of it as an instrument to preserve a relevant private domain from interference by others.

Pure instrumentalism is a popular conception of law's value[2], whether or not it comes coupled with the view that law is a neutral instrument. One might think that law, as an institution, is biased in one way or another and still hold an instrumentalist view. From an instrumentalist point of view, therefore, law would only be the herald of connectedness if some of its features (e.g., its language) showed a bias towards the sort of connectedness described above. This writer does not believe that to be

2 An instructing summary of instrumentalist conceptions can be found in Tamanaha, 2006: 118ff.

the case and, of course, is not alone in believing that. The familiar claim that the language of individual rights, so pervasive in modern western legal systems, shows an individualist bias, for instance, seems to be perfectly sound. The argument here that law always makes a claim to connectedness is compatible with both claims about the individualistic bias of certain central features of contemporary law and with claims that certain social factions, to serve their own interests, often hijack the law.

The instrumentalist vision of the law is, of course, right in that law is an appropriate (sometimes the best or even the only) instrument to achieving certain goals. But any claim that the law should be respected regardless of its instrumental value must suppose that, at a deep level, law is an expression of the intrinsic connection between the realization of each member of the relevant community. That is what Aquinas can be taken to be saying when he claims that law is intrinsically connected to the common good (as opposed to the good of a faction within the social group).[3]

Now, it is an undeniable fact that factions of particular societies often hijack the law in order to favour their own interests in detriment of the common good. Indeed, the relation between law and connectedness does not mean that law would always be an efficient means to bring about community. What it means is simply that there is a philosophically meaningful awkwardness in using the law to destroy policies that embody that connection.

This awkwardness arises from the fact that, when the law is hijacked by someone who does not believe in that essential connectedness of people in a political community in order to try and reshape society along the lines dictated by an individualist conception of the political world, this is made in the name of the ruler's faction's interest in the well-being of *all members* of the political community. In attempting to shape institutions to mirror a people's alleged disinterest in one another's realization, the ruling faction *must* claim that it is interested in the realization of all members of the social group.

Thus, to say that the law is an expression of social connectedness or that law is intrinsically linked to the common good is neither to subscribe to an optimistic view of how law operates in the world, nor to claim that if law does not serve the common good it is not law. (The caricature of natural law that was the straw man for a generation of legal theorists.)

This is not a complete argument for the thesis that political institutions (paradigmatically, legal institutions) must always claim that there is an essential connectedness between the people in a particular political community, but rather the sketch of what one such argument would look like. In what follows, this analysis will be rather generous to its own argument so far and assume its conclusion to be true. If that is the case, the question arises as to how (and whether) the private domain might be conceived as politically relevant, that is to say, as incorporating the notion of connectedness that is a conceptually necessary condition for the political.

3 Aquinas, *Summa Theologiae* 1a2ae, question 90, art. 2.

## The Puzzle of Private Connectedness

In order to understand how the private domain positions itself against the background of the argument so far it is necessary to clarify and demarcate more precisely what is meant by the private domain. This is particularly important given Raymond Geuss's fair warning that there might be too much going on under the label 'private' which we would do better to consider separately. As he puts it:

> [T]here is no single distinction between public and private; the various senses of 'public' do not cohere very closely to one another, nor do the senses of 'private'; the various forms of opposition between 'public' and 'private' are neither absolute nor are they all, in the final instance, insubstantial and illusory. (Geuss 2001: 109)

Although Geuss's warning against the dangers of over-inclusiveness when dealing with the concept of 'private' is fundamentally sound, it is important to notice that there seem to be some common structural features of arguments about a public/private divide. To postulate a distinction between the public and the private is often the first step in an argument against a spill-over between the two realms. This is present in many of the forms of distinguishing between public and private identified by Geuss. The idea of insulation is present (a) in the conception of 'public' as the realm of non-obtrusiveness, that is, certain actions are appropriate in the private domain, but should not spill over into the public domain because they would be obstructive in relation to others (Geuss 2001: 12ff) as well as (b) in the reconstruction of the public as a domain where only reasons about the common good should prevail, as opposed to reasons of private good (Geuss 2001: 34ff) and it is, of course, (c) the main worry of a liberal theory of the private domain, which will be the focus below.

The liberal theory of the private domain is not simply an attempt to build an insulated barrier between a private realm and a public realm. It specifies another, more particular, sense in which the public/private distinction might be about insulation. For liberals, the private is a realm of non-connectedness, of insulation, in contrast with the public, as a realm predicated in connectedness. If the public/private distinction is formulated in this way, the separation between the two realms is a separation between a realm in which a person's realization is intrinsically connected to the realization of others, in which someone else's tragedy is also that person's tragedy, and a realm in which the destiny of others is not necessarily relevant to that person (although one might elect to make it so).

If the distinction is considered in this way, it might seem that the discussion is not so much about two different realms of action, but rather, about two rival ethical outlooks that cannot be easily reconciled in one single political position. It would seem that either the destiny of others is relevant to a person or else it is not. One way to try and get around that objection is to conceive of self-realization as a complex task. It might be said that certain aspects of a person's realization are not conditioned by the self-realization of others, while some others cannot be achieved if others do not achieve them as well. Taken in isolation, having enough food is certainly an aspect of personal self-realization that has only a contingent connection to other people realizing themselves (because they have enough food themselves, because they have proper education or any other aspect of their self-realization). On the other hand, it might be that a person's self-realization is also dependent on a common project that cannot be fully carried out by anyone individually, but which, if successful, would enrich everyone's life. That is the way in which Arendt thought of the public realm as a realm of equality (necessarily other-dependent), work, deeds and discourse (Arendt 2005: 122ff, Arendt 1958: 50–58). Speech and action depend on the existence of a community of equals, all freed from necessity, something that is not to be found, she thinks, in the private realm (Arendt 1958: 70–72). Of course, what is missing in this argument is a justification for taking those aspects of self-realization in isolation from one another, but this paper does not need to get into the detail of Arendt's argument.[4]

More important in the context of this paper is to discuss the liberal conception of the private domain for it is liberalism that places the private domain in opposition to the thesis of connectedness. Liberalism conceives the private domain as the domain in which the default position is that others do not have a claim on a person. It is a domain in which all the meaningful connection that might occur between individuals is freely chosen; in which the realization of others is only an issue for someone if he or she chooses it be so. In this conception, the private sphere is populated by one individual in the wilderness of objects, where the other is not conceived as having any distinct status, but as one more obstacle in the persecution of a person's freely chosen objectives. The other stands before a person in a way that is not essentially different from a tiger or a stone.

What is important here is to perceive that this objectification of the other is not as much a psychological feature of humans (or even modern western men), but the conceptual presupposition of a liberal conception of the political world.

A conception of politics as mediation does not have to be anthropologically optimist to see a way out of this objectification of the other. Political institutions are not primarily a means to make better people, who would perceive the relevance of the other and perceive the importance of the realization of others to one's own realization (as a perfectionist might be tempted to believe). Neither are political institutions cunning devices that make private vice work in favour of an independently defined criterion of justice, like in Rawls's procedural justice.

4 Arendt tries to justify the separation by reference to her conception of freedom. In Arendt's view, practical life develops in two mutually dependent fronts. In the private front, agents are moved by a drive to secure themselves against the forces of necessity, seeking to satisfy the basic needs of bare life. Freedom from necessity is a condition for political freedom. The possibility of a public front depends on the presence of the conditions that give meaning to private life: the public is the realm occupied by those who are freed from necessity. What seems to be missing is an explanation of why the satisfaction of necessity in the community should not be a worthy political task.

Political institutions (and law in particular) provide a way out of objectification by embodying, themselves, a certain conception of the connectedness. That insight seems to offer the key to understand private law in a non-purely-instrumental way.

## Private Law in the Private Sphere

This section brings together the two threads of argument presented in the previous sections. On the one hand there is a conception of political institutions, including law, as embodying a claim to connectedness, and on the other hand, a short critique of the liberal conception of the private realm as the domain of 'emancipation' from the other, of liberty to choose as one pleases, without taking others into consideration. The question that will be examined now is how (and whether) the private domain can be considered to be a realm of meaningful connection, something more than the solipsistic world of objectification of the other.

Here is the thesis of this paper in a nutshell: the key to understanding the private domain as a realm of meaningful connection is private law. Private law lends connective meaning to the interactions of private agents in the private sphere while still retaining the sense in which the private sphere is a sphere of freely chosen connection. There resides the public nature of private law and this nature, in turn, determines (or should determine) its main features.

The anthropological pessimism at the roots of the conception of politics put forward in the first section above implies that the default motivation for agents in the sphere reserved for their free choice is that of utility maximization. Agents, if let free to decide what to do, will choose a course of action that maximizes their utility to the detriment of everyone else. Now, this should not be taken as a sociological claim about how people actually behave. As MacNeil pointed out (1986: 577ff), it is often the case that people involved in contractual relations behave relatively compassionately as utility enhancers (who only transact because they are willing to obtain some gain, but are also willing to make less gain than they could in order to help others). Some people even act compassionately without a personal gain in sight. As a matter of fact, an impeccable utility-maximizer, who does not see value in others obtaining gain would be, clinically, a psychopath.

This might be sociologically or psychologically true, but Hobbes, Aristotle and other anthropologic pessimists are not simply making a sociological claim about how people normally behave. They are making a conceptual claim about the fact that, in the absence of an institutional framework that makes certain kinds of action necessarily other-regarding, it would be perfectly unremarkable for anyone involved in a discrete transaction (e.g. a particular contract) not to take the interests of the other parties in the transaction into consideration. What this institutional framework generates is the conditions for politics, in the sense that the institution should always act on behalf of its entire constituency (as explained in the first section).

Dori Kimmel makes a similar point when he argues against conceiving contracts as promises (Kimmel 2003: 60, 65, 72ff). Promises rely on a background of understanding and trust between promisor and promise, while contracts are needed in those contexts in which one cannot rely on the other party to behave in a particular way.

This is the public role of private law, to infuse the private realm, where agents cannot be trusted to take each other's needs and interests into account, with the idea of mutual respect. What private law does, primarily, is to make compulsory certain forms of behaviour that would display that respect. Private law has other functions that are only indirectly connected to this core role, for instance, it creates conditions under which it would be more easily ascertainable whether a particular behaviour displays respect to the other (for example by introducing rules as to what counts as a valid promise, about where the default time or place of payment would be, and so on). Moreover, what precisely constitutes respect for the other is as controversial as any substantive conception of justice and the community should settle it as it settles most matters of justice, through politics.

What private law does in the private domain is to make it into a space for meaningful connection between private parties. The truth in the liberal conception of the private space is that the private space does not carry in itself an antidote for the objectification of the other. And the fact that that objectification is a conceptual possibility throughout the private domain, as well as a common social fact in many discrete transactions would make the private domain into a domain in which meaningful connection to the other is purely contingent. What private law does is to make the other present to a person, despite reluctance to see the other as more than an object in the way of the satisfaction of one's own desires.

That does not mean that private law would make one see the other and respond to her appropriately. This might or might not happen and, if it does, it would be a welcome by-product of the private law. What is more important is that one's *behaviour* would be compatible with being respectful (even if one only sees the law as yet another stone blocking one's path to self-satisfaction). A person's psychological framework might or might not become more political (that is, other-regarding), but that person's action following the law would necessarily mimic the action of someone whose behaviour is other-regarding. That is the sense in which private law infuses the private domain with publicity.

It is hoped that this can shed light on how to construct an appropriate narrative of private law's development, in particular from the beginning of the twentieth century. The emergence of labour law and consumer law, the growing relevance of good faith, the rise of product liability and economic duress in contract law, among many other aspects of private law's evolution, should not be considered necessary encroachments into a system that retains its normative and conceptual independence from those grudgingly accepted impingements. Instead, the narrative of private law's unfolding is a narrative in which people (collectively, if not individually) perceive progressively more sophisticated ways to understand what it means to display respect, a sophistication that is sometimes prompted by changes in the background social conditions and sometimes are simply a deepening of understanding of how respect for others is shown. In this sense, good faith and labour law are aspects of the full realization of private law in the world, as much as the idea that one should fulfil one's promises is. The critical challenge ahead for private lawyers and for the political community in general is to recognize the next steps in this narrative of realization of an institution whose point is to inculcate the private domain with connectedness. This is not only the challenge ahead for this generation, but the horizon towards which private lawyers move.

To say that private law's narrative should be understood as a process of deepening understanding of the political connection between private parties, instead of the narrative of a core conceptual structure that, unfolding from an idea of individual freedom, is constantly embattled and trespassed by the need to cope with social needs (consumer protection and so on), is not all there is to it. That reconstructed narrative just opens up a range of other questions about how respect in the private sphere differs from respect in the public sphere, about the content of this form of respect and about the relationship between concrete private law institutions and that notion of private 'respect', none of which can be examined here.

## References

Aquinas. 1966. *Summa Theologiae Vol 28*, translated by Thomas Gilby (London: Blackfriars).

Arendt, H. 1958. *The Human Condition* 2nd ed. (1998) (Chicago: University of Chicago Press).

———. 2005. *The Promise of Politics* (New York: Schocken Books).

Aristotle. 1991. *The Complete Works of Aristotle Vol 2*, edited by Jonathan Barnes and translated by Benjamin Jowett (1885) (Princeton: Princeton University Press).

Geuss, R. 2001. *Public Goods, Private Goods* (Princeton: Princeton University Press).

Hurka, T. 1996. *Perfectionism* (New York: Oxford University Press).

Kimmel, D. 2003. *From Promise to Contract* (Oxford: Hart Publishing).

MacNeil, I. 1986. 'Exchange Revisited: Individual Utility and Social Solidarity' *Ethics* 96:3, 567–93.

Schmitt, C. 1922 (rev. 1934). *Political Theology*, translated from German by George Schwab, 2005 (Chicago: University of Chicago Press).

Schmitt, C. 1923. *The Crisis of Parliamentary Democracy*, translated from German by Elen Kennedy, 1985 (Cambridge, MA: MIT Press).

Schmitt, C. 2008. *La Tirania dei Valori*, translated by Sara Bignotti and Paolo Becchi (Brescia: Morcelliana).

Tamanaha, B. 2006. *Law as a Means to an End* (Cambridge: Cambridge University Press).

# Chapter 13
# Between the Public and the Private: Banking Law in 1830s England[1]

Iain Frame[2]

In the aftermath of the 1825 banking crisis – 'one of the most violent of the century' (Crosby 1999: 230) – reform was on the agenda. The English economy had come to 'within twenty-four hours of barter' (King 1936: 36–7), making it imperative that something be done. When something was done – courtesy of legislation enacted in 1826 – the public authorities were bold: they deprived the Bank of England of its monopoly in joint-stock banking. What happened thereafter, through until the next banking crisis in 1836, is the subject matter of this paper.

The legislation of 1826, though bold, was not the sole – nor even the most important – contribution made by the legal system towards the events of the next ten years. Altering the character of banking in the decade after 1825 was what might be described as 'financial innovation' of the type theorized by Hyman Minsky: actors, including banks, found new ways of creating debt not counter to the legal code. In this paper I argue that the legal rules and practices underpinning property and contract made this financial innovation possible. This argument is intended to counter the impression that law's primary (though at best marginal) influence on finance is through periodic legislative interventions, such as those of 1826, aimed at prohibiting behaviour.

Section 2 elaborates in greater detail on the understanding of law that is used in this paper and on how the approach to law used here can better help understanding of the resounding rather than marginal impact the 1830s legal order had on banking. Moreover, that legal order, though based on typical areas of 'private' law like property and contract, was in fact, so this paper shall argue, thoroughly public in nature. It follows that 1830s banking itself was soundly public in quality not just because it was constituted by legislation of the type passed in 1826, but, in addition, because the practices that defined banking were dependent on the backing of the public authorities. When crisis unfolded once again in 1836, therefore, the contribution of law was neither limited to further legislative intervention, nor was it confined to the margins in the built up to the collapse. Instead, the legal

---

1 This paper's focus will be limited to England owing to the largely separate developments that occurred in Ireland, Scotland and Wales.

2 I would like to thank Christine Desan for her comments on the first draft of this paper, and Jennifer Langlais and Namita Wahi for their comments on a later draft. All errors and omissions are the authors alone.

order shaped banking in profound ways throughout the period 1826–1836, a point argued in section 3.

## Financial Instability and Innovation

As the financial system spirals out of control, as it did in 1825–1826, and was to do so again in 1836, unemployment increases as businesses suffer losses. And those who played no, or little, part in causing the crisis will in all probability have to contribute toward dealing with the aftermath. Given the undesirability of crisis, attempts at moderating instability in the financial system are understandable. One way that regulators attempt to control the quantity and quality of debt created by firms and banks is through legislation aimed at banks – institutions that, after all, typically make their profits by specializing in selling debt. A difficulty, however, is that banks tend to find ways of circumventing the rules developed by regulators 'just as lawyers find new loopholes in tax laws just about as fast as legislation closes up older loopholes' (Kindleberger and Aliber 2005: 18).

According to one of the most prominent theorists of recent times dealing with financial instability, Hyman Minsky (1992: 17), '[b]ecause profit-seeking agents learn how a regulatory structure operates and because regulation means that some perceived profit opportunities are not open to exploitation, there are incentives for agents to change their behaviour to evade or avoid the constraints'. And once the rules – rules like those contained in the legislation of 1826, which will be discussed in section 3 – that are intended to encourage stability prove less effective than the regulators had anticipated, then banks are free to encourage another round of debt financing. The way that financial institutions create new debt is, according to Minsky (1980: 505), through innovation. That is, they develop new practices, or adapt old practices to a new regulatory framework, that, in the case of banks, either directly expands the money supply, or enlarges the provision of credit indirectly through the creation of money substitutes – a good example of which is, as will be shown in section 3, the bill of exchange. As a result, firms and banks find ways of creating new credit in the pursuit of profit not prohibited by the regulatory framework.

## The Delegation of Public Authority

The general impression of regulation that emerges from studies of financial and banking instability is of law as a force outside the financial system that becomes active when attempts are made to regulate the behaviour of the participants in the system – most often in the aftermath of a crisis like the one in 1825 – so as to endeavour to protect the vulnerable by prohibiting, controlling or placing constraints upon the conduct that is perceived to have been the cause of the instability (e.g., Brunnermeier et al. 2009: 2, Davies and Green 2008: 7–31, Ferguson 2008: 356–7, Edwards 1996: 6–7). Once the new regulations are in place, the legal system drifts back into the margins. Provoking the next crisis are new forms of debt outside the control of the legal system.

Yet viewing law in terms of obedience and disobedience, with an impact that is ultimately marginal, is not the only way of comprehending law. For instance, legislative enactments and court doctrine, rather than prohibiting conduct or imposing duties, frequently grant actors a greater or less degree of autonomy – or permissions to act – that enable actors to shape and re-shape their own relations (e.g., Kennedy 1993, Rubin and Sugarman 1984: 9–10, Cohen 1927, Hale 1923, Hohfeld 1913).

The legal domains where actors often have a greater rather than lesser degree of autonomy are those typically associated with private law. Yet the private law categorization of, for example, the law of contract or property law, often focuses attention away from the quasi public law quality of these domains. What gives the law of contract, through which private parties take on more or less voluntary agreements, the quality of public law is that the parties know they can depend on the sovereign power of the state – the institutionalized representation of the public – to enforce the agreement (Cohen 1933: 585–6).

Thus, where parties have considerable autonomy via the law of contract or property law, this autonomy is the result of public authority delegated – sometimes expressly though formal legislation or court doctrine, sometimes by not stamping out practices – to private actors. The result is authority that is publicly constituted yet privately exercised (Ireland 2003: 490, Hale 1920). On occasions, the grant of authority is broad, with the result that actors have considerable flexibility when determining the type of practices that predominate – practices that prosper when protected by the state. Furthermore, even when the degree of autonomy is limited by, for example, quite explicit rights and obligations, actors still retain some room for manoeuvre, on account of the ambiguities, inconsistencies and uncertainties that often permeate legislation and legal doctrine – practices that thrive when the new interpretation of the legislation or doctrine goes unchallenged by the state or others. Hence, by exploiting either explicit or finding implicit permissions to act, actors have scope to create new practices or adapt older practices to a new regulatory environment, that is, to innovate.

Thus, the point noted earlier through reference to Minsky, that participants in the financial system find ways of creating new debt by innovating, can be understood in terms of legal innovation too. Locating such legal innovation frequently requires looking beyond formal public institutions to legal regimes created through delegations of public authority to private actors. When the actions of these private actors are reflected upon, what is additionally considered is the pervasive impact of the publicly constituted legal system.

## Banking in 1830s England

This part of the paper begins with the banking legislation of 1826. Then the emergence of two practices is discussed, practices that were not prohibited by this legislation and developed, as will be argued, in large part as a result of public authority delegated to private actors – in this instance the private actors being the banks created by the new legislation. The first practice saw interest offered to current account holders, while the second practice saw banks discounting and then re-discounting bills of exchange as a means of generating the income needed to cover what they owed their new depositors. It was to a considerable extent through excessive bill (re)discounting – encouraged further by the use of the bills close relation, accommodation paper – that credit expanded beyond a prudent level. Not only were these developments carried out through the legal regime underpinning the bill of exchange and accommodation paper, but they were sanctioned explicitly in the 1830s by the courts. Consequently, the public authorities and the legal institutions of the day were neither neutral bystanders, nor occasional interventionists, but were rather complicit in the expansion of credit that began to unravel during the collapse of 1836–1837.

### *The Banking Co-partnership Act*

The financial system that had emerged in England by the beginning of the nineteenth century was structured into three tiers. At the top of the system was the Bank of England. Between the Bank of England and the rest of the country were the other London banks and the rest of the London money market. Beyond London and throughout the rest of England were the country banks. Under legislation of 1694 establishing the Bank of England, and under subsequent legislation renewing its Charter, the Bank was the only joint-stock bank in England, meaning that its shareholders benefited from transferable shares and limited liability. All other banks in England were deprived of limited liability and restricted by law to no more than six partners. These banks – both those in London and those elsewhere in England (country banks) – were known as private banks (Pressnell 1956).

On account of the legislation limiting the size of banks to partnerships of not more than six persons, the size of such banks measured by their capitalization was kept within strict bounds. Hence, in times of strain the country banks had to look beyond the personal capital of their owners. One of the few available alternative options was to appeal to the London banks for further credit. Yet the banks in London – likewise limited to not more than six partners – frequently found that they too lacked the readily available resources required to meet a large number of simultaneous demands for money. They hence in turn referred to the country's largest financial institution, the Bank of England. However, if the Bank was not forth-coming with emergency aid, the banking structure as a whole suffered.

And that's what happened in 1825–1826 – at the final count 73 banks in England collapsed (Kindleberger and Aliber 2005: 111). One response formulated by parliament – the Banking Co-partnership Act of May 1826 – challenged the Bank of England's monopoly on joint-stock banking.[3] According to those in favour of reform, permitting other banks with an unlimited number of partners, i.e., joint-stock banks, made sense as a means of stabilizing the banking system in a way that did not impair the provision of credit. Larger banks would have larger resources to call upon during times of need. Consequently, in the case of failure, unlimited liability would apply to the new joint-stock banks in the same manner as it did to the country banks and London banks; only with the difference that creditors could take legal action against many more partners in the case of joint-stock banks. It was hoped that the public would then place even more confidence in the deposit accounts and notes offered by these new banks (Collins 1988: 18). The capacity of the financial system to expand credit would thereafter increase, only now on a more secure, stable basis[4].

The introduction of new banking institutions did alter the relations between the key actors involved in transferring credit and debt across England – though the security and stability hoped for by parliament did not materialize. Undermining the reformed banking structure was the creation of new debt. The devices used to expand credit were the bill of exchange and accommodation paper, both of which were utilized by the new joint-stock banks as they sought to secure their place in the world of nineteenth century banking.

### *Interest on current accounts*

Securing a future was not a straight-forward task for the joint-stock banks formed after 1826, for they were very quickly confronted with a serious problem: established private banks had not been abolished by the recent legislation. Hence, in order for the new joint-stock banks to compete with the older private banks, they had to draw in deposits from either their rivals or from persons without a bank account. To entice people into opening an account, the joint-stock banks innovated within the system of 1830s finance. Their approach was to adapt an older practice – offering interest on deposits – to the new regulatory environment.

3 A second response involved attacking the right to issue small denomination notes. Assigning, rightly or wrongly, responsibility for the crisis to the country banks, parliament acted to ban notes of less than five pounds in England and Wales from 1829. The third and final response was to allow the Bank of England to establish branches.

4 It should be noted that the 1826 Act did not permitted the establishment of joint-stock banks within London or within a 65 mile radius of the capital. The Bank of England's monopoly within London and the surrounding area hence remained. It was via the Bank Charter Act of 1833 that joint-stock banks were permitted to operate in and for 65 miles around London. The 1833 Act did, however, prevent joint-stock banks established in London from issuing their own notes (thereby consolidating the Bank of England's monopoly over the note issue in London) and it made Bank of England notes legal tender. For more on the 1833 Act, see Thomas (1934: Chapter IV)

Offering interest to depositors was not new in the 1830s. What was different though familiar was paying interest to the holders of current accounts as well as to the holders of deposit accounts. Before the arrival of joint-stock banking, it was typical to use the term 'deposit' in a narrow sense: it referred to 'time deposits' – accounts where money was left at interest and could only be withdrawn after due notice – rather than to current accounts (sometimes also called 'credit balances', 'running accounts', 'drawing accounts'), which traditionally received no interest though withdrawals could be made on demand. Owing to the practice of the joint-stock banks, however, the distinction between time deposits and current accounts became less entrenched largely because interest was offered regardless of the type of account (Pressnell 1956: 163–5).

The legislation of 1826 permitting joint-stock banks did not explicitly outline the type of accounts or rates of interest that the new banks were to offer to the public. But that does not mean that law played no role in the new practice whereby joint-stock banks paid interest to a broader range of customers. A bank account, after all, represents a promise to pay – that is a contractual commitment – and where interest is paid, the account generates a revenue stream, and so becomes a form of property for the holder. By supporting these property and contractual relations – albeit rather indirectly through the delegation of public authority to private actors – the legal regime of the 1830s influenced the shape of banking practice.

During much of the 1830s, the rate of interest the joint-stock banks contracted to pay the holders of both deposit and current accounts was frequently generous (King 1936: 39, Scammell 1968: 136).[5] Offering competitive interest rates is clearly a cost to any bank. Consequently, the joint-stock banks had to ensure as full a utilization of their resources as possible (King 1936: 39). And that meant finding an investment with a high enough yield to cover what they owed their depositors.

When it came to choosing investments, the legislation of 1826 again allocated the joint-stock banks wide discretionary powers. That should not be understood, of course, to imply banking unregulated by law. In the same way that bank accounts are a product of property and contractual relations, the asset that the joint-stock banks turned to – the bill of exchange – is similarly defined by property and contract. That is, a bill of exchange is a type of property, or financial asset that generates a right to revenue for the party owed money, and, because the bill is negotiable, this right can be transferred to others. Moreover, because the value of the bill depends on what is owed being paid at a specified date in the future, under-pining all bills of exchange is a contractual relationship or promise to pay upon maturity.

5 According to Thomas (1934: 264), whose source of reference is the Report of the 1836 Committee on Joint Stock Banking, 'The rate of interest paid on deposits at this time ... was fixed at such a level as would attract money into banks from the pockets of the people. From two to two and a half per cent appears to have been the general rule for deposit accounts subject to notice'.

The property and contractual relations defining bills of exchange and bank accounts represent examples of public authority delegated by the state to private actors. Due to the vagueness of the legislation of 1826, bankers in the 1830s were granted considerable autonomy when structuring the banking framework – in relation to both the debts they incurred and assets they held – through the facilitative legal regime provided by property and contract. The role of the public authorities then became one of waiting in the background, ready to enforce whatever arrangements the bankers adopted.

### *Bill re-discounting*

Given, therefore, that the joint-stock banks invested in bills of exchange so as to cover their debts, in order to appreciate the problems that stretched English banking in 1836, it is essential to understand how the system of bill finance worked during the first half of the nineteenth century.

Imagine a situation where A owes a debt to B and C owes a debt to A. One way of cancelling these debts is for A to draw a bill ordering C to pay B a certain sum at a future date, say in 90 days time. If B receives payment from C, then C's debt to A is cancelled, as is A's debt to B. A potential problem, however, is that B has to wait ninety days before receiving payment. An alternative for B is to take the bill to D who has available funds. As an investment D purchases, or 'discounts' the bill from B by endorsing the bill. B then gets cash up front, rather than waiting ninety days for C's payment, minus a discount that off-sets both the fact that D will be out of pocket until the bill matures, and the risk that C might not pay up. When the bill matures, D can demand payment from C (Jacobs 1924).

The joint-stock banks of the 1830s were typically in the position of D, looking for investments. Merchants were not infrequently in the situation faced by B, unable to wait for cash. The private banks, both before the legislative changes of 1826 and after, were in the habit of holding onto the bills they discounted until maturity, unless times of strain called for the re-sale of some or all of their reserve of bills in advance. By contrast, the joint-stock banks opted to raise money up-front by selling the bills they had bought before the bills matured, and were assisted in doing so by bill brokers – agents who specialized in finding buyers for those who were looking to sell bills. By selling their bills in this way, the joint-stock banks engaged in the practice known as re-discounting (King 1936: 40). They made money when doing so – enough to cover what they owed their depositors – because the rate charged to the merchants discounting bills was higher than the re-discount rate charged to the joint-stock banks. The latter rate was generally lower because with the endorsement of a joint-stock bank on the bill, should the acceptor of the bill fail to pay as promised upon maturity, the bill was backed by the security offered by the unlimited liability of the bank's numerous shareholders (Collins 1988, 98).

As the competition for deposits amongst the joint-stock banks became more extreme, their need for bills of exchange as a liquid investment grew greater.[6] Most bills originated via the interactions between traders and merchant houses,[7] who were stimulated into creating even more bills in the knowledge that they could have them turned into cash relatively easily owing to the demand generated by the joint-stock banks. And the banks were willing to invest in an ever larger number of bills because they knew that these bills could be sold on again – re-discounted – through the service performed by bill brokers. The arrival of the joint-stock banking, therefore, brought with it an abundance of debt financing.

### *Accommodation paper*

Of course, the liberal attitude toward the creation, discounting and then re-discounting of bills of exchange on the part of traders, merchant houses, joint-stock banks and bill brokers was less likely to lead to problems if the quality of bills produced was high.[8] A bill of exchange was considered high quality if the chances were that what was owed on the bill would be paid at maturity. Conversely, the creation of bills more prone to default – such as accommodation paper – so as to meet the demand fuelled by the needs of the joint-stock banks, was more likely to, and in the mid 1830s did, contribute toward stretching English finance beyond its limits. Through pushing the boundaries of the post 1826 financial system by adapting an older practice – the use of accommodation paper – to a new institutional environment, the joint-stock banks, aided by traders, merchant houses and bill brokers, brought into existence an unsustainable quantity of debt that ultimately led to another crisis.

An accommodation bill, in the eighteenth and nineteenth centuries, was a device that was the product, not of an actual sale of goods between merchants,

---

6 The number of bills in circulation continued to increase throughout the 1830s. In 1832, just over 356 million bills were created in Britain and Ireland (with 89 million in circulation at any one time during that year). By 1836 the figure stood at almost 486 million (with more than 121 million in circulation). Following the crisis of 1837, the figure dropped to 455 million (113 million in circulation) but by 1839 had surpassed the 500 million mark (132 million in circulation). Figures from Thomas (1934: 302) are based on the returns of bills stamped as provided by the Stamp Office.

7 In the nineteenth century, merchant houses facilitated international trade through the granting of acceptance credits. The house of first class credit would agree to accept bills on behalf of someone of second class credit in return for a commission payment. These bills could then be more easily discounted on account of the fact that they had been accepted by a highly respectable merchant house (Powell 1915: 374).

8 The extension of the bill market was not just a consequence of the activities of joint-stock banks. The opening of Bank of England branches (Clapham 1944: 110–16, Roberts 1958), the new reserve policy adopted by the London banks (King 1936: 62–70), and the Bank of England's growing understanding of its responsibility for the economy as a whole (Scammell 1968: Chapters 4 and 5), also played a part.

but rather of an endeavour by trading firms to 'raise funds ... even though they had not actually engaged in sales transactions' (Rogers 1995: 225). Ensuring the wide circulation of such bills required making them look as much like 'real' bills, i.e., bills supporting a transaction with a buyer and a seller of goods, as possible. Merchants could make fictitious bills look more 'real' by finding a second merchant to 'accommodate' the transaction. The second merchant would offer a helping hand by accepting the bill despite the fact that no goods were bought or sold.

Here's an example to illustrate the process: Merchant A draws a bill on Merchant B. The amount corresponds to the cost of a typical shipment of goods. Merchant B accepts the bill. Merchant A then discounts the bill for cash. When the bill is due to mature, Merchant B raises the funds to pay the debt by this time drawing a bill on Merchant A. Merchant A accepts the bill. Merchant B then discounts the bill. With cash in hand, Merchant B pays off the debt owed on the first bill (Rogers 1995: 225). To solve the problem of the same names reappearing, the parties would simply add bogus names to the bills (Rogers 1995: 226).[9] This process of accommodation worked provided Merchant A and Merchant B could discount the bills they had created, an outcome made more likely in the 1830s on account of the demand generated by the joint-stock banks for liquid investments. Yet, of course, should Merchant A and Merchant B fail to get their bills discounted, they would find themselves with neither the money nor the tangible goods to make good their debts.

### *The English courts*

The use of accommodation paper, just like interest on bank accounts, was not new in the 1830s – though in the case of accommodation paper, their past employment as an instrument of finance had proved far from popular. Indeed, throughout the late eighteenth century and equally so during the suspension of convertibility,[10] accommodation bills were widely condemned, not least by the English courts. Mr Justice Heath, writing in 1791, captures the attitude of the judiciary at that time.

> It is agreed on all hands, that the circulation of these bills is extremely mischievous, and ought to be restrained. It is the great commercial evil of these days, which has grown to a gigantic height. It has enabled needy adventurers to engage in desperate undertakings, relying on the money which they raise on this

9 E.g., Gibson v. Minet (1791), 1 Bl. H. 569, 624–5 (Heath J.) where it was declared that 'the obvious reason of inserting the name of a fictitious payee is, that too many bills should not appear in circulation in the same name at the same time'.

10 In 1797 the requirement that bank notes be convertible into gold coin on demand by the bearer was suspended owing to the commencement of hostilities with France. Following the peace of 1815, the matter of whether the Bank of England should be obliged to resume payments in gold coin re-emerged. Legislation in 1819 followed, setting down a time-line aimed at re-establishing the convertibility of Bank of England notes into specie, which occurred in 1821.

> fictitious credit. On the present question, a million of property now depends. No wonder that this traffic has spread poverty, distress, and bankruptcy, through large districts which it has pervaded.[11]

For the next twenty years and more, the English judiciary remained without exception hostile to accommodation paper. Yet, by the early 1830s, the approach adopted by the English courts had shifted (Rogers 1995: 232–43). For instance, whereas earlier to sue on an accommodation bill (understood as a bill arising out of suspected fraud or other apparently dubious circumstances) proof was required that consideration had been given (in contrast to ordinary bills where consideration was presumed), by the 1830s the courts were coming round to the view that proof of consideration vis-à-vis accommodation paper was not so essential (Rogers 1995: 241).[12] Indeed, the forceful judicial opinions of earlier years denouncing often vehemently the ills that followed from accommodation paper are almost completely absent by the 1830s.[13]

The courts could have opted to retain their antagonistic attitude towards accommodation paper but chose differently. This altered stance of the public authorities served to enhance the degree of autonomy available to merchants, bankers and brokers, by enlarging the domain of authority delegated to them. By going beyond the acquisition of mere bills of exchange (based on the sale and purchase of a tangible good) to accommodation paper (involving no actual goods, at least initially) merchants, bankers and brokers found that the types of financial asset that they could create, or that were available to them, and, moreover, the types of contractual relations that they could enter into, had expanded. Yet, as the advantages conferred onto merchants, bankers and bill brokers by legal institutions such as property and contract increased, so too did the amount of credit they could create. And with this expansion of credit there followed a rise in the degree of exposure faced not just by bankers but by the public at large.

### *The expansion of credit*

A key aspect of the 1836 crisis was the excessive re-discounting of bills of exchange and the use of accommodation paper in the trade between England and the USA. Both of these financial instruments had been given a new lease on life by the appearance of joint-stock banking, with repercussions for others involved

11 Gibson v. Minet (1791), 1 Bl. H. at 624.

12 E.g., Sir James Parke in Heath v. Sansom (1831), 2 Barn. & Adol. 291

13 The changed stance of the courts might be partly explained by the fact that it was extremely difficult to differentiate between 'real' bills and accommodation bills. To discriminate too strictly would render local bills – containing names unfamiliar to the London market – unacceptable, despite the fact that they were otherwise sound (King 1936: 94). Moreover, in times of buoyant trade, there would be, and there was in the crisis of 1836–1837, over-trading even in bills representing tangible transactions, blurring further the distinction.

in trade financing. By late 1836 a number of financing firms engaged in trade with the US admitted to difficulties and sought help from the Bank of England. Three merchant houses, Thomas Wilson & Co., Timothy Wiggin and Co. and George Wildes & Co. – informally known as the three W's – were in a particularly delicate position.

In their role as merchant houses, the three W's accepted bills on behalf of less credit-worthy merchants in return for a commission – a lucrative business provided the bills covered where ultimately met by the merchant (Powell 1915: 374). When they weren't, accommodation finance was frequently the means adopted by the merchant houses as they attempted to fulfil the debts they had guaranteed. And once the business of the three W's came to be conducted on the basis of pure credit – made possible by accommodation paper – for that business to continue the dependence on credit tended to grow stronger and stronger, at least until investors anticipated that the merchant houses themselves were no longer credit worthy and so refused to discount or re-discount paper bearing their name (Hidy 1946: 137). Consider the position of Wiggin & Co. in December 1836. The firm was estimated to have a capital of £330,000, out of which £130,000 was held in liquid assets. Wiggins, however, had taken up obligations of £1,650,000. Wildes & Co. was in an even more precarious arrangement as of February 1837: assets – £250,000; liquid assets – £100,000; liabilities – £2,200,000 (Hidy 1946: 138). Little wonder there were problems for the financial system in 1837. And owing to the fact that many of the bills created and accepted by the three W's had been discounted and often re-discounted by joint-stock banks, the financial problems of 1837 soon engulfed the banking sector in a manner reminiscent of ten years before.

## Conclusion

When confidence in banking was shattered in 1836–1837 for a second time inside a decade, parliament again considered what had gone wrong and what options existed for possible reform through legislation. The debates that followed focused on how to better regulate the currency and form part of the background that culminated in the famous banking legislation of 1844. These legislative reforms are clearly crucial to an understanding of the structure of banking in England during the first half of the nineteenth century. Nevertheless, it would be inaccurate to suppose that such legal interventions represent the only, or even the most significant legal influence on banking during the period. Instead, it has been argued here that law's role in the regulation of banking was more pervasive than is captured by a focus on legislation alone. Other legal institutions, such as the private law domains of property and contract, also made a significant contribution to the framework of banking owing to the way that agents, like bankers, used the powers delegated to them by the public authorities: in particular, the legal regimes of property and contract were used, in innovative ways, to both underpin the bank accounts and rates of interests on offer to customers and shape the creation and use of bills of exchange and accommodation paper. The expansion of credit that resulted was thus sanctioned by the public authorities, most explicitly indeed through the judgements reached by the courts. Hence, when banks during the 1830s found themselves unable to cover their obligations in the midst of another financial crisis it is, so this paper has attempted to demonstrate, more accurate to view law as a factor at the centre of credit creation, rather than as a marginal force that merely attempts to pick up the pieces via legislation in the aftermath of the collapse.

## References

Bowen, H.V. 1995. The Bank of England during the long eighteenth century, 1694–1820, in *The Bank of England: Money, Power and Influence 1694–1994*, edited by R. Roberts and D. Kynaston Oxford: Clarendon Press, 1–18.

Brunnermeier, M., A. Crocket, C. Goodhart, M. Hellwig, A. Persaud and H. Shin. 2009. *The Fundamental Principles of Regulation*. London: Centre for Economic Policy Research.

Cameron, R. 1967. England 1750–1845, in *Banking in the Early Stages of Industrialization: A Study in Comparative Economic History*, edited by R. Cameron et al. Oxford: Oxford University Press, 15–59.

Checkland, S.G. 1975. *Scottish Banking: A History 1695–1973*. Glasgow: Collins.

Clapham, J. 1945. *The Bank of England: A History* Volume II. London: Macmillan.

Cohen, M.R. 1927. Property and sovereignty. *Cornell Law Quarterly* 13(2), 8–30.

———. 1933. The basis of contract. *Harvard Law Review* 46(4), 553–92.

Collins, M. 1988. *Money and Banking in the UK: A History*. London: Routledge.

Crosby, C. 1999. Financial, in *A Companion to Victorian Literature and Culture*, edited by H.F. Tucker. London: Blackwell, 225–43.

Davies, H. and D. Green. 2008. *Global Financial Regulation: the Essential Guide*. Cambridge: Polity Press.

Edwards, F. 1996. *The New Finance: Regulation and Financial Stability*. Washington, DC: AEI Press.

Ferguson, N. 2008. *The Ascent of Money*. New York: Penguin.

Giovanoli, M. 2000. *International Monetary Law: Issues for the New Millennium*. Oxford: Oxford University Press.

Hale, R. 1923. Coercion and distribution in a supposedly noncoercive state. *Political Science Quarterly* 38(3), 470–94.

Hale, R. 1920. Law making by unofficial minorities. *Columbia Law Review* 20, 451–6.

Hidy, R.W. 1946. Cushioning a crisis in the London money market. *Bulletin of the Business History Society* 20(5), 131–45.

Hohfeld, W. 1913. 'Some fundamental legal conceptions as applied in judicial reasoning'. *Yale Law Journal* 23, 16–59.

Ireland, P. 2003. Property and contract in contemporary corporate theory. *Legal Studies* 23(3), 453–509.

Jacobs, B. 1924. *A Short Treatise on the Law of Bills of Exchange, Cheques, Promissory Notes, and Negotiable Instruments.* London: Sweet and Maxwell.

Kennedy, D. 1993. The stakes of law, or Hale and Foucault!, in *Sexy Dressing Etc.* Cambridge, MA: Harvard University Press.

Kindleberger, C. and R.Z. Aliber. 2005. *Manias, Panics and Crashes: A History of Financial Crises.* New Jersey: John Wiley & Sons, Inc.

King, W.T.C. 1936. *History of the London Discount Market.* London: Routledge.

Minsky, H. 1975. *John Maynard Keynes.* New York: Columbia University Press.

———. 1980. Capitalist financial processes and the instability of capitalism. *Journal of Economic Issues* 14(2), 505–23.

———. 1982. The financial-instability hypothesis: capitalist processes and the behaviour of the economy, in *Financial Crises: Theory, History and Policy*, edited by C.P. Kindleberger and J-P. Laffargue. Cambridge: Cambridge University Press, 13–39.

———. 1992. Profits, deficits and instability: A policy discussion, in *Profits, Deficits and Instability*, edited by D.B. Papadimitriou. Basingstoke: Macmillan, 11–22.

Newton, L. and P.L. Cottrell. 1998. Joint-stock banking in the English provinces 1826–1857: To branch or not to branch. *Business and Economic History* 27(1), 78–90.

Powell, E.T. 1915. *The Evolution of the Money Market 1385–1915.* London: *The Financial News.*

Pressnell, L.S. 1956. *Country Banking in the Industrial Revolution.* Oxford: Clarendon Press.

Roberts, R.O. 1958. Bank of England branch discounting, 1826–59, *Economica* 25, 230–45.

Rogers, J.S. 1995. *The Early History of the Law of Bills and Notes: A Study of the Origins of Anglo-American Commercial Law.* Cambridge: Cambridge University Press.

Rubin, G.R. and D. Sugarman. 1984. *Law, Economy and Society, 1750–1914: Essays in the History of English Law.* Abingdon, Oxon: Professional Books.

Scammell, W.M. 1968. *The London Discount Market.* London: Elek.

Thomas, S.E. 1934. *The Rise and Growth of Joint Stock Banking.* London: Sir I. Pitman & Sons, Ltd.

# Chapter 14
# The Public-ness of Development in the World Trade Organization

Stephanie Switzer[1]

## Introduction

The starting point for this examination is the contention that from a normative perspective, a multilateral construct of the meaning of development within the international trade regime as encapsulated within the World Trade Organization [WTO] is to be preferred. What this means is that the understanding to be ascribed to development as both a process and a commitment should be 'public' in the sense of emanating from a community. It is axiomatic that such an understanding necessarily stands in contradistinction to unilateral or private approaches under which the meaning of the concept 'belongs to' or is in some sense accessible to a limited number of participants.

This chapter will seek to deliberate upon the question as to whether and how development is understood as both a commitment and a process within the WTO is the product of public or private decision making processes. In this regard, public is defined in relation to the community of states which comprise the WTO and hence public decision making processes relevant to how development is understood should be inclusive in that all relevant members of the WTO have the chance to participate.

It is realized that this is a somewhat narrow and, by extension, in certain respects unsatisfactory definition of 'public', given that not all states are members of the WTO. Additionally, it says nothing of non-state actors and their participation – or lack thereof – within WTO decision-making processes or the particular interests which States may, or indeed may not, represent. However, the value of such a definition lies in its capacity to act as a critical comparator through which to discern the exclusion of certain actors, including Member states, from decision making processes which are relevant to how we understand development as both a process and a commitment. As such, it will be argued that the understanding accorded to development within the WTO is at times the product of unilateral and hence private processes.

---

1 The author would like to thank Professor Joe McMahon with whom many of the ideas in this chapter were originally discussed. Any errors are the author's own.

## Why Seek a 'Public' Conception of Development?

Before attention is turned to the above arguments, it is necessary to consider the more fundamental question as to why processes linked to how we understand development as a process or commitment should not exclude certain actors. From whence does the normative proposition that a public construct of the 'meaning' of development within the international trade regime is to be preferred?

Numerous definitions abound in relation to the meaning of development within the WTO. In relation, the current Doha 'Development' Round (WTO 2001a) of multilateral trade negotiations is indicative of the contestation which surrounds the concept of development. While close analysis of the events of the Round is revelatory of the fact that certain of the main sticking points in securing agreement relate to issues such as modalities in agricultural negotiations (WTO 2008), these in part are reducible to the question of what sort of tariff cut is likely to be the most appropriate to meet the development needs of members (Bhala 2009). By extension, such debates reflect the contestation which exists surrounding the concept of development and the best policies to promote this within the international trade regime.

Contestation over the application of certain concepts may be indicative of the fact that decisions which are required to be made in their operationalization require a choice be made between options which are incommensurable. A plethora of literature exists on the subject of incommensurability and various definitions have been offered for it. One such definition relevant to this analysis sets out that where conflicts arise over a given end, incommensurability exists where rationality cannot be deployed in order to arbitrate upon the correctness of one choice over another (Alder 2006).

Raz (1986) has proposed that two values, A and B, will be incommensurable when it is not true that A is better than B, or B is better than A and indeed not true that A and B are equal. Under such a scenario, it may be that a scale does not exist upon which to compare the value of A and B (Craswell 1998). An example of a choice between incommensurables would be offering a poor, childless couple the choice of a child or a large sum of money. Intuitively, most people would agree that there is no metric upon which the couple could base their decision since a child and money are not comparable (Sunstein 1994). Using this example, it is arguable that where choices or values are incommensurable, each may be said to have an independent claim to 'rightness' (Alder 2006) with a choice offered between ends which are not comparable (Cohen and Ben-Ari 1993). In certain respects, therefore, the existence of incommensurables is very much a 'social phenomenon', reflecting the 'tendency of people in everyday life to refuse to make tradeoffs …' (Posner 1997, 1186).

## The Incommensurability of Development

The relevance of the notion of incommensurability to this work is that a myriad of incommensurable choices have long been linked with the development debate in the WTO. Hence, arbitrating between the promotion of industrial development and the protection of labour rights seemingly involves a comparison between two choices which are incommensurable in the sense of not being comparable. Similarly, environmental protection and profit maximization are not 'comparable' in that one cannot be substituted for the other (Sunstein, 1998). A further example of incommensurability is the 'choice' between the protection of human health and the promotion of intellectual property protection in respect of access to essential [patented] medicines. Again, these are intuitively incomparable and, as a consequence, WTO Members have been tasked to arbitrate upon a response to such issues which does not accord primacy to one end over another (Dunoff 1999).

However, people do make choices between 'items' which they acknowledge to be incommensurable. Choices are made between environmental protection and profit maximization, even if the individual who makes that choice would previously have professed that such a choice could not be made because the choices were incomparable. In this regard, practice shows that the protection of intellectual property rights is oftentimes chosen over the promotion of human health (Cullet 2003). In offering an explanation between this dichotomy of rhetoric and action, Eric Posner contends that not all incommensurability claims will be honest in their expression. Instead, they may simply be a response to what people think is expected of them. According to Posner, the expression of incommensurability acts as a reputational signalling mechanism that the individual concerned can be 'trusted' (Posner 1997). From this, he derives the normative conclusion that a 'government that maximizes social welfare should discount incommensurability claims made by citizens, unless such discounting would interfere with socially valuable cooperation' (Posner 1997, 1213).

What are the normative implications of this? Should claims of incommensurability simply be discarded as largely irrelevant to the decision making process if they do not impinge upon the possibility of socially valuable cooperation? What implications would this have upon the various incomparable choices which confront decision makers in the development sphere? Three points are offered in response. First, as will be seen, disregarding incommensurables in the context of development would likely impinge upon socially useful cooperation. Second, the fact that these claims are raised, even if for reputational reasons, reflects some sort of normative commitment to them. Third, it is submitted that Posner's explanation as to why individuals do in fact make a choice between incommensurables fails to reflect upon the contested nature of incommensurable values or choices. Incommensurability does not mean that valuation of such choices is impossible but rather points in the direction of a range of metrics being required to make such choices. It is in disregarding this aspect of incommensurability that socially useful cooperation may be impinged upon.

In order to shed light on what is meant here by the contested nature of incommensurables, an example provided by the law of torts/delict will be utilized. In this regard, the issue of personal injury claims whereby a monetary sum is offered for bodily harm may be considered (Radnor 1993). A commodified conception of personal injury compensation would view harms and money as commensurable. However, a noncommodified version would view each element as incommensurable. Whereas the commodified version of compensation views harm through the rhetoric of the market and therefore constructs it as a 'cost' and hence makes a direct comparison between the injury and monetary recompense, the noncommodified version constructs the issue through the lens of 'right' and 'wrong' with the grant of compensation a reflection that the wrongdoer wishes to make redress to the victim and thereby reflective of the notion that bodily harm and money are not substitutable (Radnor 1993). Under the noncommodified version, even though compensation is paid, the injury is not constructed along a single metric as substitutable [and hence, comparable] for money but rather serves a symbolic role. If this analysis is utilized in reflecting upon the incommensurability of different choices within the WTO, the extent to which they may be compared or substituted arguably depends upon the frame of reference through which the items are viewed.

Of course, the existence of a scale or frame through which to compare two items, even if others would reject the use of such a mechanism, could lead to the proposition that the objects at issue cannot be incommensurable. It could hence be proposed that bodily integrity and money are not incommensurable since, under the commodified version, it is possible to compare or substitute them. The question must then be posed as to whether the notion of incommensurability is at all helpful to this analysis regarding the concept of development. In response, it is contended that a better way of understanding incommensurability is that while legal or other social mechanisms/constructs can place objective weight upon adherence to certain choices or values over others (Chang 1998), utilizing a single metric for comparative purposes in such a circumstance would require a distinction to be made which may do an injustice to other committed beliefs (Sunstein 1994) and thereby impinge upon socially useful cooperation. Hence relying solely upon the commodified version of, for example, bodily harm would do an injustice to notions such as consent since commodification of the injury has the natural consequence of harm and money being considered as substitutable. It is only by allowing a different frame that such substitutability may be departed from.

The implications of this discussion of incommensurabilty are that when decision makers are confronted with the task of arbitrating between incommensurable choices,

> Perhaps the people entrusted with the power of decision will ask, as part of the inquiry, about the society's prevailing ideas, about ways minimally to damage relevant goods, and what decision best fits with the community's self understanding of this has been established over time. This is not merely a descriptive inquiry. It involves asking what choice puts that self-understanding

> in its best or attractive light. On this view, choice among incommensurables is an act of interpretation, one that involves a dimension of fidelity to the past, but is also constructive. (Sunstein 1994, 857)

From a normative perspective, the existence of a range of metrics through which to arbitrate upon such choices requires the decision maker to be cognisant of the importance of the values at issue when making a decision (Eeckhout 2010). Of perhaps greater significance is the notion, outlined by Sunstein and quoted in the above paragraph, that in arbitrating between incommensurables, decision makers may and perhaps even should aim to reach a decision which 'fits' most appropriately with the self understanding of the community as established over time. This does not mean that a homogenous community view needs to be established to make such decisions but rather may require the use of several analytical frames which are capable of taking into account the views of the community as a whole. This has the implication that 'privatized' procedures which exclude certain voices from the community's self understanding are normatively improper.

## A Case Study of the 'Privatization' of Development: The WTO Dispute of EC – Tariff Preferences

Taken in the abstract, the argument outlined above may lack cogency. As a consequence, a case study approach is utilized below to elaborate upon how certain WTO decision-making processes directly relevant to how development is conceived, and moreover the choices involved therein, have too often been privatized in the sense of being accessible to only a limited number of participants. A caveat to the discussion which follows is, however, required. Attention will be directed, in part, to how developing country needs are responded to within the trade regime. It is realized that the reading given to how such needs are defined and responded to cannot be conflated with how development as both a process and a commitment is defined within the WTO. However, it is argued that how such needs are conceived, particularly when they are identified as development needs, has at least some connection with the reading which is given to the concept of development within the trade regime.

The case study chosen is the WTO dispute of EC – Tariff Preferences (WTO 2004) which concerned a dispute between India and the [then] European Communities and centred upon the grant of additional tariff preferences to certain developing countries to assist them in their fight against drug trafficking and production. The disputed 'drug arrangements' were one of five tariff preference schemes available to developing countries under EC Council Regulation 2501/2001. The centrepiece of this dispute concerned the question of whether it was permissible for developed country 'donors' of preferential tariff treatment to differentiate between developing country recipients in the grant of tariff preferences (Switzer 2008). A further but related question was whether such differentiation could be made by reference to 'positive conditionalities' whereby developing countries would be required to meet some goal in order to be eligible to receive preferential tariff treatment?

The dispute was initially heard before a WTO dispute settlement Panel, the findings of which were subsequently appealed to the WTO Appellate Body. In its examination of the matter before it, the Appellate Body (WTO 2004) looked to the history and objectives of the document under which Members may grant tariff preferences to developing countries to address their financial, trade or development needs. The document, commonly referred to as the Enabling Clause (GATT 1980), provides legal authority for Members to deviate from their obligations under the most-favoured nation clause [MFN] of GATT Article I.1 pursuant to which 'any advantage, favour, privilege or immunity granted by any contracting party to any product originating in or destined for any other country shall be accorded immediately and unconditionally to the like product originating in or destined for the territories of all other contracting parties'. In essence, the Enabling Clause provides permanent legal cover for Members to grant products from developing countries more favourable tariff treatment than that granted to products from other countries.

In its examination of the matter, the Appellate Body noted that WTO Members are encouraged to deviate from their MFN commitments in the pursuit of special and differential treatment in favour of developing countries. In so doing, Members may differentiate between beneficiaries of preferential tariff treatment in a way that responds positively to the 'needs of developing countries'. The phrase 'respond positively' is derived from the paragraph 3 (c) of the Enabling Clause which mandates that treatment provided under it 'shall in the case of such treatment accorded by developed contracting parties to developing countries be designed and, if necessary, modified, to respond positively to the development, financial and trade needs of developing countries'. In this regard, the Appellate Body noted that the use of the word 'shall' in paragraph 3 (c) is indicative of an obligation for developed countries providing preferential tariff treatment to respond positively to the needs of developing countries.

While the Appellate Body refers to the 'obligation' of members to respond positively according to need, it is unlikely that this extends to an obligation either to provide tariff preferences or to differentiate between recipient countries with regard to the grant of preferences. Despite the use of the word 'obligation', the Appellate Body later uses quite negative language in referring to the ability to differentiate between beneficiary countries as a response to need, noting that the requirements of the Enabling Clause do 'not prohibit' the granting of differential treatment.

In effect, the Appellate Body appears to be stating that preferential tariff treatment measures are obliged to respond positively to the needs of developing countries. At the same time, it also provides that there is a right or authority to differentiate between developing countries in this regard. However, the Appellate Body outlined that any such differentiation should be based upon objective criteria and any advantage accorded should be available to all 'similarly situated' countries. The remaining conditions set out in the Enabling Clause must be adhered to.

The best way to understand the ruling of the Appellate Body is to think of the grant of preferential tariff treatment as involving a two step process of consideration:

1. The first stage dictates that the grant of preferences to developing countries should respond positively to their needs. It would appear that the grant of preferences in line with the conditions imposed in the Enabling Clause is presupposed to be a positive response to need as, after all, as outlined by the Appellate Body, 'the very purpose of the special and differential treatment permitted under the Enabling Clause is to foster economic development of developing countries'. The Appellate Body therefore recognized that 'enhanced market access will contribute to responding to the needs of developing countries collectively'.
2. The second stage arises out of the reality that the developing country group is far from homogeneous and certain development needs may be common to only a certain number of developing countries. The Appellate Body recognized that the 'development, financial and trade needs' of developing countries are subject to change and in accordance with paragraph 3 (c) of the Enabling Clause, the treatment accorded to developing countries may be 'modified' in order to respond positively to any change in need. Since the needs of developing countries are not necessarily 'common or shared by all developing countries', responding to need 'may thus entail treating different country beneficiaries differently'. Preference granting countries may tailor their preferences. However, if any such differentiation occurs between developing country recipients, this must be intended as a 'positive' response to the 'development, financial and trade needs' of the developing countries concerned.

While the Appellate Body explicitly authorizes differentiating measures as a positive response to the divergence in developing country need, it is noted that the Appellate reading of the text of paragraph 3 (c) of the Enabling Clause was such as to find no obligation to respond to the needs of 'all' developing countries. To put it simply, the Appellate Body is stating there is no obligation for such a measure to be responsive to the needs of 'all' developing countries. It may therefore be responsive to the needs of 'some' developing countries. This provides an implicit acceptance to measures of differentiation. If there was an obligation that a measure encompass and be responsive to the needs of all, then it would be impossible to differentiate according to need. It is therefore underlined that while the Appellate Body found against the European Communities in the dispute at issue, it did not find against the practice of differentiation itself. By allowing such differentiation, even if constructed in accordance with the notion that it should act as a positive response to a relevant need, the Appellate Body in effect sanctioned the ability of developed countries to put forward a unilateral construction of 'need' – albeit within defined limits – in the grant of the preferential tariff treatment. In addition to denying developing countries communicative space to identify their needs, it is also arguable that differentiation on the basis of a positive response to 'need' may be used to meet the preference granting country's own interests (Switzer 2008).

In this regard, the Panel and Appellate Body have been criticized for not doing enough to promote development (Qureshi 2003). Indeed, a significant critique of the Appellate Body's decision in EC-Tariff Preferences was that it 'entrenched' previous practice even though the actions of major 'donors' had largely been shaped by political priorities (Tomazos 2007). In essence, the Appellate Body's pronouncements in EC-Tariff Preferences are problematic for the acceptance that in line with the practice of developed country donor states, it is for them to articulate what constitutes a relevant development, financial or trade need. So while implicit recognition was given by the Appellate Body to the incommensurable nature of development and its 'meaning' as being more than economic development, little consideration was given to the need for processes under which development concerns are prioritized and given value to 'fit' and moreover promote the self understanding of the community as a whole.

From a normative perspective, this is troubling since it reveals a fundamental lack of consistency at the heart of the grant of tariff preferences as well as potentially perpetuating a form of procedural injustice in respect of the articulation of how developing country needs are addressed under the grant of tariff preferences. At the heart of this inconsistency is the fact that under a mechanism designed to provide a positive response to developing country trade, development and financial needs, donor countries are permitted to decide unilaterally what those needs in fact are.

The above exposition upon the legal veracity of 'conditioning' access to tariff preferences is intended to demonstrate that it is possible for the developed country 'donor' to condition access to such preferences. Conditionality in itself is not the main concern with the focus of criticism being the process through which such conditionality is agreed upon. If we accept that the task of development may involve a range of incommensurable values, it appears axiomatic that the provision of legal space for a unilateral articulation of development needs does little to promote the community's self understanding of such values. As such, the [development] needs to which preferential tariff treatment is intended to respond are the products of private as opposed to public decision-making processes. As elaborated upon above, this is not only normatively troubling but liable to produce a form of procedural injustice. Moreover, if it is accepted that there is an intrinsic link between the reading given to a relevant development need and the understanding accorded to development as both a process and commitment within the trade regime, it is clear that the construct of development has to an extent been privatized.

The foregoing analysis of the grant of tariff preferences leads naturally to the question of how the legal framework governing the grant of tariff preferences would be constructed if this could be revisited. Arguably, in order to take account of the above criticisms, in the event that a donor state decides to add conditionalities to its respective scheme of preferences, a process of deliberation should be instituted.

An 'ideal' process of deliberation on the imposition of conditionalities would involve public debate. All interested parties, including civil society representatives, would be offered an opportunity to participate on an equal basis. Validity claims could be raised over the course of the deliberation relating to whether each parties' statements are true, 'correct' in their context and finally that they are sincere (Habermas, 1990). Documents relating to proceedings would be circulated on WTO website, thereby ensuring fast dissemination. In the event of disagreement, arbitration could be sought from the WTO secretariat under the same conditions as apply under the WTO dispute settlement system.

At present, while tariff preference schemes are notified to the WTO Committee on Trade and Development (CTD) and are subject to discussion therein, dissatisfaction has been expressed by developing countries that the 'multilateral' or public forum provided by the Committee is often ignored. Hence, in a recent CTD debate on the EU tariff preference scheme, it was noted by the representative of Brazil that;

> [T]the EC had limited itself to providing partial information, declaring that the rest could only be provided on a bilateral basis ... . [T]he EC, in an apparent attempt to unilaterally put an end to the matter, had on several occasions declared that the discussions were exhausted, and that there was no further reason to maintain this matter on the CTD's agenda. (WTO 2009)

## The Unilateral 'Gift' of Development

In utilizing a case study approach to answering the core research question of this chapter, mention must be made as to the appropriateness of both this approach as well as the chosen case study. In this regard, it is to be noted that the grant of tariff preferences constitutes a unilateral 'gift' to developing countries. A gift may come with conditions and is a voluntary act with little credence seeming to have been given to the notion of such tariff preferences as a [binding] gratuitous unilateral obligation. The same reading may be advanced in relation to numerous provisions of so-called special and differential treatment in favour of developing countries which are to be found under the WTO covered agreements. An example is provided by certain provisions which task developed countries to provide technical assistance to developing countries. In this regard, Article 9.2 of the Agreement on Sanitary and Phytosanitary Measures [SPS] directs that, 'Where substantial investments are required in order for an exporting Member to fulfil the sanitary and Phytosanitary requirements of an importing Member, the latter shall consider providing such technical assistance as will permit the developing country Member to maintain and expand its market access opportunities involved.' While this provision does not seek to articulate upon the meaning or understanding to be given to development as either a process of a commitment, it is focused upon meeting developing country Members' needs and thereby has at least some link to their developmental condition, however defined.

The practice of developed Members in relation to Article 9.2 SPS has been much criticized as allowing a 'top down' construction of developing country 'needs' in this area. Hence, as observed in a 2005 report adopted by the WTO Committee on Sanitary and Phytosanitary Measures, 'such assistance is often characterized as supply-driven, and may be determined to a greater extent by the policy interests of the donor rather than the specific needs of the recipient' (WTO 2005). To the extent that policy making in the SPS arena as well as the related concern of how best to address developing country needs therein may involve a range of incommensurable values, the exclusion of certain voices and viewpoints may result in the privatization of the decision-making process which is clearly normatively troubling.

Similarly, Article 10.1 SPS mandates that, 'in the preparation and application of sanitary or phytosanitary measures, members shall take account of the special needs of developing country members.' This is justiciable in the sense that it instructs developed countries to 'take account' of developing country needs. However, to take account of something is not the same as imposing a duty upon developed countries to agree with their developing counterparts on the type of measures which are appropriate given their status as developing countries (Kessie 2007).

Developing countries have expressed considerable concern that measures tasking Members to take into account their needs have been ignored. Hence, in relation to the effectiveness of Article 10.1 SPS Agreement, a number of developing countries noted that their 'special needs' have rarely been considered (WTO 2000). Accordingly, even though the obligation under Article 10.1 is phrased in mandatory terms, such 'obligations of conduct' are difficult to enforce due to the vagueness of the manner in which they are addressed (WTO 2001b). This problem has been exacerbated by the lack of information available on the extent to which the obligation under this provision has actually been met (WTO 2002).

## The Challenge of Providing a Public Communicative 'Space' for Development

In one sense, it may be said that provisions such as the grant of tariff preferences under the Enabling Clause, Article 9.2 and 10.1 SPS left the issue of 'how' developing country needs should be taken into account incompletely theorized (Sunstein 1996) or 'open' but, as we have seen, this resulted in the direction effectively being ignored or used for strategic purposes. In certain respects, therefore, provisions such as these are 'open rules' which have been converted to 'closed rules' given the lack of communicative access routes granted to developing countries to articulate their respective needs. A much greater challenge is how to [re]open such provisions to provide access routes to encourage a process of self and collective understanding between participants in respect of how to meet developing country needs and by extension, how to understand development as both a process and a commitment. For the reasons outlined above, the privatization of how we define such concepts is not only normatively troubling but of concern due to the notion that '[t]he legitimacy of WTO rules crucially depends on the extent to which all Members feel they have participated in the process that produced these common and legally enforceable rules. Ownership of the process that leads to these rules is paramount for their recognition' (Pederson 2006, 104). By extension, deeper economic integration under the WTO cannot be sustained without an accompanying commitment to deeper political integration. Central to this is the pursuit of an iterative process premised upon constructing a deepening sense of community (Esty 2002).

## Conclusion

The starting point for this examination was the contention that from a normative perspective, a multilateral construct of the meaning of development within the World Trade Organization [WTO] is to be preferred. It was iterated that the understanding to be given to development as both a process and commitment should be 'public' in the sense of emanating from a community. By extension, the reading and understanding to be ascribed to developing country [development] needs should also be the product of public rather than privatized processes. The rationale for this was based in part upon the contention that certain incommensurable values may lie at the heart of the debate on how best to promote development within the trade regime. Where a choice is required to be made between such values, the decision maker may wish to select a path which presents the community's self understanding in its best light. Where certain voices or viewpoints have been omitted, it is clear that such a result will not be achieved. Such exclusion also has the consequence that the meaning given to developing country [development] needs, and by extension, the meaning of development becomes privatized.

Several of the provisions designed to address developing country needs under the WTO covered agreements have been the subject of review under the Doha Round of multilateral trade negotiations (WTO 2001b). While this review process is still ongoing, it appears axiomatic that provisions designed to assist developing countries should not be allowed to become 'closed' in the sense of denying them communicative access routes to articulate their respective needs. Greater attention should therefore be paid under this review process to the provision of communicative access routes to encourage understanding between participants in respect of how to meet developing country needs and by extension, how to understand development as both a process and a commitment.

**References**

Alder, J. 2006. The Sublime and the Beautiful: Incommensurability and Human Rights. *Public Law*, 697–721.

Bhala, R. 2009. Resurrecting The Doha Round: Devilish Details, Grand Themes and China Too. *Texas International Law Journal* 45, 1–125.

Chang, R. 1997. Introduction, in *Incommensurability, Incomparability and Practical Reason*, edited by R. Chang. Harvard: Harvard University Press, 1–34.

Cohen, E. and E. Ben-Ari. 1993. Hard Choices: A Sociological Perspective on Value Incommensurability. *Human Studies*, 16 (3), 267–97.

Craswell, R. 1998. Incommensurability, Welfare Economic, and the Law. *University of Pennsylvania Law Review*, 146 (5), 1419–64.

Cullet, P. 2003. Patents and Medicines: The Relationship Between TRIPS and the Human Right to Health. *International Affairs*, 79 (1), 139–60.

Dunoff, J.L. 1999. The Death of the Trade Regime. *European Journal of International Law*, 10 (4), 733–62.

Eeckhout, P. The Scales of Trade – Reflections on the Growth and Functions of the WTO Adjudicative Branch. *Journal of International Economic Law*, 13 (1), 3–26.

Esty, D. 2002. The World Trade Organisation's Legitimacy Crisis. *World Trade Review*, 1 (1), 7–22.

GATT. 1980. Differential and More Favourable Treatment Reciprocity and Fuller Participation of Developing Countries – Decision of 28 November 1979. L/4903, BISD 26S/203.

Habermas, J. 1990. *Moral Consciousness and Communicative Action* (transl. C. Lenhardt and S.W. Nicholsen). Cambridge, MA: MIT Press.

Kessie, E. 2007. *The Legal Status of Special and Differential Treatment Provisions under the WTO Agreements in WTO Law and Developing Countries*, edited by G.A. Bermann and P.C. Mavroidis. Cambridge: Cambridge University Press, 12–36.

Pederson, P.N. The WTO Decision-making Process and Internal Transparency. *World Trade Review*, 5 (1), 103–31.

Posner, E.A. 1997. The Strategic Basis of Principled Behaviour: A Critique of the Incommensurability Thesis. *University of Pennsylvania Law Review*, 146, 1184–214.

Qureshi, A. 2003. Interpreting World Trade Organization Agreements for the Development Objective. *Journal of World Trade*, 37 (5), 847–82.

Radnor, M.J. 1993. Compensation and Commensurability. *Duke Law Journal*, 43 (1), 56–86.

Raz, J. 1986. *The Morality of Freedom*. Oxford: Clarendon Press.

Sunstein, C.R. 1994. Incommensurability and Valuation in Law. *Michigan Law Review*, 92, 779–861.

———. 1996. *Legal Reasoning and Political Conflict*. Oxford: Oxford University Press.

———. 1998. *Incommensurability and Kinds of Valuation: Some Applications in Law, in Incommensurability, Incomparability and Practical Reason*, edited by R. Chang. Cambridge, MA: Harvard University Press, 234–54.

Switzer, S. 2008. 'Environmental Protection and the Generalised System of Preferences'. *International and Comparative Law Quarterly*, 57 (1), 113–47.

Tomazos, A. 2007. 'The GSP Fallacy: A Critique of the Appellate Body's Ruling in The GSP Case on Legal, Economic and Political Systemic Grounds', in *WTO Law and Developing Countries*, edited by G.A. Bermann and P.C. Mavroidis. Cambridge: Cambridge University Press, 306–23.

UN Development Programme, 1990. Human Development Report 1990. New York: United Nations.

WTO. 2000. Special and Differential Treatment – Note by the Secretariat. G/SPS/W/105.

———. 2001a. Ministerial Conference Fourth Session Ministerial Declaration. WT/MIN(01)/DEC/1.

———. 2001b. Ministerial Conference Fourth Session – Implementation – Related Issues and Concerns: Decision of 14 November 2001. WT/MIN(01)/17.

———. 2002. Information on the Utilisation of Special and Differential Treatment Provisions. WT/COMTD/W/77/Rev.1/Add.4.

———. 2004. European Communities: Conditions for the Granting of Tariff Preferences for Developing Countries – Report of the Appellate Body. WT/DS246/AB/R.

———. 2005. Report on Proposals for Special and Differential Treatment – Report Adopted by Committee on 30 June 2005. G/SPS/35.

———. 2008. Report to the Trade Negotiations Committee by the Chairman of the Special Session on Agriculture. JOB(08)/95.

———. 2009. Note on the Meeting of 3 December 2008. WT/COMTD/M/72.

# PART V
# Emerging Publics: The Role of the Victim in International Criminal Justice

# Chapter 15
# The Impact of the Distinction Between Situations and Cases on the Participation of Victims in the International Criminal Court

Ania Salinas[1] and James Sloan[2]

## Introduction

The bestowal of a role for victims in the proceedings of the International Criminal Court ('ICC' or 'Court') by the drafters of the Rome Statute (1998) ('Statute') is one of the most important achievements of the ICC and a significant step forward in international criminal justice (Jorda and Hemptinne, 2002: 1388). It ensures that victims' views will be taken into consideration – rather than only those of the accused, the Prosecutor or affected states (Stahn at al., 2006: 221) – and serves as an acknowledgement of the importance of access to justice for victims at the international level.

Article 68(3) of the Statute and Rule 93 of the Rules of Procedure and Evidence (2002) ('Rules') provide the most comprehensive statements as regards victims' participation, granting them a general right to participate in the proceedings before the Court. Moreover, the Statute and the Rules provide victims with specific participatory rights[3] in numerous ICC proceedings (Vasiliev, 2009: 638). Article 68(3) provides that, where the personal interests of the victims are affected, the Court shall permit their views and concerns to be presented and considered at various stages of the proceedings. Rule 93 gives the Court the power to seek the views of the victims on any issue. While victims are not equal players in the judicial process – they are not recognized as parties but participants[4] – neither the Statute nor the Rules unambiguously address the extent of victims' rights to participate

1 Legal Officer at the Chambers of the International Criminal Court. The views expressed herein are those of the authors alone and do not reflect the views of the International Criminal Court.

2 Lecturer at the University of Glasgow, Scotland.

3 Such as, *inter alia*, Article 15(3) in conjunction with Rule 50, Article 53(3)(a) and (b) in conjunction with Rule 92(2) and Article 19(3) in conjunction with Rule 59(1).

4 *DRC* situation, ICC-01/04-556, Judgment on victim participation in the investigation stage of the proceedings in the appeal of the OPCD against decision of Pre-Trial Chamber I of 7 December 2007 and in the appeals of the OPCD and the Prosecutor against the decision of the Pre-Trial Chamber I of 24 December 2007 (Appeals Chamber, 19 December 2008), para. 55.

in proceedings. As such, the Court has been given considerable discretion to decide the parameters of those rights (Bitti and Friman, 2001: 459, Vasiliev, 2009: 638).

In exercising its discretion, the Court faces the dilemma of balancing the need to ensure the victims' rights to access to justice with the potential negative impact of their participation on the administrative burdens of the Court (Stahn et al., 2006: 223) and the rights of the accused (Stahn et al., 2006: 223, Zappala, 2010: 137). In particular, two questions have emerged in the case law so far: 1) at what stages of the proceedings may victims participate? and 2) what is the extent of victims' right to participate? This discussion considers the Court's treatment of the issues by looking at its decision-making in relation to the participation of victims at the different stages of the proceedings and shows that whether a victim is considered a victim of a 'situation' or a victim of a 'case' can have an important effect on his or her participatory rights.

## Victims of a Case vs. Victims of a Situation: The Nature of the Distinction

The terms 'case' and 'situation' are used in the Statute but neither is defined and no formal distinction is provided therein. Based on the usage of the terms in the Statute, it would appear that its drafters (Yee, 1999: 147)[5] viewed the terms, at times, as being synonyms[6] and, at other times, as being quite distinct.[7] The distinction was however, explicitly elaborated by Pre-Trial Chamber ('PTC') I in a decision of 17 January 2006, where it considered the scope of victims' participation in the Situation in the Democratic Republic of the Congo ('DRC').[8] It held that whereas *situations* 'entail the proceedings … to determine whether a particular situation should give rise to a criminal investigation as well as the investigation as such', *cases* 'entail proceedings that take place after the issuance of a warrant of arrest or a summons to appear'.[9]

It may be noted that this situation/case distinction does not correspond exactly with the investigation/trial stages of the proceedings. However, there is some overlap. A situation involves events, which occurred in a particular territory within a specific period of time in which one or more crimes within the jurisdiction of the

5 Although the distinction was discussed at the Rome Conference, it was not explicitly incorporated into the Statute. For an in-depth analysis of the drafting history of this different terminology, see *Kenya* situation, ICC-01/09-19-Corr, Decision Pursuant to Article 15 of the Rome Statute on the Authorization of an Investigation into the Situation in the Republic of Kenya (Pre-Trial Chamber II, 31 March 2010), paras. 46–8.

6 Article 15(4), in relation with Article 15(5) and (6) of the Statute.

7 Articles 13(a), 13(b), 14(1), 17(a) and 17(b) of the Statute.

8 *DRC* situation, ICC-01/04-101-tEN-Corr, Decision on the applications for participation in the proceedings of VPRS1, VPRS 2, VPRS 3, VPRS 4, VPRS 5 and VPRS 6 (Pre-Trial Chamber I, 17 January 2006) [Hereinafter 'Participation Decision' of 17 January 2006].

9 ICC-01/04-101-tEN-Corr, para. 65.

Court appear to have been committed. It can include the pre-investigation stage and the investigation stage. A case comprises the specific actions that constitute one or more crimes under the jurisdiction of the Court that were allegedly committed by one or more persons. It extends from pre-trial through to trial and appeal. Whereas, as explained above, the issuance of an arrest warrant or a summons to appear marks the start of the case, there is some issue as to whether the trial begins with the filing in the Registry of the decision confirming the charges or when the opening statements are made.[10]

To date, five situations have come before the Court – involving Northern Uganda, DRC, Darfur – Sudan, Central African Republic (CAR) and Kenya – and they have, to date, resulted in the pursuit of nine cases against fifteen alleged perpetrators.[11]

## Victims of a Situation

In its Participation Decision of 17 January 2006, PCT I described 'situations' as entailing the proceedings to determine whether a particular situation of crisis should give rise to a criminal investigation and the investigation as such. Each aspect will be considered in turn.

---

10 See the different approaches of the Trial Chambers in *Katanga and Ngudjolo* case, ICC-01/04-01/07-1213, Motifs de la decision orale relative à l'exception d'irrecevabilité de l'affaire (article 19 du Statut) (Trial Chamber II, 16 June 2009), para. 49 (para. 50 in the English version), and *Lubanga* case ICC-01/04-01/06-1084, Decision on the status before the Trial Chamber of the evidence heard by the Pre-Trial Chamber and the decisions of the Pre-Trial Chamber in trial proceedings, and the manner in which evidence shall be submitted (Trial Chamber I, 13 December 2007). The Appeals Chamber still has not made clear its position on the matter. *See Katanga and Ngudjolo* case ICC-01/04-01/07 OA 8, Judgment on the Appeal of Mr. Germain Katanga against the Oral Decision of Trial Chamber II of 12 June 2009 on the Admissibility of the Case (Appeals Chamber, 25 September 2009), para. 38.

11 In the situation in the DRC, three cases have been opened: one against Thomas Lubanga Dyilo (ICC-01/04-01/06), one against Germain Katanga and Mathieu Ngudjolo Chui (ICC-01/04-01/07) and one against Bosco Ntaganda (ICC-01/04-02/06). In the situation in CAR only one case has been opened against a single individual, Jean-Pierre Bemba Gombo (ICC-01/05-01/08). With the situation in Northern Uganda, a single case has been opened featuring four alleged perpetrators (a fifth has since deceased): Joseph Kony, Vincent Otti, Okot Odhiambo and Dominic Ongwen (ICC-02/04-01/0). In the situation in Darfur, there are four cases: one against Ahmad Muhammad Harun (Ahmad Harun) and Ali Muhammad Ali Abd-Al-Rahman (Ali Kushayb) (ICC-02/05-01/0), one against the President Omar Hassan Ahmad Al Bahir (ICC-02/05-01/09), one against Bahar Idriss Abu Garda (ICC-02/05-02/09) and the last one against Abdallah Banda Abakaer and Saleh Mohammed Jerbo Jamus (ICC-02/05-03/09).

*Pre-investigation stage: proceedings to petermine whether an investigation Sshould take place*

At the pre-investigation stage two alternate proceedings are outlined in the Statute, which may occur in certain prescribed circumstances. Whether a review of the Prosecutor's decision regarding the need for an investigation may take place depends on whether the situation was referred to the Court by a State Party or the Security Council (UNSC) or initiated by the Prosecutor *proprio motu*.

***Review of prosecutor's decision not to proceed with an investigation where the matter has been referred by a state party or the UNSC (Article 53(3))***

Where a situation is referred to the Prosecutor by a State Party or the UNSC, and the Prosecutor finds that there is no reasonable basis to proceed, a proceeding may be held to review this decision.[12] The participation of victims is specifically provided for in such proceedings. Rule 92(2) provides that the Court must notify victims of a decision of the Prosecutor not to commence an investigation in 'order to allow victims to apply for participation in the proceedings in accordance with Rule 89.'[13] Such notification shall be given to victims who have already participated in the proceedings or, as far as possible, to those who have communicated with the Court in respect of the situation in question (Rule 92(2)).[14] Additionally, Rule 93 gives the PTC the power to seek the views of victims on any issue arising at this proceeding.[15] At this early stage of the proceedings, the only victims that could seek participation or be asked for views would be victims of the situation. Given that in each of the four matters referred to the Prosecutor, to date, there has been found to be a reasonable basis to proceed with an investigation, there have been no proceedings of this nature and, as such, no judicial consideration of the parameters of victims' participation therein.

12 See Article 53(1) and (3). A referring party may request a review of the Prosecutor's decision not to proceed on several bases (Article 53(3)(a)); the PTC may conduct such a review on its own initiation (though only where the Prosecutor's decision not to prosecute was motivated by the interests of justice) (Article 53(3)(b)).

13 Rule 89(1) provides that victims may make application to the Registrar to present their views and concerns. Rule 89(2), however, provides that the Chamber may reject such an application if 'it considers that the person is not a victim or that the criteria set for the in article 68, paragraph 3, are otherwise not fulfilled'.

14 In addition, Rule 107(5), which sets out the procedure for a request by a reviewing party of the Prosecutor's decision that there is no reasonable basis to commence an investigation, refers to Rule 59, which, in turn, guarantees victims who have already communicated with the Court the right to be notified of an admissibility or jurisdiction challenge under Article 19(3), as well as the right to a summary of the grounds of the challenge and the right to make written representations.

15 Rule 93 refers, *inter alia*, to issues referred to in Rule 107; Rule 107 deals with a request for review under Article 53(3)(a).

***Authorization to the prosecutor to initiate a* Proprio Motu *investigation (Article 15(3))***

Where the Prosecutor, on a *proprio motu* basis, decides that there *is* a reasonable basis to proceed with an investigation, he or she must request an authorization to do so. Article 15(3) of the Statute specifically provides that victims may make representations to a PTC in accordance with the rules during such a proceeding (Stahn et al., 2006, pp. 228–9). Again, at this early stage only victims of the situation may make use of this specific participatory right. Rule 50 orders the Prosecutor to inform victims of the impending proceeding, to allow them to make written representations within a set time (Rule 50(3)).[16] The PTC may request additional information from the victims who have made representations and, where it considers it appropriate, may hold a hearing. Under Regulation 87 of the Regulations of the Court (2004) ('Regulations'), the Prosecutor has the duty to notify the PTC of information provided pursuant Rule 50(1).

PTC II's 31 March 2010 authorization of the Prosecutor's request to open an investigation in Kenya is, to date, the only instance of such an authorization proceeding.[17] Before the request, the Prosecutor notified victims by posting a public notice and called for written representations.[18] In an Order dated 10 December 2009, PTC II set the conditions for the victims' representations and stressed that because Article 15(3) and Rule 50(3) use the term 'victim' as defined in the Rule 85,[19] representations must only come from those qualifying as 'victims' within the meaning of that Rule.[20]

16 Regulation 50 provides for a period of 30 days and Regulation 35 provides for the possibility to modify the time limit where good cause is shown.

17 The note was posted on the website of the Court and notification was provided to Kenya media outlets and NGOs. See ICC-01/09-19-Corr.

18 *Kenya* situation ICC-01/09-3-Anx1F, Annex 1F of the Request for authorization of an investigation pursuant to Article 15. The notice advised victims that they could 'send their comments to the Judges of PTC II on whether an investigation on such alleged crimes should be opened'.

19 Rule 85(a) defines victims for the purposes of the Statute and the Rules as natural persons who have suffered harm as a result of the commission of any crime within the jurisdiction of the Court. Rule 85(b) provides that a victim may also include organizations or institutions that have sustained direct harm to any of their property which is dedicated to religion, education, art or science or charitable purposes, and their historic monuments, hospitals and other places and objects for humanitarian purposes.

20 *Kenya* situation ICC-01/09-4, Order to the Victims Participation and Reparations Section Concerning Victims' Representations Pursuant to Article 15(3) of the Statute (Pre-Trial Chamber II, 10 December 2009), para. 7. This clarification may have been necessary due to the broad and confusing approach adopted by the Prosecutor when referring to the victims and their interests. See ICC-01/09-3 para. 59. When describing the impact of the crimes on the victims, the request referred to the impact on the local communities in terms of security, social structure, economy and persistence of impunity in the country. It even went so as far as to refer to the fall in the rate of the Kenyan Gross Domestic Product growth from 7% in 2007 to 1.7% in 2008. While certain of these aspects may be relevant

In the 31 March 2010 authorization, PTC II highlighted the significant guidance provided by the victims' representation to its assessment of the impact of the crimes and the harm caused to the victims and their families. These factors were relied upon by PCT II in its analysis of the requirements of gravity according to Article 17(1)(d).[21] Further, victims' representations were decisive in the PCT's ruling that the investigation had to encompass a temporal scope that was broader than the one originally envisaged by the Prosecution.[22]

*Investigation stage*

The Statute and Rules are rather confusing in relation to the right of victims to participate at the investigative stage. Article 68(3) is placed in Part VI of the Rome Statute dealing with the trial, but Rules 89 to 92 are contained in Chapter IV of the Rules, together with the provisions relating to the various stages of the proceedings. Nevertheless, from its earliest decisions the Court has read Article 68(3) as providing for a general participatory right in all stages of the proceedings (Vasiliev, 2009: 641).[23] Since PTC I's Participation Decision of 17 January 2006,[24] both PTC I and PTC II have granted victims broad participatory rights at the investigative stage of the proceedings.[25] On appeal, this broad approach was

---

to demonstrate the gravity of the situation as a whole, they must not be confused with the impact on the victims, lest the misimpression be created that victims' direct interests and claims for justice are merely secondary and not a factor that warrants ICC's intervention. What if the Kenyan GDP had risen to 10%? Are economically stable regimes where international crimes are committed less deserving of international concern? This debatable Prosecutorial approach to the interests of the victims is further elaborated in the Prosecutorial Policy. See OTP 2007 *Policy Paper on the Interest of Justice* [online] Available at: http://www.icc-cpi.int/NR/rdonlyres/772C95C9-F54D-4321-BF09-73422BB23528/143640/ICCOTPInterestsOfJustice.pdf [accessed: 26.90.10], pp. 5–6, which sets the standard for the OTP to determine the interests of the victims, and makes reference *inter alia* to: 'the different views of victims, their communities and the broader societies in which it may be required to act.'

21 ICC-01/09-19-Corr, paras. 62 and 196.

22 ICC-01/09-19-Corr, paras. 204–7.

23 However, in early commentaries the participation of victims was envisaged as taking place at the trial or upon the confirmation of charges.

24 ICC-01/04-101-tEN-Corr.

25 See *Uganda* situation ICC-02/04-101, Decision on victims' applications for participation a/0010/06, a/0064/06 to a/0070/06, a/0081/06 to a/0104/04 and a/0111/06 to a/0127/06 (Pre-Trial Chamber II, 10 August 2007), paras. 88–9. *Darfur–Sudan* situation ICC-02/05-111, Decision on the Applications for Participation in the Proceedings of Applicants a/011/06 to a/0015/06, a/0021/07, a/0023/97 to a/0033/07 and a/0035/07 to a/0038/07 (Pre-Trial Chamber I, 6 December 2007). The approaches adopted by the PTCs differed in what is been called *systematic versus casuistic* approach. While PTC I granted victims a general right to be heard and file documents during the investigation stage, PTC II specified in which judicial proceedings during the investigative stage victims could participate.

partially overruled. Confusingly, the Appeals Chamber ('AC'), while precluding victims from intervening in the investigation conducted by the Prosecutor, expressly recognized their right to seek participation in any judicial proceeding that may take place at the investigative stage.

In the Participation Decision of 17 January 2006, PTC I took the view that the term 'proceedings' as used in Article 68(3) 'does not necessarily exclude the stage of investigation of a situation'.[26] As regards Article 68(3)'s requirement that the 'personal interest of the victims' be affected, the Chamber was of the view that 'personal interests of victims are affected in general at the investigation stage, since the participation of victims at this stage can serve to clarify the facts, to punish the perpetrators of crimes and to request reparations for the harm suffered'.[27]

When ruling on the participation of victims at the investigative stage, PTC I adopted a two-fold procedure. It was to be decided in first place whether certain victims were able to participate at the investigation stage as such. If so, they would be granted the procedural 'status of victims'. At a second stage, the Chamber would consider the extent of their participation on a case-by-case basis.[28] Accordingly, persons granted the 'status of victims' were authorized 'notwithstanding any specific proceedings being conducted in the framework of such an investigation, to be heard by the Chamber in order to present their views and concerns and to file documents pertaining to the ... investigation'.[29] With regard to specific proceedings, the PCT held that it would 'decide at the time of the initiation of such proceedings whether persons having the status of victims may participate in them. In reaching such a decision, the Chamber will take into account the impact that such specific proceedings could have on their personal interests'.[30] Furthermore, those having the status of victims were also 'entitled to

26 ICC-01/04-101-tEN-Corr, para. 38.

27 ICC-01/04-101-tEN-Corr, para. 63.

28 As to the role of victims with regard to specific proceedings, PCT I posited the following approaches: (i) when specific proceedings are initiated proprio motu by the Pre-Trial Chamber under Articles 56(3) and 57(3)(c) of the Statute, the PCT 'will decide at the time of initiation of such proceedings whether persons having the status of victims may participate in them', taking into account 'the impact that such specific proceedings could have on their personal interests'; (ii) when specific proceedings are initiated by Prosecutor or Defence Counsel, the PCT will distinguish between a) proceedings that must be conducted confidentially or in closed session and b) public proceedings. 'In the latter case, victims will be entitled to participate unless the Chamber decides otherwise after determining the impact that such proceedings might have on their personal interests. In the case of other specific proceedings that must remain confidential, persons having the status of victims will not be entitled to participate unless the Chamber decides otherwise in the light of the impact of such proceedings on their personal interests'; and (iii) when victims request the Pre-Trial Chamber to order specific proceedings pursuant to Article 68(3) of the Statute, the PCT will rule on a case-by-case basis, after assessing the impact of such proceedings on the personal interests of the applicants.

29 ICC-01/04-101-tEN-Corr, para. 71.

30 ICC-01/04-101-tEN-Corr, para. 73.

request the Pre-Trial Chamber, pursuant to article 68(3) of the Statute, to order specific proceedings'.[31]

In December 2008, the AC observed that 'the notion of *procedural status of victims* is nowhere defined, and it is difficult to attach a specific meaning to it'.[32] In interpreting Article 68(3), it distinguished between prosecutorial or investigative steps conducted by the Prosecutor and judicial proceedings:

> [A]rticle 68(3) of the Statute correlates victim participation to 'proceedings', a term denoting a judicial cause pending before a Chamber. In contrast, an investigation is not a judicial proceeding but an inquiry conducted by the Prosecutor into the commission of a crime with a view to bringing to justice those deemed responsible.[33]

The AC stated that victims' participation could take place 'only within the context of judicial proceedings'. It held further that:

> [the] authority for the conduct of the investigations vests in the Prosecutor. Acknowledgment by the Pre-Trial Chamber of a right to victims to participate in the investigation would necessarily contravene the Statute by reading into it a power outside its ambit and remit.[34]

There was, according to the AC, an 'ample scope within the statutory scheme of the Statute for victims and anyone else with relevant information to pass it on to the Prosecutor without first being formally accorded "a general right to participate"'.[35] The AC recalled that 'participation pursuant to article 68(3) of the Statute is confined to proceedings before the Court, and aims to afford victims an opportunity to voice their views and concerns on matters affecting their personal interests'.[36] It also held that 'victims are not precluded from seeking participation in any judicial proceedings, *including proceedings affecting investigations,* provided their personal interests are affected by the issues arising for resolution'.[37]

According to the AC Decision, victims are not entitled to make submissions and file documents with the PTC in relation to the Prosecution's investigation.[38] Moreover, the PTC will have to decide whether victims can participate in those specific judicial proceedings held during the investigation stage. The decision will be taken on a case-by-case basis, depending on the impact of such proceedings

31 ICC-01/04-101-tEN-Corr, para. 75.
32 ICC-01/04-556, para. 43 [emphasis added].
33 ICC-01/04-556, para. 45.
34 ICC-01/04-556, para. 52.
35 ICC-01/04-556, para. 53.
36 ICC-01/04-556, para. 55.
37 ICC-01/04-556, para. 56 [emphasis added].
38 ICC-01/04-556, paras. 41–6. See also Appeals Chamber 2 February 2009 Decision, para. 7.

on the victim's personal interests.[39] The AC therefore distinguished between investigative steps (conducted by the Prosecutor) and judicial proceedings, viewing them as different spheres within the investigation stage. While victims could not intervene in the investigation conducted by the Prosecutor, they would be able to seek participation in judicial proceedings.[40]

Again, the only victims who could intervene at this stage – when no arrest warrant or summons to appear has been issued – would be the victims of the situation under investigation. The types of proceedings that may occur at the investigative stage in which victims of a situation may have a role are numerous and can include appeals of PTC decisions where appropriate.[41] Certain proceedings must, by their very nature, occur before a case has come into existence;[42] others may occur either at the situation stage or at the case stage (or not at all), depending on the nature of the particular proceeding.[43]

---

39 ICC-01/04-556, paras. 46–55. See also Appeals Chamber 2 February 2009 Decision, para. 7.

40 ICC-01/04-556, para. 57.

41 Additional proceedings regarding appeals of certain findings of the PTC may also be brought and the victims may also have a role in them.

42 For example, a proceeding to review a decision of the Prosecutor not to commence a prosecution as provided for at Article 53(3) will necessarily occur at the investigation stage. Similarly, where the OTP initiates an investigation – either based on a referral of a State Party or based on a authorized *proprio motu* basis – he must defer to states who would normally exercise jurisdiction over the crimes if they so request unless the PTC, on the application of the OTP, decides otherwise (Art. 18(1) and (2)). This procedure, which is described as 'preliminary', must be instigated by the affected State within one month of being notified (Article 18(2)); Article 18(1) appears to imply that the notification must take place immediately upon instigation of the investigation. While a role for victims is not specifically set out in Article 18, some have taken the view that Rule 59 (which appears to deal with a proceeding regarding jurisdiction and admissibility under Article 19 only) extends to proceedings under Article 18 (Bitti and Gonzalez, 2005: 676, Hall, 2008: 411–12). To date there have been no such proceedings.

43 The wording of the various paragraphs of Article 19 indicates that a determination regarding the admissibly and jurisdiction of a case may be made at either the situation stage or the case stage, depending on who is requesting the determination. Article 19(7) provides that where a challenge is made by an affected state 'the Prosecutor shall suspend the investigation until such time as the Court makes a determination in accordance with article 17.' Other provisions speak of challenges prior to the confirmation of charges (Article 19(6)), at any time up to the start of the trial (Article 19(4)), at the start of the trial (Article 19(4)) or, exceptionally, after the start of the trial (Article 19(4)). PTC II, however, took a contrary view, holding that proceedings under Article 19(1) (i.e., initiated by the Court), 'must have reached the stage of a case (including "specific incidents during which one or more crimes within the jurisdiction of the Court seem to have been committed by one or more identified suspects"), as opposed to the preceding stage of the situation'. See *Kony et al. case* ICC-02/04-01/05-377 Decision on the admissibility of the case under article 19(1) of the Statute (Pre-Trial Chamber II, 10 March 2009), para. 14. This reasoning appears to be based on the use of the word 'case' in Article 19(1). Given that the word 'case' is also

As noted, an application for an arrest warrant or a summons to appear may be brought at any time after the initiation of an investigation (Article 58(1)). Given the Court's view that a case comes into existence when a PTC issues an arrest warrant or summons to appear,[44] this is the last proceeding at the situation stage of events (other than an appeal of such a determination). Because such a proceeding is *ex parte* in nature – as a general rule victims will only be aware of the existence of an arrest warrant or a summons to appear after it has been issued, unless under the exceptional circumstances in which the Prosecutor publicly announces the request, as it was in the case against Omar Al Bashir – a request for victim participation in the process, while possible, seems highly unlikely.[45]

What the AC has not made clear in its decisions is whether or not victims are entitled to trigger judicial proceedings at the investigation stage. While many take the view that the jurisprudence of the Court means that victims' participation is confined to judicial proceedings initiated by the Chamber or the parties, this just one possible interpretation.[46] Another contested issue is the current situation of

used in Article 19(2), this reasoning, if correct, would rule out any such proceedings at the situation stage initiated by an affected state. Caution must be exercised in reading too much into the terms 'case' and 'situation' in the Statute; as discussed above, the Statute is not consistent in this regard. Proceedings under Article 19 are discussed further below.

44 See PTC I Decision of 17 January 2006, ibid, at para. 65. An argument could be made that a matter becomes a case when the Prosecutor applies for an arrest warrant or summons to appear under Article 58 rather than when such an order is issued. After all, unlike other proceedings occurring during the situation phase, here the PTC must consider whether there are reasonable grounds to believe a named individual (or more than one) has committed the crimes as alleged rather than considering the situation in general.

45 Some victims applied for participation in the proceedings arising out of the AC's ruling that PCT I must review the threshold applied when deciding whether to issue a warrant of arrest for genocide in the *Bashir* case. However, those victims' applications were rejected because the Chamber held that to implement the Appeals Decision it was only needed to apply the standard of proof of Bashir's genocidal intent, as identified by the AC, and neither a reassessment of the materials originally supporting the application for an arrest warrant nor analysis of other material was warranted. It is arguably however that in different circumstances PTCs should consider the views and concerns of victims in such proceedings. See *Bashir* case ICC-02/05-01/09-77, Victims' Application for Participation in the Proceedings arising out of the Appeal Judgment of 3 February 2010 (ICC-02/05-01/09-73) (Pre-Trial Chamber I, 24 March 2010) and ICC-02/05-01/09-75, Application of Legal Representatives of Victims a/0011/06, a/0012/06, a/0013/06 and a/0015/06 to Participate in and Submit Observations on the Proceedings on Remand in Connection with the Application for a Warrant for the Arrest of Omar Hassan Ahmad al-Bashir (Pre-Trial Chamber I, 12 March 2010) in relation to ICC-02/05-01/09-94, Second Decision on the Prosecution's Application for a Warrant of Arrest (Pre-Trial Chamber I, 12 July 2010), paras. 2–3.

46 A recent request by victims in the DRC will require the PTC I to decide on the legal standing of victims to trigger specific proceedings before the Chamber. *See* ICC-01/04-564 'Demande du représentant légal de VPRS 3 et 6 aux fins de mise en cause de Monsieur Jean-Pierre Bemba en sa qualité de chef militaire au sens de l'article 28-a

those victims of a situation whose status had already been recognized at the time of the AC decisions; has it been revoked? These issues together with many other unsettled questions are yet to be decided by the Chambers. Contrary to what it may appear, the legal framework for the role of the so-called 'victims of the situation' is, as yet, far from crystallized.

## Victims of a Case

With the issuance of a warrant of arrest or a summons to appear, specific crimes and alleged perpetrators are identified and the second stage of judicial proceedings, 'the case', begins. At this stage, the participation of victims is narrowed to those victims of the specific crimes allegedly committed by the suspect(s), i.e., the 'victims of the case'. As shall be seen, the Court has not always imposed this rather obvious limitation.

During the case stage, it is helpful to distinguish between two sets of proceedings: 1) those that take place between the issuance of the warrant of arrest or summons to appear and the commencement of the trial, the 'pre-trial stage' of a case, and 2) those that take place after the commencement of the trial, i.e., the 'trial stage' of the case. Each will be considered in turn. However, before analysing the victims' general participatory rights during the pre-trial and trial stages of cases, it is helpful to turn to the victims' right to participate in the proceedings under Article 19 relating to issues of jurisdiction and admissibility. Such proceedings may occur at either the 'situation' stage or the 'case' stage[47] and have been treated by the Court as featuring a different participatory regime than the general one of Article 68(3).

### *Proceedings for the Determination of the Jurisdiction of the Court and/or the Admissibility of the Case (Article 19)*

Article 19 of the Statute provides for a determination regarding the jurisdiction of the Court or the admissibility of a case[48] and Article 19(3) provides that victims may submit observations to the Court in such proceedings.[49] Rule 59 guarantees the

---

su Statut pour les crimes dont ses troupes sont présumées ocupables en Iturri (Pre-Trial Chamber I, 28 June 2010).

47 PTC II, in the 31 March 2010 authorization to open an investigation in Kenya, underlined that the Statute is drafted in a manner which tends to solve questions related to admissibility at different stages of the proceedings, beginning with a 'situation' and ending with a concrete 'case'. See paras. 41–7.

48 This may occur where the Court, on its own motion, considers the matter (Article 19(1)), where a challenge is made by an accused or affected state (Article 19(2)) or where a ruling is sought by the Prosecutor (Article 19(3)).

49 Because the provision for victim participation is located in Article 19(3) – which deals with the Prosecutor seeking a ruling regarding a question of jurisdiction or admissibility – rather than as a separate subparagraph of Article 19, it has been argued that victim participation is limited to such a case (rather than cases where the issue arises on the

victims 'who have already communicated with the Court in relation to that case or their legal representatives' the right to be notified of an admissibility or jurisdiction challenge (Rule 59(1)(b)), to be provided with a summary of the grounds of the challenge (Rule 59(2)) and to make written representations (Rule 59(3)).

In the case against *Joseph Kony et al.*,[50] PTC II held that the reference in Rule 59(1)(b) to 'victims who have already communicated with the Court in relation to that case' included: 'a) Those victims who have been admitted to participate in the Case or their legal representatives; and b) those applicants who have submitted applications to be admitted to participate with respect to the Case or their legal representatives',[51] and invited all such individuals to submit their observations on the admissibility of the case. As a result, the Office of Public Counsel for Victims (OPCV) presented the views and concerns of 86 victims,[52] including those victims who had been authorized to participate in the pre-trial stage and those applicants for whom such a decision had been deferred. The views of these individuals were taken into account by PTC II[53] and the AC[54] if their decisions found that the case was admissible. In addition, PTC II granted *amicus curiae* status to two victims' rights organizations, allowing them to submit written observations on certain issues.[55]

In the 31 March 2010 authorization to open an investigation in Kenya, PTC II stressed that admissibility should be assessed against the backdrop of a 'case'. Therefore, when there is no concrete case involving identified suspects

---

instigation of the Court, the accused or an affected state). The general nature of victims' participation, however, is clear from the Rule 59. Moreover, the reliance of PTC II on Article 19(3) as affording victims the right to participate in the *Kony* case – where it was acting on its own motion in accordance with Article 19(1) – made it clear that that PTC did not consider that victims' participation was limited to situations where the Prosecutor was initiating a motion under Article 19(3) (*Kony et al.* case ICC-02/04-01/05-320, Decision initiating proceedings under article 19, requesting observations and appointing counsel for the Defense (Pre-Trial Chamber II, 21 October 2008) [hereinafter '*Kony et al.*, Decision of 21 October 2008']), para. 7.

50 *Kony et al.*, Decision of 21 October 2008.

51 *Kony et al.*, Decision of 21 October 2008, para. 7.

52 *Kony et al.* case ICC-02/04-01/05-349, Observations on behalf of victims pursuant to article 19(1) of the Rome Statute with 55 Public Annexes and 45 Redacted Annexes (Pre-Trial Chamber II, 18 November 2008).

53 *Kony at al.* case ICC-02/04-01/05-377, Decision on the admissibility of the case under article 19(1) of the Statute (Pre-Trial Chamber II, 10 March 2009), para. 9.

54 *Kony et al.* case ICC-02/04-01/05-408, Judgment on the appeal of the Defense against the 'Decision on the admissibility of the case under article 19(1) of the Statute' of 10 March 2009 (Appeals Chamber, 16 September 2009), paras. 42–5.

55 ICC-02/04-01/05-377, para. 2. The approach of granting *amicus curiae* status to such organizations may, on certain occasions, represent a means by which to put forward victim-focused positions. However, the Court should remain careful not to rely too heavily on the positions advanced by these organizations, whose members have not passed the rigorous examinations currently carried out by the Registry and the Chambers for recognition of an individual as a victim before the ICC.

'the admissibility assessment ... actually refers to the admissibility of one or more potential cases within the context of a situation'.[56] It can be inferred from this finding that when Article 19 proceedings are initiated at the stage of the investigation of the situation, because the assessment cannot be constructed in the abstract but must take place in relation to potential cases, the victims who may participate according to Rule 59 are those victims of potential cases within the context of the situation.

*Pre-trial stage of the Case*

The proceedings that may take place during the pre-trial stage of a case are numerous. They include (but are not limited to) proceedings dealing with: disclosure for the purposes of the confirmation hearing (Article 61(3)); assistance to the accused in the preparation of his or her defence (Article 57(3)(b)); protection and privacy of victims and witnesses (Article 57(3)(c)); preservation of evidence (Article 57(3)(c)); protection of the person arrested (Article 57(3)(c)); protection of national security information (Article 57(3)(c)); matters related to the release or detention of the person subject to a warrant of arrest (Article 60 and Rule 119(3)); and the confirmation hearing as such (Article 61 and Rule 92(3)).

When dealing with the modalities of participation of victims at the pre-trial stage of cases, PTCs have applied the general participatory regime of Article 68(3), but in a somewhat inconsistent way. This inconsistency arises in part due to the fact that the decisions are rather unclear as to whether participation is granted only in relation to the confirmation of charges hearing or in relation to all pre-trial proceedings. In addition, there have been different approaches by the PTCs in relation to the rights conferred upon the victims allowed to participate. Whereas PTC I made a clear distinction between anonymous and non-anonymous victims, PTCs II and III made no such distinction. Therefore, the rights of victims to participate may differ depending on which PTC decides the matter.

Article 61 of the Rome Statute provides that a PTC must confirm the charges against an accused within a reasonable time after the person's surrender or voluntary appearance before the Court. Although Article 61 does not specifically provide for the participation of victims,[57] Rule 92(3) requires the Court to notify victims of its decision to hold the confirmation hearing 'in order to allow victims to apply for participation in the proceedings in accordance with Rule 89'. In its jurisprudence, the Court has addressed participation at the confirmation hearing through reliance on the general provision on victims' participation in Article 68(3): Article 68(3) provides for consideration of whether 'the personal interests of the victims are affected' and whether victim participation would be 'prejudicial to or inconsistent with the rights of the accused and a fair and impartial trial'.

56 Authorization to open an investigation in Kenya, para. 48.

57 It provides only that the confirmation hearing 'shall be held in the presence of the Prosecutor and the person charged, as well as his or her counsel'.

The first decision on the role of victims in a confirmation hearing was issued by PTC I on 22 September 2006, in the *Lubanga* case.[58] Characterizing the confirmation hearing as 'an essential stage of the proceedings',[59] PTC I granted the victims the right to participate in the confirmation hearing. As the victims in this case wanted to remain anonymous, they were granted limited rights: to access public documents, to attend public status conferences and to attend the public sessions of the confirmation hearing.[60] Additionally, they were allowed to make opening and closing statements at the hearing. While they were entitled to request leave to intervene, this was to be decided upon on a case-by-case basis.[61] Reflecting the Court's desire to preserve the fundamental principle prohibiting anonymous accusations, victims were not permitted to add any point of fact, submit evidence or question witnesses.[62]

Judge Politi, acting as Single Judge of PTC II, considered the participatory rights of victims at the pre-trial stage of the case of *Kony et al.*[63] He observed that Article 68(3) vests in the Court a broad discretion to determine at what stage and in what manner victims should be allowed to participate in the proceedings, and noted that the 'paramount criterion for participation to be allowed is that the "*personal interests*" of the applicant victims have to be affected'.[64] He held that there seemed to be little doubt (unless the Chamber decided otherwise in a specific proceeding) that this requirement was met whenever a victim applied for participation in proceedings following the issuance of a warrant of arrest or a summons to appear for one or more individuals relating to the very crime in which the victims was allegedly involved.[65] Subject to the need for the PTC to determine whether the victims met the definition set out in Rule 85, Judge Politi decided to grant the applicants the 'status of victim in the case', thereby allowing them to

58 *Lubanga* case ICC-01/04-01/06-462-tEN, Decision on the Arrangements for Participation of Victims a/0001/06, a/0002/06 and a/0003/06 at the Confirmation Hearing (Pre-Trial Chamber I, 22 September 2006).

59 ICC-01/04-01/06-462-tEN, 5.

60 ICC-01/04-01/06-462-tEN, 6.

61 ICC-01/04-01/06-462-tEN, 6–7.

62 ICC-01/04-01/06-462-tEN, 7.

63 The decision also considered the participation of victims in the Uganda situation generally, applying different considerations. *Kony et al.* case ICC-02/04-01/05-252, Decision on victims' applications for participation a/0010/06, a/0064/06 to a/0070/06, a/0081/06 to a/0104/06 and a/0111/06 to a/0127/06 (Pre-Trial Chamber II, 10 August 2007).

64 ICC-02/04-01/05-252, para. 9 [emphasis in original].

65 ICC-02/04-01/05-252, paras. 9–10. To assess the merit of the applications, Judge Politi considered it necessary to analyse: (i) whether the identity of the applicant as a natural person appeared duly established; (ii) whether the events described by each applicant constituted a crime within the jurisdiction of the Court; (iii) whether the applicant claimed to have suffered harm; and, *most crucially*, (iv) whether such harm appeared to have arisen 'as a result' of the event constituting the crime within the jurisdiction of the Court (ICC-02/04-01/05-252, para. 12).

participate generally in the proceedings at the pre-trial stage of the case – unless the PTC decided otherwise in relation to a specific proceeding.[66]

In the lead-up to the confirmation hearing in the *Katanga and Ngudjolo* case, Judge Steiner, acting as a Single Judge of PTC I, considered the rights of victims at the confirmation hearing, as well as at the pre-trial stage generally.[67] Judge Steiner adopted Judge Politi's reasoning regarding the constituent elements required by Rule 85 to grant the 'procedural status of victim in the proceedings concerning the pre-trial stage of a case'.[68] According to Judge Steiner, the guilt or innocence of the persons charged before the Court affected the core interests of the victims, i.e., the satisfaction of their right to truth and justice.[69] She held that 'victims' central interest in the search for the truth can only be satisfied if (i) those responsible for perpetrating the crimes for which they suffered harm are declared guilty; and (ii) those not responsible for such crimes are acquitted, so that the search for those who are criminally liable can continue.[70] [T]he interests of victims go beyond the determination of what happened and the identification of those responsible, and extend to securing a certain degree of punishment for those who are responsible for perpetrating the crimes for which they suffered harm.[71] She observed that 'when [the right to justice] is to be satisfied through criminal proceedings, victims have a central interest in [ensuring] that the outcome lead [sic] to the identification, prosecution and punishment of those who have victimized them'.[72]

Judge Steiner rejected the Prosecutor's request for a 'casuistic' approach to victim's participation at the pre-trial stage of the case – according to which 'each time victims wish to conduct a specific procedural activity, they must show that it relates to issues specific to their interests'[73] – and instead embraced a 'systematic approach which consists of a clear determination of the set of procedural rights that those granted the procedural status of victim in the pre-trial stage of the ... case may exercise'.[74] Judge Steiner held that 'granting victims a procedural status at the pre-trial stage of a case is neither mandatory nor prohibited by internationally recognized standards concerning the rights of the accused and a fair and impartial trial'.[75] An exhaustive contextual interpretation of Article 68(3) and Rules 91 and

66 ICC-02/04-01/05-252, para. 9.

67 *Katanga and Ngudjolo* case ICC-01/04-01/07-474, Decision on the Set of Procedural Rights Attached to Procedural Status of Victim at the Pre-Trial Stage of the Case (Pre-Trial Chamber I, 13 May 2008).

68 *Katanga and Ngudjolo* case ICC-01/04-01/07-357, Decision on the Applications for Participation in the Proceedings of Applicants a/0327/07 to a/0337/07 and a/0001/08 (Pre Trial Chamber I, 2 April 2008), 8.

69 ICC-01/04-01/07-474, para. 41.

70 ICC-01/04-01/07-474, para. 36.

71 ICC-01/04-01/07-474, para. 38.

72 ICC-01/04-01/07-474, para. 41.

73 ICC-01/04-01/07-474, para. 48.

74 ICC-01/04-01/07-474, para. 49.

75 ICC-01/04-01/07-474, para. 73.

92, led her to conclude that the specific procedural rights attached to the 'procedural status' of victims were to be divided into six groups. As in the *Lubanga* case, in the *Katanga and Ngudjolo* case the victims who were granted anonymity had limited rights.[76] However, for those victims who did not request anonymity, Single Judge Steiner generously extended the scope of their participation.[77]

In *Prosecutor v. Jean-Pierre Bemba Gombo*, PTC III, acting through Single Judge Kaul, moved away from Judge Steiner's and Judge Politi's treatment of the issue. While pointing out that the matter arose at the stage of proceedings 'leading to the confirmation of charges',[78] Judge Kaul recognized victims of the case only 'for the purpose of participating in the proceedings concerning the confirmation hearing'.[79] This decision adopted the four requirements for the granting of victims' participation laid down by Judge Politi,[80] and limited the participation of victims to those whose harm appeared to have arisen from the crimes charged.[81] Nevertheless, Judge Kaul did affirm Judge Steiner's position to an extent: he held that 'the personal interest of victims stem from at least two motivations, namely the *right to reparations* and the *right to justice*'.[82] Judge Kaul held that there

76 ICC-01/04-01/07-474, para. 184.

77 The participatory rights were divided into the following 6 groups: 1) the right to access the record of the case kept by the Registry, including the evidence filed by the Prosecution and the Defense, regardless of whether they are classified as public or confidential but excluding access to those filings and decisions classified as *ex parte*; 2) the right to (i) make submissions on all issues relating to the admissibility and probative value of the evidence on which the Prosecution and the Defense intend to rely at the confirmation hearing and (ii) examine such evidence at the confirmation hearing; 3) the right to examine, at the confirmation hearing, any witness proposed by the Prosecution and the Defense; 4) the right to attend all public and closed sessions convened in the proceedings leading to the confirmation hearing and all public and closed sessions of the confirmation hearing, with the sole exception of the hearings held on an *ex parte* basis; 5) the right to participate by way of oral motions, responses and submissions in (i) all hearings that they can attend and (ii) all matters other than those in which their intervention has been excluded; and, 6) the right to file written motions, responses and replies in accordance with Regulation 24, in relation to all matters other than those in which victims' interventions have been excluded. Still, Judge Steiner emphasized that the 'procedural rights' can be limited by the Chamber *proprio motu*, or at the request of the parties, the Registry or any other participant, if it is shown that the relevant limitation is necessary to safeguard another competing interest protected by the Statute or the Rules. Judge Steiner justified her position by stressing the importance of what she called a 'meaningful and independent role' for victims in pre-trial proceedings before the Court (ICC-01/04-01/07-474, paras. 127–8, para. 134, para. 137, and paras. 140–42).

78 *Bemba* case ICC-01/05-01/08-320, Fourth Decision on Victims' Participation (Pre-Trial Chamber III, 12 December 2008), para. 83.

79 ICC-01/05-01/08-320, para. 37.

80 ICC-01/05-01/08-320, para. 30, 11.

81 ICC-01/05-01/08-320, para. 62.

82 ICC-01/05-01/08-320, para. 90 [emphasis added].

was to be no differentiation between victims whose identity was known to the Defence and those for whom anonymity was granted.[83] Taking into consideration the limited purpose and scope of the pre-trial proceedings and the need to ensure a fair, efficient and expeditious trial, Judge Kaul limited the participatory rights of victims.[84] He limited rights of access to public documents and hearings on the confirmation of charges, echoing the approach taken by PTC I in the decision in the *Lubanga* case.[85]

In the *Abu Garda* case, PTC I, acting through Judge Monageng, followed Judge Steiner's systematic approach and recognized victims 'for the purpose of participating during the pre-trial stage of the case'.[86] As to the modalities of participation, Judge Monageng conferred participatory rights upon the victims which were similar to those conferred in the *Katanga and Ngudjolo* case. Judge Monageng did distinguish between victims who had applied for anonymity and those who had not. His decision further expressly recognized the right of victims' legal representatives to participate by way of oral motions, responses and submissions 'in relation to all matters other than those in which their intervention has been excluded by the Statute and the Rules'.[87]

### *Trial stage of the Case*

At the time of writing, while three cases have reached the stage of trial, only two trials have begun.[88] In the *Lubanga* case, an 18 January 2008 decision of Trial Chamber ('TC') I provided general guidelines on the participation of victims throughout the proceedings.[89] TC I took the view that proceedings before the Court were '*sui generis*' and that the Court must 'develop trial procedures that meet the particular exigencies of the international cases. … [T]he opportunities for participation by victims must be given meaningful effect by applying the plain language of the relevant provisions, but always ensuring that the implementation

---

83 ICC-01/05-01/08-320, para. 99.

84 ICC-01/05-01/08-320, para. 95.

85 ICC-01/05-01/08-320, para. 100.

86 *Abu Garda* case ICC-02/05-02/09-121, Decision on the 34 Applications for Participation at the Pre-Trial Stage of the Case (Pre-Trial Chamber I, 25 September 2009), para. 31; and *Abu Garda* case ICC-02/05-02/09-147-Red, Public Redacted Version of 'Decision on the 52 Applications for Participation at the Pre-Trial Stage of the Case' (Pre-Trial Chamber I, 9 October 2009), para. 40.

87 *Abu Garda* case ICC-02/05-02/09-136, Decision on victims' modalities of participation at the Pre-Trial Stage of the Case (Pre-Trial Chamber I, 6 October 2009), para. 18.

88 The trial of *Thomas Lubanga Dyilo* started on 26 January 2009 and the trial of *Germain Katanga and Mathieu Ngudjolo* began on 24 November 2009. The trial of *Jean-Pierre Bemba Gombo* is currently expected to begin at the end of 2010.

89 *Lubanga* case ICC-01/04-01/06-1119, Decision on victims' participation (Trial Chamber I, 18 January 2008), para. 84.

of this objective does not result in an unfair trial'.[90] The majority of TC I took a remarkably broad view of the role of the victims. It held that for a victim to be able to participate in the trial proceedings (i) the applicant must be a victim of a crime under the jurisdiction of the Court and (ii) the interests of the victim must be affected in the proceedings.[91] In relation to the first element, the majority held that once the TC has determined that an applicant was a natural or legal person it was necessary to consider the evidence regarding whether or not 'the applicant suffered *any harm* as a result of the commission of *a crime* within the jurisdiction of the Court'.[92] It observed that people may be direct or indirect victims of such crimes. As Rule 85 does not provide for a definition of harm, TC I relied on Principle 8 of the Basic Principles and Guidelines on the Right to a Remedy and Reparation for Victims of Gross Violations of International Human Rights Law and Serious Violations of International Humanitarian Law.[93] It found that the harm victims may suffer – individually or collectively – can be physical, mental, emotional or economic or can consist of a substantial impairment of their rights.[94] As to the second element – the need for the interests of the victim to be affected by the proceedings – the majority held that Rule 85,[95] when read in conjunction with Article 68(3), 'does not have the effect of restricting the participation of victims to the crimes contained in the charges confirmed by PTC I'; nor was such a restriction provided for anywhere in the Rome Statute framework.[96] As a result, TC I ruled that 'a victim of any crime falling within the jurisdiction of the Court can potentially participate'.[97] With regard to the modalities of participation, TC I granted participant victims the right to lead evidence pertaining the guilt or innocence of the accused, and to challenge the admissibility or relevance of evidence in the trial proceedings.[98]

---

90 ICC-01/04-01/06-1119, para. 85.

91 ICC-01/04-01/06-1119, para. 86.

92 ICC-01/04-01/06-1119, para. 90 [emphasis added].

93 UN General Assembly Resolution 60/147, 16 December 2005.

94 ICC-01/04-01/06-1119, paras. 91–2.

95 See the definition of victim under Rule 85 at note 17 above.

96 ICC-01/04-01/06-1119, para. 93.

97 ICC-01/04-01/06-1119, para. 95. This position was strongly opposed by Judge Blattmann in his dissenting opinion. To him, the scope of the Chamber's authority to make rulings in relation to a specific case was defined by the charges. As such, he was of the view that the Chamber in this case was only authorized to allow the participation of victims who were directly connected to the charges confirmed against the accused (ICC-01/04-01/06-1119. Separate and Dissenting Opinion of Judge Blattmann), para. 32.

98 This was later confirmed by the AC. See *Lubanga* case ICC-01/04-01/06-1432, Judgment on the appeals of The Prosecutor and The Defence against Trial Chamber I's Decision on Victims' Participation of 18 January 2008 (Appeals Chamber, 11 July 2008), paras. 3–4.

On appeal, much of TC I's reasoning was reversed.[99] The AC held that 'harm' involves 'injury, loss or damage'[100] that may be material, physical or psychological in nature. While the harm suffered by victims did not have to be direct, it needed to be personal. It acknowledged, however, that 'harm suffered by one victim as a result of the commission of the crime within the jurisdiction of the Court can give rise to harm suffered by other victims', such as when 'there is a close personal relationship between the victims'.[101] The AC rejected TC I's view that neither Rule 85 nor the Statute itself had the effect of restricting the participation of victims to crimes contained in the charges as confirmed. It stressed the limited competence of the TC, observing that 'once the charges in a case against an accused have been confirmed in accordance with Article 61 of the Statute, the subject matter of the proceedings in that case is defined by the crimes charged'.[102] It continued: 'the parameters set forth in the charges define the issues to be determined at trial and limit the Trial Chamber's authority to the determination of those issues'.[103] It clarified beyond doubt the need for a causal link between the crimes charged and the harm alleged by the victim, stating that 'only victims who are victims of the crimes charged may participate in the trial proceedings'.[104]

The TC I's decision of 8 April 2009 – which addresses the issue of 'indirect victims' – provides additional insight into the reasons underlying its 18 January 2008 decision and the broad approach taken with regards to victims' participation in trial.[105] The 8 April 2009 decision was the result of a request by the Registry for clarification as to whether individuals who were victims of crimes committed by individuals who had been conscripted or enlisted whilst under the age of fifteen by the accused could be classified as indirect victims.[106] Taking into account the AC's decision, TC I ruled that 'the harm suffered by indirect victims must arise out of the harm suffered by direct victims, brought about by the commission of

99 ICC-01/04-01/06-1432.

100 ICC-01/04-01/06-1432, para. 31.

101 ICC-01/04-01/06-1432, para. 32.

102 ICC-01/04-01/06-1432.

103 ICC-01/04-01/06-1432, para. 63.

104 ICC-01/04-01/06-1432, para. 62. In a subsequent proceeding, TC I granted participant status only to victims who alleged personal harm as a result of crimes set out in the charges against the accused (*Lubanga* case ICC-01/04-01/06-1556, Decision on the applications by victims to participate in the proceedings (Trial Chamber I, 15 December 2008)).

105 *Lubanga* case ICC-01/04-01/06-1813, Redacted version of 'Decision on "indirect victims"' (Trial Chamber I. 8 April 2009). The matter resulted from a submission by the Registry dealing with more than 200 applications for participation in the *Lubanga* case that could not be accepted. The applicants were claiming to have suffered harm as a result of crimes committed by the Union of Congolese Patriots (UPC), including pillage, murder, rape, enslavement or inhuman treatment. Based on the Trial Chamber I's 18 January 2008 decision, it was possible to accept those applications, but not any more after the reversal by the Appeals Chamber in July 2008.

106 ICC-01/04-01/06-1813, para. 2.

the crimes charged'.[107] It also indicated that a close personal relationship with the direct victim was a 'precondition of participation by indirect victims'.[108] It specifically excluded from the category of indirect victims those 'who suffered harm as a result of the (later) *conduct* of direct victims'.[109] TC I relied on the AC's view that the purpose of the trial proceedings was the determination of the guilt or innocence of the accused for the crimes charged and only victims of those crimes were able to participate. Accordingly, it found that indirect victims were 'restricted to those whose harm is linked to the *harm* of the affected children when the confirmed offences were committed, not those whose harm is linked to any subsequent conduct by the children, criminal or otherwise'.[110]

In the *Katanga and Ngudjolo* case, TC II held that Regulation 86(8) should be construed to mean that in a specific case and at all stages of the proceedings, a previous decision by a Chamber under Rule 89 must be applied by a Chamber subsequently seized of the matter; however that Chamber would not be deprived of the right to exercise the power available to it under Rule 91(1).[111] Therefore, when assessing the status of the victims already authorized to participate in proceedings at the pre-trial stage, a distinction should be made between a decision that grants or denies victim status and a decision defining the modalities of his or her participation. In the interests of the proper administration of justice, the TC II held that victims authorized to participate in proceedings at the pre-trial stage must, in principle, automatically be authorized to participate in proceedings at the trial stage.[112] The same does not apply, however, to the modalities of participation, which must be reassessed, taking into account the stage of the proceedings and the prejudice which may be caused to the rights of the Defence, as well as the requirements of a fair trail.[113]

TC II ruled that participation was, nevertheless, subject to the victim having been authorized to participate on the basis of a crime confirmed by the PTC,[114] unless new information demonstrated that the victim was wrongly authorized to participate.[115] For new applicants, TC II endorsed the previous jurisprudence and demanded a direct link between the applications for participation and the charges confirmed. It observed that it was for the Chamber (not the Registry) to assess whether a causal link existed between the harm suffered and the alleged commission of the crimes.[116]

107 ICC-01/04-01/06-1813, para. 49.

108 ICC-01/04-01/06-1813, para. 50.

109 ICC-01/04-01/06-1813, para. 52 [emphasis in original].

110 ICC-01/04-01/06-1813, para. 52.

111 *Katanga and Ngudjolo* case ICC-01/04-01/07-933-tENG, Decision on the treatment of applications for participation (Trial Chamber II, 26 February 2009), para. 9.

112 ICC-01/04-01/07-933-tENG, para. 10.

113 ICC-01/04-01/07-933-tENG.

114 ICC-01/04-01/07-933-tENG, para. 11.

115 ICC-01/04-01/07-933-tENG, para. 12.

116 ICC-01/04-01/07-933-tENG, paras. 17–19.

TC II applied the provisions of Rule 85(a) and (b) and the criteria set by the AC. Thus, when analyzing applications for participation it considered: (i) whether the applicant was a natural or legal person; (ii) whether he or she had suffered harm; (iii) whether the crime that caused the harm fell within the jurisdiction of the Court and was included in the decision on confirmation of charges; and iv) whether there was a causal link between the harm and the crime.[117] The TC stressed that applications were to be analysed to ensure compliance with these four criteria, which were to be met on a *prima facie* basis, without the Chamber having to engage in a deep examination of the credibility of the victims' statements.[118]

With regard to the modalities of participation, TC II stressed that Article 68(3) of the Statute authorizes victims to present 'their views and concerns'. The Statute and the Rules, however, do not give a comprehensive definition of 'views and concerns'. As such, it fell to the TC to exercize discretion as to the meaning of the phrase depending on the circumstances of each case. It held that same discretion applies as regards its determination of the appropriate opportunity and modalities for the exercize of such a right, 'in a manner which is not prejudicial or inconsistent with the rights of the accused and a fair and impartial trial'.[119] The approach taken by TC II recognized that victims do not only seek to obtain reparations but also seek the truth regarding the events they have experienced.[120] It ruled however, that victims could only participate in seeking to establish the facts of the prosecution and contributing to the manifestation of the truth, thereby helping to establish what exactly happened.[121] Therefore, victims were not allowed, during the substantive discussions, to attempt to demonstrate their personal interests; the TC considered that such interests were already recognized given the fact that the victim had been granted the right to participate in the proceedings pursuant Rule 89.[122]

### *Appeal*

There has, to date, been no appeal judgement on the merits of a case. Nevertheless, a number of interlocutory appeals have taken place under Article 82(1) of the Statute, with victims frequently claiming a right to participate. The AC has made

117 *Katanga and Ngudjolo* case ICC-01/04-01/07-1491-Red, Motifs de la décision relative aux 345 demandes de participation de victimes à la procédure (Trial Chamber II, 23 September 2009), para 57; see also *Katanga and Ngudjolo* case ICC-01/04-01/07-1737, Motifs de la deuxiéme décision relative aux demandes de participation de victimes à la procédure (Trial Chamber II, 22 December 2009), para. 11.

118 ICC-01/04-01/07-1491-Red, para. 57.

119 *Katanga and Ngudjolo* case ICC-01/04-01/07-1788, Décision relative aux modalités de participation des victimes au stade des débats sur le fond (Trial Chamber II, 22 January 2010), para. 53.

120 ICC-01/04-01/07-1788, para. 59.

121 ICC-01/04-01/07-1788, para. 60.

122 ICC-01/04-01/07-1788, para. 61.

clear that 'there is no automatic right of participation in interlocutory appeals'.[123] Victims' participation will be determined according to the considerations set out in Article 68(3) of the Statute on a case-by-case basis.[124] In short, the following four criteria must be fulfilled:

> (i) the individuals seeking participation must be victims in the case, (ii) their personal interests must be affected by the issues on appeal, (iii) their participation must be appropriate, and (iv) the manner of participation should neither cause any prejudice to, nor be inconsistent with the rights of the accused and a fair and impartial trial.[125]

The requirement at (i), that the victims must have been victims in the case before they may participate in proceedings, was justified by the AC based upon the limited role of the interlocutory appeal proceedings. The AC observed that, as the PTCs and TCs often have an in-depth familiarity with the facts underlying the case, they are in a better position to assess whether or not an applicant may be recognized as a victim. It follows, according to the AC, 'that during the pre-trial and trial phases of the proceedings the Pre-Trial or Trial Chambers should ordinarily make the determination of victim status, and not the Appeals Chamber'.[126] With regard to the manner of participation, the AC has limited victims to 'presenting their views and concerns respecting their personal interests solely to the issues raised on appeal. Observations to be received by the victims must be specifically relevant to the issues arising in the appeal and to the extent that their personal interests are affected by the proceedings'.[127]

---

123 *Al Bashir* case ICC-02/05-01/09-70, Decision on the Second Application by Victims a/0443/09 to a/0450/09 to Participate in the Appeal against the 'Decision on the Prosecution's Application for a Warrant of Arrest against Omar Hassan Ahmad Al Bashir' (Appeals Chamber, 28 January 2010), para. 9.

124 *Lubanga* case ICC-01/04-01/06-925, Decision of the Appeals Chamber on the Joint Application of Victims a/0001/06 to a/0003/06 and a/0105/06 concerning the 'Directions and Decision of the Appeals Chamber' of 2 February 2007 (Appeals Chamber, 13 June 2007), para. 28.

125 ICC-02/05-01/09-70. See also ICC-01/04-01/06-1335, Decision, in limine, on Victim Participation in the appeals of the Prosecutor and the Defence against Trial Chamber I's decision entitled 'Decision on Victims' Participation' (Appeals Chamber, 20 May 2008), para. 36.

126 *Al Bashir* case ICC-02/05-01/09-48, Decision on the applications by Victims a/0443/09 to a/0450/09 to participate in the Appeal against the 'Decision on the Prosecution's Application for a Warrant of Arrest against Omar Hassan Ahmad Al Bashir' and on the Request for an extension of time (Appeals Chamber, 23 October 2009), para. 10.

127 ICC-01/04-01/06-1335, para. 50.

## Conclusions

The elaboration of the role of the victim in proceedings before the ICC has been – and continues to be – an exercize calling for the careful balancing of competing interests. Although the drafters of the Rome Statute made a great leap forward in international criminal justice in guaranteeing the victims' right to participate in ICC proceedings, insufficient regard was had to the particulars of the right, including, importantly, at what stages of the process the right could be exercized and the modalities of the exercize. The devil was in the details. And it was to the judges of the Court that the articulation of these details fell, representing one of the most important functions of the Court in its early years.

The approach of the Judges of the Court to victims' rights has varied considerably over the years; nevertheless, the role of victims in proceedings before the ICC is gradually beginning to become clear. A body of law has developed whereby the issues of whether an individual may participate as a victim and, if so, the modalities of such participation, are affected by the nature of the proceeding and whether it takes place during the 'situation' stage or the 'case' stage.

While the limitations on victim participation discussed above may be considered overly-restrictive by some – in particular, perhaps, by those from domestic jurisdictions where the right of victim participation has long been recognized – the Court has managed to arrive at a workable compromise: one which recognizes that meaningful victim participation is tremendously important not only to the victims themselves but to the overall success of international criminal proceedings, while, at the same time, recognizing that given the ICC's finite resources and its need to vigilantly safeguard the rights of the accused, certain limitations on the right must necessarily be imposed.

## References

Bitti, G. and H. Friman. 2001. Participation of Victims in the Proceedings, in *The International Criminal Court. Elements of Crimes and Rules of Procedure and Evidence*, edited by R.S. Lee. New York: Transnational Publishers, Inc.

Bitti, G. and G. González. 2005. La participación de las víctimas ante la Corte Penal Internacional, in *La Corte Penal Internacional: Una visión Iberoamericana*, edited by J.A. Guevara and T.D. Maso. Ciudad de Mexico: Editorial Porrúa.

Hall, C.K. 2008. Article 19, in *Commentary on the Rome Statute of the International Criminal Court*, edited by O. Triffterer. München: C.H. Beck – Hart – Nomos.

Jorda, C. and J.D. Hemptinne. 2002. The Status and Role of the Victim, in *The Rome Statute of the International Criminal Court: A Commentary*, edited by A. Cassese.

Stahn, C., H. Olasolo, and K. Gibson. 2006. Participation of Victims in Pre-Trial Proceedings of the ICC. *Journal of International Criminal Justice*, 4, 219–38.

Vasiliev, S. 2009. Article 68(3) and Personal Interests of Victims in the Emerging Practice of the ICC, in *The Emerging Practice of the International Criminal Court*, edited by C. Stahn and G. Sluiter. Leiden: Martinus Nijhoff Publishers.

Yee, L. 1999. The International Criminal Court and the Security Council: Articles 13(b) and 16, in *The International Criminal Court. The Making of the Rome Statute. Issues. Negotiations. Results*, edited by R.S. Lee. The Hague: Kluwer Law International.

Zappala, S. 2010. The Rights of Victims v. the Rights of the Accused. *Journal of International Criminal Justice*, 8.

*Table of Cases*

*DRC Situation*

ICC-01/04-101-tEN-Corr, Decision on the Applications for Participation in the Proceedings of VPRS1, VPRS 2, VPRS 3, VPRS 4, VPRS 5 and VPRS 6 (Pre-Trial Chamber I, 17 January 2006).

ICC-01/04-556, Judgment on Victim Participation in the Investigation Stage of the Proceedings in the Appeal of the OPCD against Decision of Pre-Trial Chamber I of 7 December 2007 and in the Appeals of the OPCD and the Prosecutor against the Decision of the Pre-Trial Chamber I of 24 December 2007 (Appeals Chamber, 19 December 2008).

ICC-01/04-564, Demande du représentant légal de VPRS 3 et 6 aux fins de mise en cause de Monsieur Jean-Pierre Bemba en sa qualité de chef militaire au sens de l'article 28 – a su Statut pour les crimes dont ses troupes sont présumées ocupables en Iturri (Pre-Trial Chamber I, 28 June 2010).

*Uganda Situation*

ICC-02/04-101, Decision on Victims' Applications for Participation a/0010/06, a/0064/06 to a/0070/06, a/0081/06 to a/0104/04 and a/0111/06 to a/0127/06 (Pre-Trial Chamber II, 10 August 2007).

*Darfur–Sudan Situation*

ICC-02/05-111, Decision on the Applications for Participation in the Proceedings of Applicants a/011/06 to a/0015/06, a/0021/07, a/0023/97 to a/0033/07 and a/0035/07 to a/0038/07 (Pre-Trial Chamber I, 6 December 2007).

*Kenya Situation*

ICC-01/09-4, Order to the Victims Participation and Reparations Section Concerning Victims' Representations Pursuant to Article 15(3) of the Statute (Pre-Trial Chamber II, 10 December 2009).

ICC-01/09-19-Corr, Decision Pursuant to Article 15 of the Rome Statute on the Authorization of an Investigation into the Situation in the Republic of Kenya (Pre-Trial Chamber II, 31 March 2010).

*Lubanga Case*

ICC-01/04-01/06-462-tEN, Decision on the Arrangements for Participation of Victims a/0001/06, a/0002/06 and a/0003/06 at the Confirmation Hearing (Pre-Trial Chamber I, 22 September 2006).

ICC-01/04-01/06-925, Decision of the Appeals Chamber on the Joint Application of Victims a/0001/06 to a/0003/06 and a/0105/06 concerning the 'Directions and Decision of the Appeals Chamber' of 2 February 2007 (Appeals Chamber, 13 June 2007).

ICC-01/04-01/06-1084, Decision on the Status before the Trial Chamber of the Evidence Heard by the Pre-Trial Chamber and the Decisions of the Pre-Trial Chamber in Trial Proceedings, and the Manner in which Evidence shall be Submitted (Trial Chamber I, 13 December 2007).

ICC-01/04-01/06-1119, Decision on Victims' Participation (Trial Chamber I, 18 January 2008).

ICC-01/04-01/06-1335, Decision, in Limine, on Victim Participation in the Appeals of the Prosecutor and the Defence against Trial Chamber I's Decision entitled 'Decision on Victims' Participation' (Appeals Chamber, 20 May 2008).

ICC-01/04-01/06-1432, Judgment on the Appeals of The Prosecutor and The Defence against Trial Chamber I's Decision on Victims' Participation of 18 January 2008 (Appeals Chamber, 11 July 2008).

ICC-01/04-01/06-1556, Decision on the Applications by Victims to Participate in the Proceedings (Trial Chamber I, 15 December 2008).

ICC-01/04-01/06-1813, Redacted Version of 'Decision on "Indirect Victims"' (Trial Chamber I, 8 April 2009).

*Katanga and Ngudjolo Case*

ICC-01/04-01/07-357, Decision on the Applications for Participation in the Proceedings of Applicants a/0327/07 to a/0337/07 and a/0001/08 (Pre Trial Chamber I, 2 April 2008).

ICC-01/04-01/07-474, Decision on the Set of Procedural Rights Attached to Procedural Status of Victim at the Pre-Trial Stage of the Case (Pre-Trial Chamber I, 13 May 2008).

ICC-01/04-01/07-933-tENG, Decision on the Treatment of Applications for Participation (Trial Chamber II, 26 February 2009).

ICC-01/04-01/07-1213, Motifs de la décision orale relative à l'exception d'irrecevabilité de l'affaire (article 19 du Statut) (Trial Chamber II, 16 June 2009).

ICC-01/04-01/07 OA 8, Judgment on the Appeal of Mr. Germain Katanga against the Oral Decision of Trial Chamber II of 12 June 2009 on the Admissibility of the Case (Appeals Chamber, 25 September 2009).

ICC-01/04-01/07-1491-Red, Motifs de la décision relative aux 345 demandes de participation de victimes à la procédure (Trial Chamber II, 23 September 2009).

ICC-01/04-01/07-1737, Motifs de la deuxième décision relative aux demandes de participation de victimes à la procédure (Trial Chamber II, 22 December 2009).

ICC-01/04-01/07-1788, Décision relative aux modalités de participation des victimes au stade des débats sur le fond (Trial Chamber II, 22 January 2010).

*Kony et al. Case*

ICC-02/04-01/05-320, Decision Initiating Proceedings under Article 19, Requesting Observations and Appointing Counsel for the Defense (Pre-Trial Chamber II, 21 October 2008).

ICC-02/04-01/05-349, Observations on Behalf of Victims Pursuant to Article 19(1) of the Rome Statute with 55 Public Annexes and 45 Redacted Annexes (Office of the Public Counsel for Victims, 18 November 2008).

ICC-02/04-01/05-377, Decision on the Admissibility of the Case under Article 19(1) of the Statute (Pre-Trial Chamber II, 10 March 2009).

ICC-02/04-01/05-408, Judgment on the Appeal of the Defense against the 'Decision on the Admissibility of the Case under Article 19(1) of the Statute' of 10 March 2009, (Appeals Chamber, 16 September 2009).

*Bemba Case*

ICC-01/05-01/08-320, Fourth Decision on Victims' Participation (Pre-Trial Chamber III, 12 December 2008).

*Abu Garda Case*

ICC-02/05-02/09-121, Decision on the 34 Applications for Participation at the Pre-Trial Stage of the Case (Pre-Trial Chamber I, 25 September 2009).

ICC-02/05-02/09-147-Red, Public Redacted Version of 'Decision on the 52 Applications for Participation at the Pre-Trial Stage of the Case' (Pre-Trial Chamber I, 9 October 2009).

ICC-02/05-02/09-136, Decision on Victims' Modalities of Participation at the Pre-Trial Stage of the Case (Pre-Trial Chamber I, 6 October 2009).

*Al Bashir Case*

ICC-02/05-01/09-48, Decision on the Applications by Victims a/0443/09 to a/0450/09 to Participate in the Appeal against the 'Decision on the Prosecution's Application for a Warrant of Arrest against Omar Hassan Ahmad Al Bashir' and on the Request for an Extension of Time (Appeals Chamber, 23 October 2009).

ICC-02/05-01/09-70, Decision on the Second Application by Victims a/0443/09 to a/0450/09 to Participate in the Appeal against the 'Decision on the Prosecution's Application for a Warrant of Arrest against Omar Hassan Ahmad Al Bashir' (Appeals Chamber, 28 January 2010).

ICC-02/05-01/09-77, Victims' Application for Participation in the Proceedings Arising out of the Appeal Judgment of 3 February 2010 (ICC-02/05-01/09-73) (Pre-Trial Chamber I, 24 March 2010).

ICC-02/05-01/09-75, Application of Legal Representatives of Victims a/0011/06, a/0012/06, a/0013/06 and a/0015/06 to Participate in and Submit Observations on the Proceedings on Remand In Connection with the Application for a Warrant for the Arrest of Omar Hassan Ahmad al-Bashir (Pre-Trial Chamber I, 12 March 2010).

ICC-02/05-01/09-94, Second Decision on the Prosecution's Application for a Warrant of Arrest (Pre-Trial Chamber I, 12 July 2010).

## Table of Statutes and Statutory Instruments

The Rome Statute for the International Criminal Court Adopted by the United Nations Diplomatic Conference of Plenipotentiaries on the Establishment of an International Criminal Court, 17 July 1998, A/CONF.183/9 (1998).

Rules of Procedure and Evidence of the International Criminal Court, Adopted by the Assembly of States Parties First Session, New York, 3–10 September 2002. Official Records ICC-ASP/1/3.

Regulations of the Court, Adopted by the judges of the Court on 26 May 2004, Fifth Plenary Session, The Hague, 17–28 May 2004, Official Documents of the International Criminal Court ICC-BD/01-01-04.

## Chapter 16
# Addressing the Interests of Victims: Perspectives from the Office of the Prosecutor

Olivia Swaak-Goldman[1]

### 'Victims' in the Rome Statute System

*The new role given to victims in the Normative Framework of the ICC*

The International Criminal Court (ICC) was established in 1998 by the Rome Statute with the dual purpose of bringing justice and accountability to victims and affected populations through prosecution and to contribute to the prevention of crimes, and to the victimization of additional generations and communities.[2] Victims are the first and the most important beneficiaries of the work of the ICC in general, and of the Office of the Prosecutor (OTP) in particular. As stressed in the Report of the Court on the strategy in relation to victims,

> The decision of the drafters to recognize the importance of victims is rooted in an understanding of the devastating effect that crimes can have on victims and those close to them. The Preamble to the Statute recalls that during the last century, millions of children, women, and men have been victims of unimaginable atrocities that deeply shock the conscience of humanity. The drafters recognized also that positive engagement with victims can have a significant effect on how victims experience and perceive justice and, as such, contribute to their healing process. Victims also bring a unique perspective to the judicial process.[3]

A key feature of the system established in the Rome Statute is the recognition that the ICC has not only a punitive but also a restorative function. It reflects growing

---

1 The author wishes to thank Antonia Pereira De Sousa, Satoko Ikeda and Judit Otvos for their assistance in preparing this contribution.

2 Policy Paper on Preliminary Examinations ('Preliminary Examinations'), 4 October 2010, para. 21, http://www.icc-cpi.int/NR/rdonlyres/E278F5A2-A4F9-43D7-83D2-6A2C9CF5D7D7/282515/OTP_Draftpolicypaperonpreliminaryexaminations04101.pdf (last visited 3 February, 2011).

3 Report of the Court on the strategy in relation to victims ('Court's Victims Strategy Report'), ICC-ASP/8/45, 10 November 2009, para. 2, http://www.icc-cpi.int/iccdocs/asp_docs/ASP8/ICC-ASP-8-45-ENG.pdf (last visited 28 January 2011).

international consensus that participation and reparations play an important role in achieving justice for victims.[4]

On this basis, the Rome Statute marks two landmark evolutions:

- first, it contains a commitment of the international community to provide justice for victims of the most serious crimes, should national States fail to uphold their responsibility to do so. To achieve this goal, the Statute gives a mandate to an independent Prosecutor to investigate and prosecute the crimes, protecting the rights of the victims, respecting their interests, contributing to full and effective reparation and respecting the rights of the accused, while at the same time contributing to the prevention of future crimes; and
- second, it empowers victims as an actor in the international criminal justice system, with a right to express their views and concerns independently in proceedings where their personal interests are affected.

The framework thus established in the Rome Statute regarding victims represents a key innovative feature of this Court and is, in the view of the OTP, a milestone in international criminal justice. It is part of the consistent evolution of international law, including but not limited to international criminal law, which recognizes victims as actors and not only passive subjects of the law, thus granting them specific rights.

This article will explore four aspects regarding the role and the interests of victims before the ICC: the strategies, regulations, policy papers and best practices developed by the Office regarding its interaction with victims, from the early stages to the reparations phase; the issue of witness and victim protection in situations of ongoing conflict; the question of victims' participation in the proceedings and the issue of victims' reparations.

*The court-wide strategy*

In November 2009, the Court finalized its Victims Strategy Report and submitted it to the Assembly of States Parties, the Court's governing body.[5]

This report detailed the common strategy that the different organs of the Court adopted in order to operationalize its commitment towards victims. The strategy is based on eight principles and aims to achieve six intertwined policy objectives to achieve these principles: Objectives 1 and 4 relate to the practice associated with the participation of victims in the proceedings; Objectives 2 and 3 relate to protection; Objective 5 refers to reparations; and Objective 6 addresses legal representation.[6]

---

4 *Ibid.*, para. 3.

5 Article 112 of the Rome Statute of the International Criminal Court ('Statute'), ICC-A/CONF.183/9, 1 July 2002, http://www.icc-cpi.int/NR/rdonlyres/EA9AEFF7-5752-4F84-BE94-0A655EB30E16/0/Rome_Statute_English.pdf (last visited 31 January 2011).

6 Court's Victims Strategy Report, paras. 16–61. Objective 1: Ensure that the role of the Court and its judicial activities are clearly communicated to all victims of a situation or case potentially falling within the jurisdiction of the Court, including their right to petition the Court to participate in proceedings at the Court or to seek reparation.

The strategy also emphasizes the wide range of definitions for the term 'victim' under the Rome Statute. The statutory provisions enable different modes of interaction for victims with the Court, and these modalities become more delimited and complex as the level of interaction increases. Indeed Rule 85 of the Rules of Procedure and Evidence enumerates the basic definition, noting that a victim is 'a natural person who has suffered harm as a result of the commission of any crime within the jurisdiction of the Court, or in certain circumstances an organization or institution that has sustained certain harm to its property'.[7] Importantly, whenever determining who qualifies as a 'victim', the jurisprudence of the Court is taken into consideration.

Further, the term 'victim' is a fluid concept that may refer to a variety of individuals, as specific persons interact with different organs of the Court at different phases of the proceedings. For instance, the term is used to describe *inter alia*: 1) persons having sent communications/information of crimes to the Office of the Prosecutor, 2) persons allowed by the relevant Chamber to participate in the proceedings, 3) persons who receive reparations as a result of an order of a Trial Chamber following a conviction, 4) persons who require specific measures of protection or psycho-social support related directly to their appearance before the Court, 5) persons who receive assistance directly or indirectly from the Trust Fund for Victims, and 6) members of a community affected by crimes in the context of a particular situation or case who as a result are targeted by outreach activities of the Court.[8]

Since the start of its activities, the Office of the Prosecutor has fully participated in the Court's undertakings with regard to victims. In particular, the Office aims to achieve the four most relevant objectives mentioned in the Court's Victims Strategy Report that will help increase the effective role of victims in court proceedings. The Office is in particular committed to ensuring that the Court and its judicial activities are communicated to all victims of a situation or potential case, enabling

---

Objective 2: To enable victims to interact with the Court without suffering further harm as a result of this interaction, including by providing protective measures and security arrangements at all stages; Objective 3: Provide support and assistance to victims in order to safeguard their psychological and physical integrity and well-being, ensure respect for their dignity and privacy, and prevent them from suffering further harm as a result of their interaction with the Court; Objective 4: To ensure that victims are able to fully exercise their right to participate in ICC proceedings, in a manner that is sensitive to their rights and interests and consistent with the rights of the Defense and the need to ensure a fair trial; Objective 5: To ensure that as many victims as possible are able to exercise their rights as regards reparation and to benefit from assistance; Objective 6: To ensure that victims obtain high-quality legal representation before the Court.

7 Rules of Procedure and Evidence ('Rules'), ICC-ASP/1/3, 9 September 2002, http://www.icc-cpi.int/NR/rdonlyres/F1E0AC1C-A3F3-4A3C-B9A7-B3E8B115E886/140164/Rules_of_procedure_and_Evidence_English.pdf (last visited 28 January 2011).

8 Court's Victims Strategy Report, para. 8. The Chamber held that 'indirect victims' are restricted to those whose harm is linked to the harm of the affected children when the confirmed offences were committed, not those whose harm is linked to any subsequent conduct by the children, criminal or otherwise. *Prosecutor v. Thomas Lubanga Dyilo*, Redacted version of 'Decision on "Indirect Victims."' ICC-01/04-01/06-1813, 8 April 2009, para. 52.

victims to interact with the Court without suffering further harm, providing support and assistance to victims in order to safeguard their psychological and physical integrity and well-being and ensuring that victims are able to fully exercise their right to participate in ICC proceedings in a manner sensitive to their rights and interests and the rights of the Defense.[9]

## OTP Interaction with Victims

### *OTP strategies, regulations and policies on interaction with victims*

Given its independent mandate to investigate and prosecute massive crimes and to contribute to their prevention, the Office of the Prosecutor is usually the first organ of the Court to be in touch with victims' group and affected communities in countries under preliminary examination or under investigation.

#### ***The Prosecutorial Strategy***

One of the four fundamental principles guiding the Office's work, as laid out in its Prosecutorial Strategy for 2009–2012, is to systematically address the interests of victims, seeking their views before an investigation is even launched, and to continue to assess their interests throughout the proceedings. The OTP does this by proactively monitoring and considering communications from victims' groups and NGOs.[10] During the preliminary examination and investigation phase, victims may send 'communications' or information on alleged crimes and make representations to the Prosecutor on matters pertaining to the opening of an investigation, which the OTP in turn assesses as part of its determination of the interests of justice under Article 53, in deciding whether to open an investigation.[11] The need to address the

9 Court's Victims Strategy Report, paras. 16–61.

10 Article 15 (2) states that 'The Prosecutor shall analyse the seriousness of the information received. For this purpose, he or she may seek additional information from States, organs of the United Nations, intergovernmental or non-governmental organizations, or other reliable sources that he or she deems appropriate, and may receive written or oral testimony at the seat of the Court'. Statute, Article 15 (2). Also Article 15 (6) states that 'If after the preliminary examination … the Prosecutor concludes that the information provided does not constitute a reasonable basis for an investigation, he or she shall inform those who provided the information. This shall not preclude the Prosecutor from considering further information submitted to him or her regarding the same situation …', Statute, Article 15 (6).

11 Article 53: 'The Prosecutor shall, having evaluated the information made available to him or her, initiate an investigation unless he or she determines that there is no reasonable basis to proceed under this Statute. In deciding whether to initiate an investigation, the Prosecutor shall consider whether … taking into account the gravity of the crime and the interests of victims, there are nonetheless substantial reasons to believe that an investigation would not serve the interests of justice.' Statute, Article 53 (c).

interests of victims at all stages is a principle embodied in the Court-Wide ICC Strategy in Relation to Victims which the Office fully abides by.[12]

In addition to this specific principle, the Office's approach to victims is informed by other principles and policies. For example, another fundamental principle in the Prosecutorial Strategy is the policy of focused investigations and prosecutions. Based on the Statute, the Office adopted a policy of focusing on the most serious crimes and on those who bear the greatest responsibility for these crimes. Determining which individuals bear the greatest responsibility for these crimes is done according to, and dependent on, the evidence that emerges in the course of an investigation.

It should be clarified briefly here (and in more detail below), that the Office does not select situations; if the clear criteria established by the Rome Statute are met – jurisdiction, admissibility and interests of justice – then the Office will initiate an investigation into a given situation. The Office will, however, select specific cases within each situation based on its policy of focusing on those most responsible for the most serious crimes.

This policy also means that cases inside a situation are selected according to gravity, taking into account factors such as the scale, nature, manner of commission, and impact of the alleged crimes. A limited number of incidents is selected. This allows the Office to carry out short investigations; to limit the number of persons put at risk by reason of their interaction with the Office; and to propose expeditious trials while aiming to represent the entire range of victimization. While the Office's mandate does not include the production of comprehensive historical records for a given conflict, incidents are selected to provide a sample that is reflective of the gravest incidents and the main types of victimization.[13]

Under its second objective, 'Investigations', the Office committed to 'continue to improve the quality of its work by, [inter alia], increasing reliance on new types of evidence, in particular, financial information to prove the role of those most responsible and to assist in reparations to victims….' This is also highlighted in the Regulations of the Office of the Prosecutor, under Regulation 49: 'the Office shall pay particular attention in its investigations to the identification, tracing and freezing or seizure of proceeds, property and assets and instrumentalities of crimes, in particular for the ultimate benefit of victims'.[14] Relying on financial information as evidence will also allow the Office to limit the number of witnesses called and consequently the potential number of persons put at risk by reason of their interaction with the Office.

---

12 Prosecutorial Strategy, 1 February 2010, para. 22, http://www.icc-cpi.int/NR/rdonlyres/66A8DCDC-3650-4514-AA62-D229D1128F65/281506/OTPProsecutorialStrategy20092013.pdf (last visited 31 January 2011).

13 *Ibid.*, para. 20.

14 Regulations of the the Office of the Prosecutor ('Regulations'), ICC-BD/05-01-09, 23 April 2009, p. 23, http://www.icc-cpi.int/NR/rdonlyres/FFF97111-ECD6-40B5-9CDA-792BCBE1E695/280253/ICCBD050109ENG.pdf (last visited 31 January 2011).

It is also part of the Prosecutorial Strategy that the Office will pay particular attention to the investigation and the prosecution of crimes committed against children, sexual and gender-based crimes.

Further, under objective 5, 'Maximizing the impact of the Office's work', the Office clarified that its work 'must be relevant to victims, to affected communities, and more broadly to all relevant communities in order to foster conciliation and prevent future crimes. Visits to situation countries by representatives of the Office will continue to include town hall meetings with victims and meetings with key actors such as women's associations, community leaders, and 'chefs de quartiers'. In doing so, the Office will ensure that those involved are not exposed to any foreseeable risks, pursuant to its obligations under Article 68.[15]

### *The Regulations of the OTP*

Through its Regulations, the Office works to support and respect victims' rights at all levels. Regulation 16 and 37, respectively, ensure effective coordination with the Victims Participation and Reparation Section (VPRS) of the Registry and guarantee that all victims are informed of their ability to participate in the court proceedings. Regulation 16 states that the 'Office shall, in coordination with the Victims Participation and Reparations Section (VPRS) of the Registry, as appropriate, seek and receive the views of the victims at all stages in order to be mindful of and take into account their interests'.[16] Regulation 37 instructs OTP staff to inform victims of their role in the Court, the procedures of their participation, the access to reparations under the Statute and the existence of the VPRS.[17]

The relationship between the victims' legal representatives and the OTP is also regulated in the framework, with regulation 52 stating that 'the Office shall constructively engage with the legal representatives of victims in order to promote the efficient conduct of proceedings'.[18]

### *The Policy Paper on Victims' Participation*

As part of the Office's efforts to enhance predictability and consistency, the Office is adopting and widely disseminating its policy papers on key issues. In April 2010, after several rounds of consultations with States, international organizations and civil society, the Office adopted a policy paper on victims' participation.[19] This paper aims to ensure a clear and consistent approach of the Prosecution in its

---

15 Prosecutorial Strategy, para. 69.

16 Regulations, Regulation 16.

17 *Ibid.*, Regulation 37. Under regulation 37, the Office also informs victims that it forwards their personal data to the VPRS, subject to the need to protect their safety, well-being and privacy, as well as the integrity of investigations.

18 *Ibid.*, p. 24.

19 Policy Paper on Victims' Participation ('Victims' Participation'), 12 April 2010, http://www.icc-cpi.int/NR/rdonlyres/BC21BFDF-88CD-426B-BAC3-D0981E4ABE02/281751/PolicyPaperonVictimsParticipationApril2010.pdf (last visited 31 January 2011).

activities, legal submissions and positions on victims' participation under article 68(3), building upon the experience of the activities of the Office in recent years.[20]

The Office believes that victims bring a unique and necessary perspective to the activities of the ICC and contribute to fair and efficient trials. Under the Rome Statute, victims are actors of international justice rather than its passive subjects. As such, the Office considers that procedures for implementation of their rights must be defined in a clear and consistent manner.

The OTP has stressed the important role victims have within the ICC, from sending information directly to the OTP to participating in specific proceedings, emphasizing that 'participation is a right under the Statute and not a privilege bestowed upon victims on an ad hoc basis'.[21] Importantly, the OTP does not consider bureaucratic or resource-related arguments, such as the number of victims or costs involved, to be an obstacle to participation per se, but rather fully supports victims' participation when all statutory requirements are met.[22] Further, the OTP considers 'victims' to include natural persons who are both direct and indirect victims of crimes, so long as the harm suffered is personal to the individual.[23]

Regarding participation at different stages of the proceedings, for participation in pre-trial or trial proceedings, the harm alleged by a victim must be linked with the charges alleged.[24] For reparations, by contrast, the OTP takes a broader

---

20 Article 68(3) states 'Where the personal interests of the victims are affected, the Court shall permit their views and concerns to be presented and considered at stages of the proceedings determined to be appropriate by the Court and in a manner which is not prejudicial to or inconsistent with the rights of the accused and a fair and impartial trial. Such views and concerns may be presented by the legal representatives of the victims where the Court considers it appropriate, in accordance with the Rules of Procedure and Evidence'. Rome Statute of the International Criminal Court ('Statute'), ICC-A/CONF.183/9, 1 July 2002, http://www.icc-cpi.int/NR/rdonlyres/EA9AEFF7-5752-4F84-BE94-0A655EB30E16/0/Rome_Statute_English.pdf (last visited 31 January 2011).

21 Policy Paper on Victims' Participation, p. 1.

22 Victims' Participation, p. 5.

23 Ibid., pp. 10–11.

24 *See e.g., In the Case of the Prosecutor v. Abdallah Banda Abakaer Nourain and Saleh Mohammed Jerbo Jamus*, Decision on Victims' Participation at the Hearing on the Confirmation of Charges, ICC-02/05-03/09, 29 October 2010, para. 2, http://www.icc-cpi.int/iccdocs/doc/doc959401.pdf (last visited 31 January 2011); *Prosecutor v. Thomas Lubanga Dyilo*, Judgment on the Appeals of The Prosecutor and The Defence against Trial Chamber I's Decision on Victims' Participation of 18 January 2008 ('Judgment on Appeals of The Prosecutor'), ICC-01/04-01/06-1432, 11 July 2008, para. 2; The Appeals Chamber also confirmed that any modification of the legal characterization of the facts by the Trial Chamber pursuant to regulation 55 of the Regulations of the Court must be limited to the facts and circumstances described in the charges and any amendments thereto; *Prosecutor v. Thomas Lubanga Dyilo*, Judgment on the Appeals of Mr Lubanga Dyilo and the Prosecutor against the Decision of Trial Chamber I of 14 July 2009 entitled 'Decision giving notice to the parties and participants that the legal characterization of the facts may be subject to

approach and supports applications by individuals and entities other than those linked to the charges for which the accused is being prosecuted.[25]

With regard to the modalities of participation the Office has stated that 'while an assessment will need to be made on a case by case basis, the Office considers that the overall modalities should be consolidated to the largest extent possible in order to ensure certainty and consistency for victims themselves'.[26] More information on how the Office supports victims' participation in the proceedings is included in Part 4 of this article.

*Institutional integration*

Attention to victims is embedded in the organizational and management structure of the office, especially for particularly vulnerable victims, such as children, and sexual and gender-based crime victims. As noted above, it is part of the Prosecutorial Strategy to pay particular attention to the investigation and the prosecution of these crimes, which is evident in the working methods of the teams. In this regard, Professor Catharine A. MacKinnon was appointed as Special Gender Adviser to the Prosecutor on 26 November 2008. Her role is to provide strategic advice to the Office on sexual and gender violence, an area where expertise is required under Article 42(9) of the Rome Statute. Professor MacKinnon assists Prosecutor Moreno-Ocampo and Deputy Prosecutor Fatou Bensouda (OTP focal point for gender-related aspects), and works with the Office's Gender and Children Unit (GCU), the specialized unit working on gender issues across all of the Office's cases. The Unit is comprised of advisers with legal and psycho-social expertise to deal specifically with gender and children issues. The GCU advises the Prosecutor directly and provides support to the Office's divisions, from preliminary examination through to prosecution phases.

As stressed in the Court Strategy in relation to victims, 'Interviews with investigators and any other interactions between victims and staff members of the Court must be carefully managed in order to avoid retraumatization or other problems. The OTP will conduct assessments before interviewing vulnerable witnesses in order to determine if they are physically and psychologically fit to go through the interview, and will ensure that a psycho-social expert is available in case an intervention is needed. The OTP, as well as other relevant organs and bodies of the Court, will also ensure that their staff receive training on techniques when interviewing children and victims of sexual violence. External counsel interacting with victims are also engaged in this regard'.[27]

change in accordance with Regulation 55(2) of the Regulations of the Court', ICC-01/04-01/06-2205, 8 December 2009.

25 Victims' Participation, p. 9.

26 Victims' Participation, p. 1.

27 Court's Victims Strategy Report, para. 38.

In this sense, training is provided within the OTP on methodologies in collection of gender-based crimes and the legal framework for such crimes and on cultural issues related to each country of investigation, for all investigation staff. Interpreters also receive briefings and a sheet of relevant terminology.

Questionnaires, guidelines and policies have been developed since 2004 which provide questions to be routinely asked about all sexual and gender-based crimes under the Court's jurisdiction to all types of witnesses by all investigators so that gender-based issues are covered in all interviews. These guidelines also address issues such as the composition of the team, with choices to be given to the witness on the gender of the interviewing team, location, ensuring informed consent, use of a support person, etc.

### *Victims considerations in case selection*

The position of the OTP in regard to victims is a unique one. Prior to proceeding with an investigation, the Prosecutor must evaluate three criteria. According to the legal framework for preliminary examinations as established in article 53(1)(a)-(c) of the Statute, the Prosecutor must consider jurisdiction (temporal, material, and either territorial or personal jurisdiction); admissibility (complementarity and gravity); and the interests of justice prior to proceeding with an investigation.[28]

While the two tests for jurisdiction and admissibility 'are positive requirements that must be satisfied, the "interests of justice" is not. The interests of justice test is a potential countervailing consideration that might produce a reason not to proceed even where the first two are satisfied'.[29] This difference is indeed important: the Prosecutor is not required to establish that an investigation or prosecution is in the interests of justice. Rather, he should proceed with investigation unless there are specific circumstances which provide substantial reasons to believe it is not in the interests of justice to do so at that time.

Article 53(1) of the Statute addresses the initiation of an investigation. If the Prosecutor is satisfied that there is a reasonable basis to believe that the case is within the jurisdiction of the Court and is or would be admissible under Article 17 of the Statute, he must determine whether, *taking into account the gravity of the crime and the interests of the victims, there are nonetheless substantial reasons to believe that an investigation would not serve the interests of justice.* The interests of victims is thus a critical component of the interests of justice.

Article 53(2) addresses the initiation of a prosecution. It indicates that the Prosecutor may conclude that there is not sufficient basis to proceed because it

28 Article 53(1)(a)-(c) lists factors for the Prosecutor to consider whether the information available to the Prosecutor provides a reasonable basis to believe that a crime within the jurisdiction of the Court has been or is being committed. The case is or would be admissible under article 17; and taking into account the gravity of the crime and the interests of victims, there are nonetheless substantial reasons to believe that an investigation would not serve the interests of justice. Statute, Article 53(1)(a)-(c).

29 The Interests of Justice: Internal OTP Discussion Paper, 16 March 2007, p. 3.

'is not in the interests of justice, taking into account all the circumstances, including the gravity of the crime, the interests of victims and the age or infirmity of the alleged perpetrators, and his or her role in the alleged crime'.

There is thus a presumption in favor of investigation or prosecution and only in exceptional circumstances would the Prosecutor conclude that an investigation or a prosecution may not serve the interests of justice.[30]

## Victims Protection and OTP Contribution

### *Avoiding the risks*

The best way to achieve the security of victims is by minimizing their exposure to risks arising from their interaction with the Court. This is *inter alia* achieved through the Office's policy of focused investigations and prosecutions.[31] By allowing speedy investigation and prosecution and minimizing the number of witnesses called to testify, the Office is able to minimize the number of persons put at risk.

To further limit the risk to victims, the OTP has sought to increase its reliance on new types of evidence such as financial information and forensic evidence. This policy enables the Office to establish criminal responsibility without increasing the risk to victims and other witnesses.

The Office is developing its capacity to gather such evidence by continuously exploring cooperation with specialized institutes, national authorities and existing cooperation networks in financial, forensic and other fields.[32] One example of such a successful multilateral cooperation with national authorities was the investigation and arrest of Callixte Mbarushimana in Paris on 11 October 2010.[33] Mr. Mbarushimana was the Executive Secretary of the Forces Démocratiques pour la Libération du Rwanda – Forces Combattantes Abacunguzi (FDLR), a group engaged in armed conflict with the Forces Armées de la République Démocratique du Congo (FARDC) and the Rwandan Defence Forces (RDF). He is charged with crimes against humanity and war crimes committed when deciding to launch an offensive targeting the civilian population of the Kivu regions in order to ultimately obtain political concessions in the DRC.[34] His arrest followed the arrests of Mr. Murwanashyaka

30 *Ibid.*, at p. 3.

31 Prosecutorial Strategy, paras. 18–21.

32 *Ibid.*, para. 34.

33 'Callixte Mbarushimana arrested in France for crimes against humanity and war crimes allegedly committed in the Kivus (Democratic Republic of the Congo)', ICC-CPI-20101011-PR581, 11 October 2010, http://www.icc-cpi.int/menus/icc/situations%20and%20cases/situations/situation%20icc%200104/related%20cases/icc01040110/press%20releases/pr581 (last visited 31 January 2011).

34 Ibid. *See also* Case Information Sheet, http://www.icc-cpi.int/iccdocs/PIDS/publications/MbarushimanaENG.pdf (last visited 3 February 2011).

and Mr. Musoni, President and First Vice-President of the FDLR respectively, in Germany for crimes committed under German law. All three of these arrests were the result of coordination and cooperation between the Office and four countries: Germany, France, the DRC and Rwanda. As the DRC Coalition for the ICC stated: 'The victims, the affected communities and the whole of the Congolese population support this arrest and think that the Court's action will contribute to the stabilization of the East of the DRC.'[35] UN Secretary General Ban Ki-moon elaborated that 'this cooperative burden-sharing in prosecuting individuals for serious international crimes will greatly advance the fight against impunity. Legal action against FDLR leaders also reinforces efforts to demobilize and repatriate FDLR fighters, which would significantly contribute to stabilizing the eastern DRC'.[36]

### *Protection duty*

Although all organs of the Court are responsible for the protection of persons at risk on account of the activities of the Court, including victims who interact with the Court, the Registry plays an important role in this regard.[37] The Victims and Witnesses Unit (VWU) within the Registry arranges protective measures and security arrangements for testifying witnesses and also ensures that 'mechanisms are in place, in line with established clear, transparent and consistent criteria, to respond to requests for support or assistance, including medical and psychological support or counseling' throughout the proceedings.[38] Under Article 68 of the Statute, the OTP has a duty to take 'appropriate measures to protect the safety, physical and psychological well-being, dignity and privacy of victims and witnesses .... The Prosecutor shall take such measures particularly during the investigation and prosecution of such crimes'.[39]

The activities of the OTP begin before 'a crime' has been identified, thus expanding the scope of persons for the OTP to protect to 'any person'[40] at risk on

---

35 OTP Weekly Briefings, Issue #59, 12–18 October 2010, http://www.icc-cpi.int/NR/rdonlyres/B694680F-671A-4B52-892D-2220787DE758/282565/WBENG.pdf (last visited 31 January 2011).

36 *OTP Weekly Briefings*, Issue # 71, 18-25 January 2011, http://www.icc-cpi.int/NR/rdonlyres/12221416-FADA-45AF-A442-2923C7EBC4DC/282959/OTPWeeklyBriefing1825January2011Issue71.pdf (last visited 3 February 2011).

37 Court's Victims Strategy Report, para. 26.

38 Ibid., paras. 32, 39.

39 Statute, Article 68(1).

40 Article 54(3)(f) states the Prosecutor may 'take necessary measures, or request that necessary measures be taken, to ensure the confidentiality of information, the protection of any person or the preservation of evidence'. Statute, Article 54(3)(f). Also, the Appeal Chamber in the Katanga case found that the provisions of the Statute and the Rules protects not only 'witnesses and victims and members of their families, but also of others at risk on account of the activities of the Court' and thus an overarching concern of the whole system is 'to ensure that persons are not unjustifiably exposed to risk through the activities of the

account of his or her interaction with the OTP and not just to victims as defined in Rule 85. Under the OTP Regulations, the Investigation Division is the main division responsible for the necessary preparation for security plans and protection policies for each case. As explained in Regulation 46, the Office has the primary duty of ensuring adequate measures for the safety of victims. Through planning and in coordination with VWU when appropriate, the Investigation Division ensures the safety and well-being of victims, witnesses, office staff, and all persons put at risk by their interaction with the OTP.[41] Regulation 47 also provides for the need of the OTP to collaborate with the VWU to ensure that the Office remains committed to ensuring that the protective measures taken remain adequate.[42] The Investigation Division also develops various levels of precautions on security prior to conducting investigative activities[43] and upon selecting external persons to contact.[44] In order to maximize the safety of victims and gain a better idea of the security threats, the Office collaborates with the VWU to develop a Situation Threat and Risk Assessment for each area of operation in situations under investigation.[45] In addition, the Office continues to prioritize all other measures to increase the protection, safety and well-being of witnesses pursuant to article 68(1) of the Statute.[46]

---

Court'. *Prosecutor v. Germain Katanga*, Judgment on the Appeal of the Prosecutor Against the Decision of Pre-Trial Chamber I entitled 'First Decision on the Prosecution Request for Authorization to Redact Witness Statements', ICC-01/04-01/07-475, 13 May 2008, para. 54.

41 Regulation 8(a) states that the Investigation Division shall be responsible for 'the preparation of the necessary security plans and protection policies for each case to ensure the safety and well-being of victims, witnesses, Office staff, and persons at risk on account of their interaction with the Court, in adherence with good practices and in cooperation and coordination with the Registry, when required, on matters relating to protection and support', Regulations, Regulation 8(a).

42 Regulation 46: 'The Office shall maintain a full and accurate record of all protective measures sought and obtained by the Office for each witness and, to the extent possible, of all other protective measures implemented. The Office shall ensure that the measures remain adequate and necessary given the circumstances of each case.' Regulations, Regulation 46.

43 Regulation 25(2) states: 'In support of investigations, the Office shall prepare additional plans related to administration, security and communication, in consultation with the Registry as appropriate.' Regulations, Regulation 25(2).

44 Regulation 36(2): 'Prior to contacting a person to be questioned in connection with an investigation, the Office shall collect as much information as possible on the level of risk involved for that person as well as for others who may be at risk on account of such questioning, including those who facilitated contact between the Office and the person to be questioned. Based upon its determination of the level of risk, the Office may consider alternatives to questioning as well as the possibility of additional security measures, in consultation with the Victims and Witnesses Unit (VWU) as appropriate.' Regulations, Regulation 36(2).

45 Regulation 44: 'The Office shall develop, in consultation with VWU, an Area-Specific Threat and Risk Assessment for each area of operation related to a situation under investigation.'

46 Regulation 45: 'In order to protect the safety and well-being of witnesses pursuant to article 68, paragraph 1, the Office shall: (a) create a database containing relevant

Through initiatives such as the Office's internal operational manual, which details the above Regulations, the OTP continues to implement all the necessary precautions to ensure the safety of those who come in contact with the Office. In addition, the OTP has appointed a focal point within the Prosecution Division regarding protection.

## Supporting Victims' Participation in Proceedings

### *Legal framework*

As a policy, the OTP fully supports the participation of those victims who fulfill the statutory requirements. The Statute provides as a general rule for victims' participation that 'where the personal interests of the victims are affected, the Court shall permit victims' views and concerns to be presented and considered at stages of the proceedings determined to be appropriate by the Court and in a manner which is not prejudicial to, or inconsistent with, the rights of the Accused'.[47]

### *'Personal interest'*

As stated in filings to the Appeals Chamber, the Office considers that the 'personal interest' in the context of Article 68(3) must be more specific than the general interest of any victim in the progress and outcome of the proceedings. It is the core of the Prosecutor's mandate that crimes should be effectively investigated and prosecuted, and the victims' interests on effective investigation and prosecution should not be confused with the interest of the victims under Article 68.[48] Consistent with the Appeals Chamber's decision,[49] the Office considers that 'once a criminal case is brought against a person, the proper determination of personal interests for the purposes of victim participation requires a showing that the applicant's personal

information on persons who have provided evidence and information to the Office; (b) ensure that only expressly authorized staff have access to the database containing relevant information on persons who have provided evidence and information to the Office; (c) ensure discreet and secure contact with witnesses in adherence to good practices and the Code of Conduct for Investigators; (d) collect security information; (e) update regularly the general and individual security risk assessments; and (f) implement or, where relevant, participate in the implementation of other preventive measures taken on the basis of the security risk assessment in accordance with the Statute, the Rules, these Regulations, relevant Court decisions and good practices.' Regulations, Regulation 45.

47 Statute, Article 68(3).

48 *Situation in Darfur, Sudan*, Prosecution's Document in Support of Appeal against the 6 December 2007 Decision on the Victims' Applications for Participation in the Proceedings, ICC-02/05-125, 18 February 2008, para. 24.

49 *Dyilo*, Judgment on the Appeals of The Prosecutor, para. 1.

interests are affected in connection to the charges, which form the subject-matter of the proceedings in which he or she seeks to participate'.[50]

*Notifications to enable participation*

Pursuant to Article 15(3) of the Statute, victims are allowed to make representations to the Prosecutor and the Court bearing on their interests[51] upon the opening of an investigation.[52] Moreover, in the context of proceedings related to the *proprio motu* initiation of an investigation pursuant to Article 15, the Prosecutor is required to give notice of the application to victims in order to allow them to make representations to the Pre-Trial Chamber.[53]

The situation in Kenya was the first example of the initiation of an investigation on a *proprio motu* basis. In compliance with Rule 50(1),[54] on 23 November 2009, the Prosecutor provided notice to victims and their legal representatives of his intention to request authorization to open an investigation through a widely publicized notification.[55]

---

50 *Prosecutor v. Thomas Lubanga Dyilo*, Prosecution's Document in Support of Appeal against Trial Chamber I's 18 January 2008 Decision on Victim Participation, ICC-01/04-01/06-1219, 10 March 2008, para. 18.

51 Article 15(3): 'If the Prosecutor concludes that there is a reasonable basis to proceed with an investigation, he or she shall submit to the Pre-Trial Chamber a request for authorization of an investigation, together with any supporting material collected. Victims may make representations to the Pre-Trial Chamber, in accordance with the Rules of Procedure and Evidence.' Statute, Article 15(3).

52 Rule 92 also requires the Court to notify the victims on all proceedings to enable the victims to make informed decisions of whether or not to participate. Rules, Rule 92. Rule 92(8) requires the Registrar to give adequate publicity to the proceedings. at the request of a Chamber and in the following circumstances: 1. Prosecutor's decision not to initiate an investigation or not to prosecute. Rules, Rule 92(2); Regulations, Regulation 87(2); 2. Hearing to confirm charges. Rules, Rule 92(3); 3. Proceedings subsequent to the proceeding which the victim or the representative participated. Rules, Rule 92(4).

53 Cf., Statute, Article 15(3); Rules, Rule 50.

54 Rule 50(1): 'When the Prosecutor intends to seek authorization from the Pre-Trial Chamber to initiate an investigation pursuant to article 15, paragraph 3, the Prosecutor shall inform victims, known to him or her or to the Victims and Witnesses Unit, or their legal representatives, unless the Prosecutor decides that doing so would pose a danger to the integrity of the investigation or the life or well-being of victims and witnesses. The Prosecutor may also give notice by general means in order to reach groups of victims if he or she determines in the particular circumstances of the case that such notice could not pose a danger to the integrity and effective conduct of the investigation or to the security and well-being of victims and witnesses. In performing these functions, the Prosecutor may seek the assistance of the Victims and Witnesses Unit as appropriate.' Rules, Rule 50(1).

55 OTP Public Notice: Victims of post-election violence in Kenya have 30 days to make representations to ICC in the Hague, 23 November 2009,

*Modalities to participate*

Article 68(3) gives victims the right to present 'views and concerns'[56] where their personal interests are affected. Rule 89 requires victims to apply for the permission of the Chamber for their participation in proceedings.[57] According to Article 68(1) of the Statute and the Court's jurisprudence, the modalities of such participation must be specified by a Chamber 'in a manner not prejudicial to the rights of the person under investigation or the Accused, and in a way non-antagonistic to a fair and impartial trial'.[58]

Other manners of participation described in the Rules include the presentation of views and concerns in oral or written format,[59] questioning a witness[60] and the

---

http://www.icc-cpi.int/NR/rdonlyres/7A34B336-9611-430F-A668-CA5D209471CA/281270/Notificationtovictims_231120091.pdf (last visited 3 February 2011).

56 Statute, Article 68(3).

57 Rule 89 '(1): In order to present their views and concerns, victims shall make written application to the Registrar, who shall transmit the application to the relevant Chamber. Subject to the provisions of the Statute, in particular article 68, paragraph 1, the Registrar shall provide a copy of the application to the Prosecutor and the Defence, who shall be entitled to reply within a time limit to be set by the Chamber. Subject to the provisions of sub-rule 2, the Chamber shall then specify the proceedings and manner in which participation is considered appropriate, which may include making opening and closing statements. (2) The Chamber, on its own initiative or on the application of the Prosecutor or the Defence, may reject the application if it considers that the person is not a victim or that the criteria set forth in article 68, paragraph 3, are not otherwise fulfilled. A victim whose application has been rejected may file a new application later in the proceedings. (3) An application referred to in this rule may also be made by a person acting with the consent of the victim, or a person acting on behalf of a victim, in the case of a victim who is a child or, when necessary, a victim who is disabled. (4) Where there are a number of applications, the Chamber may consider the applications in such a manner as to ensure the effectiveness of the proceedings and may issue one decision.' Rules, Rule 89.

58 *Situation in Darfur*, Judgment on Victim Participation in the Investigation Stage of the Proceedings in the Appeal of the OPCD against the Decision of Pre-Trial Chamber I of 3 December 2007 and in the Appeals of the OPCD and the Prosecutor against the decision of Pre-Trial Chamber I of 6 December 2007, ICC-02/05-177, 2 February 2009, para. 45.

59 Rule 91(2): 'A legal representative of a victim shall be entitled to attend and participate in the proceedings in accordance with the terms of the ruling of the Chamber and any modification thereof given under rules 89 and 90. This shall include participation in hearings unless, in the circumstances of the case, the Chamber concerned is of the view that the representative's intervention should be confined to written observations or submissions. The Prosecutor and the defence shall be allowed to reply to any oral or written observation by the legal representative for victims.' Rules, Rule 91(2).

60 Rule 91(3)(a): 'When a legal representative attends and participates in accordance with this rule, and wishes to question a witness, including questioning under rules 67 and 68, an expert or the accused, the legal representative must make application to the Chamber. The Chamber may require the legal representative to provide a written note of the questions and in that case the questions shall be communicated to the Prosecutor and, if appropriate,

consultation of a record of the proceedings[61] subject to relevant restrictions and the Chamber's approval.

The Office considers that overall modalities of victims' participation should be consolidated to the largest extent possible in order to ensure certainty and consistency for victims themselves.

*Victims' submission of evidence*

The submission of evidence and the lodging of challenges against the admissibility or relevance of evidence are rights reserved for the parties to the proceedings.[62] 'While the Statute enables victim participants to present their personal views and concerns, it does not grant them rights equivalent to that of parties as such. In particular, the Office considers that victims do not have the right to introduce additional evidence at the pre-trial stage.'[63] This principle has been established by the Pre-Trial Chamber I in *Katanga and Ngudjolo*.[64]

---

the defence, who shall be allowed to make observations within a time limit set by the Chamber. (b) The Chamber shall then issue a ruling on the request, taking into account the stage of the proceedings, the rights of the accused, the interests of witnesses, the need for a fair, impartial and expeditious trial and in order to give effect to article 68, paragraph 3. The ruling may include directions on the manner and order of the questions and the production of documents in accordance with the powers of the Chamber under article 64. The Chamber may, if it considers it appropriate, put the question to the witness, expert or accused on behalf of the victim's legal representative.' Rules, Rule 91(3).

61 Rule 131(2): 'Subject to any restrictions concerning confidentiality and the protection of national security information, the record may be consulted by the Prosecutor, the defence, the representatives of States when they participate in the proceedings, and the victims or their legal representatives participating in the proceedings pursuant to rules 89 to 91.' Rules, Rule 131(2).

62 Article 69(3): 'The parties may submit evidence relevant to the case, in accordance with article 64. The Court shall have the authority to request the submission of all evidence that it considers necessary for the determination of the truth.' Statute, Article 69(3).

63 Victims' Participation, p. 18.

64 *Prosecutor v. Germain Katanga and Mathieu Ngudjolo Chui*, Decision on the Set of Procedural Rights Attached to Procedural Status of Victim at the Pre-Trial Stage of the Case ('Decision on Procedural Rights at Pre-Trial'), ICC-01/04-01/07-474, 13 May 2008, para. 113. The Chamber has held that 'the statutory framework provided for by the Statute and the Rules for the pre-trial stage of a case leaves no room for the presentation of additional evidence by those granted the procedural status of victim'. The Chamber noted that according to article 61(7) of the Statute, the power of the Pre-Trial Chamber is confined to 'requesting the consideration by the Prosecution of the opportunity to provide additional evidence' in contrast to article 69(3) which gives the competent Chamber 'the authority to request the submission of all evidence that it considers necessary for the determination of the truth'. Ibid., paras. 107–9.

The OTP is also of the opinion that it should be a rare exception for victims to present evidence other than for reparation purposes or to challenge the admissibility or relevance of a piece of evidence before the Trial Chamber.

However, the Appeals Chamber has held that the Statute and the Rules do not 'preclude the possibility for victims to lead evidence pertaining to the guilt or innocence of the accused and to challenge the admissibility or relevance of evidence during the trial proceedings'.[65] Nevertheless the Chamber emphasized that victims are not granted an unfettered right to lead or challenge evidence; 'instead victims are required to demonstrate why their interests are affected by the evidence or issue, upon which the Chamber will decide, on a case-by-case basis whether or not to allow such participation'.[66]

Victims must comply with the six criteria established by the Appeals Chamber, which are subject to the Chamber's case-by-case determination: '(i) a discrete application by victims to that effect; (ii) notice to the parties; (iii) demonstration of personal interests that are affected by the specific proceedings; (iv) compliance with disclosure obligations and protection orders; (v) a determination of appropriateness; and (vi) consistency with the rights of the accused and a fair trial.'[67]

Even with the careful application of the Chamber's criteria, the Prosecutor remains concerned that allowing victims to collect or present evidence in their possession can create risks for their own security as well as that of other persons at risk.[68] This is particularly relevant when the information is collected in the absence of relevant duties of protection, or the means or expertise to ensure such protection. The Office recommends to those victims who are in the possession of meaningful evidence necessary to establish the truth to contact the Prosecution.

65 *Prosecutor v. Thomas Lubanga Dyilo*, Judgment on the Appeals of The Prosecutor, para. 3. For the submission of evidence, the Chamber based its decision on the authority of the Trial Chamber to request the presentation of all evidence necessary for determining the truth pursuant to article 69(3). For the rights to challenge the admissibility or relevance of evidence, the Chamber relied on its general powers under article 69(4) to declare evidence admissible or relevant and rule 91(3) under which the Chamber may authorize, upon request, the legal representatives to question witnesses or produce documents. *Ibid.*, paras. 108–9.

66 *Ibid.*, para. 4. 'With these safeguards in place, the grant of participatory rights to victims to lead evidence pertaining to the guilt or innocence of the accused and to challenge the admissibility or relevance of the evidence is not inconsistent with the onus on the Prosecutor to prove the guilt of the accused nor is it inconsistent with the rights of the accused and a fair trial. … the Trial Chamber did not create an unfettered right for victims to lead or challenge evidence, instead victims are required to demonstrate why their interests are affected by the evidence or issue, upon which the Chamber will decide, on a case-by-case basis whether or not to allow such participation.'

67 *Ibid.*, paras. 4, 104.

68 Indeed, victims could potentially be allowed to present evidence through the Chamber's authority, pursuant to Articles 64(6)(b) and (d).

***Questioning of witnesses***
Likewise, examination of witnesses by legal representatives permitted by a Chamber pursuant to rule 91(3) should be limited to issues directly relevant to the interests of the victims.[69] Examinations to address issues of guilt or innocence of the accused should be limited to exceptional circumstances.[70] The manner of questioning should be neutral.[71]

***Access to records and evidence***
The OTP considers that victims do not have the right to access records and evidence under the Statute. The right to access material in the Prosecution's possession 'goes to the heart of the Prosecution's independence and its right to exercise control over its evidence, which is only subject to the provisions of the Statute and the Rules on disclosure and inspection to the defense'.[72] Nonetheless, pursuant to OTP regulation 52, which provides that there should be constructive engagement with legal representatives the Office provides them access to its filings and evidence, including those classified as confidential where appropriate. However, the sharing of this evidence with the legal representatives is subject to the requirements of confidentiality and of witness protection.[73]

Pre-Trial Chambers have generally granted legal representatives access to the public evidence contained in the record of the case[74] and filed by the Prosecution

69 *See supra* note 55.

70 *Prosecutor v. Germain Katanga and Mathieu Ngudjolo Chui,* Prosecution's Observations on the Anonymity and the Modalities of Participation in the Proceedings of Applicants a/0327/07 to a/0337/07 ('Prosecution's Observations on Anonymity'), ICC-01/04-01/07-392, 14 April 2008, para. 22.

71 Trial Chamber I stated that 'there is a presumption in favour of a neutral form of questioning, which may be displaced in favour of a more closed form of questioning, along with the use of leading or challenging questions, depending on the issues raised and the interests affected and if a representative of victims wishes to depart from a neutral type of questioning, an oral request should be made to the bench'. *Prosecutor v. Thomas Lubanga Dyilo,* Decision on the Manner of Questioning Witnesses by the Legal Representatives of Victims, ICC-01/04-01/06-2127, 16 September 2009, paras. 29–30. *See also Prosecutor v. Katanga and Ngudjolo,* Decision on the Modalities of Victim Participation at Trial ('Decision on Modalities of Victim Participation'), ICC-01/04-01/07-1788-tENG, 22 January 2010, para. 78.

72 *Prosecutor v. Thomas Lubanga Dyilo,* Application for Leave to Appeal Trial Chamber I's 18 January 2008 Decision on Victims' Participation, ICC-01/04-01/06-1136, 28 January 2008, para. 18. On this issue, the application was dismissed by the Trial Chamber. *Prosecutor v. Thomas Lubanga Dyilo,* Decision on the Defense and Prosecution Requests for Leave to Appeal the Decision on Victims' Participation of 18 January 2008, ICC-01/04-01/06-1197, 26 February 2008, para. 49.

73 Victims' Participation, p. 21.

74 *Katanga and Chui,* Decision on Procedural Rights at Pre-Trial, para. 132; *Prosecutor v. Bahar Idriss Abu Garda,* Decision on victims' modalities of participation at the Pre-Trial Stage of the Case, ICC-02/05-02/09-136, 6 October 2009, para. 13.

and the Defense. 'In relation to those filings that are marked confidential and are not notified to the victims' legal representatives [...] the Chamber retains the option to decide, on a case by case basis and upon receipt of a specific and motivated request, whether to grant victims' legal representatives access thereto.'[75]

The Pre-Trial Chamber in *Katanga and Ngudjolo* decided that 'the Legal Representatives of non-anonymous victims shall be prohibited from transmitting to their clients copies of any document or evidence included in the confidential part of the case record, as well as any transcript of hearings held in closed session'.[76] In cases where the legal representatives establish that they require further access to confidential portions of the record and request the intervention of the Chamber, the Office is of the opinion that access should only be granted 'in highly exceptional

75 *Katanga and Chui*, Decision on Procedural Rights at Pre-Trial, para. 147. Upon request by the Prosecution, the Chamber subsequently set limitations to the procedural rights of the victims recognized in its decision in light of risks to the safety of witnesses and/or family members. It decided that the legal representatives of non-anonymous victims shall be prohibited from transmitting to their clients' copies of any document or evidence included in the confidential part of the case record, as well as any transcript of hearings held in closed session. The Chamber also prohibited the legal representatives from discussing with their clients the information which would allow the victims to identify the specific witnesses in the confirmation hearing of the case. See *Prosecutor v. Germain Katanga and Mathieu Ngudjolo Chui*, Decision on Limitations of Set of Procedural Rights for Non-Anonymous Victims ('Decision on Limitations for Non-Anonymous Victims'), ICC-01/04-01/07-537, 30 May 2008, pp. 12–13; *Prosecutor v. Germain Katanga and Mathieu Ngudjolo Chui*, Public Redacted Version of the 'Decision on the 97 Applications for Participation at the Pre-Trial Stage of the Case' ('Decision on the 97 Applications'), ICC-01/04-01/07-579, 10 June 2008, p. 48.

76 *See Katanga and Chui*, Decision on Limitations for Non-Anonymous Victims, pp 12–13; *Katanga and Chui*, 'Decision on the 97 Applications', p. 48. The Pre-Trial Chamber I, at first, held that victims have the right to access all filings and decisions contained in the record of the case regardless of whether they are classified as public or confidential, except for those classified ex parte. *Katanga and Chui*, Decision on Procedural Rights at Pre-Trial, para.128. Due to the security concerns of witnesses and their family members, the Prosecution requested the single judge to limit access to the confidential material that identifies Prosecution witnesses who have not consented to the disclosure of their identity beyond that of the Defence. *Prosecutor v. Germain Katanga and Mathieu Ngudjolo Chui*, Prosecution's Request for Limitations pursuant to the Decision on the Set of Procedural Rights Attached to Procedural Status of Victim at the Pre-Trial Stage of the Case, ICC-01/04-01/07-485, 20 May 2008, paras. 5–14. In addition, the Prosecutor also supported 'any mechanism that may be employed that will enhance the security of witnesses and confidential information in the case record and permit victims to participate in the proceedings pursuant to the "Decision on the set of Procedural Rights Attached to Procedural Status of Victim at the Pre-Trial Stage of the Case"', *Prosecutor v. Germain Katanga and Mathieu Ngudjolo Chui*, Prosecution's Observations on Registry's 'Registry's considerations on victims' rights to access the record of the case and to attend closed session hearings', ICC-01/04-01/07-506, 26 May 2008.

situations and only after an applicant has established a compelling case that the material in question directly affects his or her interests'.[77]

Any decision must take into consideration the protection of confidential information, the safety and security of victims and witnesses, and the risks associated with the dissemination of information capable of endangering persons or the integrity of ongoing investigations.[78]

### *Anonymous victims*

The Office considers that anonymous victims can be permitted to participate in pre-trial and trial proceedings, subject to the imposition of strict limitations on their procedural rights in light of considerations of fairness to the accused.

In order to allow for a proper response by the Defense,[79] basic considerations of fairness vis-à-vis the accused person require that they be informed of the identities of individuals who have been granted the procedural status of participants and who may bring allegations prejudicial to their interests.

It is the Office's general position that the legal representatives ought to be entitled to participate, in the pre-confirmation and confirmation hearings, in various forms which relate to issues specific to their interests. Such participation must be performed in a manner that respects the rights of the victims and all the rights granted to the accused. The participation of anonymous victims and the manner of their participation should also follow the same principle.

In this respect, it is the prosecution's view that the *Lubanga* Pre-Trial chamber struck an appropriate balance between the rights of the parties and the exercise of meaningful procedural rights by victims' participants at the pre-trial stage.[80] The Chamber decided that in principle,[81] the rights of legal representatives of anonymous victims at confirmation hearings include: i) access to the public

---

77 *Situation in the Democratic Republic of the Congo*, Prosecution's response to the 'Request of the OPCV to access documents in the situation record related to applicants a/0004/06 to a/0008/06, a/0019/06, a/0020/06, a/0022/06 to a/0024/06, a/0026/06, a/0027/06, a/0029/06, a/0030/06, a/0033/06, a/0035/06, a/0036/06, a/0039/06 to a/0041/06, a/0043/06, a/0046/06 to a/0052/06, a/0072/06 to a/0080/06 and a/0110/06', ICC-01/04-413, 8 November 2007, para. 3.

78 *Katanga and Chui*, Prosecution's Observations on Anonymity, para. 17.

79 *Prosecutor v. Thomas Lubanga Dyilo*, Prosecution's Response to 'Observations Concernant les Modalités de la Participation des Victims', ICC-01/04-01/06-353, 25 August 2006, para. 21. The Prosecution submitted that while the parties should know the identity of victims participating as the proceedings lead up to trial but also acknowledged that protective concern calls for victims need to maintain their anonymity toward the public. *Prosecutor v. Thomas Lubanga Dyilo*, Prosecution's Submissions of the Role of Victims in the Proceedings Leading up to, and During, the Trial, ICC-01/04-01/06-996-Anx1, 23 October 2007 (refilling of 19 October 2007 submission), paras. 25–9.

80 *Ibid.*, para. 7.

81 The Chamber retained the option to make an exception to limitation to the records to access and the hearing they may attend in the event of exceptional circumstances.

documents only; ii) the ability to attend at public hearings only; iii) the inability to add any point of fact or any evidence or question the witnesses presented by Parties. The Prosecution submitted that anonymous victims participating in the *Katanga* proceeding are to be treated similarly.[82] Accordingly, the *Katanga* Pre-Trial Chamber afforded the same procedural rights granted to anonymous victims at the pre-trial stage of the *Lubanga* case.[83]

The stake is higher at the trial stage than at the confirmation of charges proceedings. In the latter, the proceeding is simply a check to see if the Prosecution's evidence is adequate to confirm the charges, while the former is where determination of guilt or innocence takes place. To ensure a balance, Trial Chamber I in *Lubanga* indicated that it would 'scrutinize carefully the precise circumstances and the potential prejudice to the parties and other participants' in order to 'determine whether steps that fall short of revealing the victim's identity can sufficiently mitigate the prejudice'.[84] Trial Chamber II in *Katanga and Ngudjolo* did not rule out the possibility of anonymous victims participating in proceedings, but emphasized that it will not authorize victims who wish to remain anonymous to the Defense to testify as witnesses.[85]

***Personal interventions***

The Office considers that victims should ordinarily present their views and concerns before a Chamber through their legal representatives. An application for personal victim participation should be made in writing and set out the particular circumstances where it is both necessary and appropriate for the person to appear in person rather than through a legal representative.

Although the opportunity is expressly created for legal representatives to undertake this task on victims' behalf, Trial Chamber I in *Lubanga* held that article 68(3) gives victims the unequivocal statutory right to present their views and concerns in person when their personal interests are affected.[86] The Chamber nevertheless indicated that any intervention by victims must be conducted 'in a manner which is not prejudicial to, or inconsistent with, the rights of the accused and a fair and impartial trial', particularly where a significant number of victims

82 *Katanga and Chui*, Prosecution's Observations on Anonymity, para. 12.

83 *Katanga and Chui*, Decision on Procedural Rights at Pre-Trial, paras. 182–3.

84 *Prosecutor v. Thomas Lubanga Dyilo*, Decision on Victims' Participation, ICC-01/04-01/06-1119, 18 January 2008, para. 131. See also *Prosecutor v. Thomas Lubanga Dyilo*, Decision on the Application by Victims to Participate in the Proceedings, ICC-01/04-01/06-1556, 15 December 2008, para. 131. The Chamber is to consider whether any victims are to remain 'anonymous' and if so, the extent of the anonymity. Ibid.

85 *Katanga and Chui*, Decision on Modalities of Victim Participation, paras. 92–3.

86 *Prosecutor v. Thomas Lubanga Dyilo* Decision on the Request by Victims a/0225/06, a/0229/06 and a/0270/07 to Express their Views and Concerns in Person and to Present Evidence during the Trial ('Decision on the Request by Victims to Express their Views'), ICC-01/04-01/06-2032-Anx, 26 June 2009, para. 17.

are participating.[87] Trial Chamber II in *Katanga* also stated that it will grant the legal representatives an opportunity to call victims to give evidence under the oath at trial.

## Victims' Reparations

The full system of reparations envisioned in the Statute, including through the Trust Fund for Victims, is a critical aspect of the Rome system.

Upon request by the victims or on the Trial Chamber's own motion, proceedings regarding reparations for victims may be initiated. The Chamber's powers in terms of reparations are rather limited: reparations proceedings will take place only after a Trial Chamber has entered a conviction against an accused. In addition, the Trial Chamber may award (individual) reparations only to those victims who suffered harm as a consequence of a crime of which the accused was convicted. By contrast, the Trust Fund's scope and powers are broader than the functions of the Trial Chamber with respect to reparations. It may make awards for reparations other than against the accused; uses resources other than those obtained by way of fines or secured by forfeiture; and also act prior to a conviction (see in this sense Article 79(1) and Rule 98(5)). However, the Statute and the Rules provide for a number of ways in which the Trial Chamber may avail itself of the assistance of the Trust Fund to comply with its duties with respect to reparations to victims. Moreover, the Trial Chamber has the power to oversee the exercise of the Trust Funds functions with respect to other resources, so as to provide that the Trust Fund's activities do not interfere with any pending proceedings (Article 75(2), Rule 98).

The Office believes that victims need to receive individual or collective reparations to ensure the full cycle of justice. As not all victims will participate, the role for the Trust Fund as a tool able to reach any victim is key. The policy of the Office is to request freezing of assets early on in proceedings, in order to provide for future reparations. It is a standing instruction of the Prosecutor to the teams.

## Conclusion

The role of victims in the ICC framework is one of the distinguishing features of the Court. While most criminal proceedings allow for victims to be called as witnesses and share their experiences, the ICC is the only international criminal institution where the victims themselves have a right to actively participate in all stages of a criminal trial. Their participation is rooted in the notion that these

87 *Lubanga*, Decision on the Request by Victims to Express their Views, paras. 17, 24, 27. While the Chamber granted the three victims the right to give evidence, it decided that once they have completed their evidence, it will determine, if relevant, when and by whom any views and concerns are to be presented. Ibid., para. 40.

crimes have a devastating impact on victims' lives and their participation in the proceedings not only contribute to the promotion of justice and fight against impunity but also serve as a healing process for the victims themselves. The OTP's position on victims is included from the structure of the organization to its policy on focused investigations and prosecutions.

The OTP specifically recognizes the important role victims have and as reflected in the Regulations, the OTP supports and respects victims' rights in relation to the Court. The OTP stresses that the procedures for implementation of victims' rights should be clearly defined. Further, the OTP emphasizes the importance of having mechanisms in place to protect the psychological and physical well-being of victims and cooperates fully with the VWU to ensure their protection through every stage of the proceedings, including pre and post-trial. Specifically, the OTP is aware of the trauma inflicted upon child victims and sexual or gender based crime victims and has established a unit that specifically deals with these issues. It is in relation to the role of victims that the International Criminal Court is truly ground-breaking.

# Chapter 17
# Victim's Access to the International Criminal Court: Much Remains to be Done

Gilbert Bitti and Leïla Bourguiba[1]

Non-governmental organizations ('NGOs') were the driving force for the inclusion of the provisions on victims' rights in the Rome Statute (the 'Statute') of the International Criminal Court (the 'ICC' or the 'Court').

Their statement in this respect at the beginning of the Rome Conference on 17 June 1998 was very clear:

> Punishing criminals is not enough. There will be no justice without justice for victims. And in order to do justice for victims, the ICC must be empowered to address their rights and needs.[2]

Thus, it was time to create a permanent international criminal court which would offer to the victims a better role than that of a simple tool to move forward its cases as the *ad hoc* Tribunals for the Former Yugoslavia and Rwanda were perceived to do. This should no longer be tolerated in a permanent system of international criminal justice where victims' rights ought to be recognized as such and protected.

The NGOs efforts were not in vain at the Rome Conference: the Court has a duty to allow victims to exercise their right to participate at all stages of the proceedings, represented by their own lawyers, who they may choose freely.[3] Victims are no longer just witnesses used by the Prosecutor.

The crucial article in the Statute in this respect is the much disputed in Rome article 68(3), which reads as follows:

> Where the personal interests of the victims are affected, the Court shall permit their views and concerns to be presented and considered at stages of the proceedings determined to be appropriate by the Court and in a manner

1 The views expressed are solely those of the authors.

2 Statement by Fiona McKay, representing REDRESS, on behalf of *The Victims Rights Working Group* delivered to the Rome Conference on 17 June 1998, reprinted in Bitti, G. and H. Friman (2001), Participation of Victims in the Proceedings, in Roy S. Lee, *The International Criminal Court, Elements of Crimes and Rules of procedure and Evidence* (456–74), Transnational Publishers.

3 Rule 90(1) of the Rules of Procedure and Evidence (the 'Rules').

> which is not prejudicial to or inconsistent with the rights of the accused and a fair and impartial trial. Such views and concerns may be presented by the legal representatives of the victims where the Court considers it appropriate, in accordance with the Rules of Procedure and Evidence.

But this article was not the only step towards establishing a victim's general right to participate in proceedings before the ICC. Other articles of the Statute give them more specific procedural rights such as articles 15(3) and 19(3). Article 15(3) provides a right for victims to participate at a *specific stage* of the proceedings, i.e., the decision of the Pre-Trial Chamber on the question of whether or not to authorize a *proprio motu* investigation by the Prosecutor, whereas article 19(3) provides a right for victims to participate in proceedings with regard to *specific issues*, i.e., questions in relation to jurisdiction or admissibility.

Article 75 is also a major victory for victims' rights for which NGOs, and especially REDRESS, invested a lot of efforts before and during Rome. For the first time in the history of international criminal justice, an international criminal court was given the power to decide on awards for reparations, including restitution, compensation and rehabilitation. In addition, article 79 of the Statute provides for the establishment of a Trust Fund for the benefit of victims. However, the Court has yet to conclude its first trial and article 75 remains 'untested'.

Yet, despite this success on paper, it is interesting to notice that ten years after their major victory, NGOs are still complaining, and rightly so, about the way the Court is handling its mandate towards victims. It is worth having a look at their complaints voiced at the first Review Conference of the Statute in Uganda, Kampala, between 31 May and 11 June 2010, during a very interesting stocktaking exercise conducted, on victims' issues, among other topics.

The present contribution will therefore focus on the challenges faced by victims in exercising their right to participate in the proceedings before the ICC,[4] in particular by casting light on the obstacles to victims' effective access to the Court (I) and the issue of challenges to their protection and the impact of those challenges on participation (II).

## The 'Arduous' Access to Court

Although the Court *shall* permit victims to appear before it, obstacles to their participation remain numerous such as the lack of proper information (A), the complexity of the process for them to apply for participation (B) and more

4 For an extensive and comprehensive review of the Court's jurisprudence in relation to the participatory rights of victims see 'The impact of the distinction between situations and cases on the participation of victims in the International Criminal Court', Ania Salinas and James Sloan. See also the comprehensive and exhaustive article of Silvestro Stazzone, 'Victims' participation in the International Criminal Proceeding: the Early Jurisprudence of the International Criminal Court' *in L'Observateur des Nations Unies* (2010–2011, vol. 28), pp. 93–119.

generally the 'dramatic' geographical distance between the Court and the affected communities (C).

*The lack of proper information*

NGOs have praised the efforts made by the Court with regard to the early involvement of victims in the situation in the Republic of Kenya.[5] Indeed, for the first time in the history of the ICC, victims were invited to participate in the process leading to the opening of the investigation in that situation.

In November, 2009, when the Prosecutor announced that he would ask the authorization of the Pre-Trial Chamber to open an investigation in Kenya pursuant to article 15, he decided to inform victims by 'general means through a widely publicized notification', in accordance with article 15(3) and rule 50 of the Rules, as he thought that direct contact with victims would pose a danger to the integrity of a future investigation or to their lives or well-being.

Pre-Trial Chamber II, seized with the Prosecutor's request, decided that such a public notice would not be enough to properly allow victims to participate in the proceedings. The Chamber therefore requested the Victims Participation and Reparations Section (the 'VPRS'), a section within the ICC Registry in charge of assisting victims before the Court, to organize urgently a field mission to Kenya in order to *inter alia*: 1) identify the community leaders of the affected groups to act on behalf of those victims who might wish to make representations to the Court (collective representations), and 2) receive victims' representations (either collective and/or individual).[6]

Although the VPRS was ordered to submit a report by 21 December 2009, it requested more time and finally submitted its report in March 2010[7] together with 396 'victims' representations', including 76 collective representations made by groups comprising from 100 to 10,000 victims. The vast majority of victims supported the Prosecutor's request to open an investigation in Kenya but added that the time-frame of the investigation should be broader than the one suggested by the Prosecutor, a request which was taken into consideration by the Chamber when it authorized the investigation on 31 March 2010.[8]

---

5 International Federation of Human Rights, *ICC Review Conference: Renewing Commitment to Accountability*, May 2010, p. 9 (the 'FIDH Report to the ICC Review Conference').

6 *Situation in the Republic of Kenya*, ICC-01/09-4, Order to the Victims Participation and Reparations Section Concerning Victims' Representations Pursuant to Article 15(3) of the Statute (Pre-Trial Chamber II, 10 December 2009).

7 *Situation in the Republic of Kenya*, ICC-01/09-17-Corr-Red, Victims Participation and Reparations Section, Public Redacted Version of Corrigendum to the Report on Victims' Representations (ICC-01/09-17-Conf-Exp-Corr) and annexes 1 and 5, 29 March 2010.

8 *Situation in the Republic of Kenya*, ICC-01/09-19, Decision Pursuant to Article 15 of the Rome Statute on the Authorization of an Investigation into the Situation in the Republic of Kenya (Pre-Trial Chamber II, 31 March 2010), para. 204.

However, early involvement of victims in the proceedings has been the exception before the Court rather than the rule. Indeed, article 15(3) does not apply when the Prosecutor receives a referral either by a State Party[9] in accordance with articles 13(a) and 14 of the Statute, or by the Security Council[10] in accordance with article 13(b) of the Statute.

In those situations, rule 92(2) provides for notification to victims of a decision of the Prosecutor not to investigate or not to prosecute. However, in all those situations, the Prosecutor, first, decided to start an investigation and, second, never took any decision not to prosecute, probably in order to avoid the eventual judicial review by the Pre-Trial Chamber of those decisions provided for in article 53(3)(b) of the Statute. Rule 92(2) has therefore never been applied.

Otherwise, Rule 92(3) provides for victims' notification for the purposes of allowing them to apply for participation at the confirmation of charges' hearing. However, such a notification is both late and limited.

It is late because it occurs only when the Prosecutor has selected a case and when such a case has reached the stage of the hearing on the confirmation of charges. For example, whereas the investigation in the Democratic Republic of the Congo (the 'DRC') started in June 2004, the confirmation of charges in the first case arising out of that situation, the case of Thomas Lubanga Dyilo, took place in November 2006. Thus, during more than two years after the start of the investigation, no notification to victims was made.

It is limited because only the victims related to the specific case at stake are notified, which, for example in the case of Thomas Lubanga Dyilo, solely concerned crimes committed within one district (Ituri) of one of the eleven provinces of the DRC, between July 2002 and December 2003, and related to conscripting and enlisting children under the age of 15 years into armed forces or using them to participate actively in hostilities. It therefore concerned an infinitely more limited group than the one of the victims of the entire situation under investigation.

In this respect, NGOs, in the reports submitted to the Review Conference in Kampala,[11] complained about the lack of information for victims in the situations where the Court was investigating, many victims being totally unaware of the existence of the Court, especially women. The Court's efforts in its outreach program should be strengthen and Chambers should envisage resorting to rule

9 Uganda (2003), the Democratic Republic of the Congo (2004) and the Central African Republic (2004).

10 Darfur, Sudan (2005).

11 See in this regard the discussion paper researched and written by Eric Stover, Camille Crittenden and Alexa Koening (University of California, Berkeley), Victor Peskin (Arizona State University) and Tracey Gurd (Open Society Justice Initiative), in coordination with the focal points (Finland and Chile) on the stocktaking topic concerning victims before the ICC and in consultation with a wide range of civil society actors and victims representatives, as well as the Court: RC/ST/V/INF.4, 'The Impact of the Rome Statute System on Victims and Affected Communities', Review Conference of the Rome Statute, 30 May 2010.

92(8) of the RPE to request the Registrar to take necessary measures to give adequate publicity to the proceedings at any stage of those proceedings, a power which has not yet being used by the chambers.

*The complexity of the application process*

Rule 89(1) of the RPE states that '[i]n order to present their views and concerns, victim shall make written application to the Registrar' and regulation 86 of the Regulations of the Court adds that the standard forms developed by the Registry 'shall, to the extent possible, be made available to the victims ... and be used by victims.' The Chambers have further developed requirements as to the completeness of such application forms.[12] Nevertheless, NGOs[13] have underlined that the Court's requirements with regard to the proof of identity for victims presenting applications to participate have been sometimes almost impossible to meet.

In this regard, the jurisprudence of Pre-Trial Chamber II raised serious concerns when, in 2007,[14] it requested victims to present, as proof of identification, a document: 1) issued by a recognized public authority; 2) stating the name and the date of birth of the holder; and 3) showing a photograph of the holder.

Pre-Trial Chamber I was, one week later, more generous as it noted that 'in regions which are or have been ravaged by conflict, not all civil status records may be available, and if available, may be difficult or too expensive to obtain'.[15]

Pre-Trial Chamber I accepted as proof of identity the submission of the following documents: 1) national identity card, passport, birth certificate, death certificate, marriage certificate, family registration booklet, will, driving license, card from humanitarian agency; 2) voting card, student identity card, pupil identity card, letter from local authority, camp registration card, documents pertaining to medical treatment, employee identity card, baptism card; 3) certificate/attestation of loss of documents (loss of official documents, school documents, church membership card, association and political party membership card, documents issued in rehabilitation centers for children associated with armed groups, certificates of nationality, pension booklet; or, in case the victim is not in a position to present any of the above mentioned documents; 4) a statement signed by two witnesses attesting to the identity of the applicant or the relationship between the victim and the person acting on his or her behalf, providing that there is consistency between

12 *Situation in the Democratic Republic of the Congo*, ICC-01/04-374, Decision on the Requests of the Legal Representative of Applicants on application process for victims' participation and legal representation (Pre-Trial Chamber I, 17 August 2007), paras. 4 to 15.

13 See the FIDH Report to the ICC Review Conference, May 2010, p. 10.

14 *Situation in Uganda*, ICC-02/04-101, Decision on victims' applications for participation a/0010/06, a/0064/06 to a/0070/06, a/0081/06 to a/0104/04 and a/0111/06 to a/0127/06 (Pre-Trial Chamber II, 10 August 2007), para. 16.

15 *Situation in the Democratic Republic of the Congo*, ICC-01/04-374, Decision on the Requests of the Legal Representative of Applicants on application process for victims' participation and legal representation (Pre-Trial Chamber I, 17 August, 2007), paras. 13 and 15.

the statement and the application. The statement must be accompanied by proof of identity of the two witnesses.

This jurisprudence was later followed by Trial Chamber I in the case of Thomas Lubanga Dyilo.[16] This maybe prompted Pre-Trial Chamber II to modify its previous jurisprudence in March 2008,[17] as meanwhile that Chamber had also received a report from the VPRS with respect to the situation in Uganda, explaining that most of the victims would be unable to present documents meeting the requirements established in its 10 August 2007 decision.

The ICC chambers now seem to have a more 'situation-specific' jurisprudence as explained by Pre-Trial Chamber III[18] in its decision in the Bemba case:

> Each victim applicant must prove his or her identity satisfactorily. The Single Judge considers that some kind of proof meeting basic requirements must be submitted. However, bearing in mind the principle that victims apply to the Court from different regions of the world in which different security situations, political, social and personal circumstances prevail, the Single Judge is of the view that it is appropriate to take a flexible approach which is adapted to the realities in the individual situation country. An official identity document which may be obtainable easily in one situation country, may not be in another. Taking into account these considerations, the Single Judge holds the view that the Victims Participation and Reparations Section (the 'VPRS') will be requested also in the future to submit a thorough report on the availability of official identity documents in the situation country in question when submitting to the Chamber the first applications for participation.

Although Judges have been slowly trying to adapt to the realities of victims' difficulty in obtaining identity documents, the process remains complex and long as evidenced by the fact that, for example, in the situation in Uganda, as of April 2010,[19] only 62 victims were recognized as victims before the Court out of 701 applications to participate presented.

The NGO REDRESS[20] has also

16 *Situation in the Democratic Republic of the Congo*, in the case *of The Prosecutor v. Thomas Lubanga Dyilo*, ICC-01/04-01/06-1119, Decision on victims' participation (Trial Chamber I, 18 January 2008), paras. 87 and 88.

17 *Situation in Uganda*, ICC-02/04-125, Decision on victims' applications for participation a/0010/06, a/0064/06 to a/0070/06, a/0081/06, a/0082/06, a/0084/06 to a/0089/06, a/0091/06 to a/0097/06, a/0099/06, a/0100/06, a/0102/06 to a/0104/06, a/0111/06, a/0113/06 to a/0117/06, a/0120/06, a/0121/06 and a/0123/06 to a/0127/06, (Pre-Trial Chamber II, 14 March 2008), para. 6.

18 *Situation in the Central African Republic*, in the case of *The Prosecutor v. Jean-Pierre Bemba Gombo*, ICC-01/05-01/08-320, Fourth Decision on Victims' Participation (Pre-Trial Chamber III, 12 December 2008), para. 34.

19 RC/ST/V/INF.3, *Registry and Trust Fund for Victims, Fact Sheet (as of April 2010)*, Review Conference of the Rome Statute, 1 June 2010.

20 RC/ST/V/INF.4, *The Impact of the Rome Statute System on Victims and Affected communities*, Review Conference of the Rome Statute, 30 May 2010, p. 4.

highlighted the long processing time for applications for victim participation in the Democratic Republic of the Congo, leading to backlogs and diminishing the access for victims. The organization noted in its November 2009 report that since 2006 over two hundred applicants in the Democratic Republic of the Congo situation alone have been waiting for a response to their application to participate in the proceedings.

*The distance between the Court and the affected communities*

Taking into consideration, as stressed by NGOs, the logistical obstacles, including the 'sheer geographical divide between the Court and affected communities',[21] NGOs have continuously advocated for strong outreach program in favor of victims and the need for the Court to envisage trials *in situ*.

Such cases of 'geographical divide', but also the lack of court personnel in the countries under investigation, have prompted problems for the victims' access to Court especially with regard to the need to resort to intermediaries and to the way to organize legal representation.

Indeed, local NGOs have sometimes been the link between victims and the Court and have proven to be very useful to 'bridge the physical, cultural and linguistic gap between the Court and members of the community'.[22]

The Court itself in its jurisprudence[23] has recognized the usefulness of those 'intermediaries':

> The Single Judge notes that, with respect to victim applications, the intermediaries who assist applicants in accessing the Court are essential to the proper progress of the proceedings. Intermediaries who assist victims do not only explain the relatively complicated 17-page[24] application form to applicants who are, for the most part, wholly unfamiliar with the Court's proceedings, but also provide logistical support to the applicants to ensure that the application, which is often filled out in relatively inaccessible villages in the DRC, is filed with the Court.

NGOs have however stressed that although those intermediaries are carrying out functions which should normally be vested upon the ICC Registry, they do not receive any funding from the Court to perform those functions and they may be at risk on account of those activities. In this respect the FIDH 'repeatedly expressed

---

21 Ibid., p. 8.

22 See the FIDH Report to the ICC Review Conference, May 2010, p. 10.

23 *Situation in the Democratic Republic of the Congo*, ICC-01/04-545, Decision on the Applications for Participation Filed in Connection with the Investigation in the Democratic Republic of the Congo by Applicants a/0189/06 to a/0198/06, a/0200/06 to a/0202/06, a/0204/06 to a/0208/06, a/0210/06 to a/0213/06, a/0215/06 to a/0218/06, a/0223/06, a/0332/07, a/0334/07 to a/0337/07, a/0001/08, a/0030/08 and a/0031/08 (Pre-Trial Chamber I, 4 November 2008), para. 25.

24 The Court has now developed a new application form which is only seven pages long.

concerns about the precarious situation of all intermediaries who are often human rights defenders'.[25]

Indeed, the Court has acknowledged that the mere fact that an intermediary is assisting the Court is enough for his or her safety and security to be threatened.[26] Nonetheless, for the moment no solution has been found with regard to appropriate funding or protection for those intermediaries.

Due to the distance between the victims and the Court, legal representation has also proven to be complex to organize in order to ensure proper communication between the counsels acting before the Court in The Hague, and the victims who remain in their respective countries.

The recent jurisprudence of the Court has tried to tackle this problem by imposing that each team representing victims before the Court be composed of at least two persons, one counsel based in The Hague, and one assistant based in the country where the victims are residing. As stated by Trial Chamber III in the Bemba case:[27]

> Indeed, the Chamber is convinced that, for a meaningful participation of victims, it is of crucial importance that the legal representatives are enabled to maintain effective contacts with the victims in the CAR. The Chamber thus emphasises that the support teams should be composed so as to facilitate regular exchanges between the legal representatives appearing in Court in The Hague and their respective assistants based in the field who will liaise with the victims.

Assuming that victims are properly informed and are successful in approaching the Court in order to submit their applications for participation, all obstacles to their participation are not yet overcome. The issue of their protection is a further challenge which must be surmounted in order to give full effect to the right of victims to access justice.

## The Challenges of Victims' Protection

The Court is faced with situations of ongoing violence or very recent conflict, the consequences of which are still vividly imprinted in the minds of the victims, victims of what the preamble to the Rome Statute describes as the 'most serious crimes of concern to the international community as a whole'. The activities of the Court are, therefore, of a highly sensitive nature. Yet, it is also important that the activities of the Court are, to the greatest extent possible, conducted in public. As a

25 See the FIDH Report to the ICC Review Conference, May 2010, p. 11.

26 *Situation in the Democratic Republic of the Congo*, ICC-01/04-374, Decision on the Requests of the Legal Representative of Applicants on application process for victims' participation and legal representation (Pre-Trial Chamber I, 17 August 2007), paras. 30–31.

27 *Situation in the Central African Republic, in the Case of the Prosecutor v. Jean-Pierre Bemba Gombo*, ICC-01/05-01/08-1005, Decision on common legal representation of victims for the purpose of trial (Trial Chamber III, 10 November 2010), para. 26.

result, the risk of reprisals against victims is increased. Thus, if the victims are to be given access to justice and the opportunity to resort to article 68(3) of the Statute, allowing them to participate in a meaningful manner, consideration must be given to the protection that may be afforded to those who take the risk to approach the Court and to express their views and concerns. Consideration must also be given to the suffering they have endured and, in this regard, it is incumbent upon the Court to ensure that their participation does not lead to any further victimization.

### *The Court's duty to protect victims and the means available to comply with this duty*

Article 68 of the Statute is often referred to as the seminal provision on victims' participation.[28] It is, however, equally important to underline that this provision also provides for the right of victims to be *protected*. Indeed, article 68(1) of the Statute imposes a general obligation on 'the Court' to protect not only witnesses but also victims, stating that '[t]he Court shall take appropriate measures to protect the safety, physical and psychological well-being, dignity and privacy of victims and witnesses'.

While Article 68(1) of the Statute refers to the Court in general, several other provisions of the Statute make specific reference to different organs in this regard.

The prosecutor is the first presence of the Court on the field, as his office is the organ responsible for conducting investigations. From the opening of an investigation into a situation through to the issuing of a warrant of arrest or a summons to appear and to the conducting of a trial, public awareness of the proceedings before the Court increases, as does the awareness of those who may wish to disrupt the Court's work. It is, therefore, of paramount importance to ensure that, in conducting its investigations, the Prosecutor does not unnecessarily put at risk the individuals with whom he may enter into contact and who may be somehow perceived as cooperating with the Court. Special care should be taken before victims are approached and victim protection issues should be identified and addressed as soon as investigations start and not only when a suspect has been surrendered to the Court.

The Statute vests the Prosecutor with a general mandate to protect victims and witnesses during his investigations.[29] The Appeals Chamber clarified the extent of the Prosecutor's mandate by stating that he 'takes general measures that ordinarily might be expected to arise on a day-to-day basis during the course of an investigation or prosecution with the aim of preventing harm from occurring to victims and witnesses'.[30] Therefore, his mandate should not extend to the

28 Thus, only addressing the importance of paragraph 3 of article 68 of the Statute.

29 Article 68(1) and 54(3)(f) of the Statute.

30 *Situation in the Democratic Republic of the Congo*, case of *The Prosecutor v. Germain Katanga and Mathieu Ngudjolo Chui*, ICC-01/04-01/07-776 OA7, 'Judgment on the appeal of the Prosecutor against the "Decision on Evidentiary Scope of the Confirmation

preventative relocation of an individual without however barring him from taking temporary emergency measures in situations of urgency, notably when the urgency is such that he is precluded from approaching the Chamber before taking action.[31]

In addition, articles 57(3)(c) and 64(6)(e) state that the Pre-trial Chamber and Trial Chamber, respectively, may take, where necessary, measures to provide for the protection and privacy of victims.[32] It has to be noted that article 68(1) of the Statute expresses this in mandatory terms ('shall') while articles 57(3)(c) and 64(6)(e) of the Statute adopt a more permissive tone ('may').[33] Despite this unfortunate difference in the wording, victims' protection should still considered to be an obligation, a view which was underlined by Trial Chamber I in its decision of 13 June 2008: 'once constituted [the Chamber has] a statutory responsibility for the protection of victims and witnesses throughout the entirety of the period it is seized of the case'.[34]

This obligation applies to all stages of the proceedings, including the investigative stage, since a Pre-Trial Chamber is obliged, when carrying out a review of the Prosecutor's decision not to investigate or prosecute,[35] to 'protect the safety of witnesses and victims and members of their families'.[36] Thus, individuals put at risk on account of the Court's activities are entitled to protection, regardless of whether they have already been recognized as such, pursuant to rule 85 of the RPP, and authorized to participate, pursuant to article 68(3) of the Statute.

An organ has been established to that effect within the remit of the Registry and in order to advise the Prosecutor and the Court on the appropriate measures.[37] The Registry has indeed created pursuant to article 43(6) of the Statute, the Victims and Witnesses Unit ('VWU') which shall provide, in consultation with the Office of the Prosecutor, 'protective measures and security arrangements, counseling and other appropriate assistance for witnesses, victims who appear before the Court, and others at risk on account of testimony given by such witnesses'.

---

Hearing, Preventive Relocation and Disclosure under Article 67(2) of the Statute and Rule 77 of the Rules" of Pre-Trial Chamber I' (Appeals Chambers, 26 November 2008), para. 98.

31 Ibid., paras. 103–4.

32 While article 68(1) mentions that the Court *shall* take such measures, articles 57(3)(c) and 64(6)(e) only states that the relevant Chamber *may* take these measures.

33 *The International Criminal Court, A Commentary on the Rome Statute*, William A. Schabbas, Oxford University press, p. 768 (Article 64. Functions and powers of the Trial Chamber).

34 Trial Chamber I, Decision on the consequences of non-disclosure of exculpatory materials covered by Article 54(3)(e) agreements and the application to stay the prosecution of the accused, together with certain other issues raised at the Status Conference on 10 June 2008, para. 41, cited in Shabbas, *The International Criminal Court, A Commentary on the Rome Statute*, p. 768 (Article 64. Functions and powers of the Trial Chamber).

35 Article 53(3)(a) of the Statute.

36 Rule 107(3) of the Rules of Procedure and Evidence.

37 Article 68(4) of the Statute.

There are a number of possible protective and special measures, any of which may be resorted to, depending on a consideration of a number of relevant factors, *including* age, gender as defined in article 7, paragraph 3, and health of the victim, and the nature of the crime, in particular, *but not limited to*, where the crime involves sexual or gender violence or violence against children. A sample of such measures are contained in rules 87(3) and 88(1) of the Rules of Procedure and Evidence and include measures such as maintenance of anonymity vis-à-vis the public or even the parties, the use of pseudonyms or the conduct of part of the proceedings in camera. The measures listed in these two provisions are not exhaustive and this allows the Judges some leeway in this regard.[38] The Court may also request the cooperation of States Parties to provide assistance in relation to victim protection.

It goes without saying that the primary obligation to protect individuals rests on the State of which they are nationals. Obviously, when officials of the State are allegedly involved in the criminal conduct investigated by the Prosecutor, it is doubtful that the State could be trusted with the task of protecting victims against reprisals. The Court has to protect them.

In light of the involvement of different organs, coordinated action and expeditious communication of information is essential to prevent duplication of workload and contradictory efforts to the ultimate detriment of the safety of the individual concerned. The dispute between organs such as the one of 2008 between the VWU and the Prosecutor in relation to the preventive relocation should not re-occur.[39] For instance, the VWU must be promptly informed as to whether a victim will also act as the witness of one of the parties so that a proper risk assessment may be carried out in relation to this individual. In the event of divergence between the views of the VWU and the Prosecutor, the Chamber is the 'ultimate arbiter'.[40]Resorting to such measures without going through the VWU would expose the Prosecutor, or the Defence as the case might be, to 'allegations of unduly influencing, inducing or rewarding the witnesses for their testimony'.[41]

38 Michael E. Kurth, Anonymous Witnesses before the International Criminal Court: Due Process in Dire Strates in *The Emerging Practise of the International Criminal Court*, Martinus Nijhoff Publishers, edited by Carsten Sthan and Göran Sluiter, p. 628.

39 *Situation in the Democratic Republic of the Congo*, case of *The Prosecutor v. Germain Katanga and Mathieu Ngudjolo Chui*, ICC-01/04-01/07-776 OA7, 'Judgment on the appeal of the Prosecutor against the "Decision on Evidentiary Scope of the Confirmation Hearing, Preventive Relocation and Disclosure under Article 67(2) of the Statute and Rule 77 of the Rules" of Pre-Trial Chamber I' (Appeals Chambers, 26 November 2008).

40 Ibid., para. 97.

41 *Situation in the Democratic Republic of the Congo*, case of *The Prosecutor v. Germain Katanga and Mathieu Ngudjolo Chui*, Victims and Witnesses Unit's considerations on the system of witness protection and the practice of 'preventive relocation', ICC-01/04-01/07-585 (Registry, 12 June 2008).

*Impact of protection issues on the victims' access to the Court and on their effective participation at the proceedings*

The availability and implementation of protective measures have an enormous impact on the lives of victims, on their decision as to whether to approach the Court and on their participatory rights.[42]

The Statute puts an emphasis on the fact that protective measures should not adversely affect the rights of the Defense.[43] This gives rise to a difficult and delicate balancing exercise between the duty to protect victims and the duty to safeguard the rights of the Defense. The balance ultimately struck between these two conflicting obligations has a dramatic impact on the set of participatory rights that are granted to victims.

The weight of this balancing exercise and its results vary depending on the stage of the proceedings involved. Also, the jurisprudence on this issue has evolved considerably.

*The application stage*

The application stage is designed to allow a victim to apply to the relevant Chamber for authorization to participate in the proceedings by the expression of his or her views and concerns. At that stage, the victim is a 'victim applicant' whose application may or may not be granted. The number of applications for participation in the proceedings, to a large extent, depends on how successful the outreach program has been in explaining to victims the processes of the Court and on the publicity of Court's proceedings.

Recently, in the case of Mr Jean-Pierre Bemba, more than 1500 victims applied for participation before Trial Chamber III. This figure will only increase as the Court is mandated to prosecute mass crimes. This raises serious practical problems for the Court in terms of its ability to protect such a high number of applicants and then victims. Such a high number of victims, combined with the often hazardous security situations in regions under investigation results in a drastic reduction of the range of protective measures practically available. It is unrealistic to believe that individualized measures can be afforded to victims in such circumstances.

42 This part focuses on those who intend to approach the Court for the purposes of participation. This is notwithstanding the fact that other victims who might be referred to in these victims' applications for participation or also in the parties' evidence are also entitled to protection. In this respect, the Appeals Chamber inter alia held that the Prosecutor may apply to the Pre-Trial Chamber, pursuant to rule 81(4) of the Rules of the Procedure and Evidence, for a ruling as to whether the names, identifying information and whereabouts of alleged victims must be disclosed to the Defence, 'so as to protect the safety of such alleged victims as "persons at risk on account of the activities of the Court"' Judgment on the appeal of Mr Mathieu Ngudjolo against the decision of Pre-Trial Chamber I entitled 'Decision on the Prosecution Request for Authorisation to Redact Statements of Witnesses 4 and 9', 27 May 2008, ICC-01/04-01/07-521 OA5.

43 Articles 64(2), 68(1) and (5) and 69(2) of the Statute.

Non-disclosure of the information which could lead to the identification of the applicants (i.e., redaction) remains, therefore, the only protective measure capable of practical implementation in order to protect victim-applicants.

Interestingly, the Defense for Mr Katanga filed a request for leave to appeal a decision of Pre-trial Chamber I authorizing such redactions, raising *inter alia* the issue as to whether the Chamber had exceeded its discretionary powers in ordering such redactions and whether, in relying on the general insecurity in the DRC and particularly in the Ituri district, rather than the insecurity of the specific applicants to justify the need for redactions, the single judge had failed to respect the exceptional nature of this protective measure.

> In deciding on the Defence's request for leave to appeal, Pre-trial Chamber I recalled that an order to redact identifying information is a decision which may be taken *proprio motu* by the Chamber pursuant to article 68(1) of the Statute and reiterated that, in light of the security situation in Ituri, DRC, the redaction of the identities and identifying information of the applicants was 'the only protective measure available.... which might have been implemented to duly protect the applicants who have not yet been granted the status of victims'.[44]

The Chambers have repeatedly held that such redactions should not exceed what is strictly necessary to preserve the anonymity of the 'victim-applicant' and, in any event, should allow the defence or the parties to exercise their right to respond[45] effectively to the application for participation.

Nevertheless, the procedure applied for implementing redactions has been consistently criticized by the Defence, mainly on the grounds that the applications were unnecessarily heavily redacted and that redactions should not be made when a victim does not wish to remain anonymous.[46] Such arguments should not be entertained. The fact remains that an applicant's safety should not be unduly jeopardized in circumstances where their right to participate in the proceedings has not yet been granted. Such redactions may subsequently be reduced or eliminated when the applicant is ultimately granted the right to participate as a victim and this is sufficient to safeguard the rights of the Defense.

Once applicants have been recognized as victims and authorized to participate in the proceedings, the balance between their rights and the rights of the Defense evolves. It is thus of utmost importance that during the application process, the proceedings before the Court have been thoroughly explained to the victim and,

---

44 Situation in the Democratic Republic of the Congo, the case of *The Prosecutor v. Germain Katanga*, ICC-01/04-01/07-241, Decision on the Defence Application for Leave to Appeal the 'Decision authorising the filing of observations on the applications for participation in the proceedings a/0327/07 to a/0337/07 and a/0001/08' (Pre-Trial Chamber I, 27 February 2008).

45 Rule 89(1) of the Rules of Procedure and Evidence.

46 A specific section of the application gives the opportunity to the victim applicants to tick boxes and inform by this way against whom they request anonymity, provided again that they do understand the meaning of such a technical question.

crucially that they have been made aware of the fact that it cannot be guaranteed that their identities will never be disclosed to the parties.

Here again, it is important to properly informing the victims. Contact with the applicant to explain to them the protective measures available and the possibility of them changing in the course of the proceedings is essential as these are fundamental issues for a victim to consider before deciding whether to apply for participation. In balancing their fear with their will to participate, they should also be made aware that the fact that they choose not to participate throughout what may be lengthy proceedings will not prevent them from applying for reparations before a Trial Chamber at the appropriate time and up until the reparation hearing.

*Impact of victims' anonymity on the extent of their participation*

In the early jurisprudence of Pre-Trial Chamber I, victims' participatory rights were limited where they retained anonymity. Thus, because victims were in need of protection and such protection was provided through redactions, the Chamber decided that, in order to avoid any violation of the fundamental principle prohibiting anonymous accusations, participatory rights of anonymous victims would be limited.

Accordingly, Pre-Trial Chamber I did not permit anonymous victims to add any point of fact or evidence to the Prosecutor's case, or to question witnesses.[47] On the other hand, when victims consented to the disclosure of their identity to the Defence they were authorised *inter alia* to access confidential documents and the evidence of the case as well as to question witnesses.

This approach was, however, deviated from in subsequent cases. Indeed, Pre-Trial Chamber II, in the case against Mr Jean-Pierre Bemba, held that there should not be any differentiation between victims whose identity is known to the Defence and those for whom anonymity has been granted, as a 'differentiation in participatory rights should not be made to the detriment of those requesting protective measures'.[48]

As for the Trial Chambers, Trial Chamber I has highlighted, in the case against Mr Thomas Lubanga Dyilo, that submissions from parties to the effect that anonymous victims should never be permitted to participate in the proceedings should be rejected. It went on to hold that:

---

47 Situation in the Republic Democratic of the Congo, case of *The Prosecutor v. Germain Katanga and Mathieu Ngudjolo Chui*, Decision on the Set of Procedural Rights Attached to Procedural Status of Victim at the Pre-Trial Stage of the Case, ICC-01/04-01/07-474 (Pre-Trial Chamber I, 13 May 2008), paras. 182–3; See also Situation in the Republic Democratic of the Congo, case of *The Prosecutor v Thomas Lubanga Dyilo*, Decision on the Arrangements for Participation of Victims a/0001/06, a/0002/06 and a/0003/06 at the Confirmation Hearing, ICC-01/04-01/06-462-tEN (Pre-Trial Chamber I, 22 September 2006), p. 8.

48 Situation in the Central African Republic, case of *The Prosecutor v. Jean-Pierre Bemba Gombo*, Fourth Decision on Victims' Participation, ICC-01/05-01/08-320 (Pre-Trial Chamber III, 12 December 2008), para. 99.

> although [it] recognizes that it is preferable that the identities of victims are disclosed in full to parties, the Chamber is also conscious of the particularly vulnerable position of many of these victims, who live in an area of ongoing conflict where it is difficult to ensure their safety.[49]

However, the Trial Chamber emphasized the need to ensure that such anonymity does not impact on the Defense's rights, thus adding:

> [w]hile the safety and secrutity of victims is a central responsibility of the Court, their participation in the proceedings cannot be allowed to undermine the fundamental guarantee of a fair trial. The greater the extent and the significance of the proposed participation, the more likely it will be that the Chamber will require the victim to identify himself or herself. Accordingly, when resolving a request for anonymity by a victim who applied to participate, the Chamber will scrutinise carefully the precise circumstances and the potential prejudice to the parties and other participants.[50] [emphasis added]

*Impact of holding the so-called dual status as a victim-witness on the individual's right to protective measures*

Trial Chamber I held that 'the fact that an individual has dual status does not grant him or her rights in addition to those of someone who is only a victim or a witness'.[51]

However, it seems relevant to underline that, in assessing the risk to which an individual is exposed, VWU also takes into consideration whether an individual is a witness before the Court. Being identified as a witness in proceedings before the Court theoretically increases the risk of retaliation.

Theoretically, because this is assuming that the author of the threat makes the distinction between a victim participating in the proceedings and a witness called by a party or the Chamber to testify. The author of the threat might well put both individuals within one and the same category: a person cooperating with the Court. As a result, a victim holding dual status may be in a more advantageous position, as threats to her or his safety will be considered to have greater substance and therefore warrant the application of protective measures. In any event, anonymity *vis-à-vis* the public and the conduct of hearings *in camera*, when necessary, remain the default measures applied to protect the victim from retaliation, although they represent a derogation from the principle of publicity of the proceedings.

---

49 Situation in the Republic Democratic of the Congo, case of *The Prosecutor v Thomas Lubanga Dyilo*, Decision on victims' participation, ICC-01/04-01/06-1119 (Trial Chamber I, 18 January 2008), para. 130.

50 *Ibid.*, para. 131.

51 Situation in the Republic Democratic of the Congo, case of *The Prosecutor v Thomas Lubanga Dyilo*, Decision on certain practicalities regarding individuals who have the dual status of witness and victim, ICC-01/04-01/06-1379 (Trial Chamber I 5 June 2008), p. 20.

## Conclusion

Despite the adoption of the Rome Statute and article 68 therein, criticisms as to victims' participation before the ICC are recurrent. The arguments in favor and against victims' participation in proceedings are numerous. It is vain to further delve into the soundness of any of these positions: victims' participation in the proceedings has been recognised in the Statute of the International Criminal Court. The Court is slowly and cautiously establishing its case law in relation to the system for participation. Many questions in this respect remain either unsolved or are not uniformly answered by the Chambers.

However all these efforts will be vain if we do not primarily secure victims' access to the Court, to justice. In this respect, much remains to be done to give an effective meaning to their right to participate in the proceedings. If victims are to be actors in these proceedings rather than simple walker-on, to ease their access to the Court and to ensure their protection are the preliminary conditions.

# Index


Alvarez, Jose Enrique 69, 76
Arendt, Hannah 3, 35, 39, 42, 43, 44, 47, 92, 201
    conception of public sphere 92–3

banking 6, 205, 206, 208–12, 214–15,
    Banking Co-partnership Act (1826) 208–9
    and private law 205, 210–13
Barry, Brian 138, 144
Berlin, Isaiah 2, 35, 38, 43, 50, 97
    negative and positive liberty distinction 38, 43
Bernard Connolly v Commission 4, 115, 120–24, 125, 127, 128; *see also* civil disobedience
Bovens, Mark 120, 127, 128
    civic conception of responsibility 127; *see also* civil disobedience
British Empire 5, 161, 162, 163, 164, 165, 166, 167, 168, 169, 170, 171
    constitutional history of 161
    imperial-national distinction 168
    'British' polity 162–3
Brownlee, Kimberley 100–101
Brugidou, Mathieu 151, 155
    notion of the public 151
De Burca, Grainne 118

capitalist production and social reproduction 185–6
    and the public/private dichotomy 186
capitalist society as class society 187
citizenship 5, 43, 90, 111, 118, 126, 127, 135, 143, 156, 157, 170
    and categories of prisoners 156
    and prisoners' rights 5, 156–7
civil disobedience 3, 4, 99, 100, 101, 105, 106, 109, 110, 115, 116, 117, 119, 120, 121, 122, 123, 124, 125, 126, 127, 128
    and active citizenship 5, 118, 126, 127
    and civic conception of responsibility 125, 127, 128
    communicative nature of 100–103, 107
    Connolly v Commission; *see also* Bernard Connolly v. Commission
    and European Union 4, 115–29
    and guilty plea 3–4, 99–111
    and hierarchical conception of responsibility 4, 118, 120
    and the judiciary 106, 116, 119, 128
        and judicial reasoning 122, 125, 127
        traditional judicial approach to 115, 117, 119
    and political action 3, 111, 116,
    and public consensus 115–17, 119–20, 125–9
    and the renovation of institutional politics 117
colonial conference of 1887 161–4
Constant, Benjamin 2, 35, 36, 38, 50
    ancient and modern liberty 2, 35, 36, 38, 39, 40, 43, 48,
    and publicity 48, 49
    and republican moment 2, 48–50
constituent power 3, 4, 46

democracy 1, 2, 4, 5, 22, 23, 24, 25, 26, 28, 39, 53, 54, 55, 56, 57, 58, 59, 60, 61, 62, 63, 64, 77, 118, 156, 157, 184, 197
    and elections 53, 54, 56, 57, 64, 147
    electoral 2, 53, 54, 56, 57, 59, 62
    and freedom as non-domination 39–43, 46; *see also* liberty
    liberal 4, 54, 56, 60, 62, 63
    militant, theory of 56, 62
    and political parties; *see also* political parties; Refah Partisi
    and the protection of rights 55, 62–4

and republicanism; *see also* republicanism 38–43
and secularism 2, 4, 54, 58, 62, 63, 140n5, 141, 142
and the will of the people 53, 54
development and incommensurability 223–4
Dewey, John 148, 151, 153, 154, 155
passive and active public 151
*The Public and Its Problems* 154
Dilke, Charles 162
*Greater Britain* 162
Disenfranchisement 4, 148, 149, 150, 152, 153, 155, 156, 157
arguments for 149–51
Duff, Antony 101, 102, 103, 104
notion of blame 101–2

Englishness 161, 162, 164, 169
European Convention on Human Rights (ECHR) 59, 121, 122, 123, 124, 139
European Court of Human Rights (ECtHR) 78, 136, 138, 139, 140, 141, 147, 149, 152n13
Behrami and Behrami v France 78
Frodl v. Austria 147
Grand Chamber 55, 56, 58, 63, 139, 140
Hirst v. The United Kingdom 147, 149, 152
Mathieu-Mohin and Clerfayt c. Belgium 147
Refah Partisi; *see also* Refah Partisi
Saramati v France, Germany and Norway 78
European Court of Justice (ECJ) 115, 118, 120, 121, 123, 124, 125, 128
Connolly v Commission 4, 115, 120–30
Kadi v. Council and Commission 77–8

Finnis, John 138, 139, 140, 141, 142, 143, 144
Fraser, Nancy 153, 154
Fuller, Lon 90

Geuss, Raymond 12, 13, 14, 200
public/private distinction according to 12–14, 200
Glenn, Patrick 19
common law and *ius publicum* 19

Habermas, Jurgen 27, 92, 93, 94, 96, 148, 153, 154, 155
conception of public sphere 92–3
Hildebrandt, Mireille 101, 158
idea of fair trial 101

imperial federalists 161, 164, 166
institutions 3, 20, 22, 36, 49, 50, 57, 69, 73, 74, 75, 76, 77, 89, 116, 124, 138, 141, 162, 163, 164, 169, 170, 191, 196–202, 204, 206, 207, 208, 209, 214, 215
banking 208, 211
international 3, 26n
legal 199, 210, 216, 215
logic of 3, 91
political 116, 196–9, 201–2
public 209
intergovernmental organizations (IGOs) 3, 69, 70, 72–3, 74, 76–80
functional public role of 80
International Court of Justice (ICJ) 72, 76
International Criminal Court (ICC) 6, 235, 249, 257, 264, 264, 269, 285, 287, 288, 289, 291, 293, 295, 296, 297, 299, 301, 302
access to justice, and 7, 235–6, 289–95, 298
as a right 7, 235–6, 250, 295, 302
Office of the Prosecutor, of 7, 240n20, 243n42, 263–85
proceeding criteria 271
restorative function 261
and Rome Statute 7, 235–40, 247, 252, 257, 263–7, 287–90, 302
definition of victim 265
victim participation, on 235, 242–57, 275–83, 293
anonymous victims 282–3
challenges faced by 289–94
statutory requirements 275–9
victims anonymity 300
victims of a case 236, 245
victims protection 272–5, 295
victims' reparations 284
victims of a situation 236, 237, 238, 243, 245, 266
International Law 3, 19, 20, 69, 70, 71, 72, 73, 74, 75, 76, 77, 78, 79, 80

institutional approach to 70–71
legitimacy of and intergovernmental organizations 69–78
as public law 70–73
and publicness 73–4
and Scelle's theory of 'dedoublement fonctionnel' 71–2
Westphalian, transformation of 74
ius publicum 18, 19, 20, 21, 23, 25
and legal authority 19–25
in post-Westphalian states 20

Katz, Richard 56, 57
Krisch, Nico 27, 28
and pluralistic public autonomy 27–8

law
authority of 108, 110
connectedness, claim to 196, 198, 199, 202
and economics 6, 7, 50, 177–80, 182–6, 192
and institutional logics 91
private; see also private law
public; see also public law
public in 50, 76, 90, 95, 97
as an adjective 90
as a body of people 89
Sharia 54, 55, 61
legal authority 19, 20, 21, 26, 28, 224
beyond the state 19–26
and ius publicum 19–21
Legrand, Pierre 97
liberal democracy 4, 56, 62, 63
principle of equal respect 56, 60–63
liberty 2, 35, 36, 38, 39, 40, 42, 43, 44, 45, 46, 47, 48, 49, 50, 60, 164, 202
ancient 2, 35, 36, 39, 40, 43, 48; *see also* Constant, Benjamin
freedom as non-domination 39, 40, 42, 43, 46
and democracy 2, 39, 54
as neo-Roman 40, 44, 46; *see also* Skinner, Quentin
and republicanism 2, 38, 39, 42–3; *see also* Pettit, Philip; *see also* republicanism
modern 2, 35, 36, 38, 39n4, 40, 43, 48, 50; *see also* Constant, Benjamin
negative 38, 39n4, 40, 42, 43, 46, 47
political 2, 35, 40, 43, 44, 48, 49, 50
positive 38, 39, 39n4, 40, 42, 43, 44, 47
and public space 47, 49, 50
Locke, John 137, 138, 141, 143, 144
logical unity of private and public law 190–91
Loughlin, Martin 15, 15n7, 16, 17, 18, 20, 21, 23, 24, 25, 25n11, 63, 79, 80, 89, 96; *see also* public law as a constitutive discipline
criticism of postnational constitutionalists 21

Machiavelli 45, 46, 47
Mackinnon, Catharine 270
Madison, James 61
Marx, Karl 5, 38, 91, 95, 96, 177, 178, 180, 181, 183, 191
conception of political economy 5, 177, 178
conception of political equality 91, 95
master and servant law of 1823 182

neo-liberalism 184
new British man ('*civis Britannicus*') 170
normal public 148, 153–5, 156, 157

Oakeshott, Michael 79, 79n6, 80
*societas* and *universitas* distinction 79

Pashukanis, Evgeny 5, 187, 190
*Law and Marxism* 187
legal subject 188
'public' and 'private' persons 188
Pettit, Philip 2, 35, 39, 40, 41, 42, 43, 44, 46, 47, 50
and citizen contestation 42, 43
secession 43
and freedom as non-domination; *see also* liberty
and special treatment under the law 43
political equality 91, 95
and property 91, 95

political parties 53, 54, 55, 56, 57, 60, 61, 64
and democratic process 53
and elections 53–61
and majority rule 56–8
popular sovereignty, principle of 53, 56, 58, 59, 60
private law 5, 6, 9, 10, 11, 14, 69, 89, 188, 190, 192, 195, 201, 202, 203, 204, 207, 215
concept of 10, 14, 89, 195
and the private sphere 202
public aspect of 195
public character of law 24
necessarily 9, 15, 19, 21, 25
and global administrative law 25
and global constitutional law 25
and Habermasian approach to public autonomy 27
and state-centred positions 25
selectively 9, 11
as a disciplinary division (disciplinary) 2, 11, 15, 17
in relation to legal doctrine (doctrinal) 2, 11, 13, 15, 17
public conception of development 222
'public' in and out of the law 95
public interest 14, 26, 90, 92, 124
and civil disobedience; *see also* civil disobedience
and international institutions 79
public law 1, 10, 11, 14, 15, 16, 17, 18, 19, 21, 25, 26, 70, 77, 79, 80, 177, 178, 190, 191, 195, 207
as a constitutive discipline 15–22
and common law 19–20
and globalization 21
and *ius publicum* 18–28
and the written constitution 18–19
and international law 19, 70–72, 77–80
and public/private persons 188
public of prisoners 147–57
negative identities 148, 152, 155
public/private divide 2, 4, 5, 12, 13n2, 14, 95, 133, 134, 136, 137, 177, 186, 187, 188, 189, 190, 200
and capital accumulation 5, 177, 189–91
liberal divide 4, 13, 133–7, 141–4
and liberal neutrality 134–44
and religious observance 4, 136
public space; *see also* political liberty
public sphere 4, 5, 12, 13, 17, 91, 92, 93, 94, 95, 96, 97, 133, 134, 135, 136, 137, 141, 142, 143, 144, 153, 154, 155, 190, 191, 204
Arendt's conception of 92–3
autopoietic quality of the 93
Habermas conception of 92–6, 153–5
potential of 91–7
publicity, virtue of 48
publicness of law; *see also* public character of law
as democratic ideal and aspiration 22–8
disciplinary 2, 10–12, 14–15, 17
doctrinal 2, 11–14, 17, 70
legal doctrine in 10–15
and international law 70, 73, 80, 86
and the non-public sphere 94–5

Rand, Ayn 35
virtue of selfishness 35
Rawls, John 90, 116, 117, 119n6, 122, 123, 201
conception of civil disobedience 116–17
public reason according to 90
Raz, Joseph 109n8, 116n2, 222
notion of incommensurability 222
Refah Partisi 2, 53, 54, 55, 56, 58, 59, 60, 61, 62, 63, 64, 139
and democracy 2, 53–6, 58–64
and electoral democracy 2, 54, 56, 59, 61, 62
and majority rule 2, 53, 56–61
and popular sovereignty 53, 56, 58–60
republicanism 2, 38, 39, 42, 43, 136
and democracy 39–46
and freedom as non-domination; *see also* liberty
Rousseau 38, 53, 64
and the will of the people 53

Sandel, Michael 39
Sartori, Giovanni 60
popular sovereignty 60
Schmitt, Carl 47, 197
*Political Theology* 197
secularism 2, 4, 54, 58, 62, 63, 140n5, 141, 142

Seeley, John 162
definition of Greater Britain 162
Sen, Amartya 22
the democratic ideal as universal commitment 22
Skinner, Quentin 2, 39, 40, 41, 42, 44, 45, 46
freedom as non-domination; *see also* liberty
Smith, Adam 182, 189

Taylor, Charles 38, 39
Teubner, Gunter 28n14
Touraut, Caroline 156
classification of different categories of prisoners 156
Turkey 53, 54, 61, 62, 63, 139, 140,
Constitution of the Republic of 54, 63
Constitutional Court 54
tyranny 49, 50, 60, 63

Universal Declaration of Human Rights 101

Waldron, Jeremy 22, 23, 24, 26n, 138n4, 141
publicness of law as an ideal 22
Walker, Neil 177, 192
Walzer, Michael 26
reiterative universalism 26
Weiler, Joseph 75
geological layering in international law, notion of 75
World Trade Organization (WTO) 6, 20, 73, 76, 77, 79, 219, 220, 221, 222, 223, 224, 227, 228, 229
EC-Tariff Preferences dispute 226
Committee on Trade and Development (CTD) 227

For Product Safety Concerns and Information please contact our EU representative GPSR@taylorandfrancis.com
Taylor & Francis Verlag GmbH, Kaufingerstraße 24, 80331 München, Germany

www.ingramcontent.com/pod-product-compliance
Ingram Content Group UK Ltd.
Pitfield, Milton Keynes, MK11 3LW, UK
UKHW022011180926
475701UK00003B/313
* 9 7 8 1 1 3 8 2 7 3 9 6 2 *